CW01666597

From the editor

Microsoft's operating system (OS) has come a long way since the early days of Windows 3.1. Gone are the crude colours, blocky text and boxy graphics, replaced by smooth animations, sharp fonts and intuitive navigation systems.

But Windows 10's improvements are much more than just skin deep. And once you've got used to its flashy new features, such as the revamped Start menu and Cortana the voice-controlled assistant, there are dozens of other, more profound enhancements and tools to discover. And these are the things we'll be focusing on in this guide – ways to customise Windows 10 so it works the way *you* want it to, settings *you* can change to make your PC safer, tools and hacks that *you* can use to improve the OS, and much more.

Although we think Windows 10 is great, it's far from perfect. That's why, over the course of this book, we'll explain how you can overcome some of its major shortcomings. We'll show you how to protect your privacy from Microsoft's prying eyes, how to take back control of key settings and how to fix dozens of frustrating Windows 10 problems.

In addition, we'll be exploring some of the big new changes brought about by Windows 10's latest updates. Microsoft has pledged to keep bringing new features to Windows 10 and it has delivered on its promise by constantly improving the operating system with useful new tools and refinements that keep Windows 10 feeling fresh.

Windows 10 might not be free any more, but it's undoubtedly the best computer operating system around. And, whether you've just upgraded or you were one of the early adopters back in July 2015, there's still so much to uncover – as you're about to find out by reading this guide.

Jonathan Parkyn
Editor
The Advanced Guide to Windows 10

The Advanced Guide to Windows 10

EDITORIAL

Editor: Jonathan Parkyn
Art Editor: Ian Jackson
Consulting Editor: Robert Irvine
Group Editor: Daniel Booth
Digital Production Manager: Nicky Baker

MANAGEMENT

MagBook Publisher: Dharmesh Mistry
Operations Director: Robin Ryan
MD of Advertising: Julian Lloyd-Evans
Newstrade Director: David Barker
MD of Enterprise: Martin Belson
Chief Operating Officer: Brett Reynolds
Group Finance Director: Ian Leggett
Chief Executive: James Tye
Founder: Felix Dennis

MAGBOOK

MAGBOOK The 'MagBook' brand is a trademark of Dennis Publishing Ltd, 30 Cleveland Street, London W1T 4JD. Company registered in England. All material © Dennis Publishing Ltd, licensed by Felden 2016, and may not be reproduced in whole or part without the consent of the publishers.

The Definitive Guide to Windows 10 ISBN 1-78106-522-5

LICENSING AND SYNDICATION

To license this product please contact Carlotta Serantoni on +44 (0) 20 7907 6550 or email carlotta_serantoni@dennis.co.uk
To syndicate content from this product please contact Anj Dosaj-Halai on +44 (0) 20 7907 6132 or email anj_dosaj-halai@dennis.co.uk

LIABILITY

While every care was taken during the production of this MagBook, the publishers cannot be held responsible for the accuracy of the information or any consequence arising from it. Dennis Publishing takes no responsibility for the companies advertising in this MagBook.

The paper used within this MagBook is produced from sustainable fibre, manufactured by mills with a valid chain of custody.

Printed at Southernprint

Contents

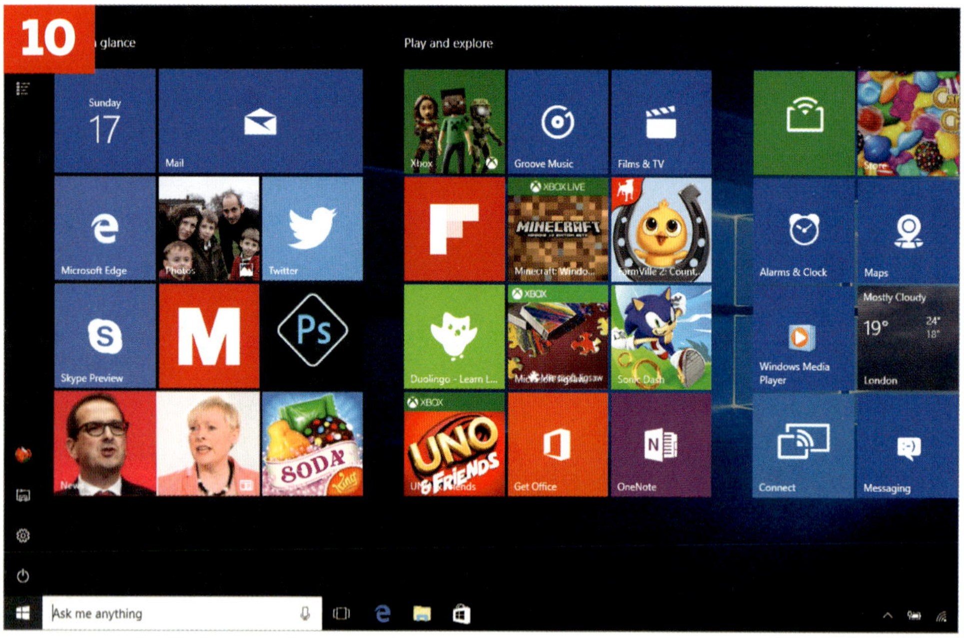
10
Play and explore
Sunday
17
Mail
Xbox
Groove Music
Films & TV
Microsoft Edge
Photos
Twitter
Alarms & Clock
Maps
Skype Preview
Duolingo - Learn L...
Mostly Cloudy
19°
London
Windows Media Player
Get Office
OneNote
Connect
Messaging
Ask me anything

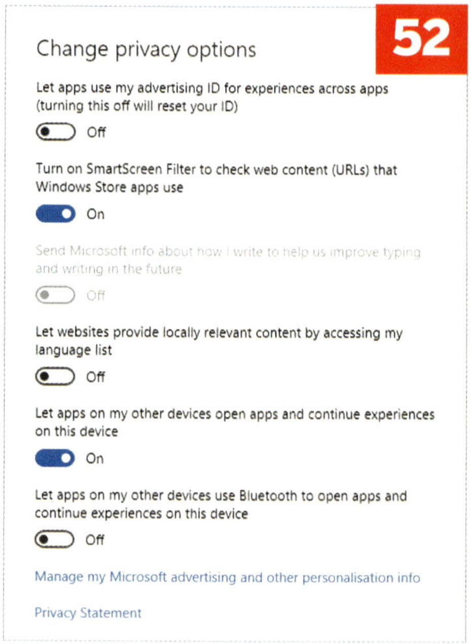
52
Change privacy options
Let apps use my advertising ID for experiences across apps (turning this off will reset your ID)
Off
Turn on SmartScreen Filter to check web content (URLs) that Windows Store apps use
On
Send Microsoft info about how I write to help us improve typing and writing in the future
Off
Let websites provide locally relevant content by accessing my language list
Off
Let apps on my other devices open apps and continue experiences on this device
On
Let apps on my other devices use Bluetooth to open apps and continue experiences on this device
Off
Manage my Microsoft advertising and other personalisation info
Privacy Statement

Jargon buster
Plain English definitions for all technical terms
Turn to page 193

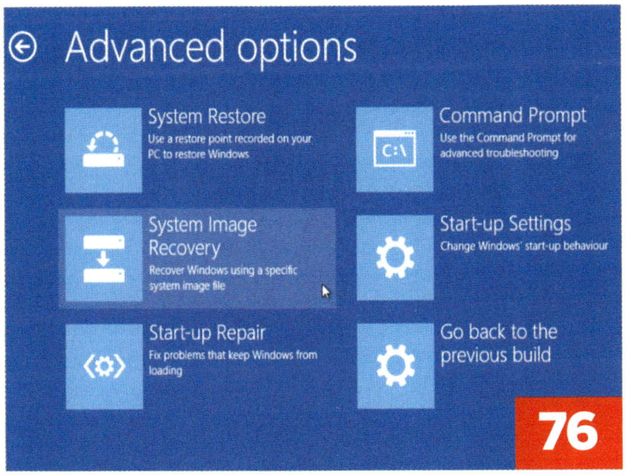

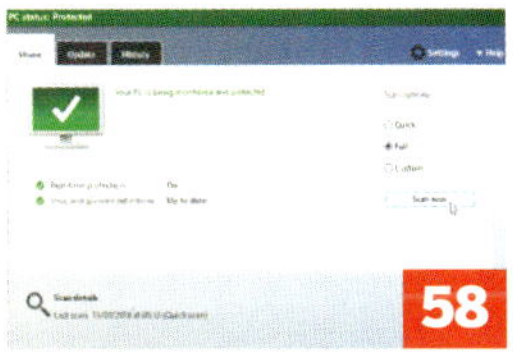

Chapter 1

What's new in Windows 10?

We examine the biggest changes that Windows 10 brings – including all the brand new features in the big Anniversary Update

Unlike previous versions of Microsoft's operating system, Windows 10 is changing all the time, regularly adding all-new features as well as continuing to refine the way the old ones work. That's why we're going to kick off our Advanced Guide to Windows 10 with an in-depth look at all the great new things the OS has to offer. We'll be introducing features and abilities that you might not be aware of if you've recently upgraded from Windows 7 or 8, as well as examining all the brand new tools, options and settings that were recently added to Windows 10 as part of its Anniversary Update.

IN THIS SECTION

Windows 10's Anniversary Update: every new feature

Windows 10 received a major overhaul in August, thanks to Microsoft's Anniversary Update. We examine all the best (and worst) new features and tools

By the time you read this, Windows 10 will be well into its second year of life. The bad news is that since its first birthday, Windows 10 stopped being free – a new copy of the OS now costs the tidy sum of £100. But the good news is that, as a bit of a birthday present, Microsoft has provided every Windows 10 user with a selection of brand new features to play with and settings to tweak – all free, courtesy of the Anniversary Update (AU).

Windows 10 has received many updates over its lifetime (some might say too many), but the AU (formerly known as 'Redstone') is different. It's effectively Windows 10.1 – an overhaul so all-encompassing that it affects everything from the look of the Start menu to the way the taskbar works.

Before you get too worried about having to relearn how to use your PC from scratch all over again, we should point out that Microsoft's changes, though significant, don't change the fundamental way the OS works. Many are minor evolutions that'll be easy to get the hang of, while others are big improvements we think you'll love.

Not all of the AU's changes will be welcome, though, while some potentially useful features haven't made it to the update at all. And, since all Windows updates are now mandatory, you're stuck with all the changes, whether you want them or not (though it's possible to delay the update if you've not already received it – see page 12). Over the next few pages we'll walk you through the main changes the AU brings with it – good and bad – explaining what's new, how it all works, and what settings you need change to make sure the update doesn't disrupt your work or leave your privacy exposed.

What you can do

- Explore the new features that have been added to the OS
- Learn about privacy problems and new settings you must change
- Find out how to get the latest update to Windows 10
- Discover which features Microsoft has dropped and why

WHAT'S NEW?

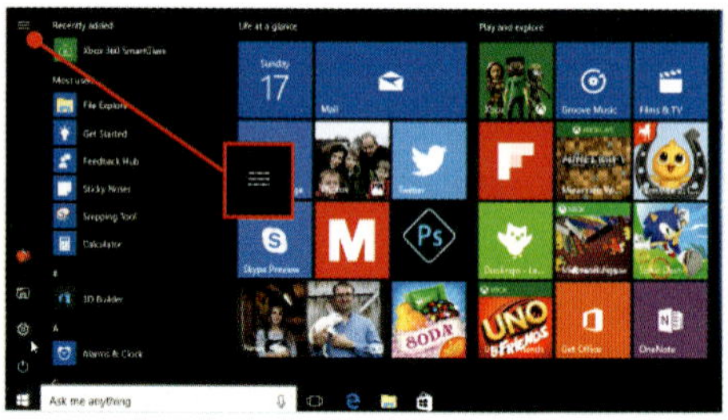

1 The new Start menu

The Start menu famously made a return in Windows 10 after Microsoft thought it would be a good idea to pretend everyone was using a tablet in Windows 8. But the AU shows that Microsoft's not finished refining the Start menu yet.

There are no radical changes, thankfully, but it has changed from a two-pane menu to a three-pane menu, with the addition of a slim strip on the left (expandable by clicking the hamburger icon top left), which houses icons for account, settings and power. You can add further icons here (including File Explorer) by going to Settings, Personalisation, Start, then clicking 'Choose which folders appear on Start'.

Also, the 'All apps' option is gone and now all your programs are permanently listed in the middle pane, just under 'Recently added' and 'Most used'.

2 New full-screen Start

If you do like to pretend that you're using a tablet (or if you actually are using a tablet), then you may be pleased to hear that Windows 10's optional full-screen Start mode has also had a bit of a redesign.

The tiles have been rearranged to take more advantage of the increased space offered in full-screen mode and, as with the standard Start menu, there's now a new strip of icons running down the left-hand side. You can click the hamburger icon at the top of the strip to see what each icon is. Clicking the 'All apps' icon here now switches the entire screen to an all apps view (before these appeared in a scrollable panel on the left), with 'Recently added' and 'Most used' at the top.

3 Improved notifications

So-called 'toast' notifications are the ones that pop up (see what they did there?) in the bottom right-hand corner of the screen in Windows 10 and can be reviewed in the Action Centre. Up until now, they've been pretty basic but the AU makes these more dynamic, allowing app developers to include more information in them, as well as images and clickable links. Some notifications now look and work more like Live tiles.

In addition, users get more control

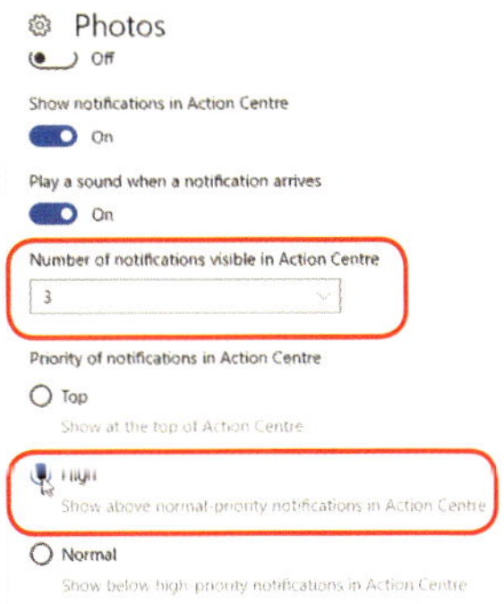

over how notifications work for individual apps. Head to Settings, System, 'Notifications & actions', then scroll down and click an app to see the options available. You can now specify how many notifications the app is allowed in the Action Centre and what priority they should be given.

4 Changes to the Settings app

Assuming you haven't switched on dark mode (see below), the Settings app doesn't look too different at first. But click one of the nine category icons on the main screen and you'll notice that each sub-category now has its own unique icon, too.

There are more settings now as well. The System category, for example, now houses 11 settings (13 if you're using a laptop), compared to just 9 in the pre-AU era, including a new entry for 'Apps for websites,' which lets you open certain sites in their associated apps, rather than in your browser.

And, just to keep you on your toes, some of the settings in each category have been re-ordered and options re-worded.

5 New dark theme

Previously, Windows 10's 'hidden' dark theme was only available by manually hacking away at the Registry. But now it's available right from the Settings app – click Personalisation,

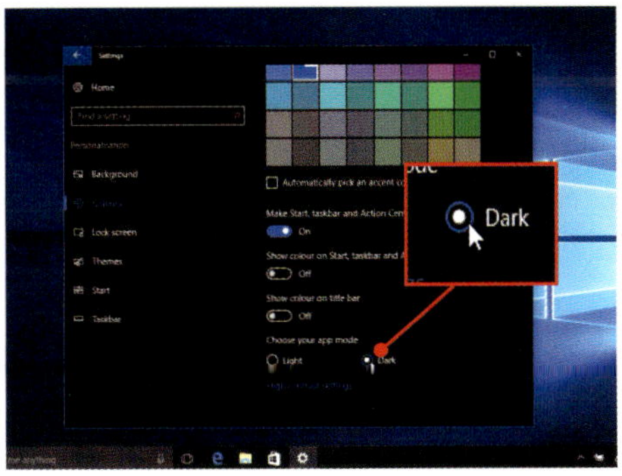

Colours and then select Dark under 'Choose your app mode'. Aside from changing the interface cosmetically, it works a little like one of Windows high-contrast modes, making it easier to read text. Unfortunately, the theme isn't entirely system-wide – it only works in apps and settings, not desktop programs and tools.

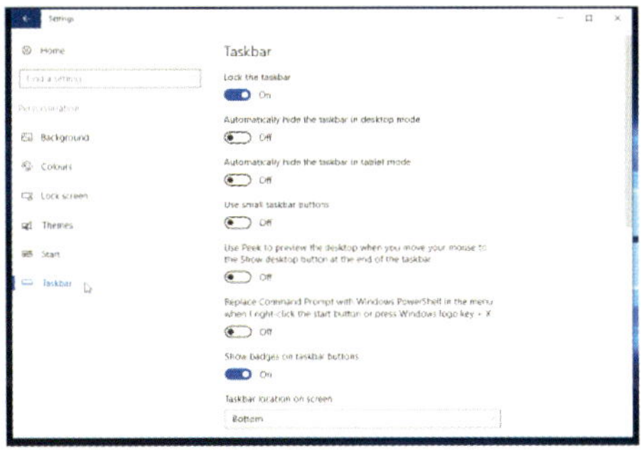

6 New taskbar options

The taskbar looks and works much as it did before though, as well see in a moment, the icons that live on it behave a little differently than before.

What has changed, though, is the way you customise the taskbar. Pre-AU, the options for changing the taskbar and Notification area were spread awkwardly throughout the OS. Now, a quick right-click brings up a Settings option – click this for a dedicated one-stop shop for all your taskbar needs (which you can also get to by clicking Settings, Personalisation, then Taskbar), including automatically hiding the taskbar, and whether or not you show the taskbar on all displays in a multi-monitor set-up.

7 Badges

If you've ever used an iPhone or an iPad, then you'll be familiar with the concept of badges. These are little mini-notifications that sit on top of icons to draw your intention to something in particular, such as the number of new

mail messages or Facebook notifications. Well, now Windows 10 has badges, too. They appear over your taskbar and Notification area icons and they're a bit of an acquired taste. Some people may find them genuinely useful to see how many thousands of unread emails there are sitting in their inbox, but others may find this a little oppressive. Thankfully, it's possible to disable them if you prefer, by clicking Settings, Personalisation, Taskbar, then switching 'Show badges on taskbar buttons' off.

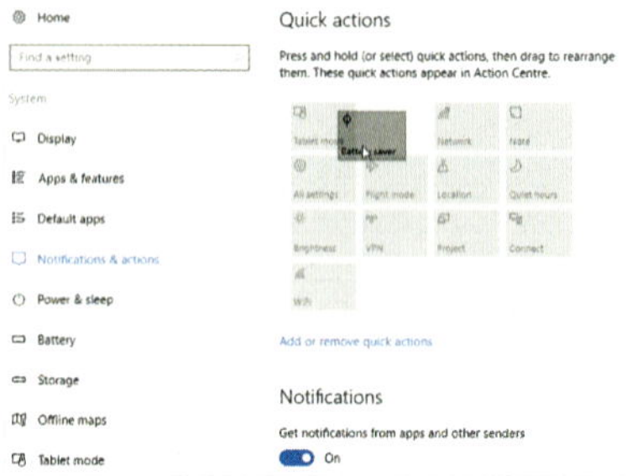

8 Better Quick actions in the notification area

Quick actions – the shortcuts that appear in the bottom of the Action Center panel – were somewhat underused in Windows 10's original incarnation, so we were pleased that Microsoft decided to revamp them for the AU. Now, in Settings, System, 'Notifications & actions' you can click 'Add or remove quick actions' to choose which ones you want to appear and you can also drag and drop them into any order you like with, for example, your most-used ones first. We reckon Microsoft could go a bit further with the customisation options next time, though. It would be good to be able to choose any action here, rather than just those in Microsoft's predefined list.

9 Extensions in Edge

One of the potentially more significant additions in the AU, is the ability to add extensions to Edge (also celebrating its first birthday). We say 'potentially', since the benefits of this depend somewhat on whether or not you actually use Microsoft's browser. If you're one of the many who stuck with (or turned back to) Chrome, Firefox or Microsoft's own Internet Explorer, then the ability to add mini-tools, such as ad blockers and password managers, to Edge may hold limited appeal. On the other hand, it may be just enough to lure you back to give Edge another spin, if only to see how they work in practice.

Currently, there's only a modest selection of Extensions available, all via the Windows Store, including LastPass, AdBlock, Adblock Plus, Evernote Web Clipper and Office Online web apps. Doubtless this selection will grow over time. Installed extensions appear as little icons to the right of the address bar in the browser window and can be managed by clicking the Menu (three dots) icon and selecting Extensions.

10 Other Edge improvements

Less momentous but also worth noting are some minor tweaks to Edge that help bring it in line with other modern browsers. New right-click options, for example, allow you to 'Paste and go' when pasting a URL or 'Paste and search' when pasting search terms into the address bar, which make navigation a lot easier. You can now pin tabs (right-click a tab and select Pin) so these pages always remain open whenever you launch the browser (unless you right-click and Unpin). And – at long last – you can change the browser's default download location (click Menu, Settings, 'View advanced settings' and click Change under 'Save downloaded files to'). All these make using Edge feel better, but is it too little too late for Microsoft's beleaguered browser?

11 Windows Ink

A brand new feature, unique to the AU, Windows Ink is, as the name suggests, intended to improve the use of pen devices. Which brings us to our first problem. It's unlikely that you own a pen device unless you're lucky enough to have one of Microsoft's expensive Surface Pro tablets – and even then, the Surface Pen is a £50 optional extra. It's possible to use your mouse or your finger, if you have a touchscreen PC, but Windows Ink won't be enabled by default. In fact (problem #2), it's actually quite well hidden and won't appear in the OS at all unless you right-click the taskbar and select 'Show Windows Ink Workspace button'.

Tap the new button, and a panel of options (the 'Workspace') will fly out from

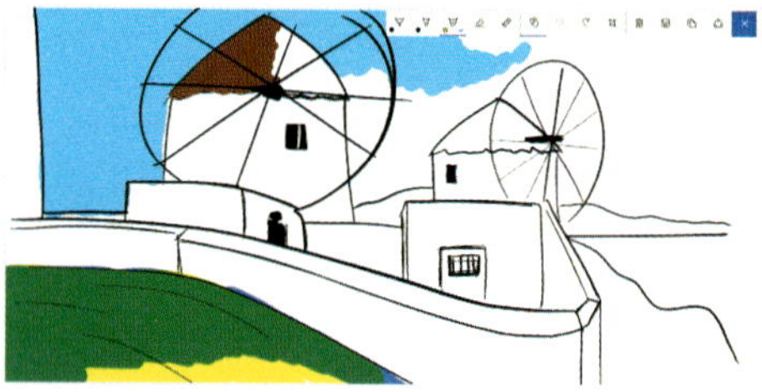

the right, where the Action Centre would normally be. It contains three main tools: Sticky Notes (Post-Its you can scribble notes on), Sketchpad (blank pages you can draw on) and 'Screen sketch' (which lets you annotate what's on-screen).

As it stands, Windows Ink is great if you have a Surface Pro and a Surface Pen, but the feature doesn't work well with a mouse or finger (problem #3) and appears to be a bit buggy. In fact, it managed to crash the entire Start menu twice while we were testing it out (problem #4).

Where's my AU?

Haven't received the Anniversary Update yet? Microsoft has been rolling out the free update to all Windows 10 users "in waves" since 2 August and it should simply get picked up by Windows Update and downloaded automatically as it's rolled out to your PC.

If you haven't received it yet, try clicking Settings, 'Update & security', then 'Check for updates'. If it doesn't come through straight away, keep trying. You might also want to check that you haven't accidentally set your PC to defer updates or configured your internet connection as 'metered' (see the box on page 14), as these could also delay the update.

If all else fails, you could try downloading the update manually from Microsoft. Visit www.snipca.com/21195 to find out how.

12 Calendar integration

If you use Windows 10's Calendar app, then you may have been frustrated by its apparent inability to talk to the calendar in your taskbar – the one that pops up when you click the time and date in the Notification area. The AU addresses this failing by making the two inexplicably separate calendars one and the same. So now you don't have to open the app to check upcoming appointments; just click the date in the bottom right of your screen for a snapshot of the day ahead.

13 New accessibility features

Microsoft has included a heavily revamped text-to-speech tool among the AU's 'Ease of Access' options in the Settings app. New voices in Narrator offer a much faster top rate of speech – approximately 800 words per minute, compared to roughly 400 words per minute in previous versions. Improved keyboard navigation (more in keeping with other screen-reading hardware) and automatic verbal suggestions when you start typing search terms are among the other improvements – see www.snipca.com/21197 for full details.

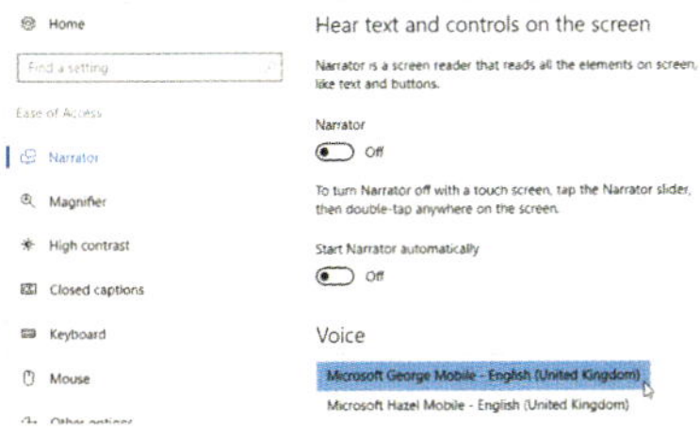

14 More control over updates

No, sadly Microsoft hasn't relented on its compulsory updates rule. But what the AU does provide is a little more control over when updates are installed, thanks to Active hours. This new feature allows you to specify a period of every day when you can be certain that Windows Update won't suddenly interrupt what you're doing with a random request to restart following an update. It's not an ideal situation, but it's better than it was. To configure Active hours, go to Settings, 'Update & security', Windows Update, then click 'Change active hours' and set your time period.

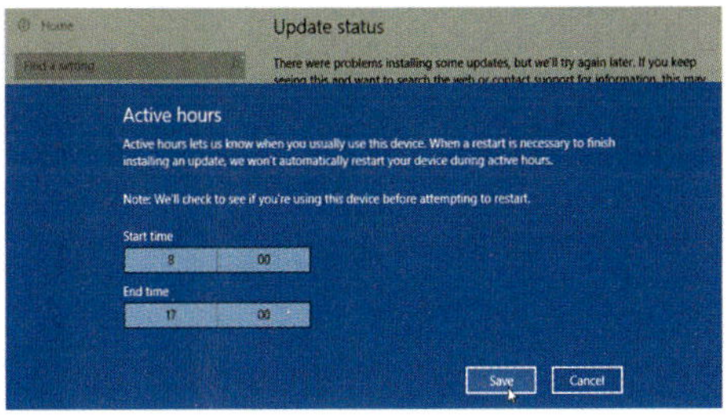

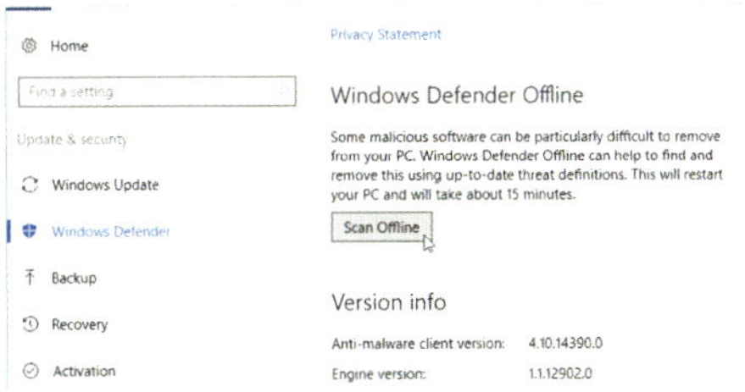

15 Improvements to Defender

We've yet to test the new version of Defender properly, so we don't know whether Windows 10's built-in protection is any safer than it was. But a number of new features make the tool more useful, even if you're using third-party security software instead. Chief among these is a new type of scan that can help root out hard-to-find malware by restarting your PC in offline mode – click Settings, 'Update & security', Windows Defender, then Scan Offline. Security conscious users can also opt for enhanced notifications in Defender's options, for more regular updates on the health of their system.

And if you'd rather use an alternative antivirus tool, such as Kaspersky Internet Security, it's now possible to set Windows Defender as a second layer of protection without causing conflicts with your other security software – see Chapter 3 for more on Defender.

16 Linux command line

At its Build 2016 conference, Microsoft made a surprise announcement that it was adding the Linux command line to Windows 10 via the AU. In practice, this isn't anything like running a virtual version of Linux within Windows. There's no friendly user interface, for example – it's literally just the Linux command line console. Disabled by default, this is an optional feature, aimed at developers rather than everyday users.

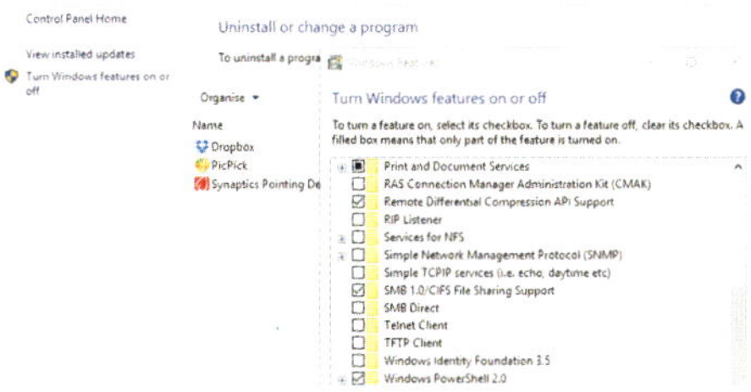

If you want to experiment with it, you'll need to enable it by right-clicking Start and selecting 'Programs and Features', then clicking 'Turn Windows features on or off' on the left. Scroll down to 'Windows Subsystem For Linux (Beta)' and tick this, then click OK and restart your PC when prompted. This will add a new app called Bash to your PC – click Start, type bash and press Enter to launch it and you'll be given the option to install Ubuntu on your computer.

17 Other new features

On laptops and tablets, you can now choose how much battery life background apps are allowed to use. Click Settings, System, Battery, 'Battery usage by app', then click an app and select whether to always allow the app, never allow it, or let Windows manage it.

Meanwhile, Cortana is now available from the lock screen, which we're not necessarily sure is a good thing (see over the page). And if you have Cortana on your Android phone (which you probably don't, since Cortana for Android isn't available in the UK yet), then it's possible to see your phone's notifications – incoming SMS alerts and so on – on your PC desktop.

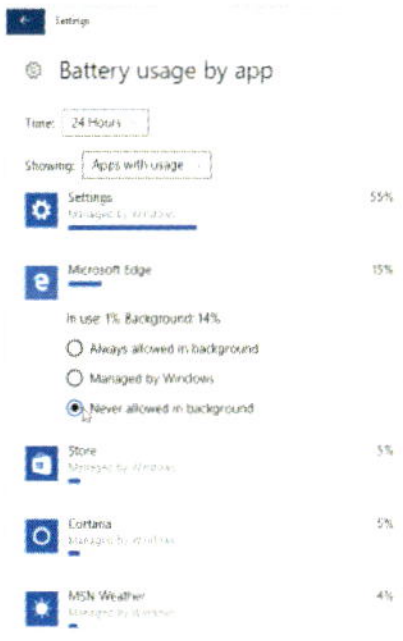

Windows Phone owners get a new feature that lets them 'project' their device to a Windows 10 PC without having to connect any cables – the phone's display appears in a window on the desktop.

Windows Hello – Microsoft's password-less login system – is extended further into the OS, allowing you to unlock to apps and web pages (in Edge) using your fingerprint or iris scan, though you'll need the relevant biometric hardware in order to make use of this.

IT'S NOT ALL GOOD – WHAT YOU MUST CHANGE NOW

More ads!

Upon its initial release, Windows 10 failed to endear itself to large amounts of the population, thanks to the overabundance of adverts – and adverts masquerading as apps and 'suggestions' – found throughout the OS. This was bad enough when Windows 10 was free, but it's even more galling now that the OS is officially a pay-for product.

The bad news for anyone who hates ads (in other words, everyone except advertisers) is that the Anniversary Update features more of them than ever before. You'll find double the amount of adverts in the Start menu, along with many more scattered around in various other parts of the operating system.

The Start menu in the AU contains no less than 10 tiles for 'promoted apps', including Flipboard, Adobe Photoshop Express and games like Minecraft, Sonic Dash and Uno. Clicking on any of these opens the app's page in the Windows Store. Annoyingly, there's currently no way to turn these off all in one go, so instead you'll just need to right-click each one in turn and select 'Unpin from Start'. As far as we can tell, those updating existing Windows 10 PCs won't suffer the extra Start menu ads – they'll only appear if you reinstall Windows from scratch or buy a new PC.

▲ There are more ads in the Start menu now

Whichever way you've installed the AU, you'll find that adverts have also invaded the Windows Ink Workspace – there's a 'Suggested' panel towards the bottom that promotes apps from the Windows Store, and there currently doesn't appear to be any way of disabling this without hacking your Registry.

More privacy problems!

Windows 10's privacy is leaky at the best of times – see Chapter 3 for our advice on what you need to do to protect your personal information. But the AU brings fresh opportunities for Microsoft – and others – to harvest your data.

For example, Cortana's location tracking is a lot more sophisticated in the AU, able to store and call upon past locations you've visited – a bit like having your very own desktop stalker. Cortana can also now potentially take proactive action, carrying out tasks in certain apps without your interaction, which is fine in theory, but could potentially cause problems if the apps in question were malicious.

Cortana is also now available from the lock screen – this is enabled by default. If you use Cortana, having access to it from the lock screen could be useful, but this could be abused, should your computer fall into the wrong hands – criminals could potentially carry out actions and access your data without the need to unlock your PC. You can disable this by clicking in the Search box, then clicking the Settings (cog) icon and switching off 'Use Cortana even when my device is locked'.

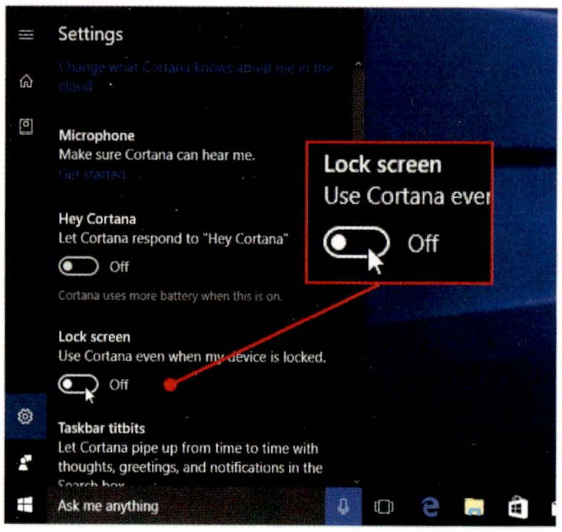

▲ Stop Cortana appearing on the lock screen

Finally, a new feature in Edge called 'Web notifications' allows websites to send you desktop notifications. This is all very well for sites and services that you want to keep up to date with, but it's easy to see how you could end up being inundated with notifications you don't want. Thankfully, websites can't send you anything unless you agree to let them do so first. To block notifications, you no longer want, open Edge, click the menu (three dots) button and select Settings, then 'View advanced settings', then click Manage under Notifications.

More hassle!

It's worth mentioning that, since the AU effectively installs an entirely new build of Windows 10 on your PC, it will take some time to download – the files needed will exceed 3GB. The process of updating could take a long time, too, as the new version will need to be installed over the top of your old OS. And it goes without saying that any major update such as this has the potential to go horribly wrong.

If you have problems with the update, be sure to check out the troubleshooting section of this guide (Chapter 6) for help and advice. In the meantime, if you haven't already installed the update, then we strongly advise you to back up your entire system before you do so. And, if you'd prefer to delay installing the Anniversary Update, check the options on the left.

How to delay the update

On page 12 we showed you how to get the Anniversary Update, but not everyone will be as eager to invite all the disruption and hassle that installing such a big update inevitably brings. Since updates are mandatory in Windows 10, you'll need to install it sooner or later, but if you haven't received it already, there may be a way to put it off until you're ready.

If you're running Windows 10 Pro, you can use the 'Defer upgrades' option (under Settings, 'Update & security', Windows Update, 'Advanced options'), which lets you postpone updates that bring new Windows features for "several months" – this should prevent the AU installing automatically.

If you're running Windows 10 Home and your PC uses Wi-Fi to connect to the web, you can defer major updates, including the AU, by setting your connection as metered. To do this, click Settings, 'Network & internet', then WiFi. Click 'Advanced options', then click to switch 'Set as metered connection' on.

THE FEATURES THAT ARE MISSING

1 Wi-Fi Sense

A deeply unpopular feature in Windows 10's original release, Wi-Fi Sense – which automatically shared your Wi-Fi password with anyone in your Contacts list – has been unceremoniously dropped from the AU.

Microsoft always maintained the feature was safe, but since it stored a copy of your password on the company's servers, and since it offered no control over which of your contacts the password was shared with, we always felt that the security of the feature was flawed and we're glad to see the back of it.

The name Wi-Fi Sense lives on, but it now only refers to the feature that connects you automatically to 'suggested' Wi-Fi hotspots. But guess what – we don't think this is safe, either, because it could lead you to unknowingly send sensitive data while connected to an unsecured hotspot, allowing hackers to intercept it. So we recommend disabling it by going to Settings, 'Network & internet', then Wi-Fi and switching off 'Connect to suggested open hotspots'.

2 Messaging Everywhere

Microsoft promised Messaging Everywhere as part of the Anniversary Update back in April and Windows Insiders even got to try it out in previous preview builds of the OS. The rather handy feature allowed you to send and receive text messages from your phone via your Windows 10 desktop. Sadly, however, Messaging Everywhere never made to the final update and it looks unlikely that it'll ever see the light of day. In a blog post, Windows Insider chief Dona Sarkar explained that, while the feature was well-received by Insiders, "we believe we can deliver an even better experience through the Skype app," though we've yet to see equivalent features turn up in Skype.

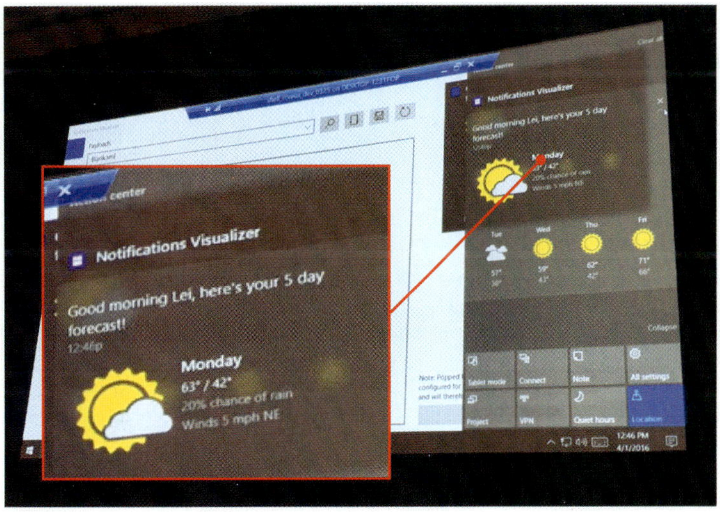

▲ The 'widgets' shown in Microsoft's early demo turned out to be just notifications

3 'Floating' Cortana

When Redstone was originally announced, there were rumours that a more integrated version of Cortana was going to be imbued with the ability to move around the OS, appearing 'contextually', while you browsed the web or typed up documents. But Microsoft appears to have dumped this idea – or perhaps it was never true in the first place. Either way, we're grateful that Cortana remains where it is, and doesn't pop up randomly, like some kind of voice-controllable Clippy the animated paper clip

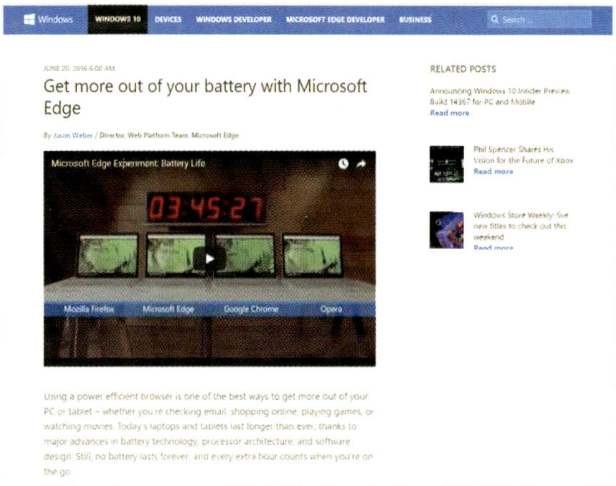

▲ Microsoft's battery claims have been largely debunked

4 Action Centre widgets

Several months ago, Microsoft demoed a build of the AU that showed off what appeared to be widgets in the Action Centre, displaying weather forecasts and more. Sadly, however, these turned out to be nothing like the handy desktop widgets included in Windows 7 – they're just slightly fancier notifications (see page 11) and can't be pinned in place or dynamically refreshed, like true widgets can.

5 Massively longer battery life with Edge

In June this year, Microsoft made the bold claim that Edge consumed much less power than other browsers, allowing you to run your device on battery power for dramatically longer than if you used Chrome, Firefox or Opera. It even displayed a video of its tests (www.snipca.com/21199) and suggested that the Anniversary Update would "make sure you can stay online longer with Microsoft Edge." Just two days later, however, Microsoft's claims were blown out of the water by Opera, who questioned Microsoft's methodology and revealed its own test (www.snipca.com/21200), inviting Microsoft – and anyone else – to replicate their findings. A subsequent independent test carried out by US website PC World (www.snipca.com/21202) appears to give Edge a small lead over its rivals but nothing like the huge advantages originally claimed by Microsoft.

5 Chaseable' live tiles

The AU was supposed to make live tiles cleverer by allowing them to know specifically what you clicked on and take you directly to that content, rather than just opening the app. If Microsoft has implemented this improvement, we've yet to see any evidence of it. On our test PC, for example, clicking on particular news story on the News app's live tile still fails to open the story in the News app.

The best new things Windows 10 can do (that Windows 7 and 8.1 can't)

We reveal 19 reasons why Windows 10 is so much better than its predecessors

Windows 10 has come in for its fair share of flak since it launched in July 2015, with many naysayers citing installation problems, flawed privacy settings and compulsory updates among the reasons why they're sticking with Windows 7 or 8.1.

But these problems can usually be overcome with a little patience and the odd settings tweak. Follow our advice throughout this guide and you should be left with a secure, modern operating system (OS) that will be supported by Microsoft for years to come – and which offers many tangible benefits over previous versions of Windows.

It shouldn't be forgotten that a number of Windows 10's biggest plus points are actually older features that weren't included in Windows 8.1. But, while it's good to see Microsoft had enough sense to restore features like the Start menu and Shutdown button, it's actually Windows 10's brand new features that are more likely to win you over if you're still in two minds about upgrading.

We're not talking about those gimmicky, heavily hyped features that Microsoft never stops harping on about, either. For every Cortana personal assistant or Xbox games-streaming app, there are dozens of genuinely useful features, tools and additions that you won't find in any version of Windows that came before.

Whether you're a Windows 7 or 8.1 user who's still undecided about upgrading, or you have already taken the leap and are looking for new features to explore, we'll show you 19 things – some significant, some quite nuanced – that Windows 10 does better than its predecessors.

What you can do

- Download maps to use when you're offline
- Pin the settings you access most to the Start menu
- Install apps to an external hard drive
- Chat live to Microsoft support
- Send photos and videos to your TV

GET MORE FROM YOUR WINDOWS APPLICATIONS

1 'Cast' photos and videos to your TV

If you own a Miracast-enabled TV or set-top box, then you can use Windows 10 to send media – including music, photos and videos – from your PC to your TV. It's true that Windows 8.1 can do something similar, but Windows 10 adds the ability to stream media directly from the Edge browser.

Launch Edge and navigate to the page you want – this could be, for example, a photo slideshow, YouTube video, or even files you've stored in Dropbox or OneDrive. Next, click the menu button (three dots at the top right) and select 'Cast media to device'. A small window will pop up listing available screens and receivers – click your TV to cast the media to it.

If you don't see your TV or device listed, make sure your PC and the device you want to cast to are both connected to the same network and the receiving device is turned on. This tip will work for BBC iPlayer, though annoyingly other TV-streaming services, such as Netflix, don't support Edge casting.

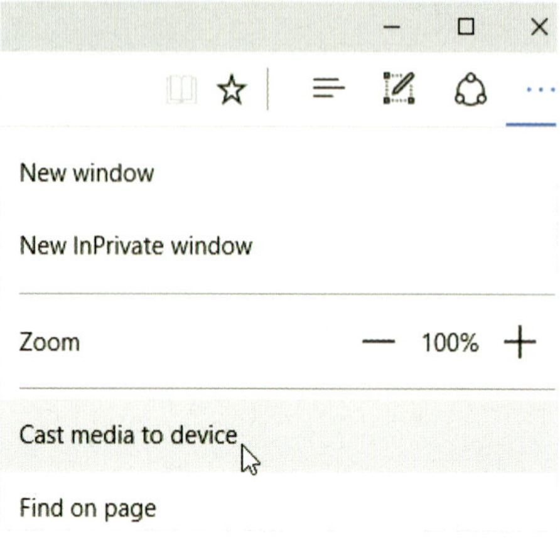

◄ Send music, photos and videos to your TV

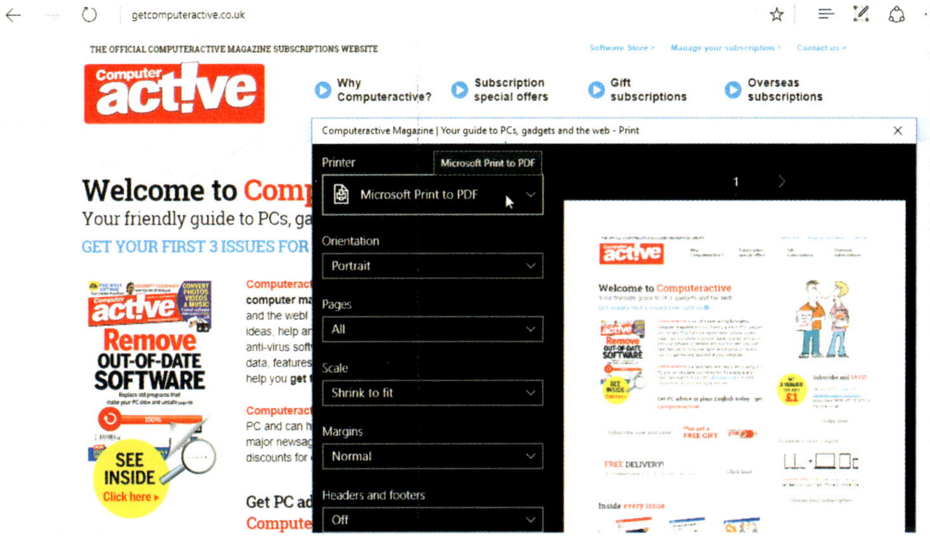

▲ Choose 'Microsoft Print to PDF' to save a PDF of a document, website, map and more

2 Create PDFs in almost any program

Converting documents, maps and other content to PDF files can make it easier to share them over email. Until now, you had to install a third-party PDF tool to carry out these conversions, but many, such as CutePDF, come crammed with adware, toolbars and other unwanted junk.

Sensibly, Microsoft has built PDF creation into Windows 10. Better still, the feature has been incorporated as a print option, meaning that any program or app that allows you to print will also allow you to create or convert your files to PDF.

Let's say you want to save a web page as a PDF. Simply click your browser's menu button (usually in the top-right corner) and select Print. Then choose 'Microsoft Print to PDF' from the list of available printers (see screenshot above). Change any other settings as needed, then click Print. You'll be prompted to give your PDF file a name and choose a location to save it in. Do so and your PDF will be created.

3 Copy and paste in the Command Prompt

Many advanced PC fixes require you to enter specific commands into the Windows Command Prompt tool (CMD) – shutdown /r /o, for example, will restart your PC and bring up the Advanced Start Options menu, from where you can launch Safe Mode. Typing complicated commands can produce errors, which is why it's great that Windows 10's revamped CMD tool finally lets users copy and paste directly using Ctrl+C and Ctrl+V keyboard shortcuts. It's astonishing that Microsoft seemingly hadn't thought of this until now.

To enable this, right-click Start and select Command Prompt. When it opens, right-click the header bar at the top of the program window and select Properties. On the Options tab under Edit Options, tick the box next to 'Enable Ctrl key shortcuts' (see screenshot below right). While you're here, you can enable some of Windows 10's other unique new features too. 'QuickEdit mode' lets you click and drag to select text in the Command Prompt window; 'Filter clipboard contents on paste' automatically removes unnecessary characters from commands you copy; 'Enable line wrapping selection' lets you select and copy multiple lines of text; and 'Extended text selection keys' provides support for even more keyboard shortcuts (such as Ctrl+A to select all text). Click OK when you've finished ticking these.

4 See all notifications in one place

The lack of a notification centre – similar to those you find on most phones and tablets – has been a bone of contention for many Windows users over the years. Windows 8.1 tried to unify the way you received notifications, but it fell short. Windows 10 finally addresses this in its new version of the Action Center.

Simply click the speech-bubble icon at the bottom right of the desktop and the Action Center will slide out from the side of the screen. The latest notifications will be displayed at the top of the panel. Once you've read a notification, click the 'X'

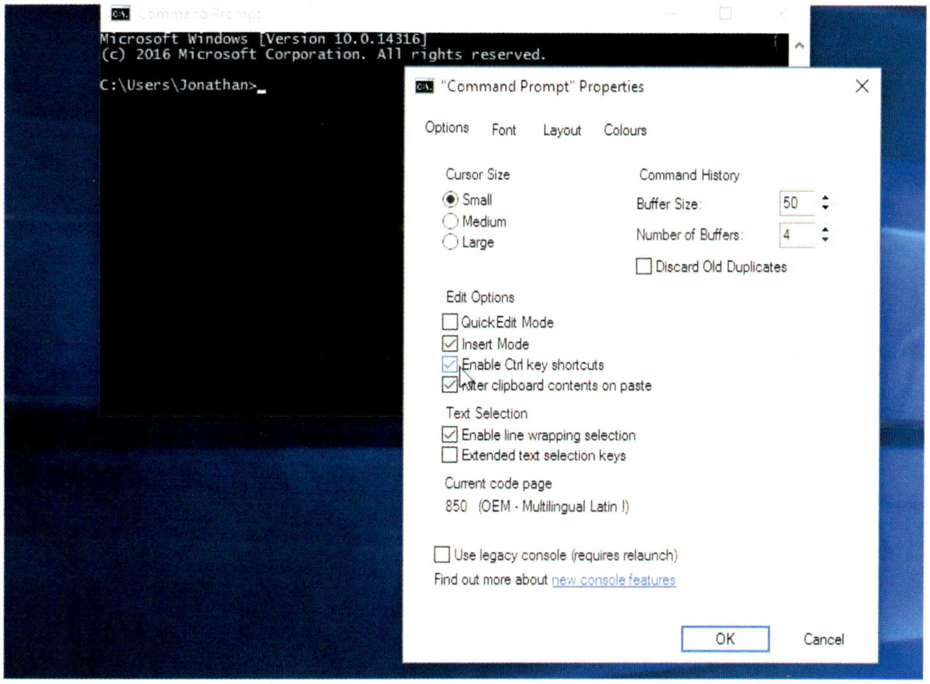

▲ Enable keyboard shortcuts and other new customisations in the Command Prompt

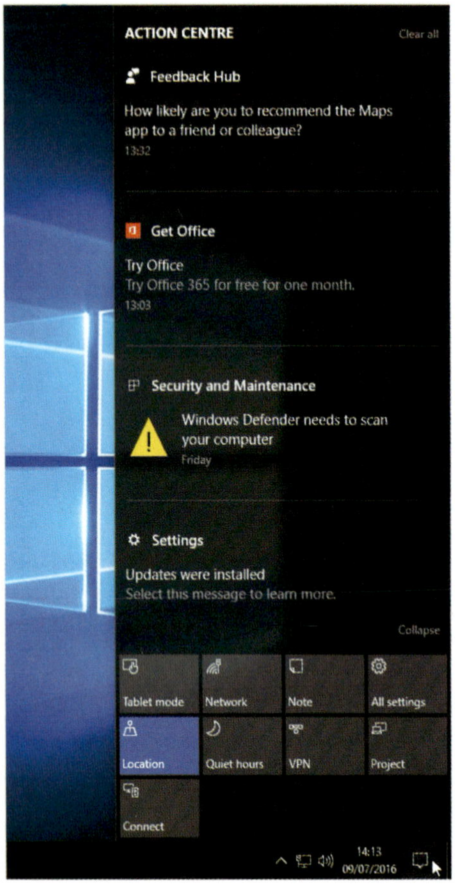

▲ Windows 10 groups all your notifications together

next to it to delete it or click 'Clear all' to delete all your current notifications.

5 Set reminders via your voice

Most Windows 10 users will probably agree that Cortana – the operating system's much-vaunted personal assistant – is nowhere near as impressive as Microsoft would have us believe. That said, there are times when Cortana's skills can actually come in very handy – for instance, when you want a quick way to set reminders.

Let's say there's something important that you need to do at a certain time of day – take some medication, perhaps. Just click the microphone icon in the taskbar and say 'set a reminder'. Cortana will ask you what it is you need to remember and when you need the reminder to pop up. You can even set up recurring reminders by saying 'every day at four o'clock,' for example. Double-check that all the details displayed in Cortana's panel are correct, adjust them if necessary, then say 'yes' or click Remind.

6 Download maps

Windows 8.1 has a map app, but Windows 10's version goes one better by letting you download maps to your PC, so you can view them without an internet

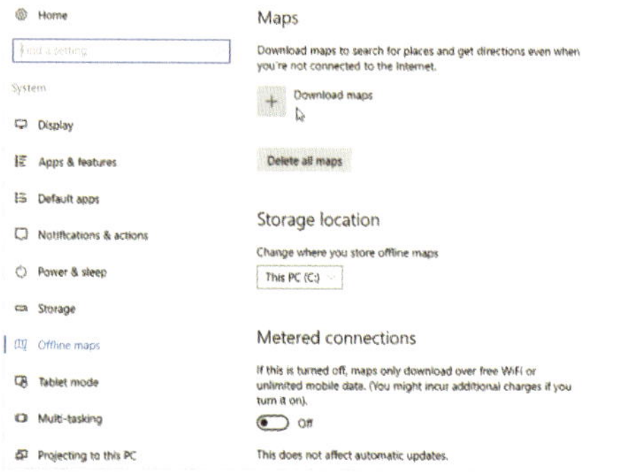

▲ Download maps to use offline

connection. Click Start, type maps and click the Maps app link. When the app opens, click the Menu (three dots) icon, top right, then Settings (cog), then 'Choose maps'.

You'll be taken to the 'Offline maps' page of the Settings app. Click 'Download maps' (see screenshot above), select your continent (Europe, for example), followed by your country, then your region.

Close the Maps app and your map will begin downloading. Navigate to Start, Settings, System, 'Offline maps' to delete maps you've downloaded or change where they are stored. It's also a good idea to enable the 'Automatically update maps' option while you're here.

CUSTOMISE YOUR DESKTOP

7 Scroll inactive windows

Another feature Microsoft should have built into Windows 7 and 8.1 is the ability to scroll program windows that aren't active. Most of us have several different windows open at any given time – an email program, a web browser and a Word document, for example. In previous versions of Windows, you'd need to click the program window to make it active before you could use the mouse wheel to scroll.

But in Windows 10 you can scroll any open window just by moving your mouse over it. On paper this doesn't sound like a big deal, but in practice, being able to scroll any open window just makes sense. Background scrolling is usually enabled by default in Windows 10, but you can check by clicking Start, Settings, Devices and making sure the 'Scroll inactive windows when I hover over them' option is enabled.

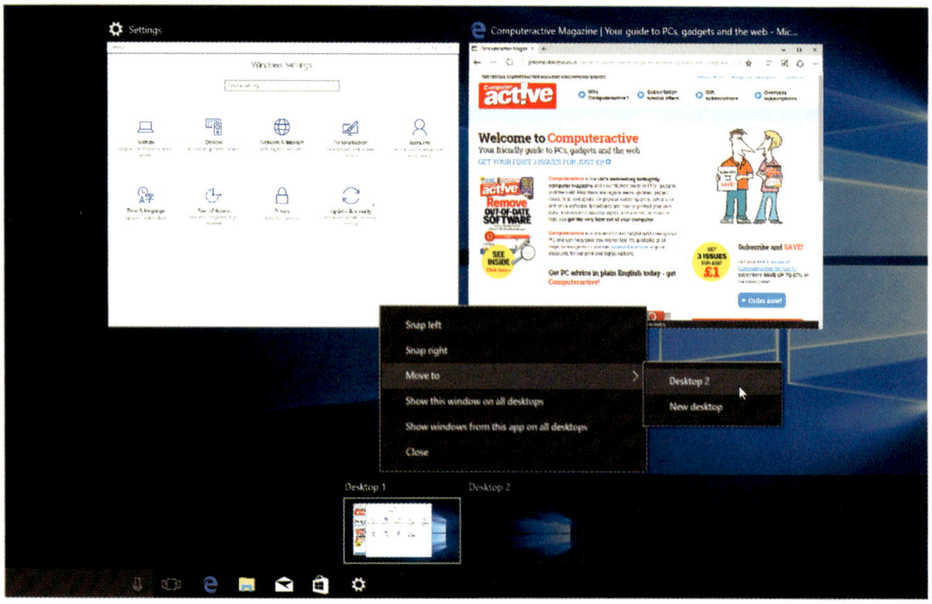

▲ Once you've created a virtual desktop, move a program to it by choosing 'Move to', then Desktop 2

8 Work across multiple virtual desktops

Windows 10 is the first version of the OS to have virtual desktops, which are a great way to organise your screen if you only have one monitor. Each desktop works a bit like a second screen, so if you have certain applications that you want to keep open but don't want them taking up too much space, you can park them on a second desktop and switch to it when you need to. For example, you could keep your email program running on a separate desktop and only switch to it when you're notified of new messages that you want to read.

To create a virtual desktop (or even multiple virtual desktops), click the Task View button next to the Search bar on the taskbar, then click 'New desktop' on the right. You can quickly move any open program window to your new desktop by clicking Task View, then right-clicking the thumbnail of the program you want to move and choosing 'Move to', then Desktop 2 (see screenshot left). To quickly jump between virtual desktops hold down the Windows Key and Ctrl, then press the left and right arrow keys.

9 Put the Recycle Bin in the Start menu

Amazingly, Windows 10 is the first version of the OS that makes it easy to add a shortcut to the Recycle Bin to the Start menu. If you want to do this in Windows 7, you need to carry out a massively convoluted hack and, of course, Windows 8.1 doesn't have a Start menu at all.
In Windows 10, you can simply right-click the Recycle Bin icon on your desktop (or click Start, type recycle and right-click the Recycle Bin link), then select 'Pin to Start'. A Recycle Bin tile will appear in the Start menu, which you can drag to position wherever you like.

10 Turn your PC into a tablet

Windows 7 was designed in an era before support for touchscreens and tablets was necessary, while Windows 8.1 arguably went too far in the other direction – by imposing tablet-based ways of working on people who just wanted to use their PC like they always had done. Windows 10, on the other hand, offers the best of both worlds.

It's set up to be used with a traditional keyboard and mouse on a PC and with touchscreen gestures on a tablet, and can automatically switch between desktop and tablet mode depending on the type of device it's being run on. But, should you want to, you can manually switch between these two modes, giving you the option of using your PC like a tablet (and vice versa).

This isn't as handy on a desktop PC, but if you're using a touchscreen laptop, it offers a useful alternative way of interacting with your device. To enable tablet mode, click Start, Settings, System, 'Tablet mode' and select either 'Use the appropriate mode for my hardware' (for automatic switching) or 'Use tablet mode' (to set tablet mode manually) from the 'When I sign in' dropdown menu.

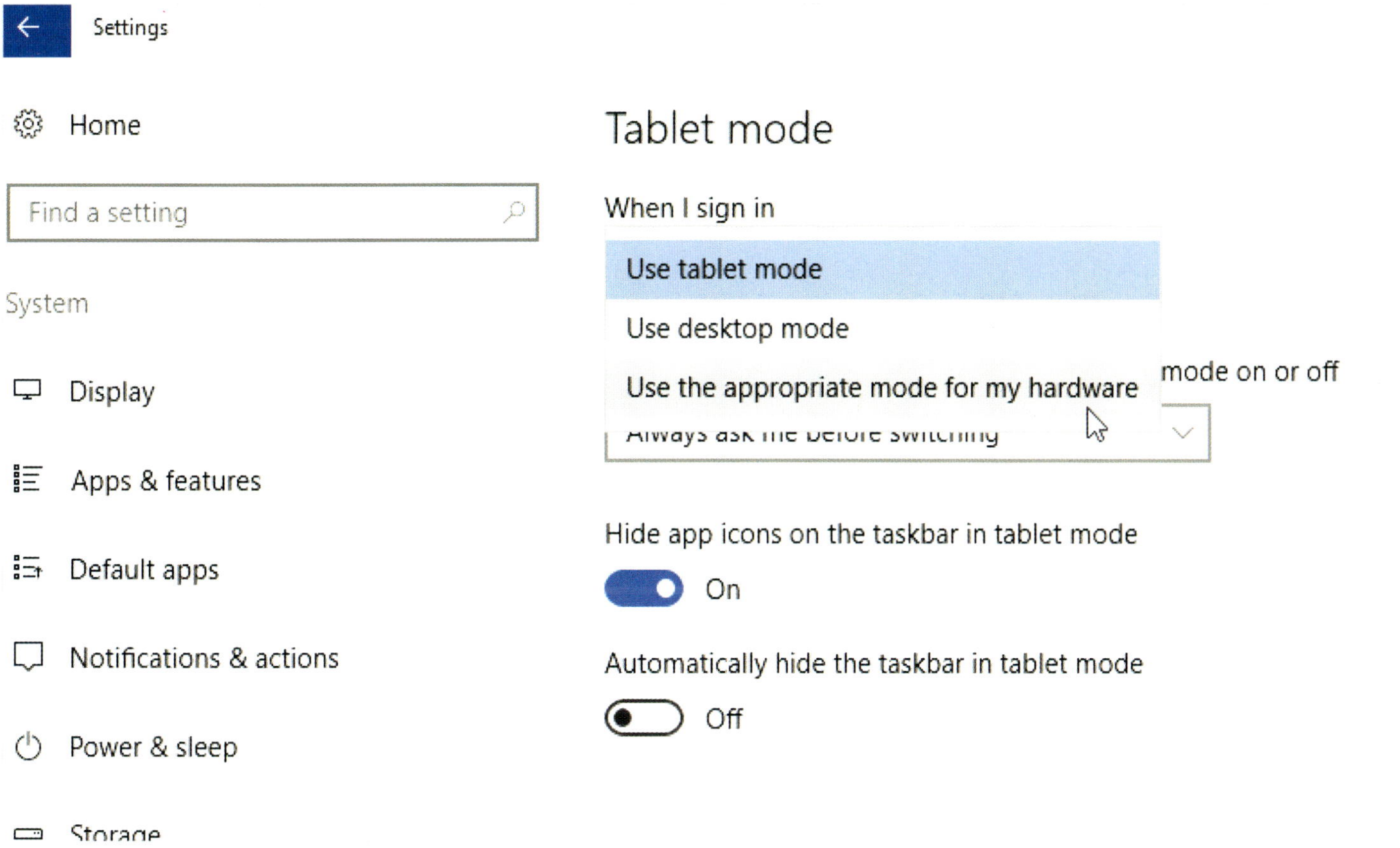

▲ If you're using a touchscreen laptop, tablet mode offers a useful alternative way of interacting with your device

THINGS WE WISH WINDOWS 10 COULD DO

Windows 10 is evolving all the time as Microsoft constantly updates it – a fresh new batch of features has just arrived as part of the Anniversary Update in August (see page 10). Here is a wish list of features we'd like to see added to Windows 10 in future updates.

LET YOU CHOOSE WHAT TO UPDATE

Microsoft has allowed us to control what gets updated on our PCs for many years, so it's galling that Windows 10 forces its updates upon us. In theory, this is the safest bet because it means you'll always have the latest security updates, but we wish the OS would allow more flexibility, particularly when it comes to updates to drivers because these can sometimes cause devices, such as printers and scanners, to stop working.

CUSTOMISE START MENU TILES

Currently, you have limited options to change how the Start menu tiles look and work. Some tiles look a bit boring – just icons in a box – and we'd love to be able to customise these or create our own.

ADD TABS TO FILE EXPLORER

The new version of File Explorer offers more features than its predecessors, including the ability to pin files and folders to the Quick Access area. But we'd like to see the addition of tabs – similar to those used in web browsers – that let you copy, paste and move files between two locations more easily.

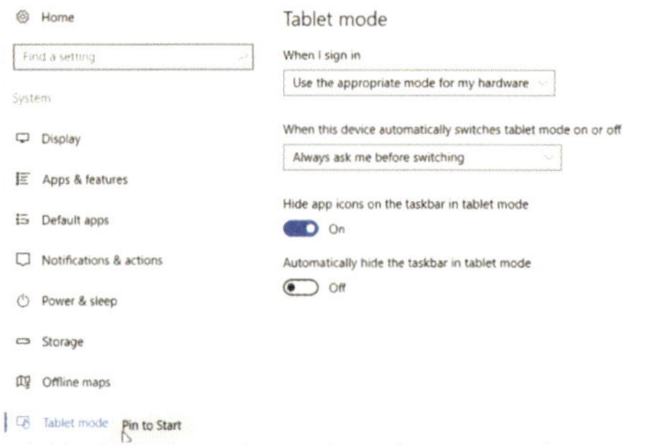

▲ You can pin almost any option to the Start menu

11 Pin specific settings to the Start menu

The Windows 10 Settings app is simpler than Windows 7's Control Panel and far easier to access and navigate than Windows 8.1's PC Settings. Not only that, but Windows 10 also includes one very useful feature that you won't find on its predecessors – the ability to add individual settings to the Start menu.

Let's say, for example, you find yourself frequently switching between tablet and desktop mode (see previous tip). Instead of laboriously navigating your way through the Settings app every time, you could add a link to quickly enable or disable tablet mode directly from the Start menu. Open the Settings app, navigate to the setting you want, then right-click the setting's subcategory on the left. Select 'Pin to Start' (see screenshot above) then click Yes.

12 Switch between open windows with a click

Anyone who multitasks will be familiar with Alt+Tab – the keyboard shortcut that has, for many years, let users switch between open windows. But Windows 10 adds a completely new way to do this – using your mouse instead. Simply click the Task View button on the taskbar and you'll see thumbnails representing each open program on your PC. Click a thumbnail to switch to the program it represents. Task View also lets you add and switch between virtual desktops (see tip 8).

13 Pin four program windows to your screen

Aero Snap, which was introduced in Windows 7 and continued in Windows 8.1, lets you pin program windows to either side of the screen. It's incredibly useful if you're working within two programs at the same time – a Word document and an Excel spreadsheet, for example – and want to copy and paste between the two.

Windows 10 takes this feature and doubles it, letting you pin not two, but four open program windows at the same time (see screenshot below). You can still snap two programs so they sit side by side if you want (drag the window to the side of the screen as before). To pin three or four programs, drag each window to a corner of the desktop. Each will automatically resize to fit the space, and Snap Assist (another exclusive Windows 10 feature) will display thumbnails of your remaining open windows – just click those you want to view to snap them to the remaining empty quadrants.

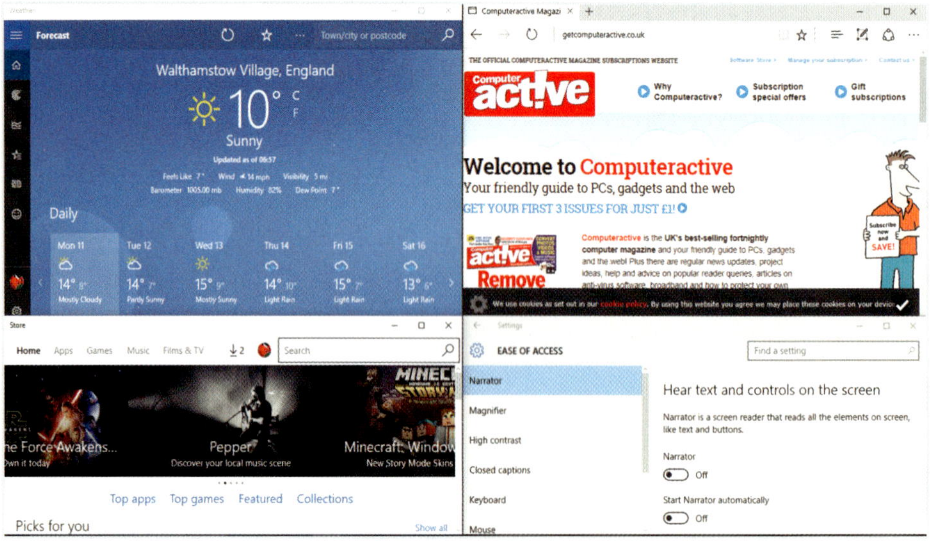

▶ Drag your open programs to the four corners of your desktop to have them 'snap' into place so you can easily view and use them at the same time

MANAGE YOUR PC'S STORAGE

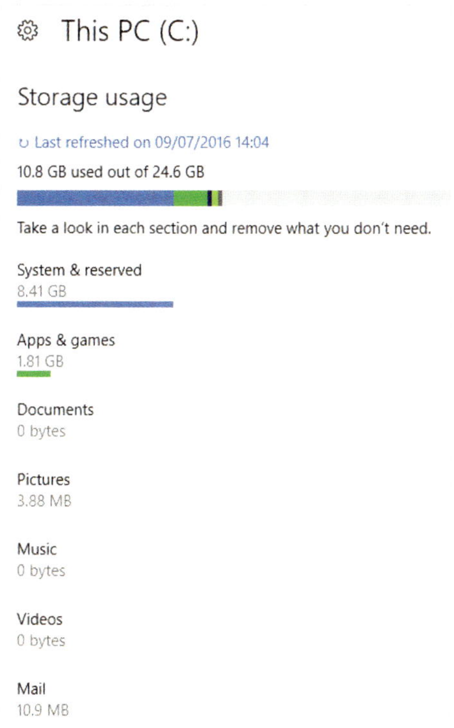

▲ See exactly what's taking up hard drive space

14 Analyse your PC's storage

When it comes to managing the data stored on your PC's hard drive, Windows 7's tools are basic by modern standards. Right-click a drive, then click Properties and you'll see a pie chart showing how much free and used space it has – and that's it. Windows 8.1 offers a little more information, with the 'Disk space' section of the PC Settings app at least breaking down the used space by types of file.

But Windows 10 goes much further than this, visualising exactly what is taking up all your precious hard-drive space, along with options for removing programs, deleting temporary files and more.

To check this out for yourself, click Start, Settings, System, Storage, then click the drive you want to analyse under Storage on the right. Click each category under the bar chart to see what you can remove.

15 Install apps on SD cards

Another new storage utility in Windows 10 (since the November 2015 update) lets users install Windows Store apps on SD cards, USB sticks and other internal and external storage devices, instead of the PC's built-in system drive. This is particularly useful for laptops and tablets that are running low on storage, because you can install the tools you want without clogging up your system drive (usually the C drive). Insert your SD card or USB stick, then click Start, Settings, System, then Storage. Scroll down to the 'Save locations' section and under 'New apps will save to', select the SD card or USB storage you want to use, then click Apply.

16 Set default save locations for specific file types

You can also use the procedure described in the previous tip to change which drive you save new documents, music files, photos and video files to. The nearest equivalent in Windows 7 or 8.1 is a somewhat complex procedure that involves defining a custom target location for each Library folder.

In Windows 10, you just click an option to set which drive you want to save each type of file to. You might want to do this if your PC uses a fast SSD for its system drive and a larger traditional hard drive for storing files.

Click Start, Settings, System, then Storage. Scroll down to the 'Save locations' section, use the dropdown menus to select the drive you want for each type of file, then click Apply (see screenshot below). Note that this won't move any existing files to the new locations – you'll still need to move these manually.

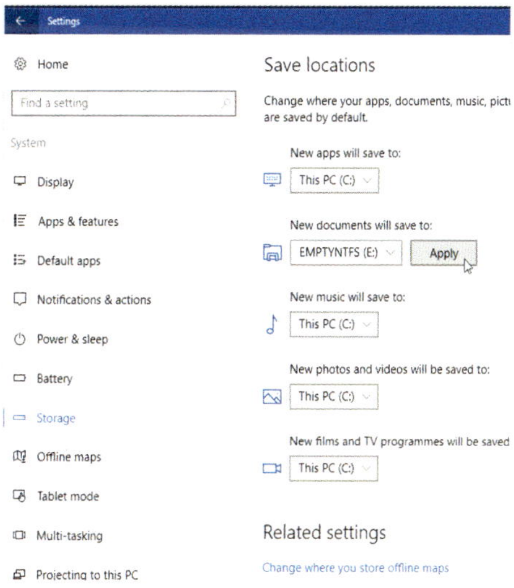

◀ Choose where you want to save specific file types on your PC by changing their default save location

WHAT WINDOWS 10 CAN'T DO THAT WINDOWS 7 OR 8.1 CAN

Windows 10 offers lots of new features, but it's also dropped a few old ones too. Here are some of our favourite Windows 7 and 8.1 functions that are missing from Microsoft's newest OS.

PLAY DVDS

As a cost-saving exercise (and to push more people towards its own movie download service), Microsoft didn't include DVD playback in Windows 10. If you have lots of DVDs, install the free VLC media player from www.videolan.org to play them on your PC.

PLAY SOLITAIRE FOR FREE

This long-serving staple is still available in Windows 10, but it has gone 'freemium', meaning you need to pay (£1.19 a month or £7.69 a year) to remove annoying adverts and unlock all of its features. We don't recommend you pay, though. Instead try a free online alternative such as www.solitaireforfree.com.

THE START SCREEN

Not everybody loved Windows 8's Start screen, but it had some benefits, including the ability to display all the programs installed on your PC on a single screen. It's replaced by the Start menu in Windows 10, but a version of the Start screen lives on in Tablet mode (see page 19).

DESKTOP GADGETS

Gadgets, a feature of Windows 7 (and Vista), let you pin mini apps – clocks, weather icons and so on – to your desktop. However, long before Windows 10, Microsoft decided gadgets were unsafe and urged users to stop using them (see www.snipca.com/20225). A safe version would still be a useful addition to W10.

MAKE YOUR PC WORK FOR YOU

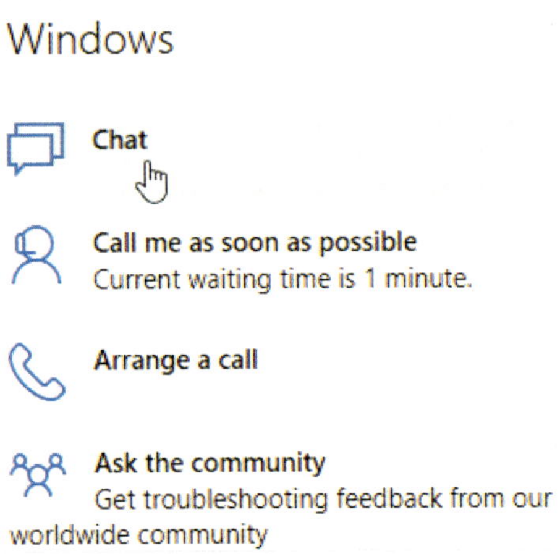

▲ Get help with PC problems from Microsoft

17 Chat directly with Microsoft's support staff

Previous versions of Windows include help files (press the F1 key) that you can browse through. But if you can't find what you need, then Windows 7 and 8.1 passes the buck by suggesting you look for a solution online.

Windows 10 is different. It offers a direct line to an actual human member of Microsoft's Answer Desk at any time via the Contact Support app. Click Start, type contact then click the Contact Support link that appears. A small window will open, asking 'What can we help you with?' In most cases, clicking 'My device' here will simply link you to your PC manufacturer's website, so click 'Windows, Office, Services & Apps' for questions about Windows, or 'Accounts & billing' for help with purchases made through your Microsoft account, for example.

Click through the categories that best describe the problem you're having (choose 'Windows' for most PC problems) and eventually you should see the option to 'Chat' online with a Microsoft tech expert. Alternatively, you can arrange for Microsoft to phone you at a specified time.

If you choose the latter option, just be sure to double-check that the Microsoft technician knows about your case before you offer any details and never reveal your bank details, because there are numerous telephone scams that involve criminals posing as Microsoft employees who demand money to 'fix' your PC – something Microsoft would never do.

18 Find a lost device

Apple has Find My iPhone, Android has Device Manager, but you'll need to rely on the kindness of strangers if you leave your Windows 7 or 8.1 device in the back of a taxi, because there's no way of tracking it remotely.

Windows 10 rectifies this omission by adding a Find My Device option. Sometimes it's switched off by default, so click Start, Settings, 'Update & security', then Find My Device. Click Change, then move the switch to On. If you can't find the Find My Device option, you may need to enable Wi-Fi (it won't work with Wi-Fi switched off). Should you ever lose your device, you can check its last known location by logging in at https://account. microsoft. com/devices.

19 Let Windows 10 manage your printers

Another addition to Windows 10 in the November 2015 update lets the operating system manage your printers. This feature is particularly useful for people who work across different locations – the home and the office, for example – because it means your PC will automatically select the correct default printer for the job.

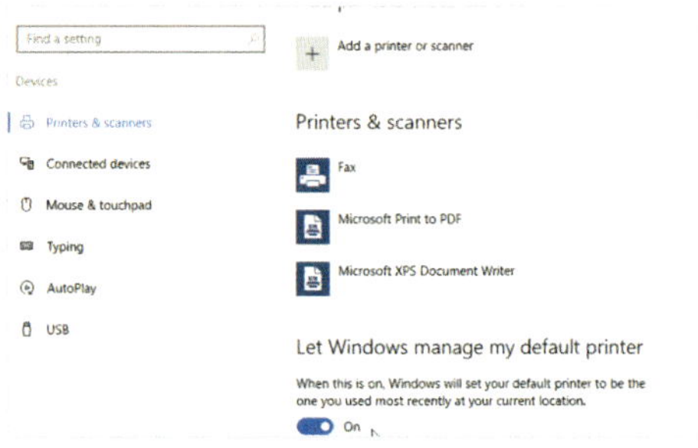

▲ Windows 10 can manage your printer for you

This feature should be enabled by default, but you can check by clicking Start, Settings, Devices, 'Printers & scanners', then scrolling down to make sure the 'Let Windows manage my default printer' option is switched on (see screenshot above). If you'd prefer to set a default printer you can switch the option off, select the printer you use and click 'Set as default'.

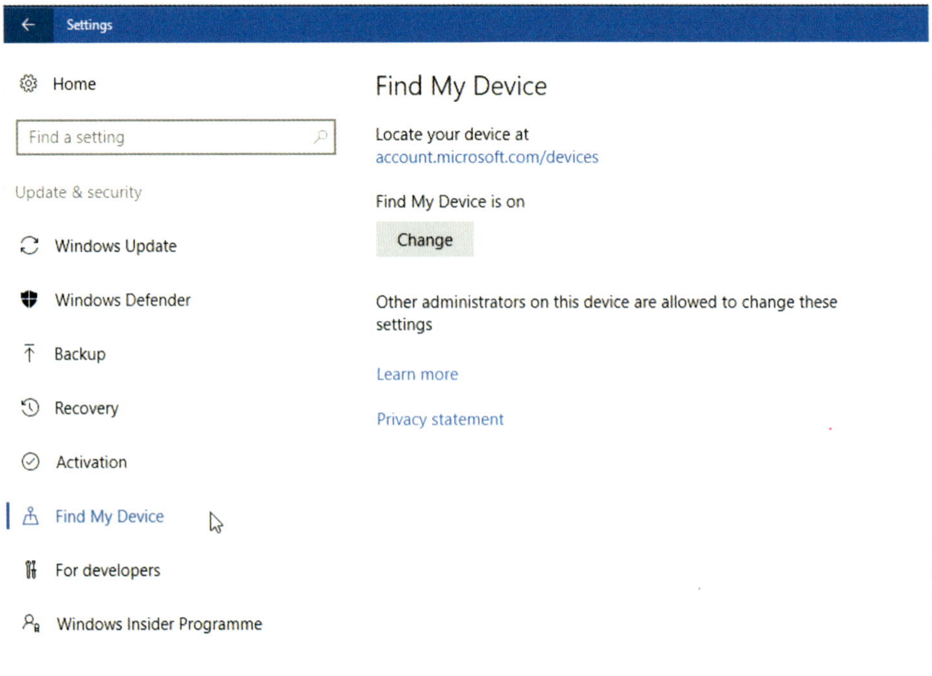

▲ Lost your Windows 10 laptop or tablet? Now you can track it down online

The biggest controversies so far

Windows 10 is great – but it's not been without its clangers and scandals. We deliver our verdict on every one

On the surface, Windows 10 feels like a return to Windows 7. But underneath the comfortingly familiar Desktop and Start menu lurk a number of radical changes – not all of which have been well received. Ever since (and even before) its release, Microsoft's new operating system (OS) has courted its fair share of controversy.

Don't get us wrong – we think Windows 10 is easily the best version of the OS to date. But not everything about it is brilliant. Here's a look at some of Windows 10's biggest blips and blunders since its launch, along with what we think in each case.

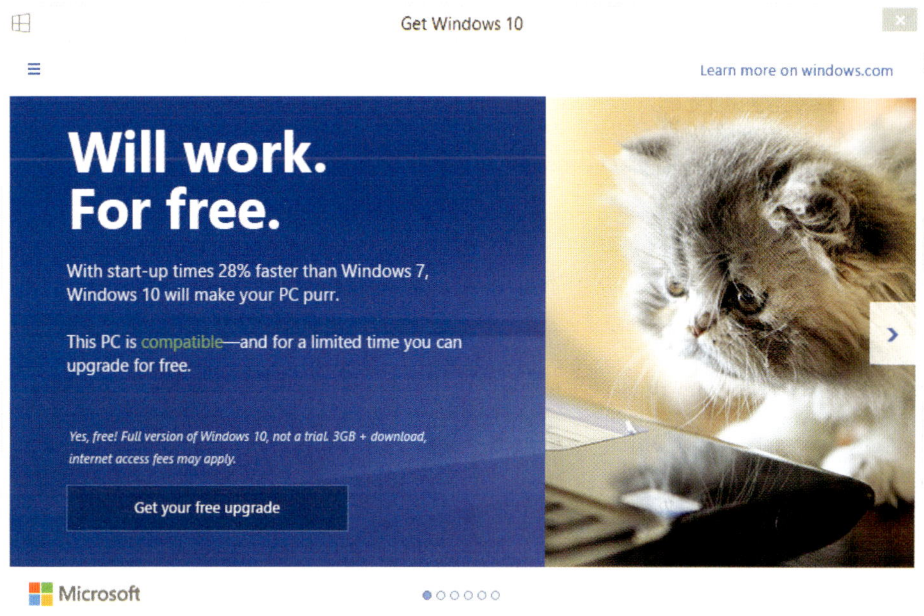

▲ The cute kittens don't fool us – Microsoft's nagging is just unacceptable

Aggressive upgrade nagging

Anyone who was still using Windows 7 or 8.1 during the first year of Windows 10's release will be familiar with the infamous nag screen telling you to upgrade for free, that popped up whenever you started your PC. If you thought they were annoying, things got a whole lot worse when Microsoft decided to re-categorise Windows 10 as a 'Recommended Update'. Basically, this meant many people who set Windows 7 or 8.1 to install updates automatically, suddenly found themselves inadvertently installing Windows 10 – whether they wanted it or not.

OUR VERDICT

It's in Microsoft's interests to have everyone running Windows 10, but the company is assuming that it's in our best interests too. Windows 10 is a great OS, but there are plenty of users who are happy with Windows 7 and 8.1 – and even Windows 8 – so we think the company's heavy-handed tactics were completely out of order.

Compulsory updates

As you probably already know, Windows 10 reduces your control over Windows Updates. In Windows 7 and 8/8.1 you could configure updates (timing, program exclusions and so on), but in Windows 10, all updates are compulsory and you have limited options over how they are installed. You can either leave Windows Update to operate entirely autonomously, restarting your PC to finish off installing updates when it likes, regardless of whether you're using your PC at the time, or you can get it to notify you when a restart is required. Getting updates automatically is mostly a good thing. But significant updates, such as the recent Anniversary Update, can take a long time to install and often cause problems. The big November 2015 update, for example, unleashed numerous problems, including a serious glitch that results in the upgrade getting stuck at the 44% mark.

OUR VERDICT

We think that Microsoft should at least tell you what's in an update. Currently, it doesn't offer any information about what updates contain and that makes us feel insecure. What will it change? What if my PC can't handle it? Moreover, automatic updates should at least work. Microsoft needs to address its apparent strategy of

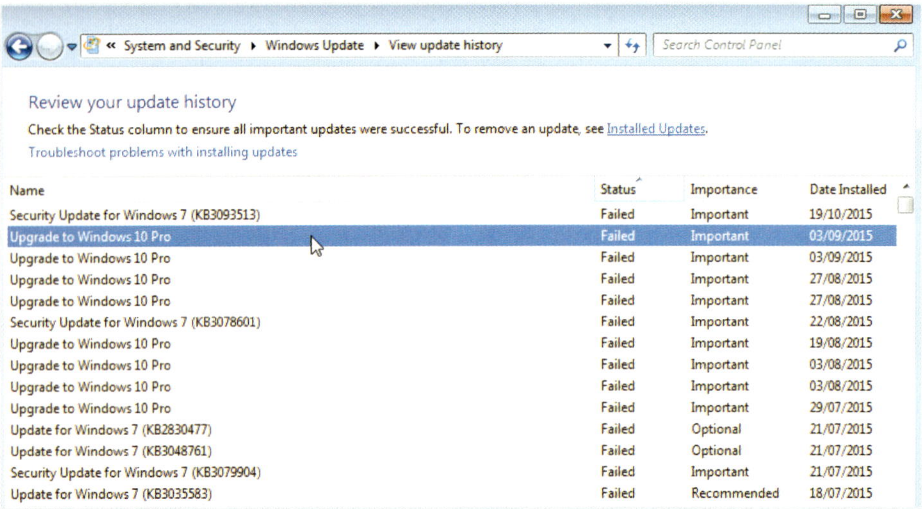

« System and Security ▸ Windows Update ▸ View update history

Review your update history

Check the Status column to ensure all important updates were successful. To remove an update, see Installed Updates.

Troubleshoot problems with installing updates

Name	Status	Importance	Date Installed
Security Update for Windows 7 (KB3093513)	Failed	Important	19/10/2015
Upgrade to Windows 10 Pro	Failed	Important	03/09/2015
Upgrade to Windows 10 Pro	Failed	Important	03/09/2015
Upgrade to Windows 10 Pro	Failed	Important	27/08/2015
Upgrade to Windows 10 Pro	Failed	Important	27/08/2015
Security Update for Windows 7 (KB3078601)	Failed	Important	22/08/2015
Upgrade to Windows 10 Pro	Failed	Important	19/08/2015
Upgrade to Windows 10 Pro	Failed	Important	03/08/2015
Upgrade to Windows 10 Pro	Failed	Important	03/08/2015
Upgrade to Windows 10 Pro	Failed	Important	29/07/2015
Update for Windows 7 (KB2830477)	Failed	Optional	21/07/2015
Update for Windows 7 (KB3048761)	Failed	Optional	21/07/2015
Security Update for Windows 7 (KB3079904)	Failed	Important	21/07/2015
Update for Windows 7 (KB3035583)	Failed	Recommended	18/07/2015

▲ If Microsoft has tried to install buggy files on your PC, they'll be marked as 'Failed'

releasing updates that contain glitches. Users of the Professional, Enterprise and Education editions of Windows 10 can defer updates until bugs are ironed out, but most of us are Home users – and we should have the same option.

Downloading Windows 10 without your permission

During Microsoft's free offer period following Windows 10's launch, many Windows 7 and 8.1 users – including those who never reserved the Windows upgrade –suddenly found massive Windows 10 installation files sitting on their PC's hard drive. This is because Microsoft smuggled these files in without asking. And when we say massive we mean up to 6GB of storage space and bandwidth. Thankfully, there were ways of uninstalling these files. There have been cases, however, in which the unwanted Windows 10 download has quietly attempted to install itself, sometimes several times. At the time, a Microsoft representative stated that automatic installation attempts are caused by a bug which the company claims was subsequently corrected.

OUR VERDICT

Microsoft's intention – to make the upgrade Windows 10 process quicker and simpler – appears to have been benign. And the failed installation bug (assuming it genuinely is a bug), is an unfortunate by-product of an ill-conceived strategy. But the initial assumption on Microsoft's part that no one will mind massive files being downloaded to their PCs without their consent was misjudged. What if you don't actually want to upgrade? And what about people who are on capped or metered broadband connections? That 6GB could have pushed you over your monthly data allowance and cost you money as well as hard-drive space.

Privacy problems

On its launch, many critics slammed Windows 10 for its blatant disregard for users' privacy. Left to its default settings, the new OS and its apps will happily gather all manner of personal data, including your current location and virtually anything you type on your keyboard. The good news is that, in most cases, it's possible to opt out of tracking and other background data-gathering aspects of Windows 10 via the Privacy section of the Settings app. But even if you disable all the data-collection settings you can find, it won't stop the OS from collecting all information about you. Microsoft's Corporate VP Joe Belfiore admitted in an interview (www.snipca.com/18847) that Windows 10 includes enforced data-collection elements that users can't opt out of. He claims these are strictly limited to your PC's performance and how you use it, and "are not personal information or are not related to privacy".

OUR VERDICT

Data collection is nothing new. Windows users have shared basic performance information with Microsoft for years via the Customer Experience Improvement Program, though it's possible to opt out of this. Meanwhile, smartphones, tablets and online services, such as Google, routinely collect information about us and our activities. But Windows 10 ramps things up by several notches compared with previous versions of the OS, and many of its data-collection settings are enabled by default. But there is an argument that protecting our privacy is, to a large degree, our own responsibility. If you're worried about your privacy in Windows 10, then we'd encourage you to follow our advice on opting out via Settings (see Chapter 3). You may also want to read Microsoft's Windows 10 privacy FAQ (www.snipca.com/18848).

Nagging users (again)

After the November 2015 update, Windows 10 started displaying 'nag' screens that attempted to dissuade users from changing their default web browser from Edge to Chrome or Firefox or any number of lesser-known, but faster browsers that are perfectly suited to tablets. The nag to 'Try it out' (see screenshot above right) smacks of desperation.

OUR VERDICT

The "please like Edge... please" nag (OK, we're paraphrasing) is a bit annoying but it

CONTROVERSIAL GESTURE

Windows 10 was involved in another outrage just before its main release in July 2015, when it emerged that the new OS would support the controversial 'middle finger' emoji. The offensive symbol has been available for more than a year as part of the current emoji standards (yes, there are 'standards'; Wikipedia has some interesting links: www.snipca.com/18910). However, the finger was not included in previous versions of Windows. This may all sound in bad taste, and be assured the controversial character is not actually included in Windows 10's on-screen keyboard (here's how to enable it: www.snipca.com/18911). The only way to use it is to copy and paste it from somewhere else.

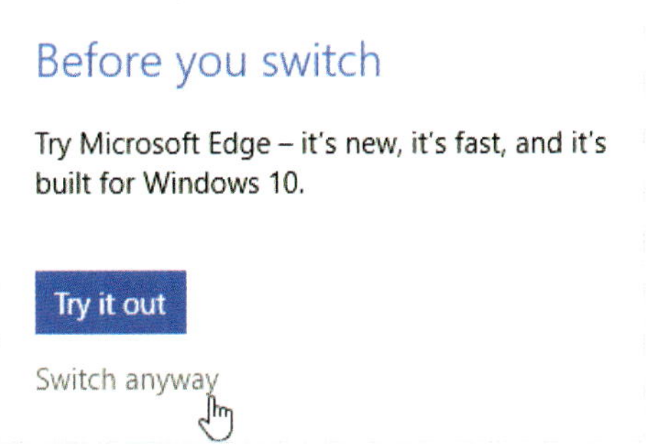

▲ **Microsoft is fiercely promoting its browser Edge**

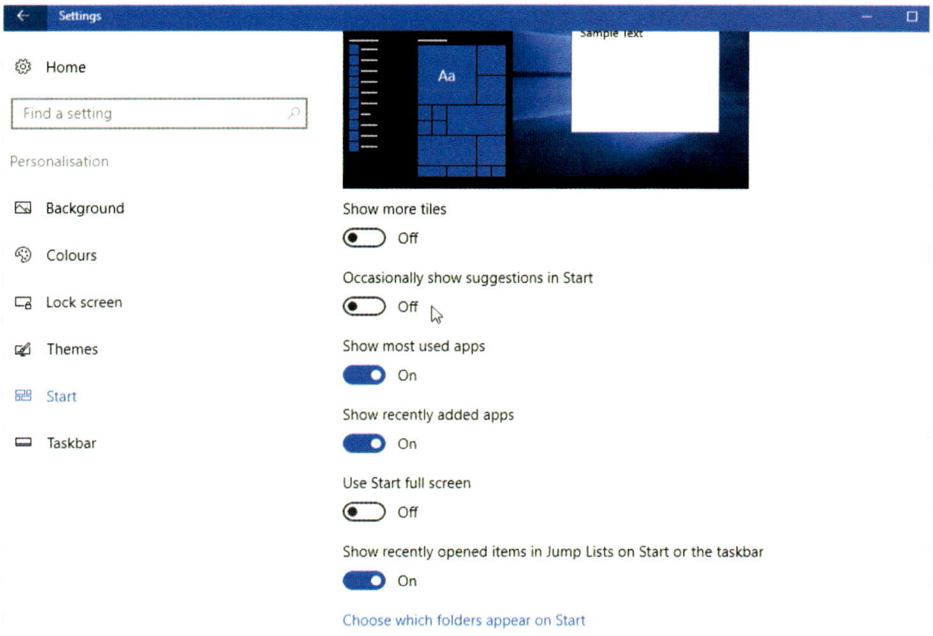

▲ **Microsoft is now littering your Start menu with adverts for products you don't want**

doesn't really cause any major problems. Hopefully, Microsoft won't try to make it harder to choose your default browser in the future. Aside from being somewhat desperate, Microsoft's behaviour may turn out to be legally dubious. After all, it wasn't long ago (2009) that Microsoft was taken to court by the European Commission and fined nearly £400 million for exactly this type of anti-competitive practice. You can find many more examples of Microsoft's legally questionable dealings on this Wikipedia page: www.snipca.com/18907.

Start menu adverts

The big November 2015 update brought fresh new features to Windows 10 – though not all were welcome. Among the most annoying was the inclusion of adverts (Microsoft prefers to call them 'suggestions') in the Start menu. You could get rid of them by clicking Start, Settings, Personalisation, then Start and click the slider next to 'Occasionally show suggestions in Start' to switch this feature off. Cortana and Edge also make money through advertising, which may explain why Microsoft is so desperate for you not to switch to another browser.

OUR VERDICT

Adverts are part and parcel of our lives these days, especially online, where they basically subsidise free services. But that doesn't always make them OK. Your Start menu is your Start menu, configured and customised to suit you. To find it littered with adverts for silly games feels intrusive, especially if you're used to hiding adverts online by using ad-blockers such as Adblock Plus (https://adblockplus.org). The sudden return of adverts on your computer, especially in your Start menu, can actually feel scary, because unexpected content is often a sign of malware.

Microsoft's ads are safe but disconcerting. And, unfortunately, this is likely to be just the start of the invasion of adverts on your desktop, in your taskbar and pretty much elsewhere in the OS.

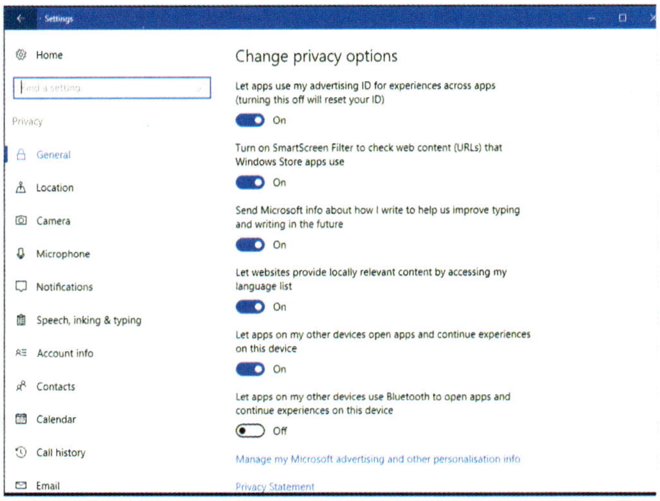

▲ **Windows 10 gathers your information even if you tell it not to**

Hidden costs

As if it's not enough that Microsoft takes a 30 per cent cut of all apps sold in the Windows Store, all Windows 10's default Microsoft apps – Groove Music, Films & TV and so on – nudge you to buy or rent music, films and other content. Meanwhile, many of Microsoft's free apps – such as Word Mobile and Solitaire (now Microsoft Solitaire Collection, www.snipca.com/18909) – attempt to push you towards coughing up for premium versions or ongoing subscriptions. Even simple DVD playback can cost you dear in Windows 10. If you've upgraded from Windows 7 Professional, Ultimate or Home Premium, you can get Windows DVD Player free "for a limited time" (www.snipca.com/18968). If you upgraded from any other version (including Windows 7 Home), the app will set you back £11.59 (www.snipca.com/18969). We strongly suggest you switch to the excellent free media player suite VLC instead (www.videolan.org/vlc).

OUR VERDICT

Savvy users will just ignore these hard-sell tactics, but inexperienced users might easily be swayed by entreaties to cough up cash to remove adverts. Many users with less confidence see Microsoft as the voice of authority, and will do whatever it tells them.

Chapter 2

Customise Windows 10

Few people would ever claim that Windows 10 is perfect the way it is. We explain all the ways you can take control of the OS and make it your own

Every version of Windows has let you change the look and feel of the operating system, but Windows 10 is different. It comes with loads of settings that you need to change straight away, as well as defaults that you need to switch – and that's just the start.

On top of that, the OS comes with a rich selection of tools and features that let you personalise your experience. In this chapter we're going to take an in-depth look at all the customisation options Windows 10 puts at your disposal, as well as ways to beat Microsoft's restrictions and take full control of the OS.

IN THIS SECTION

Customise everything

Not happy with how Windows 10 looks and works? Don't worry – you can customise almost every aspect of it to your liking. We explain how

Despite courting controversy (see Chapter 1), Windows 10 is the fastest growing operating system Microsoft has ever produced. By the end of June 2016 – just 11 months after it launched – Windows 10 was running on more than 350 million devices, according to Microsoft. To put that into perspective, it took Windows 7 almost twice as long to reach a similar number of adopters.

People the world over have embraced Windows 10 – partly because they could upgrade for free during its first year, but also because the OS looks great and is easy to use. However, even those who love it will admit that Windows 10 is far from perfect.

Perhaps you find the on-screen text too small or difficult to read, or perhaps you don't like the live tiles in the Start menu. Whatever your gripes and grievances, you'll be pleased to know there are easy ways to modify Microsoft's default settings and get Windows 10 looking and working exactly how you want. Over the next few pages we'll show you how to customise, tweak and hack your way through the OS until you've eliminated everything you don't like about it.

What you can do

- Tweak the Start menu, taskbar and more to suit you better
- Make Windows 10 easier to see and more comfortable to work with
- Hack Windows 10 with free tools to customise almost anything

CUSTOMISE THE START MENU

1 Resize the Start menu

Unlike the relatively small panel that pops up when you click Start in Windows 7 or XP, the Windows 10 Start menu can take over a sizable portion of your Desktop. But there's an easy way to cut it down to size. Click Start, then move your mouse over the menu's top or right-hand edge and the cursor will turn into a double-headed arrow. Click and drag downwards from the top edge to adjust the menu's height, or drag left from the right edge to make it narrower.

On the other hand, if you find it too cramped, you can enlarge it by dragging upwards and outwards. And, for a Windows 8-style Start screen, click Start, Settings, Personalisation, then Start, and turn on the 'Use Start full screen' option.

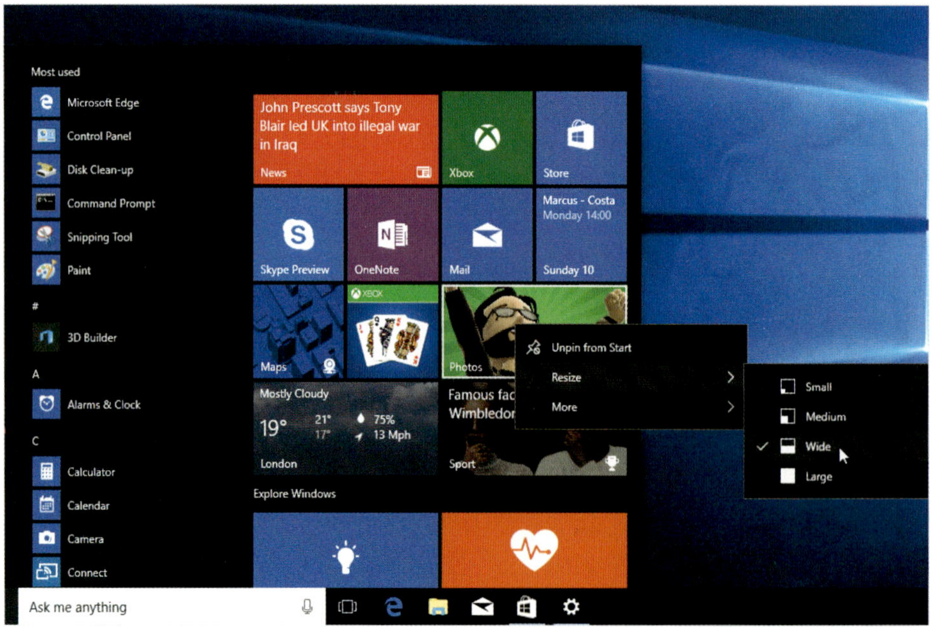

▶ Resize individual tiles or the entire Start menu

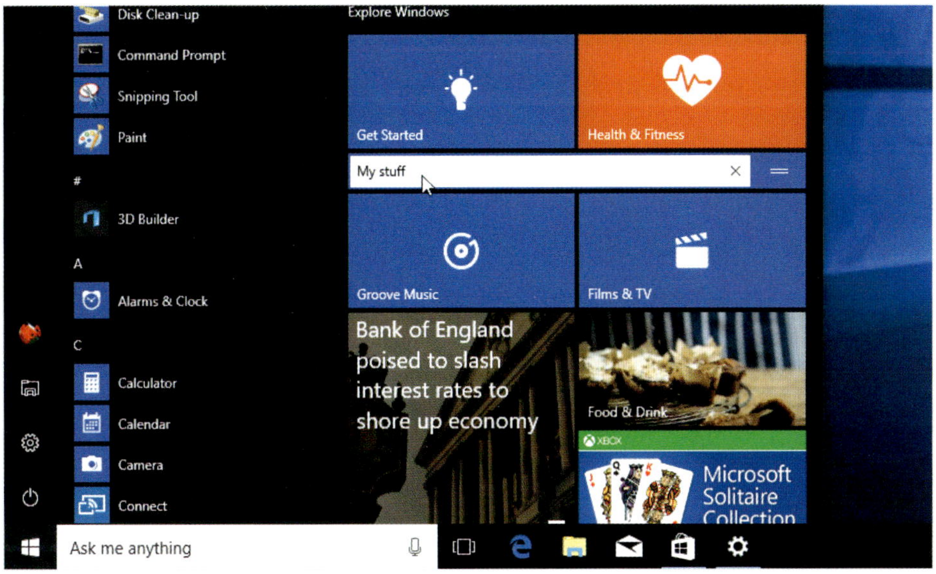

▲ Group your tiles into categories then name them

2 Move, resize, remove or add tiles

By default, the Windows 10 Start menu is divided into two halves, with colourful tiles on the right-hand side. But you don't have to stick with this arrangement. Click a tile, hold your mouse button down, then drag the tile to where you want it. To resize a tile, right-click it then select Resize. In most cases you'll be shown a selection of sizes – Small, Medium, Wide or Large (see screenshot left) – though some tiles don't have all four options.

Right-clicking also lets you 'Unpin from Start', which whisks the tile away. You can add new tiles to the Start menu by right-clicking almost anything you like (programs listed in 'All apps', files, folders, shortcuts on your Desktop and more) then selecting 'Pin to Start'.

3 Turn live tiles on or off

If you'd rather avoid the flickering distraction of animated live tiles, it's easy to switch them off. Click Start, then right-click a live tile and select More, then 'Turn live tile off'.

If, on the other hand, you find live tiles a vibrant addition to your Desktop, you can enable extra ones. Right-click a non-live tile, select More, then click 'Turn live tile on'. Be aware that not all tiles let you do this; it's usually only those that are associated with Windows Store apps and which deliver regularly updated information, such as news, sports results and weather forecasts.

4 Group tiles using your own categories

Windows 10 arranges Start menu tiles into pre-assigned groups: 'Explore Windows', 'Life at a glance' and so on. To rename an existing group, click the heading, select the current text, then type your own group name (see screenshot above left). To create a new group, click and drag a tile to the very bottom of the Start menu until a blank, coloured bar appears above it. Release the tile and move your mouse to the blank area above the tile and you'll see 'Name group' appear – click and type a category name.

Drag tiles under your category heading to add them to the group. You can move groups of tiles by clicking the heading and dragging. Removing all tiles from a group will also remove the heading.

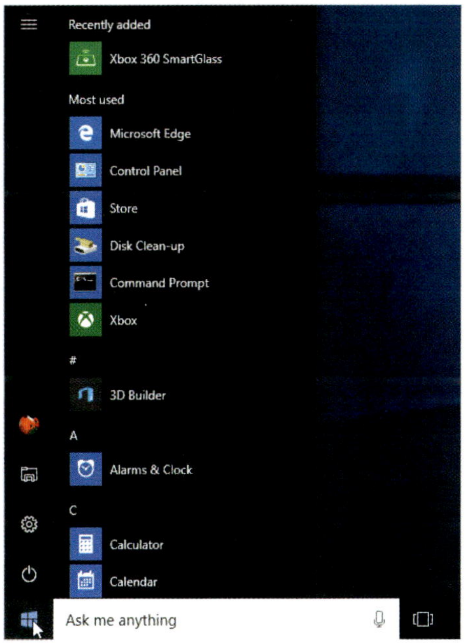

▲ You can remove all the tiles from the Start menu

5 Remove live tiles completely

If you really dislike Windows 10's tiles, then you can remove them all and shrink the Start menu down to a simple, neat, single-column panel (see screenshot left). Annoyingly, you'll need to right-click each tile individually and select 'Unpin from Start'. When you've done this, click the right edge of the menu and drag it left.

6 Banish adverts from the Start menu

By default, Microsoft advertises 'suggested' apps in the Start menu. To turn these off, open the Windows Store app, click your account icon, then Settings and click 'Show products on tile' to Off. As mentioned in Chapter 1 you can also click Start, Settings, Personalisation, Start, then click the switch under 'Occasionally show suggestions in Start' to Off.

TWEAK THE START MENU WITH FREE TOOLS

If none of the tweaks we've suggested here go far enough and you'd like even more control over your Start menu, you could consider installing a third-party tool. Anyone who has used Windows 8 will probably be familiar with Classic Shell (www.classicshell.net). It effectively banishes Windows 8's Start screen and allows you to restore a classic Windows-style Start menu. But Classic Shell is also compatible with Windows 10, where it lets you configure almost any aspect of your Start menu, including menu styles, jump lists, shutdown button behaviour and more.

There are other, Windows 10-specific alternative tools available, though these tend to cost money – Stardock's Start10 (www.snipca.com/19651), for example, costs about £4. See page 36 for more.

CHANGE THE WAY WINDOWS 10 LOOKS

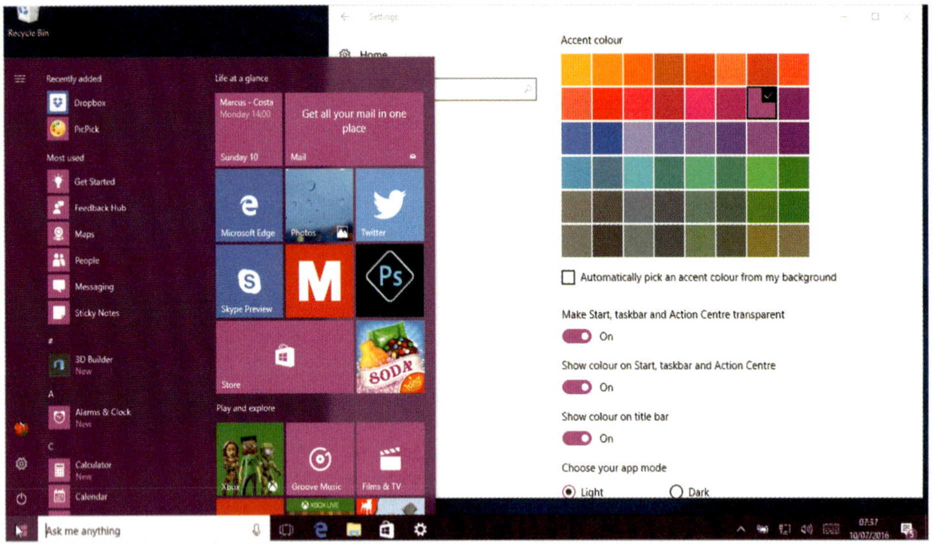

▲ Pick a colour for your interface that looks nice with your desktop

7 Change your colour scheme

Click Start, Settings, Personalisation, then Colours. Under 'Accent colour' you can change the colour of the interface's highlights, such as the Start menu tiles (see screenshot above). Or, you can allow Windows to pick a colour that complements your chosen desktop wallpaper by switching on 'Automatically pick an accent colour from my background'.

You can make the interface even more colourful by scrolling to 'Show colour on Start, taskbar, action centre and title bar', and switching it on. The other settings here let you choose between transparent effects or solid colours for the Start menu, taskbar and Action Centre, or show colour to the title bar – the strip at the top of every program window (it's white, by default).

8 Personalise your desktop and lock screen

Click Start, Settings, Personalisation, then Background. From the Background dropdown menu choose Picture, 'Solid colour' or Slideshow. For Picture and Slideshow, click Browse to locate a file or folder of pictures you want to use, then select your preference from the 'Choose a fit' menu. For Slideshows, choose how frequently the images update from the 'Change picture every' dropdown menu. Enabling Shuffle randomises the selection.

Now click 'Lock screen' on the left. Again, under Background, you can select Picture or Slideshow and browse for images. But you can also choose 'Windows spotlight' here, which will display random images from Microsoft whenever you lock your PC.

9 Download free themes

Windows 7-style themes – combinations of backdrops, colours and system sounds – are still available in Windows 10, but they're somewhat buried. Click Start, Settings, Personalisation, then Themes. Click 'Theme settings' to launch the familiar Windows 7 Personalisation Control Panel. A small selection of pre-defined default themes is offered here – click

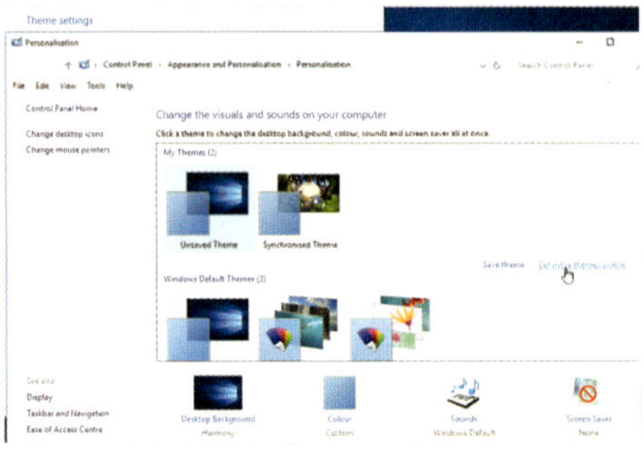

▲ Download new themes free from Microsoft

one to apply it. To download additional themes, click the 'Get more themes online' link (see screenshot below left). This will open a web page in your browser, from which you can view and download any themes that take your fancy. They're all free.

10 Add useful icons to your desktop

By default, Windows 10 only shows the Recycle Bin icon on the desktop, but it's possible to add more, including a handy link to the Control Panel. Click Start, Settings, Personalisation, then Themes. Click 'Desktop icon settings' and, in the box that opens, put a tick next to any of the icons you'd like to add (you can also choose User's Files, Network and Computer), then click Apply.

You can also change the look of the icons themselves – click one of the icons displayed, then click the Change Icon button to select a new one.

11 Change your mouse cursors

Click Start, Settings, Personalisation, Themes, then click 'Mouse pointer settings'. From the Scheme dropdown menu you can select a variety of alternative cursor styles, including larger variations on the default scheme. This can help if you're having trouble seeing the cursor on your screen. Click Apply when you've made your selection.

Alternatively, in the Customise section, you can click on each individual cursor in your scheme then click Browse to select another one. Adding a drop-shadow to the mouse by ticking the option at the bottom of the box can help make the cursor easier to see. You can also change how quickly your mouse wheel works - just click the Wheel tab at the top.

12 Get rid of check boxes on icons

Windows 10's icons display check boxes when you select them, which can be distracting. To remove them click Start, File Explorer. Then click View, Options and, in the box that appears, click the View tab. In the 'Advanced settings' section, scroll down to 'Use check boxes

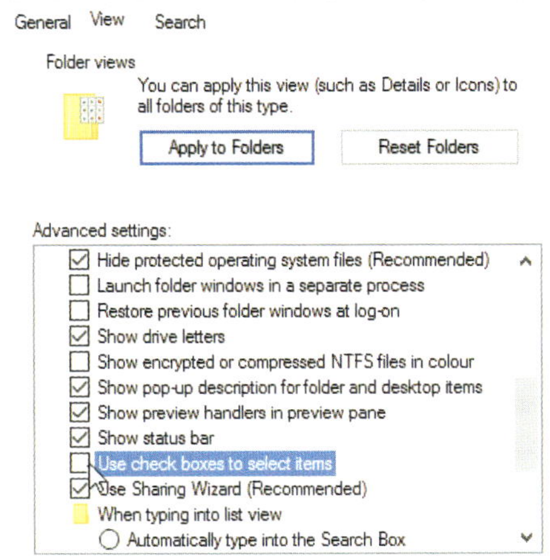

▲ If checkboxes on icons annoy you, get rid of them

to select items' – untick this, then click OK (see screenshot above).

13 Change the way File Explorer works

The new version of File Explorer is highly customisable. Click Start, File Explorer, then click the View tab for some options. Use the top-left Panes section to add or remove the Navigation, Preview or Details panes (see below). The Details pane on the right is particularly useful; it provides lots of information about any file you click without you having to open it. In the Layout section, you can choose how items are displayed in the main part of the window. You could switch to extra-large icons, for example, or choose Details, which lets you sort items by name, date, type, size and more. You can use the options in the 'Current view' section to sort or group items the way you want.

14 Add a handy shortcut to Windows PowerShell

The Windows PowerShell is a very useful command-line console that lets you do everything the Command Prompt can, and more besides. And you can customise Windows 10's shortcuts to go to PowerShell instead of the Command Prompt, if you prefer. Right-click the taskbar then select Settings. In the box that opens, switch on the 'Replace Command Prompt with PowerShell...' option (see screenshot below). Now, when you right-click the Start button, you'll find a useful shortcut to the PowerShell. You can also open the PowerShell by using the Windows key+X keyboard shortcut.

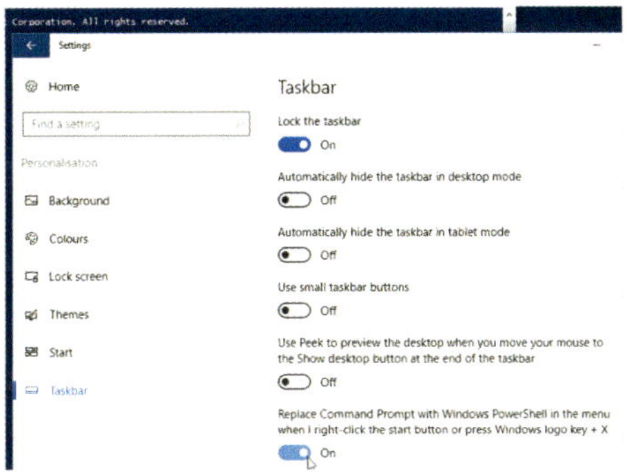

▲ Get to the PowerShell tool quicker with this trick

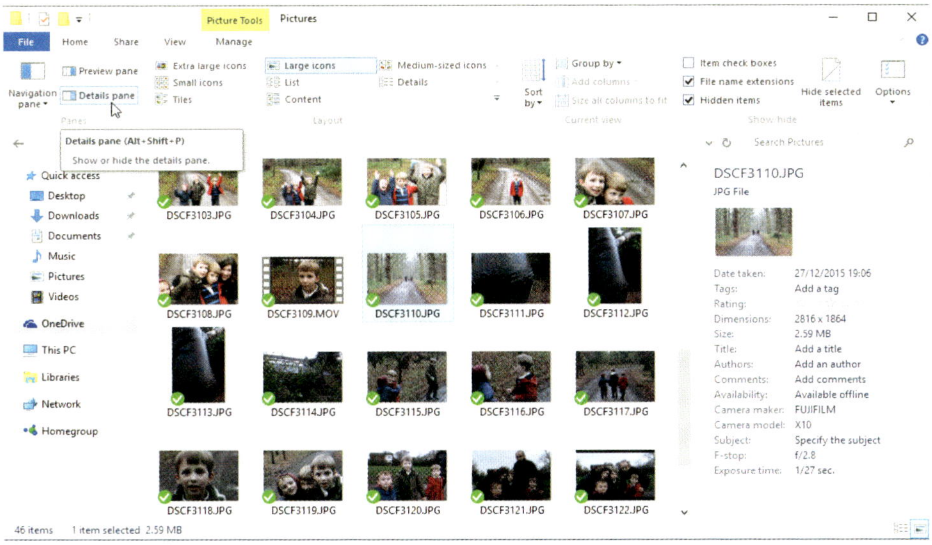

▲ Add or remove Navigation, Preview or Details from the Panes section in File Explorer

MAKE WINDOWS 10 EASIER TO SEE

1 MAKE ICONS AND TEXT BIGGER

Right-click the desktop, select 'Display settings', then use the slider to increase the size of all on-screen elements.

2 MAKE EVERYTHING BIGGER

Right-click the desktop, select 'Display settings', click 'Advanced display settings', then 'Advanced sizing of text and other items'. Under 'Change size of items', click 'set a custom scaling level'. Use the dropdown menu in the ruler window that opens to select your scaling percentage, then click OK, Apply. You'll be prompted to sign out, then sign in again for the setting to take effect.

3 MAKE ONLY TEXT LARGER

Navigate to 'Advanced sizing of text and other items' as described above, then choose the text elements you want to enlarge from the dropdown menu under 'Change the text size only'. Select the font size from the dropdown menu next to it. Click Apply for each element that you decide to change.

4 MAGNIFY TEXT

Click Start, Settings, 'Ease of Access', Magnifier and switch Magnifier on – this will magnify the section of your desktop immediately surrounding your mouse cursor. You can customise the magnification amount and the tool's behaviour by clicking the magnifying glass icon on your desktop.

5 USE A HIGH-CONTRAST THEME

Click Start, Settings, 'Ease of access', then 'High contrast' to select a high-contrast theme from the dropdown menu. Click Apply.

6 CHANGE THE CURSOR'S THICKNESS

As well as making the mouse cursor bigger (see tip 11), you can increase its thickness when it's blinking. Click Start, Settings, 'Ease of access', then 'Other options' and use the slider.

15 Switch File Explorer back to My Computer

Windows 10's new Quick Access view is how File Explorer appears when you open it. It displays a selection of frequently used folders and recently used files. Quick Access can be useful, but it's very different from the old My Computer-style view used in Windows XP and 7, which displayed your PC's drives and devices. To revert to using this instead, click Start, File Explorer, View, then click Options. On the General tab, select This PC from the 'Open File Explorer to' dropdown menu and click OK.

16 Switch to single-clicking

Double-clicking has long been the default way to launch programs and open files in Windows. But there's no reason to stick with this if you don't like it – it's easy to change to single-clicking. Click Start, File Explorer, View, then click Options.

On the General tab, click 'Single-click to open an item (point to select)' (see top-right screenshot below) to select it, then select 'Underline icon titles only when I point at them' and click OK. This will give you a more web browser-like experience, where items you point to on the desktop or in File Explorer will display a line underneath them to show you've selected them. Clicking items once will open them.

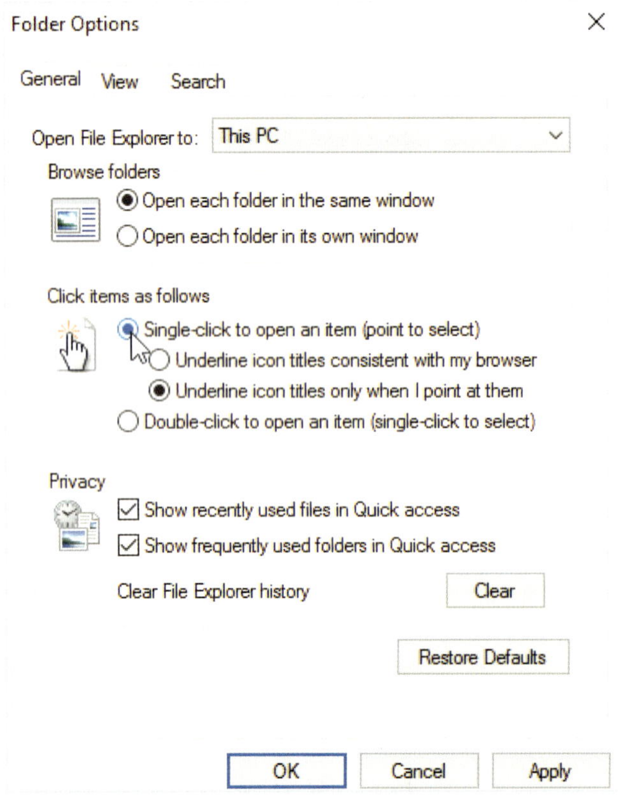

▲ Don't like double-clicking? It's easy to change to a single click

17 Customise Quick Actions

Windows 10's Quick Actions menu – not to be confused with Quick Access – is a selection of shortcuts that appears in Action Centre. To see which shortcuts you currently have, click the speech-bubble icon in the notification area. The four buttons at the bottom are your Quick Actions. You can click Expand to see more, but you can also re-organise them so that the four Quick Actions you use most are always available, without having to click Expand. Click Start, Settings, System, then 'Notifications & actions'. Here, click and drag any of the shortcuts shown to rearrange the way they appear in the Action Centre or click 'Add or remove quick actions' to change which items are displayed.

18 Create another desktop

Thankfully, the desktop is at the heart of how you use Windows 10 - a relief following Windows 8's disorientating Start screen interface. Proving that you can never get too much of a good thing, Windows 10 lets you create multiple desktops that you can switch between using the Task View button on the taskbar or via the Windows key+Tab keyboard shortcut.

This can be a very handy way to keep organised while you work. For example, it can prevent your main desktop from getting cluttered with web browsers or media players by letting you position them on a different screen - even if you have just one monitor. To create another desktop, click the Task View button, then click 'New desktop' on the right.

19 Show Libraries in File Explorer

Windows 7 trained us to use Libraries – centralised locations for files of specific types, such as Documents, Pictures, Music and Videos. But just as we were all getting used to them, Windows 10 came along and relegated them in File Explorer, leaving them out of the left-hand Navigation pane altogether. To get them back, click Start, File Explorer, then View. Click the 'Navigation pane' button then tick the 'Show libraries' option (see screenshot below).

20 Customise the Command Prompt

As we mentioned in Chapter 1, you can now change the way Windows 10's Command Prompt looks and works by clicking Start, typing cmd and pressing Enter, then right-clicking the Command Prompt window's title bar and selecting Properties.

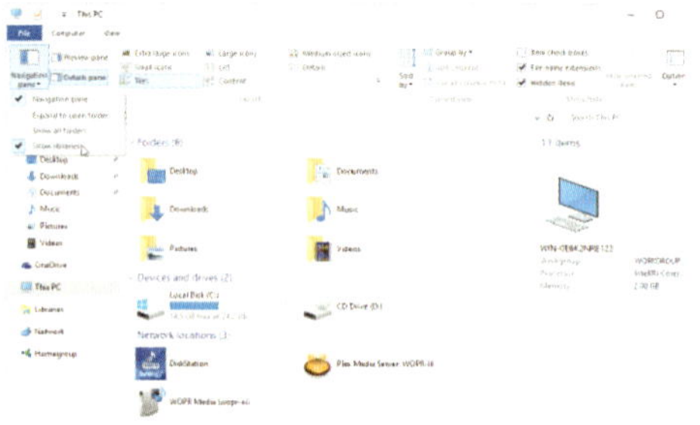

▲ Get Windows 7's libraries back in Windows 10

In the box that opens, select the 'Enable Ctrl key shortcuts' option. This lets you copy and paste text using the Ctrl+C and Ctrl+V keyboard shortcuts – handy if you're copying command lines from a web page. Click the Font tab to change the size of the text and the style of font used. You can make the text larger if you're having trouble reading it.

Also useful is the Colours tab, which lets you customise the colour of the background and text. The Opacity slider at the bottom lets you make the entire window semi-transparent. Click OK.

21 Turn any website into a Windows 10 app

This hack makes use of a feature in Chrome that lets you convert websites into app-like shortcuts that you can add

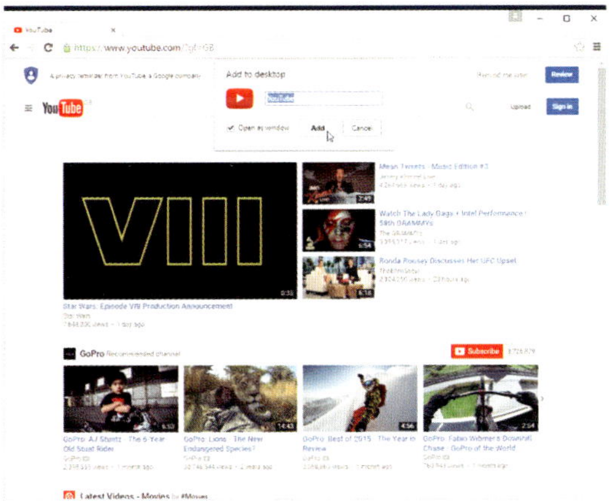

▲ If you use Chrome, turn a website into a Windows 10 app

to your taskbar or Start menu. Install Chrome from www.google.com/chrome if you don't already have it, then open the browser and navigate to the site you want to convert. Click the top-right menu button (three horizontal lines), then select 'More tools', 'Add to desktop' (this may appear as 'Add to taskbar').

In the small window that opens, give your app a name, make sure the 'Open as window' option is ticked, then click Add (see screenshot above). Now right-click on the new desktop icon that appears, then select 'Pin to taskbar'. Whenever you click your new taskbar icon, your website will open in its own window, just like an app.

22 Switch to Windows 10's 'dark' mode

Until recently, Windows 10's dark theme was hidden – in order to enable it you needed to carry out a complicated Registry hack. Since the launch of the Anniversary edition, though, the dark theme is available to anyone via the Settings app. To activate it, click Start, Settings, Personalisation, then Colours. Scroll down and, under 'Choose your app mode', select Dark. The new theme doesn't turn every window dark – just Windows Store apps. Some people think it adds a touch of class to the operating system, and it's certainly easier to read some of the text – see screenshot below. But if you decide you don't like it, it's easy to switch back. Just head back to Start, Settings, Personalisation, Colours and click Light under 'Choose your app mode'.

23 Create a toolbar of shortcuts

Open File Explorer, navigate to your Documents folder, then create a new folder. Name it 'Shortcuts'. Now open a second File Explorer window and navigate to C:\ProgramData\Microsoft\ Windows\Start Menu\Programs. Work your way through the folders to select any programs and tools that you want to add to your toolbar. In each case, right-click the icon, select Copy, then right-click in your empty Shortcuts folder and select Paste – don't drag and drop anything. You can add shortcuts for anything to your folder – programs, web pages, files and more.

When you're done, right-click the taskbar and select Toolbars, then 'New toolbar'. In the window that opens, navigate to your Shortcuts folder, then click 'Select folder'. You should see the word Shortcuts towards the right of your taskbar – click the double arrow next to it to see all your shortcuts in a menu.

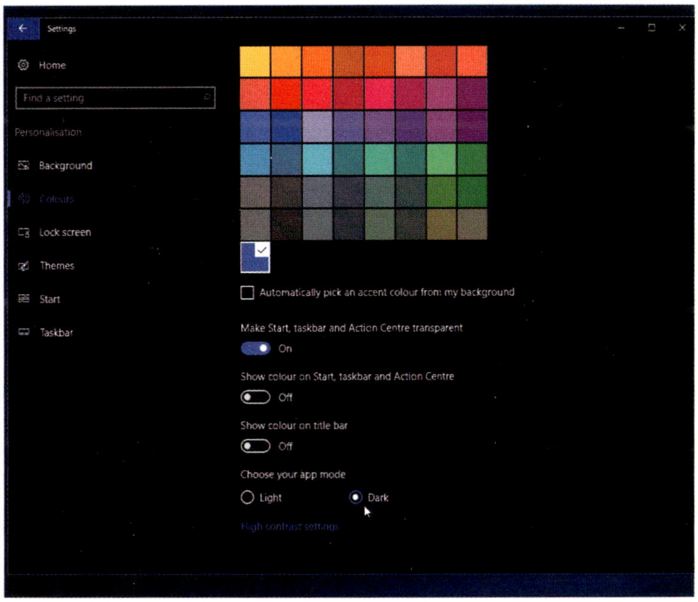

◄ You don't need to hack the Registry to turn on Windows 10's dark theme anymore

CUSTOMISE THE TASKBAR

1 DITCH UNNECESSARY ICONS Click Start, Settings, Personalisation, then Taskbar. Click 'Select which icons appear on the taskbar' to switch on or off the icons that are permanently displayed in the notification area.

2 SET THE TASKBAR TO AUTO-HIDE Right-click the taskbar, then select Settings. Switch on 'Automatically hide the taskbar in desktop mode' (and tablet mode, if you wish). Move your mouse to the bottom of the screen to make it pop up again.

3 MAKE THE TASKBAR BIGGER Right-click the taskbar and make sure 'Lock the taskbar' isn't ticked. Then move your mouse pointer to the top edge of the taskbar until it becomes a double-headed arrow. Click and drag to increase the taskbar's depth. Lock the taskbar again when you're done.

4 FIT MORE SHORTCUTS Right-click the taskbar, then select Settings. Click the switch next to 'Use small taskbar buttons' – shrinking these will let you fit more shortcuts. The Search bar will disappear but you can still click Start, then search by typing.

5 MOVE THE TASKBAR You don't have to stick with the taskbar at the bottom of the screen. Right-click it, select Settings, then choose Left, Right or Top from the 'Taskbar location on screen' dropdown menu.

Reinstall Windows 10's missing tools

We show you how to put back the features that Microsoft took out

Bring back lost games in Windows 10

Microsoft Solitaire Collection, which is bundled with Windows 10, replaces the card games that were in previous versions of Windows. It includes Klondike, Spider, Freecell, Pyramid and TriPeaks. None of the other games in Windows 7 are included, but the Windows Store makes it easy to replace the missing apps and add many more.

Minesweeper is no longer in Windows 10 but there is a new Microsoft Minesweeper app, which includes an adventure mode with weapons, monsters and traps. Microsoft Mahjong is a great new version of Windows 7's Mahjong Titans and is one of the top five free games available through the Windows Store. Microsoft has abandoned Chess, Backgammon and Checkers (Draughts), but searching in the store for these turns up dozens of alternatives, such as Backgammon Deluxe, Checkers Live and 3D Chess Game.

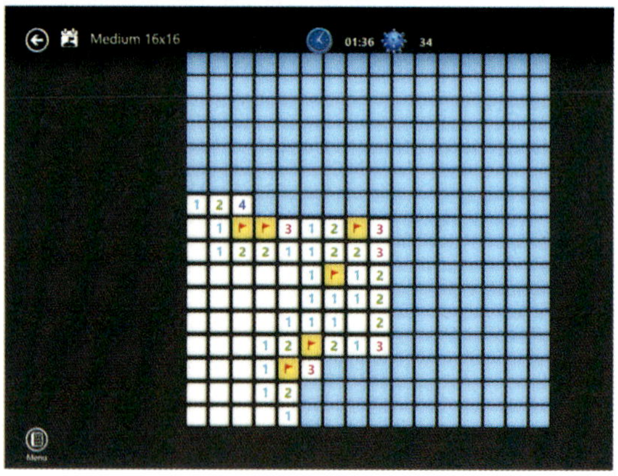

Play DVDs

Windows 10 can't play DVDs, much to the annoyance of many people. If you want to play movies and you have upgraded from a previous version of Windows that had Media Center and the ability to play DVDs, Microsoft has been giving away copies of Windows DVD Player for free, but only for a limited time. It's in the Windows Store and costs £11.59 for anyone that performed a clean install of Windows 10, bought a new PC with Windows 10 or didn't have Media Center before. It has quite a low rating from users, though, and the one-star reviews outnumber all the others combined.

A better way to play DVDs – and just about any digital video file – in Windows 10 is to use VLC Media Player (www.videolan.org). Much more than just a DVD player, VLC supports a wide range of media including music, videos, photos, DVDs and Video CDs. It will play almost any type of media file you can download from the internet.

Playing files is easy. From the View menu, select Playlist to display a file-selection window on the left. Select My Videos, My Music, My Pictures or Discs to show the files available or the disc that's in your DVD drive. Just double-click to play them. With a DVD, for example, select the View menu, then choose Minimal Interface to hide the controls. Right-click inside the video window and select Video, then Fullscreen. You can now sit back and watch the movie.

▲ Use VLC Media Player to watch your DVD library in Windows 10

Replace Windows Media Center

Around 10 years ago, Windows Media Center was a popular program on Windows for playing videos, photo slideshows, music and DVDs. You could even record and play back digital TV if your PC had a tuner installed. Not many PCs have TV tuners anymore, and DVDs are dying out, so Media Center was dropped from Windows 10. There are several alternatives that can be used to replace it, though, such as Media Portal (www.team-mediaportal.com) and Kodi (kodi.tv). They do everything that Media Center did and more. However, neither of them worked on our test PC, despite saying they were compatible with Windows 10. Other people have had success with them, so it may just have been our PC. Try them, because you might have better luck than we did.

Plex (plex.tv) is another alternative, which worked perfectly on our test PC, although it's not as straightforward to use as Media Center. It installs a server application which can then be accessed by other software and apps that run on other devices, such as phones and tablets. It can also be accessed on the PC running the server via a web browser.

To set it up, go to the Downloads section of the Plex website and download Plex Media Server for Computer (not NAS). Run it and it will add an icon in the notification area of the taskbar. It also opens a browser and prompts you to create an account and sign in. This is only necessary if you want to access your

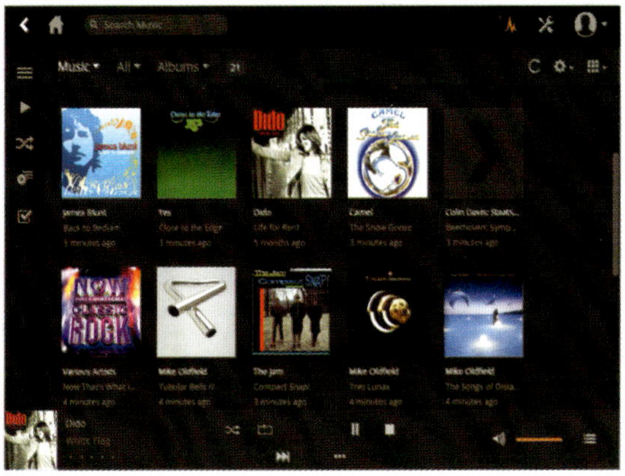

▲ Plex is a replacement for Windows Media Center. It plays music, movies and photos

media files from outside your home network, otherwise you can ignore it. If you have problems getting started (and, as we've said, the process is less obvious than with Media Center), go to the Support section of the website and read the guides on how to get Plex up and running.

Right-click the notification area icon and select Media Manager. A browser window opens that accesses the Plex server running on the PC. On the homepage, click the Plus button to add a new library and select the type you want, such as music, movies, TV shows, photos or home videos. Click Next, click 'Browse for media folder' and select your Videos, Pictures, Music or other folder. Click Add Library and all your media files will be added to Plex. It might take several minutes to add them, but once it has finished, you can browse and play them.

Resurrect desktop gadgets

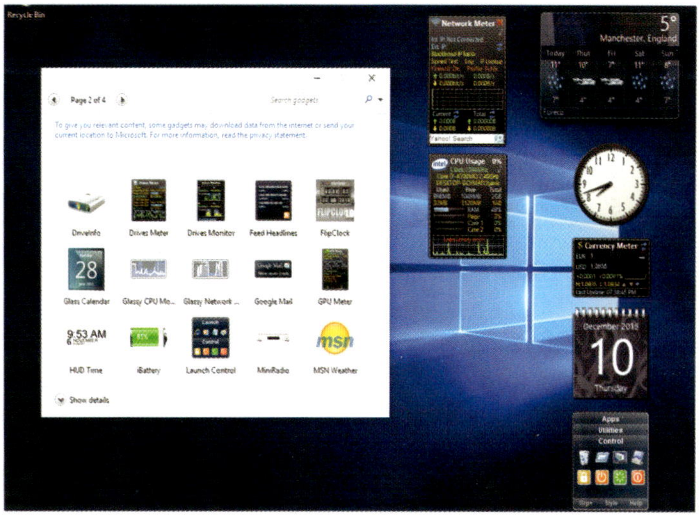

▲ Desktop gadgets are back thanks to 8GadgetPack

Gadgets were introduced in Windows Vista and continued to be supported in Windows 7. There were clocks, calendars, performance and status monitors, weather forecasts and more. They were very popular with some users and you may miss them if you've upgraded from 7 to 10.

Although gadgets are no longer supported by Microsoft, the free tool 8GadgetPack (8gadgetpack.net) lets you get gadgets back on the desktop. Download, install and run the application. It comes with an excellent collection of some of the best gadgets, but you can get more once the software is installed.

After installing 8GadgetPack, run 8GadgetPack Tools on the Start menu. This opens a window containing a list of functions. Click 'Add gadget' to open the gadget browser. There are four screens of gadgets and you simply drag them to the desktop to install them. Run 8GadgetPack Tools and click Disable/Enable Autorun to set the auto-start with Windows option.

There is a whole website full of desktop gadgets at Win7Gadgets (win7gadgets.com). They are designed for Windows 7 but they work in Windows 10 if you have 8GadgetPack installed. To add a gadget, right-click the downloaded Zip file and extract the contents. Explore the files and folders and double-click the .gadget file to install it.

Revive Windows Live Essentials

Windows Live Essentials (now called Windows Essentials) is a collection of useful programs that includes OneDrive, Movie Maker, Windows Live Mail, Windows Live Writer and Photo Gallery. However, it's less useful in Windows 10 where the new Photos app replaces Photo Gallery, the Mail app replaces Windows Live Mail (which no longer works with Hotmail and Outlook.com accounts anyway), and OneDrive is already built-in.

Movie Maker is the one application you might miss, but there are good alternatives in the Windows Store, such as Power Director Mobile Video Editor. This is designed for tablets and supports touch, but it also works with a keyboard and mouse. You can add its thumbnails of clips to a timeline in the lower half of the screen.

Special effects can be applied to the clips, music and titles can be added, and the resulting video can be saved to the hard drive or shared on Facebook or YouTube. There are also great desktop applications such as the free Serif Movie Plus Starter Edition (bit.ly/serif388).

Take back control of Windows Update

Unlike previous versions of the operating system, Windows updates are compulsory in Windows 10 and you no longer have the option to decide whether to enable or disable them.

If you've installed the new Anniversary Update, however, you'll find that it provides a way to get back some control, courtesy of something called 'Active hours', which allows you to stipulate a particular time period during the day that you don't want updates installed. We'll be covering this topic in much more detail in Chapter 3.

Customise Windows 10 with free tools

You don't have to stick with the customisation options Microsoft gives you. Here we explain how to truly make the Windows 10 desktop your own

Most people will agree that Windows 10 is an enormous improvement on Windows 8. Even if you're a fan, you'll probably still have the occasional niggle or annoyance with the way it works.

One of the best things about Windows is that you can make your own improvements, and Windows 10 is no different. Microsoft provides lots of different options to tweak the way Windows 10 works, as we saw earlier in this chapter. But the customisation options that come built in only go so far.

Thankfully there are also many great free programs and add-ons that let you change and customise the operating system even further, so that it looks and behaves exactly how you want it to.

If you're not keen on the tiled Start menu, for example, you can replace it with a tile-free version. And if File Explorer seems a little basic, swap it for a more feature-packed alternative.

Change the Start menu

After the massive outcry that followed Microsoft's decision to remove the Start menu from Windows 8, Microsoft back-tracked to avoid the same criticisms in Windows 10. The new Start menu is an interesting mix of the old and new, blending Windows 7's Start menu with the Start screen from Windows 8. It's not to everyone's taste, however, and the inclusion of live tiles can feel a little odd – you have to open the Start menu and then wait for them to update.

If you'd prefer a different Start menu, there are plenty to choose from, including IObit Start Menu 8 (bit.ly/iobit398) which,

MINI WORKSHOP
Replace the Windows 10 Start menu with Classic Shell

1 Install Classic Shell and click the Start button. You will now have a new Windows 7-style Start menu – no more tiles, just a list of regularly used programs **1** and a sidebar containing important file locations and Windows settings. **2** You can search for programs and files **3** and quickly shut down your PC. **4**

2 To customise the menu, right-click the Start button and select Settings. Classic Shell offers a choice of Start menu styles **1** and you can also replace the default Start button. **2** Customise the menu behaviour under Basic Settings and tweak its look under Skin. **3** Choose which menu items to show under Customize Start Menu. **4**

3 Classic Shell is more than just a Start menu replacement – it also makes changes to File Explorer. You can customise this by clicking the Shell button. **1** Options include changing the navigation pane style (XP or Vista) **2** and enabling or disabling the breadcrumbs feature, **3** which shows the path of your navigation.

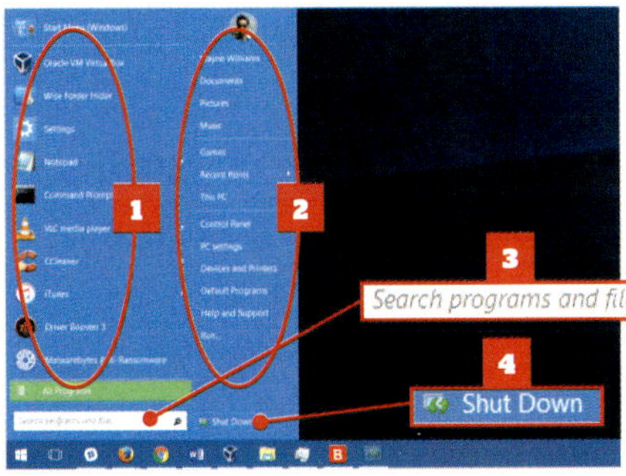

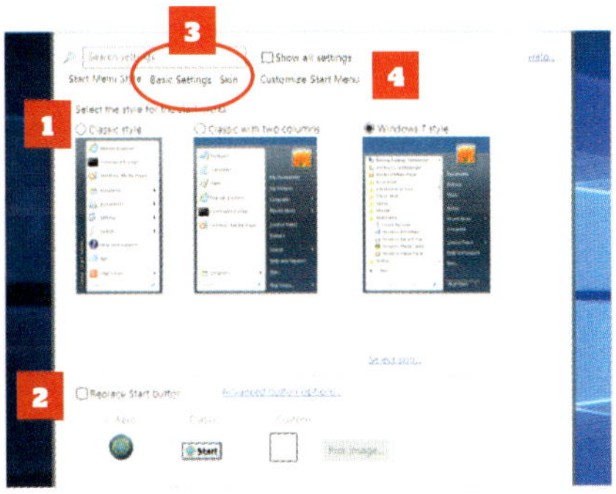

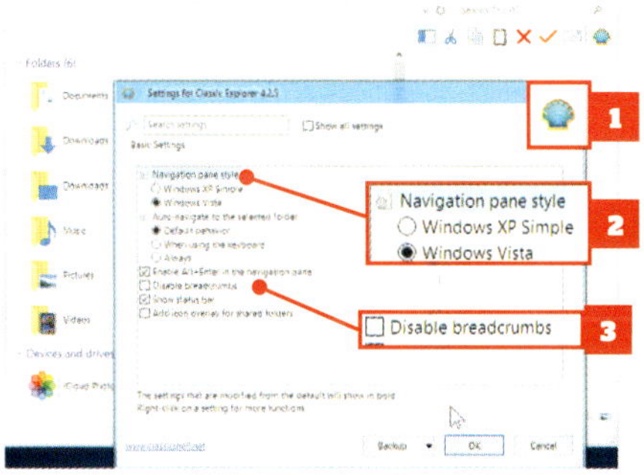

despite its name, works absolutely fine with Windows 10 (though you need to skip the bundled junk during installation), and Stardock's Start10 (bit.ly/dock398). The latter program isn't free, but it only costs $4.99 (around £3.44) and there's a 30-day trial available. It offers a good choice of menus, including one with tiles.

Our personal favourite is Classic Shell (www.classicshell.net), which offers a choice of three different menu styles – Classic, Two Columns and Windows 7 – all of which can be tweaked with different colours and designs to suit your tastes.

The program comes packed with extra options, including a dedicated shutdown button, the ability to pin programs directly from Explorer and an enhanced Windows Search tool. The latest version improves compatibility with the most recent build of Windows 10, adds transparency settings for skins and also lets you uninstall Windows Store apps directly from the Start menu.

We show you how to use Classic Shell in our Mini Workshop, above.

Customise the taskbar

You can make various changes to the taskbar setup from within Windows. If you have a widescreen monitor, moving the taskbar from the bottom of the screen to the left (or right) will free up a bit of vertical space. To do this, right-click the taskbar and untick 'Lock the taskbar'. Click a blank area of the taskbar and drag it to its new location. You can then lock it into position. This also removes the search

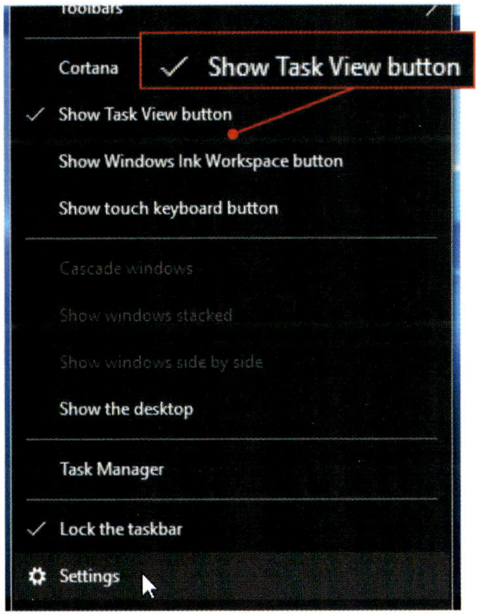

▲ Right-click the taskbar to change its settings

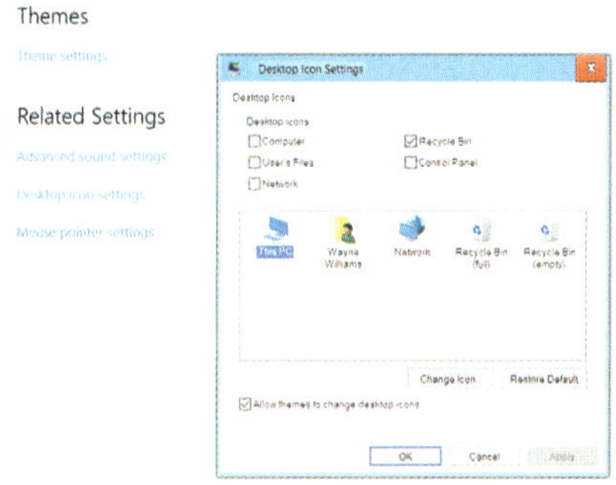

▲ Choose which shortcut icons you want to keep

box that usually sits at the left-hand side.

If you don't want to move the position of the taskbar but would like to get rid of the search box, right-click the taskbar, click the Search link and choose either Hidden or Show Search Icon. If Microsoft's personal assistant is active, go into the Cortana menu instead and tick Hidden.

You can make further customisations by right-clicking the taskbar and selecting Settings. There are options to auto-hide the taskbar, switch to smaller buttons, tweak their behaviour and customise the notification area. If you are using more than one screen, you can choose which

MINI WORKSHOP
Customise the taskbar with 7+ Taskbar Tweaker

1 7+ Taskbar Tweaker is very easy to use because everything you need is presented on a single menu screen and sorted into three main categories: 'Taskbar items', **1** 'Grouping and combining' **2** and 'Other taskbar options'. **3** Just click a taskbar setting to change it. Changes are made immediately.

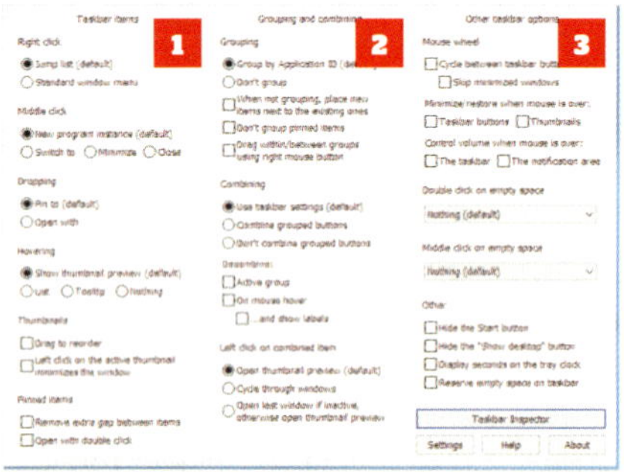

2 If you don't want the Start button on the taskbar, you can hide it. **1** Pressing the Windows key will still open the menu. You can also hide the 'Show desktop' button. **2** The Taskbar Inspector button **3** shows you all items currently open on the taskbar. **4** Right-clicking an item will let you interact with it. **5**

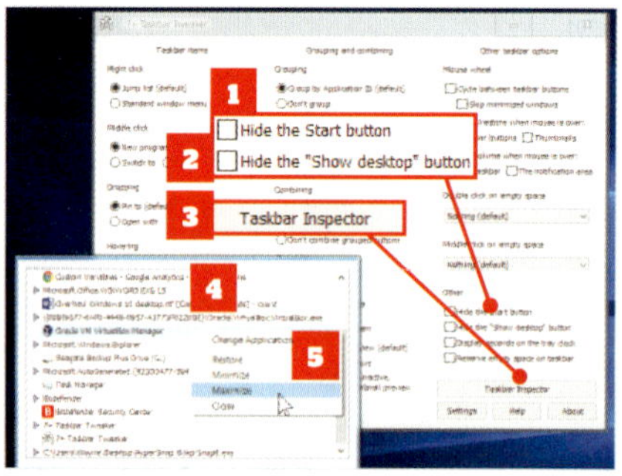

3 7+ Taskbar Tweaker also includes some hidden extras. Right-click the top of the window and select 'Advanced options'. These are less easy to use, so you should click the Help button if you need guidance. **1** Right-click an option to modify it. **2** There are tabs for Mouse Button Control **3** and Keyboard Shortcuts **4** too.

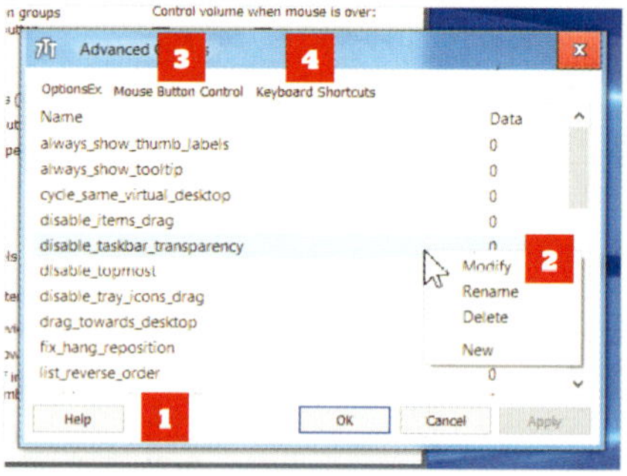

one to display taskbars on. You can also add different toolbars to the taskbar, including Address, Links, iTunes and Desktop.

If you want even greater control over the Windows taskbar, give 7+ Taskbar Tweaker (bit.ly/tweak398) a try. This was originally designed for Windows 7 but will work fine with Windows 8 and 10. It lets you make changes to the taskbar items (altering the mouse's clicking, dropping and hovering behaviour), and how it groups and combines programs. There are plenty of other taskbar options and they are all available through a single-screen interface. We show you how to use it in our Mini Workshop above.

Choose which icons to include on the desktop

Some people are happy to have only the Recycle Bin on their desktop, while others prefer to display a variety of shortcuts, including Computer, User Files and Control Panel. You can quickly decide which shortcuts you want by clicking Start and going to Settings, Personalisation, Themes. Click the 'Desktop icon settings' link and tick or untick the options in the window that opens. You can also change the icon for each one.

Get greater control over the colours

Windows 10 Color Control (bit.ly/control398) gives you greater control over the colours used in borders, the taskbar and the Start menu. It doesn't require installation – just pick your colour and apply it. You can go back to the original palette by ticking the 'New autocolour accent algorithm' box.

Replace or enhance File Explorer

The Windows file manager has seen many improvements over the years, but while File Explorer in Windows 10 is a decent

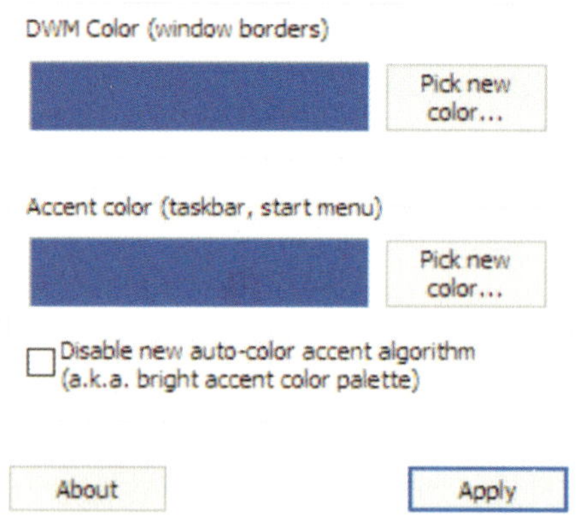

▲ Change the colours of Windows with Color Control

tool, there are better programs available that can complement or replace it. Multi Commander 6 (multicommander.com) has a dual-panel layout, making it much easier to copy files between locations. It also supports tabs, so you can have multiple folders open and within easy reach at all times. It comes with a quick-launch bar and a command field for entering commands, and has lots of options for customising the software.

XYplorerFree (bit.ly/xy398) is a cut-down but fully featured version of the paid-for XYplorer. Like Multi Commander, it has a dual-pane interface and tabs that make it easier to navigate and copy content between locations. You can also save your favourite folders for easy access in the future.

Seer (bit.ly/seer398) is another excellent option, which provides instant previews of files on your desktop or in File Explorer. Once it has been installed, you just select (single-click) a file and press the spacebar. A preview appears in a floating window.

Replace the Task Manager

The Windows 10 Task Manager, which can be summoned by right-clicking the taskbar and selecting Task Manager or by pressing Ctrl+Shift+Esc, is a very powerful tool, packed with features. There are even better replacements available, though, including AnVir Task Manager Free (www.anvir.com), which displays all running applications, processes and services in tabs across the top of its window. You can use it to disable or delay any unimportant items that start alongside Windows, and also monitor your hardware.

Process Explorer 16 (bit.ly/procex398) is also very good. It doesn't require installation and displays a list of colour-coded running processes. You can end suspicious items or scan them using the online virus checker at VirusTotal (www.virustotal.com). Process Explorer can be set as the default task manager by going into Options and selecting Replace Task Manager.

Make loads of quick changes to Windows 10

If you want a one-stop shop, Winaero Tweaker (winaero.com) is ideal. It works with various versions of Windows, including Windows 10, and can make numerous changes, including enabling the Aero Lite theme, changing the look of icons and menus, and tweaking the desktop and taskbar. We show you how

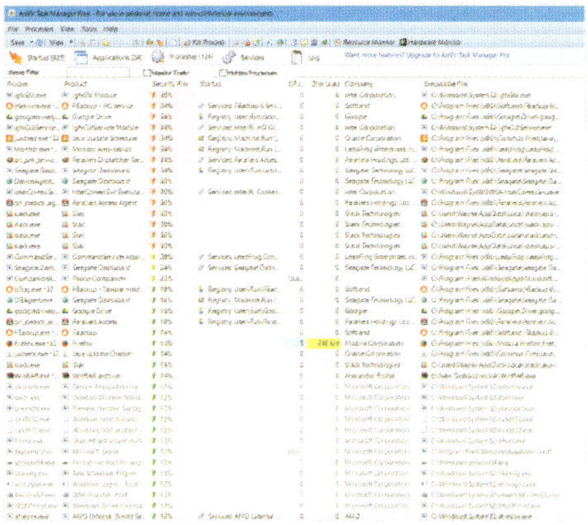

▲ AnVir Task Manager is more detailed Microsoft's

to use it in our Mini Workshop, below.

Another tool to try is the modestly named Ultimate Windows Tweaker (bit.ly/tweaker398), which offers more than 200 tweaks, all of which have been sorted into straightforward categories, such as Customisation, Performance, Security & Privacy and Context Menu.

Restore desktop Gadgets to Windows 10

Gadgets are floating mini-apps that you can arrange on the desktop and store in a handy sidebar. They were introduced in Vista and removed from Windows 8,

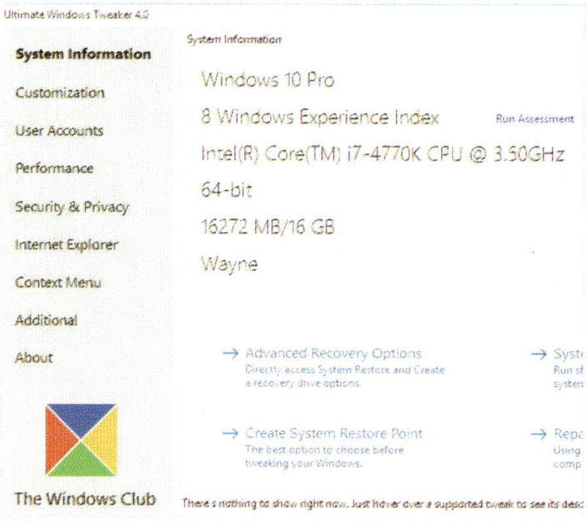

▲ Get instant access to more than 200 settings

but you can restore them by installing Gadgets Revived (gadgetsrevived.com). Download the sidebar from the site and pick the gadgets you want to run, then right-click the desktop and select Gadgets. You'll find a Control Panel option under 'Appearance and Personalisation', Desktop Gadgets.

Microsoft removed the gadget tools from Windows for security reasons but the ones that come with this program are safe.

Turn back to page 35 for more on restoring Gadgets and other missing Windows 10 features.

MINI WORKSHOP
Tweak Windows 10 with Winaero Tweaker

1 Winaero's tweaking tool provides useful information about your PC, including the version of Windows 10 you're running 1 and its Windows Experience Index (WEI) score. 2 WEI was a benchmarking feature introduced in Vista but removed in Windows 8. The higher the number, the better your overall Windows performance will be

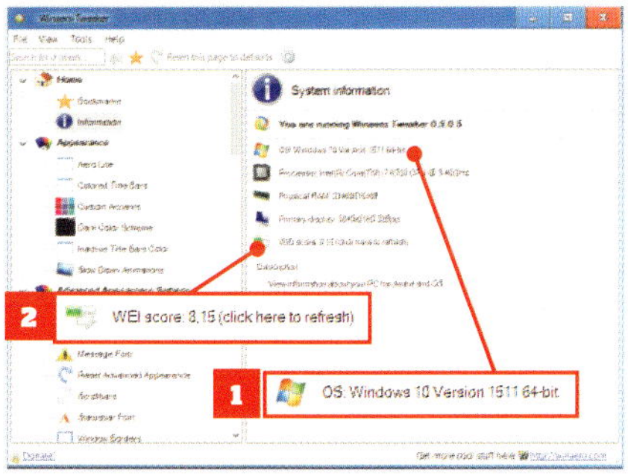

2 All the available tweaks are sorted into categories down the left-hand side. These include Appearance, 1 Advanced Appearance Settings, 2 Behavior, 3 'Boot and Logon', 'Desktop and Taskbar' and Context Menu. Select a tweak and the options for it will appear on the right. 4 Most can be actioned by ticking a box or using a slider.

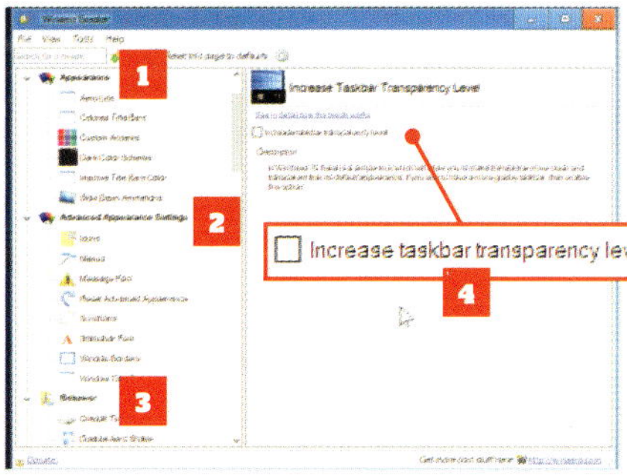

3 The Windows Apps section 1 lets you activate the Windows Photo Viewer, disable Windows Defender (although not in all versions of Windows 10), and change the default Microsoft Edge download folder. Save your favourite tweaks by clicking the Bookmark button. 2 Click the gear icon 3 to access settings.

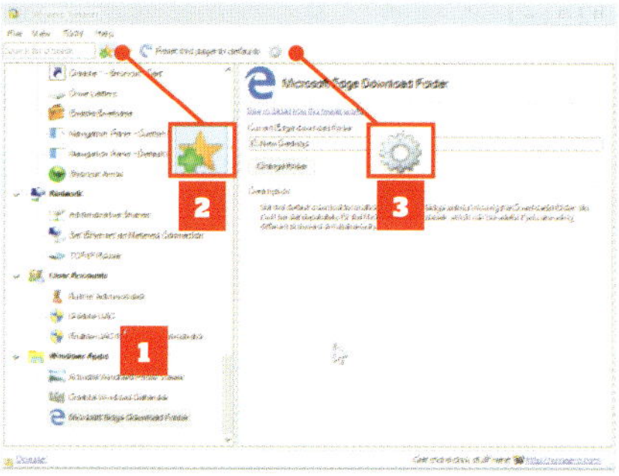

Use multiple accounts in Windows 10

In Windows 10 you can create separate accounts for everyone in the family. We reveal why this is such a great idea

In an ideal world, every member of the family would be able to have their own Windows 10 PC, fully customised so it looks and works how they want it to, and with all their files stored safely in their own folders. Kids' computers would be safe to use, and grown ups' computers would be safe from kids. Sadly, it's just not practical to buy expensive computer hardware for everyone in your house.

But there is a way of making it feel almost exactly like each person in your family has their own PC – and that's by setting them up with their very own Windows 10 account.

Before Windows 10, most PCs were operated from a single user account. That means the computer belongs to one person, and one person only.

Windows 10 now allows every family member (and friends, colleagues or people visiting for the weekend) to set up their own dedicated account. Each separate account owner can have their own private email account, document folders, desktop wallpaper, Windows apps and customised Start menu.

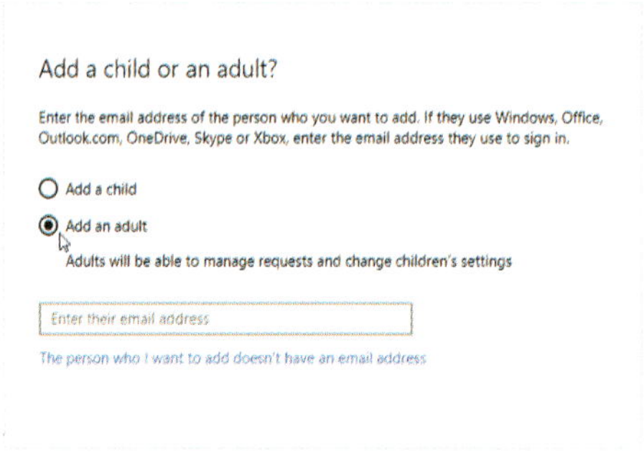

▲ **You'll be asked to choose whether the account is for a child or adult for safety features**

It's not the same as setting up virtual PCs – which is where you are effectively creating an entirely new system inside the same physical hardware – but the benefits are similar and it's much quicker and easier to do. Here we'll show you how.

Set up accounts for family members

When you're setting up a new account, Windows 10 makes a distinction between family members and 'other' users. The main reason for this is to allow adults to monitor their children's accounts; giving them permission to download apps, set times they can use the computer and so on. If you have children, or even grandchildren, see the box below to find out how to use this feature.

If you're in a household of adults and grown-up children, it doesn't really matter which option you choose. Your main decision will be whether you want to use a Microsoft account or not.

If you'd rather not, you can set up a completely local account. This means you won't be able to sync settings, bookmarks and so on across different PCs using your Microsoft account, and it can make buying Windows Store apps trickier. But if you're determined not to give Microsoft your email address and other details, choose 'Add someone else to this PC' under 'Family & other people'.

If other family members are happy to use a Microsoft account, open Settings

ACCOUNTS FOR CHILDREN

Windows 10 lets you set up child accounts. These accounts are designed to prevent youngsters installing software, moving files around and messing up your settings. Go to Settings, then Accounts, then 'Family & other people'. Select 'Add a family member', then choose 'Add a child' and follow the remaining steps.

This also gives you (as administrator) a range of controls over children's accounts, including limiting the hours in which they can use the PC, and the option to block or allow access to certain websites. Parents and grandparents will even get a full list of every website the child visits, plus an alert if they attempt to visit an 'adult' site.

Child accounts can even be managed remotely using another PC or tablet by logging in at https://account.microsoft.com/family (see screenshot).

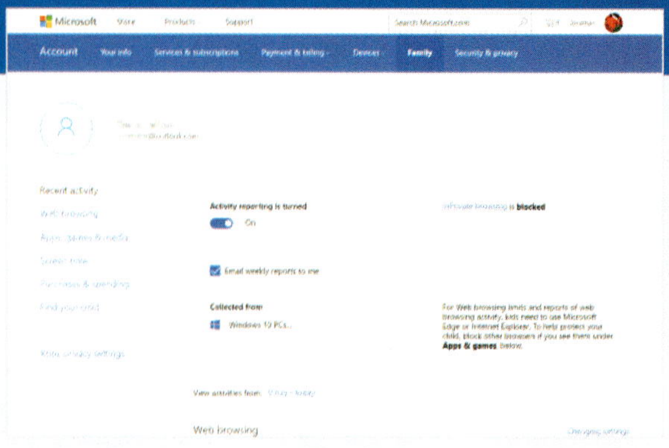

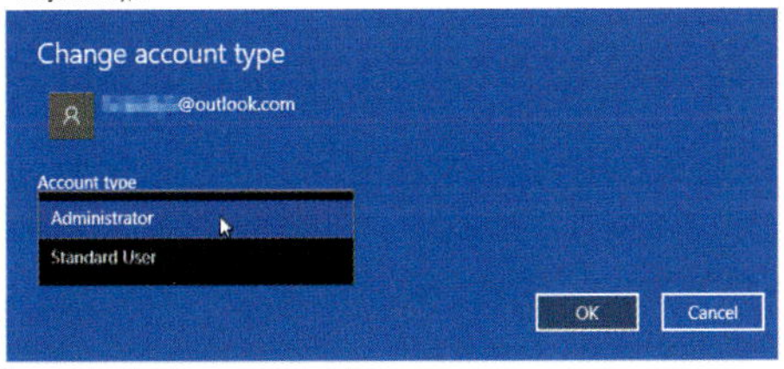

▲ **If you find standard accounts too restrictive, it's easy to switch to admin**

from the Start menu and choose the Accounts option. Click the 'Family & other people' tab on the left-hand side of the window that appears, then click 'Add a family member'. You'll now be asked whether you're setting up an account for an adult or a child, and prompted to enter the new user's email address. You'll then be asked to set up a Microsoft account (if you don't already have one registered to that email address), then follow the on-screen instructions.

Turn a standard account into an admin account

By default, the person who first set up the PC will be the 'administrator' and any secondary accounts added will be given 'standard' status.

Standard account holders have fewer privileges. They can't install most software without the administrator's password, they can't view the personal folders (documents, photos and so on) of other account holders, and they have limited access to PC settings.

The original idea was based on letting kids use their parents' computers without creating havoc, but these standard account privileges may seem somewhat restrictive for those of us who just want to share our computers with family members. For example, if you want to install a program when the administrator is out of the house, you can't.

Thankfully, you can upgrade a trusted secondary account holder to administrator status. The original administrator needs to do this. Go to Settings, Accounts, then 'Family & other people' and select the relevant account holder's name. Click 'Change account type' and select Administrator.

Add a temporary guest account

If you have friends or extended family members coming to stay, you can set them up with their own accounts on your PC. These guest accounts don't give them access to your files, email and so on.

Go to Settings, then Accounts, then 'Family & other people' and select 'Add someone else to this PC' under 'Other people'. If the guest already has a Microsoft account, they can enter their email address or phone number to retrieve all the settings, bookmarks and apps that are stored in their account.

If your guest doesn't have a Microsoft account, or if they don't want the fuss of registering an account with Microsoft, click the small 'I don't have this person's sign-in information' link at the bottom of the screen requesting an email address. Then on the next screen, click the tiny 'Add a user without a Microsoft account' link (see screenshot below) at the bottom. You'll be asked to choose a username and password for the new account.

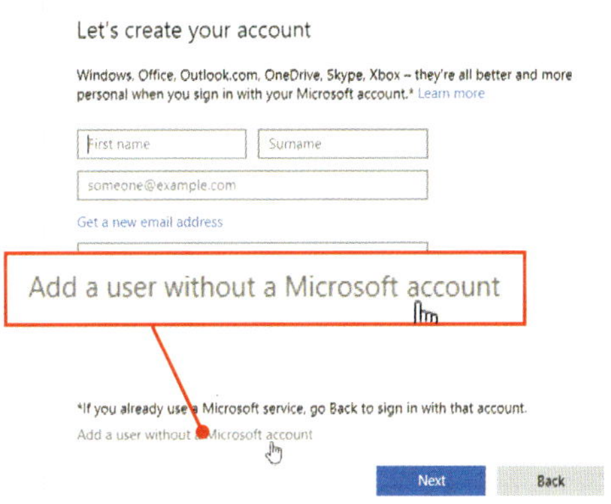

▲ **Click the tiny blue link to create a user account without handing over an email address**

Share programs and apps with other users

Any traditional PC software, such as Microsoft Office, that's already been installed on the PC by the administrator will be available to all account holders.

When the administrator installs software in future, they will be asked if they want the program to be available to every user on the PC or just to themselves.

Windows Store apps aren't automatically shared, but there is a workaround for this. If the administrator has already paid for an app or game, he or she can share it with a new account holder after taking a few steps. In the new account, open the Windows Store and then click the account holder's profile icon next to the search bar. Click the account at the top of the dropdown menu, click the account holder's name and sign them out. Then sign in again, this time with the administrator's account details.

Now go to My Library and you'll see a list of apps owned by the administrator. Click the little arrow to download any of these to the new account.

Make sure the administrator signs out again when you've got all the apps you need.

There's a new option in Windows 10 called 'Assigned access', where a user account can access only one specific Windows Store app. For example, you could create an account just for the Netflix app (www.snipca.com/18724), Dropbox (www.snipca.com/18725) or the Kindle app (www.snipca.com/18723).

To set up assigned access, create a secondary account (see above) and then go to Settings, Accounts, 'Family & other users' and click the small 'Set up assigned access' link at the bottom of the page. Choose the user account and app, then restart your PC.

FIVE BEST REASONS TO USE W10 ACCOUNTS

1 You save money by buying one Windows 10 PC and turning it into a computer everyone can use in their own way, in private.

2 No one account holder can see another account holder's browser history – so nobody's going to spot those surprise holiday plans.

3 Every family member can have their own Windows settings, desktop wallpaper and Start menu set-up, making it feel like their 'own' PC.

4 Security is greatly improved by preventing standard account holders from inadvertently installing software (including associated adware).

5 Standard account holders can't view each other's personal folders, so your files can't be accidentally deleted by other people.

Set new defaults for Windows 10 tasks

Time required: 30 minutes

If you've upgraded to Windows 10, or bought a PC running the new operating system, you may notice that Microsoft's apps are the defaults for all your PC's functions (Groove Music for playing music, Photos for viewing photos, and so on).

We'll show you how to set new defaults in just a few clicks. We'll also show you a secret way to use Gmail in Chrome as your default email service, how to set your default printer and scanner, and how to change your default search engine within Microsoft Edge.

STEP 1 First, ensure that you've installed any third-party programs or apps that you want to set as your defaults. Now open the Start menu, click Settings, System, then click 'Default apps' 1. Some programs may have automatically set themselves as defaults after you installed them. If you're happy with that, then leave it as the default. If not, click the Reset button 2 at the bottom to reset all your apps to Microsoft's defaults. You'll now see Microsoft Edge as your default web browser 3, Films & TV as your default video player 4, and so on. You can now systematically change each one.

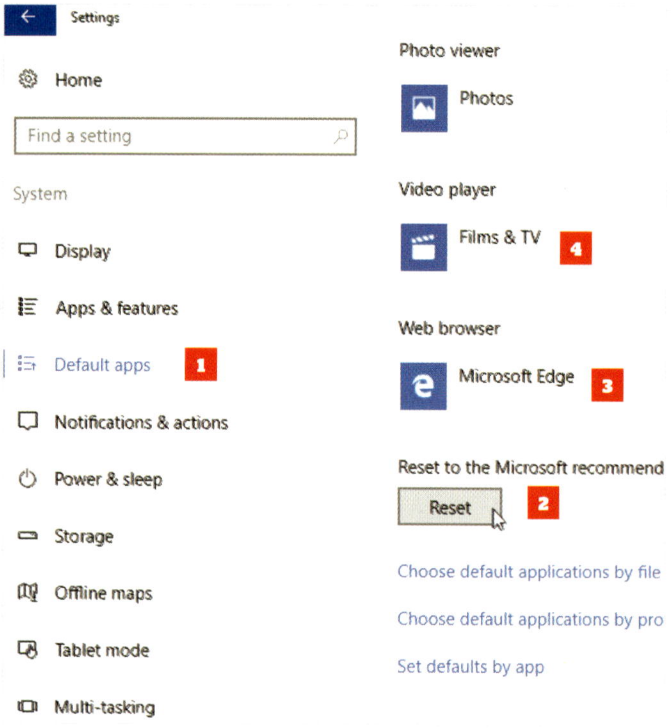

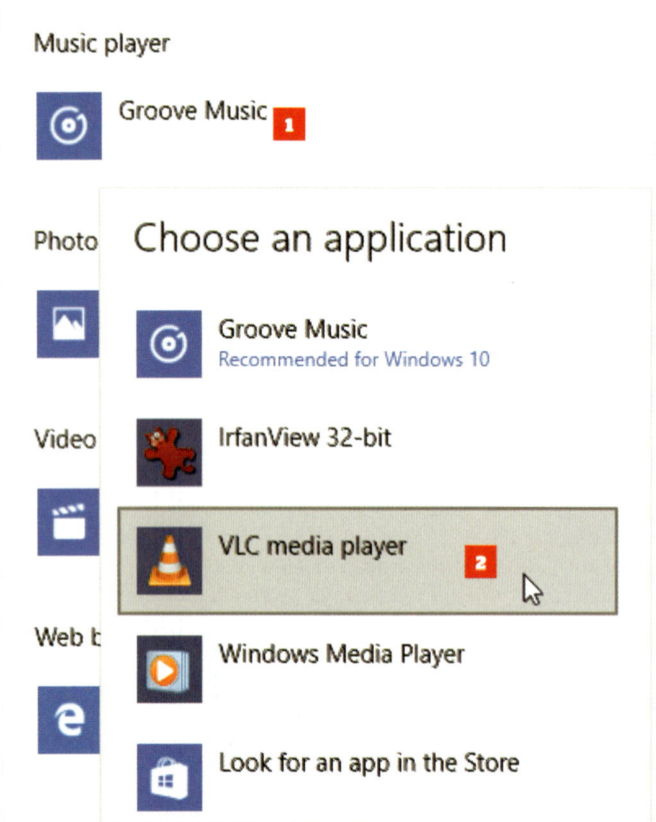

STEP 2 To change your default app for any of the functions (such as 'Music player'), click the current default (Groove Music) 1. You'll now see a list of installed programs/apps that you can use as your default for that function. Click to select the one you want (such as 'VLC media player') 2. If a program or app you want to use doesn't appear within the list, then use the method outlined in Step 6 to set it as your default.

STEP 3 Your default Email app is set to Mail. If you want to change this to Outlook, then ensure you've installed Office on your PC. To install the latest version, go to www.office.com/myaccount and log in with your Microsoft account. Next, click the Install button 1, run the downloaded setup file and wait for it to finish. This installs Office 365, which you can use for free for one month on up to five devices 2 (it costs £7.99 per month or £79.99 per year, thereafter). After installing, open Outlook and log into your account. Now return to the 'Default apps' settings and set your default Mail app to Outlook.

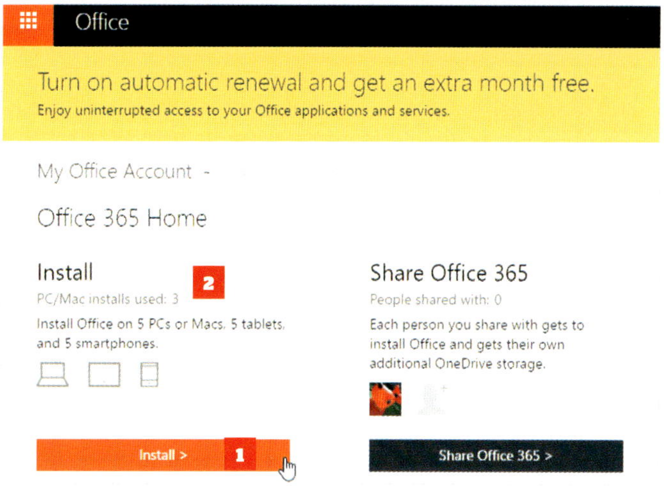

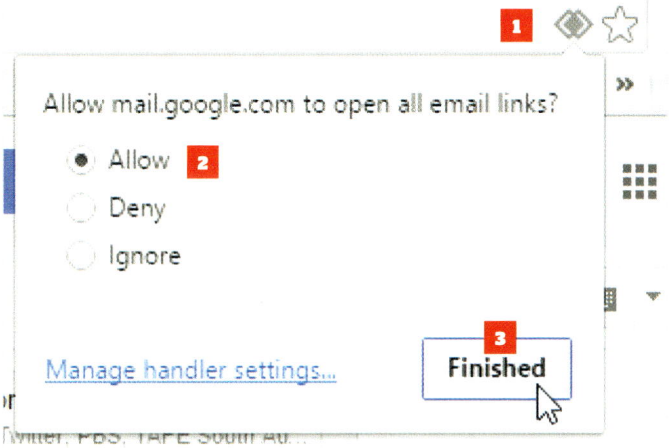

STEP 4 You can set Gmail as your default email. To do this, open Chrome (www.snipca.com/19773), go to www.gmail.com and log into your account. Next, click the Protocol Handler icon 1 (at the right of your browser bar). If you don't see this icon, skip to the next step. Now select Allow 2, then click Finished 3. Click OK if you see a pop-up message on your screen. Now return to the 'Default apps' section, click your default email app (Mail) and select Google Chrome.

STEP 5 After doing that, open Chrome again, click the three lines at the top right, Settings, then scroll to the bottom and click '+ Show advanced settings'. In the Privacy section, click the 'Content settings' button. Now scroll to the Handlers section and click the 'Manage handlers' button 1. Click the 'mailto' dropdown menu, select 'mail.google.com' 2, then click Finished twice 3. From now on, whenever you click an email address link, it'll open within Gmail in Chrome, ready for you to write your email.

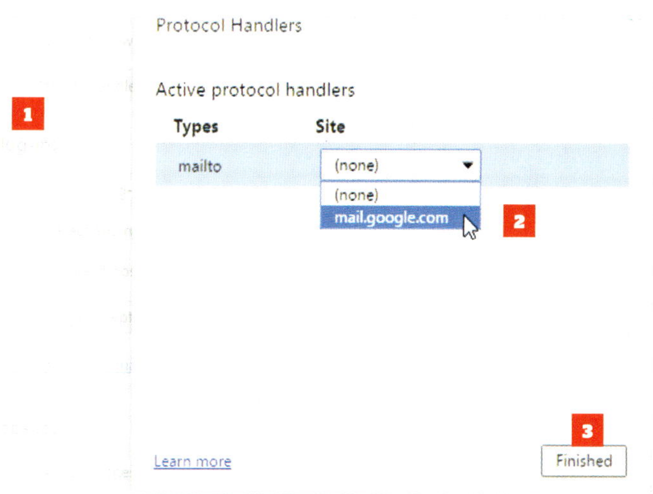

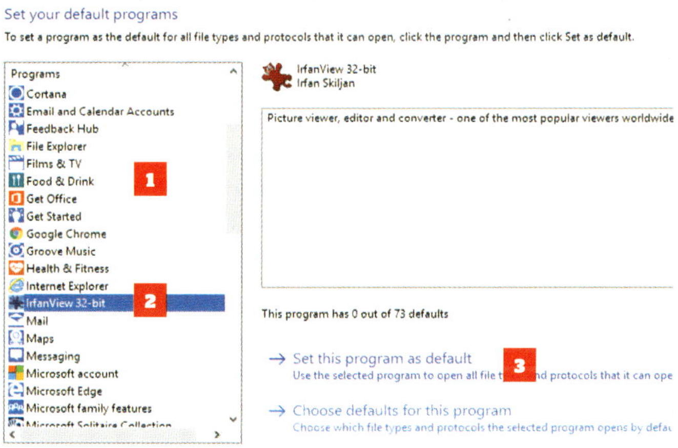

STEP 6 Photos is your default 'Photo viewer' app. If you click to change it (see Step 2), you'll see a list of alternative programs. You'll notice that some third-party programs (such as the popular IrfanView www.snipca.com/19774) won't appear, even if they're installed on your PC. Using IrfanView as an example, we'll show you how to add it to the list. First, scroll to the bottom of the 'Default apps' section and click 'Set defaults by app'. You'll now see an alphabetical list of all the programs and apps on your PC 1. Select IrfanView 2, then click 'Set this program as default' 3. This will set IrfanView as the default program for all the file types associated with it (photos, images and screenshots).

STEP 7 Alternatively, you can choose which file type you want to set IrfanView as your default for. To do this, select the program in the alphabetical list on the left, then click 'Choose defaults for this program' below. Now click the Current Default heading 1 and scroll down the list. You'll see that the Photos app is set as your default for most photo file formats. Tick the file formats you want to set IrfanView as your default for (.jpg, gif, .png, .raw and .tif are the most common image formats) 2, then click Save 3. Repeat Steps 6 and 7 to change your defaults for all the programs and apps that don't appear within your list in the 'Default apps' section.

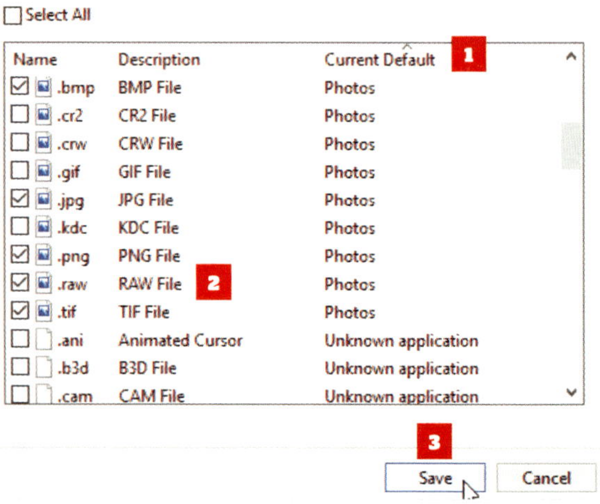

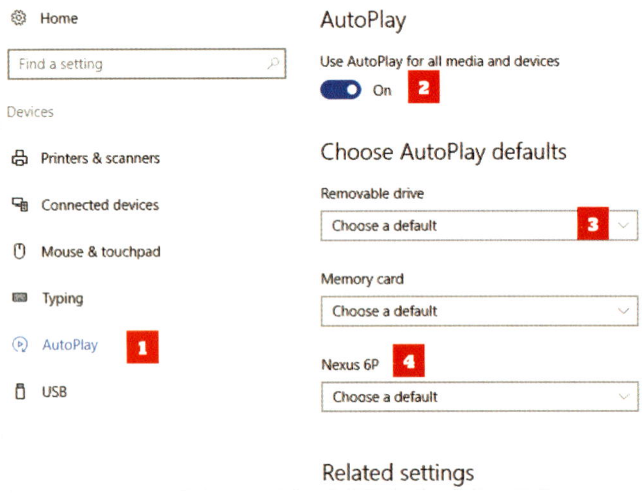

STEP 8 We'll now show you how to set default actions when you connect any device (such as a mobile phone, external hard drive, SD card, CD or DVD) to your PC. Open Settings, Devices, then click AutoPlay 1. Ensure the AutoPlay slider is turned on 2. Next, click the 'Removable device' dropdown menu and choose what you want. We recommend 'Open folder to view files (File Explorer)' 3. Next, click the 'Memory card' dropdown menu and select an action. Connect your phone or tablet to your PC to see its option appear within this list 4. Now select what you want to do when you connect it to your PC.

STEP 9 Next, let's set your default printer and scanner. Ensure both devices are connected to your PC. Now open Settings, click Devices, then click 'Printers & scanners' 1. If your device isn't listed, click the Refresh button 2 and wait for the list to update. If there's a device you no longer use, select it and click 'Remove device' 3. Now switch 'Let Windows manage my default printer' off. Select your printer and click 'Manage' 4, then click 'Set as default'. Repeat this to set your default scanner.

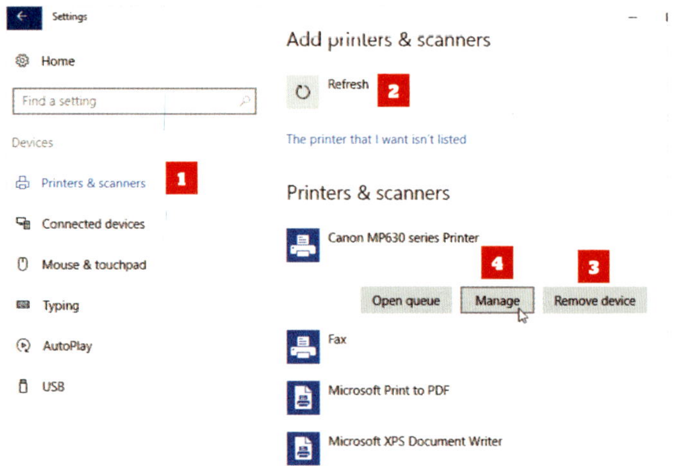

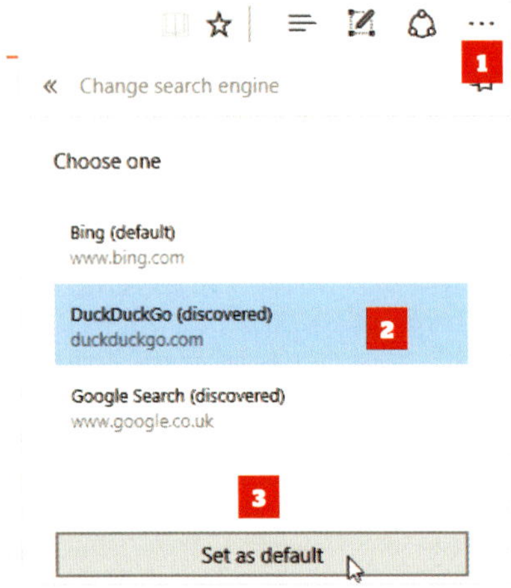

STEP 10 Bing is the default search engine in Microsoft Edge. If you prefer using another search engine (such as Google or DuckDuckGo), you can set it as the default. Launch Edge, then open the website you want to set as your search engine. Now click the three dots at the top right 1, Settings at the bottom, then scroll to the bottom again and click the 'View advanced settings' button. Click the 'Change search engine' button below Bing. You'll see the website you're on in a list. Click to select it 2, then click 'Set as default' 3.

Windows 10 settings you must change now

Microsoft's default settings in Windows 10 aren't as efficient or safe as they should be. We explain what they do, and tell you which to disable

Every version of Windows has had settings that needed tweaking, whether it's changing the desktop background to a photo of your family, or switching off a feature you don't like.

But Windows 10 takes this to a whole new level. No previous version has had more default settings that need changing straight away.

As we've said before, we love Windows 10. It's a fast, modern operating system (OS) with some great tools. But whether you've recently upgraded or you're planning to soon, there are dozens of settings you need to change. Take Microsoft's automatic updates, for example, which could randomly reboot your PC right when you're in the middle of doing something important. Or how about System Restore? This fantastically useful tool is left switched off unless you turn it on yourself.

We'll be looking at settings that affect your privacy and safety in more detail in Chapter 3. But, before then, here is our ultimate checklist of all the settings Windows 10 users need to change.

In each case, we'll explain what the Windows 10 default setting is and the reasons why Microsoft wants you to leave it that way. Then we'll show you what we recommend changing it to and explain why.

What you can do

- Change Windows 10 so that it works the way you want it to
- Re-enable the features that Microsoft doesn't want you to use
- Block unwanted updates and stop background downloads
- Banish annoying messages and nuisance notifications

SYSTEM AND UPDATES

1 Choose how updates are installed

Windows 10 default: Automatic
Microsoft is so keen to keep all its users' PCs up to date that the default setting for Windows Update is to download and install updates whether you want them or not.

We recommend: 'Active hours'
You can't turn automatic updates off, but you can choose when updates are installed, so that you don't suddenly have to stop whatever you're doing and reboot your PC. The recent Anniversary Update added a new tool for controlling when updates are installed and we'll be showing you how to use it in more detail in Chapter 3.

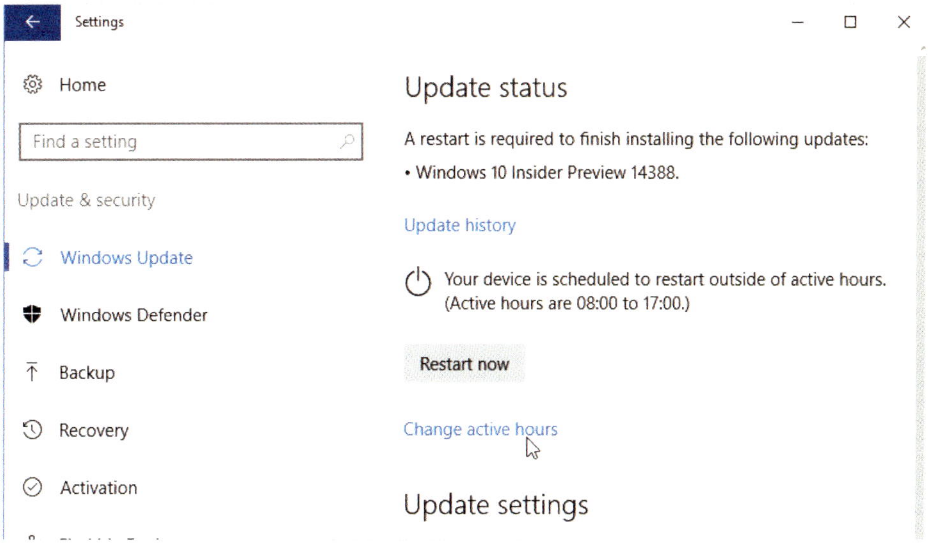

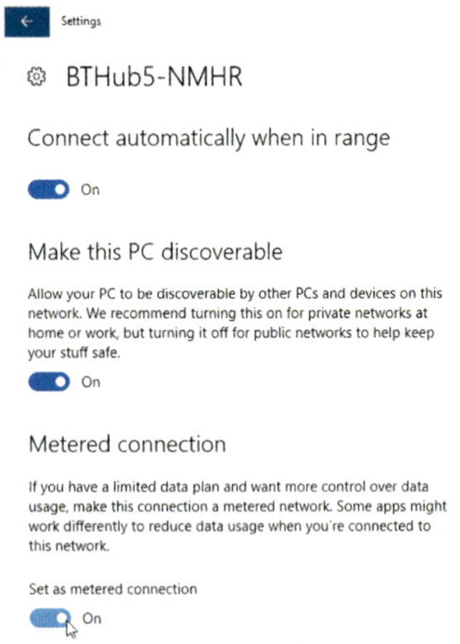

2 Metered connection

Windows 10 default: Off

Windows 10 automatically assumes that your internet connection allows for unlimited data.

We recommend: On

If you pay for your internet connection by the gigabyte, then enabling this setting will prevent background downloads eating into your data allowance. But even if your connection isn't pay-as-you-go, there's another reason you may want to switch this on. If Windows thinks your connection is metered, then it won't force updates on you unless you download them manually. Currently, this only works on wireless connections. Click Start, Settings, 'Network & internet', Wi-Fi, then click 'Manage known networks.' Click your network name, then click Properties and click the button under 'Set as metered connection'.

3 Updates from more than one place

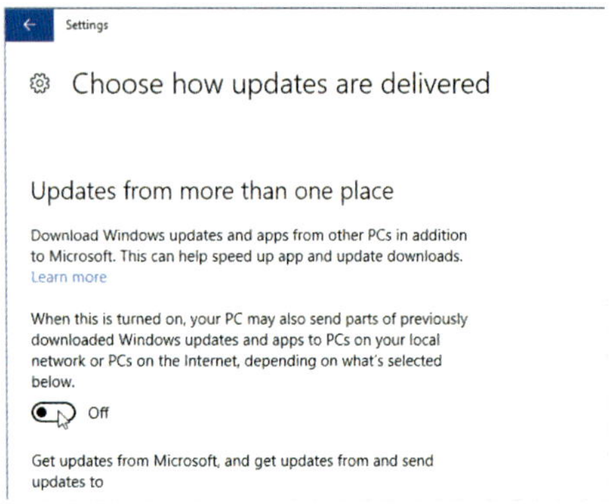

Windows 10 default: On

Windows 10 uses peer-to-peer technology – similar to BitTorrent – to take the strain off Microsoft's own servers. It does this by making Windows 10 users upload Windows and app updates to other users' PCs over the internet.

We recommend: Off

There's no evidence to suggest this setting is unsafe, but it could mean you waste gigabytes of personal bandwidth – and all just to save Microsoft money. Click Start, Settings, 'Update & security', Windows Update, 'Advanced options', then either switch the setting off altogether, or choose the 'PCs on my local network' option. The latter will actually save bandwidth if you have multiple Windows 10 PCs, because updates will be downloaded and shared with your PCs.

4 Give me updates for other Microsoft products when I update Windows

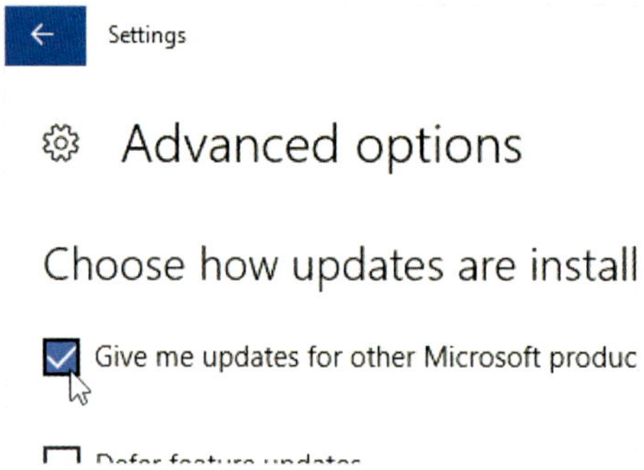

Windows 10 default: Off

Microsoft assumes you want updates for Windows 10 only, not its other products, such as Office.

We recommend: On

While Windows updates can be annoying, they're generally a good idea because they fix problems, add features and make your computer safer. The same goes for all the other software on your PC, so if you own other Microsoft programs or devices – Office, for example – it's worth switching this setting on so that you get their latest updates. Click Start, Settings, 'Update & security', Windows Update, 'Advanced options', then 'Choose how updates are delivered'.

5 Backup

Windows 10 default: Off

Despite having several different built-in backup options, Windows 10 leaves them all disabled unless you do something about it yourself.

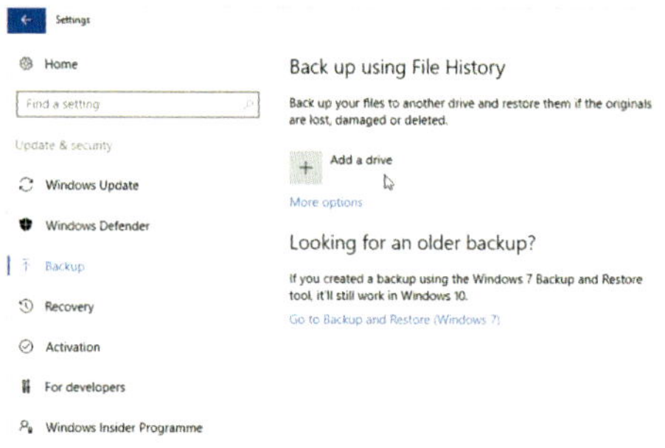

We recommend: On

Backing up is such an important part of running a PC but, amazingly, Windows 10 still fails to enable backup when you first set up your computer. To enable it yourself, click Start, Settings, 'Update & security', then Backup. To use Windows 10's File History feature, plug in a USB hard drive, then click 'Add a drive' and follow the prompts. This backs up your data continuously in the background. If you'd prefer to use a more familiar scheduled backup instead, click 'Go to Backup and Restore (Windows 7)' and click 'Set up back-up'. We'll cover backing up in more detail in Chapter 4.

6 System Restore

Windows 10 default: Off

For reasons we've yet to fathom, Windows 10 disables System Restore altogether.

We recommend: On

System Restore is a feature we've relied on since Windows XP. It provides a way

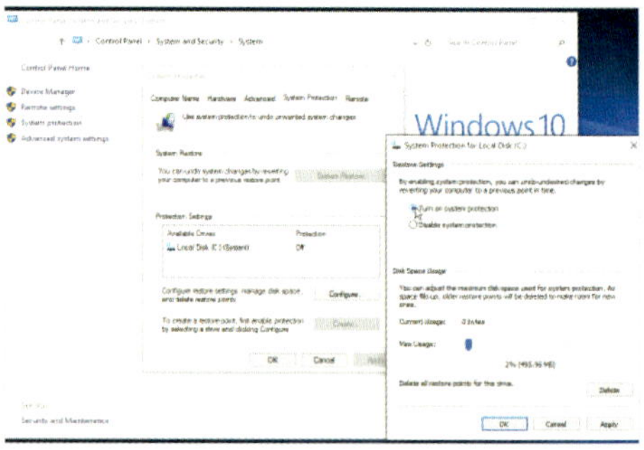

of rolling back your system to a time before a troublesome update or program was installed, instantly fixing disastrous PC problems. To re-enable it, right-click Start and select System, then click 'System protection'. In the window that opens, click your system drive (usually C:), then click Configure. Next, click 'Turn on system protection' and use the slider to allocate a small percentage of your hard-drive space (around two per cent) to System Restore, then click OK.

PERFORMANCE, SPEED AND INTERFACE

7 Visual Effects

Windows 10 default: 'Let Windows choose what's best for my computer'

Windows 10 uses a lot of fancy effects to make it attractive to use, but these all consume system resources. By default, the OS manages these automatically.

We recommend: Off

You may notice a significant improvement in performance if you disable Windows 10's visual effects. Right-click Start, then click System, 'Advanced system settings'. Now click the Settings button under Performance, select the 'Adjust for best performance' option at the top, then click OK (see screenshot below). The effect will be more noticeable on some PCs than others; if you don't notice any difference, you can always switch back.

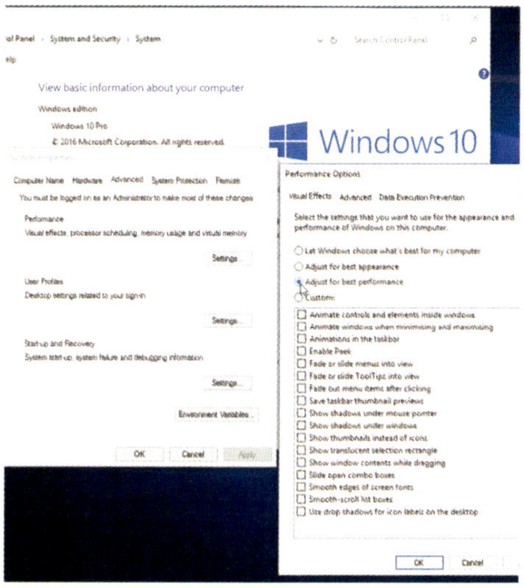

8 Start-up items

Windows 10 default: Enabled

Windows 10 allows programs to add themselves to your PC's start-up unless you choose to disable them, the idea being that important programs are ready to go as soon as your computer starts.

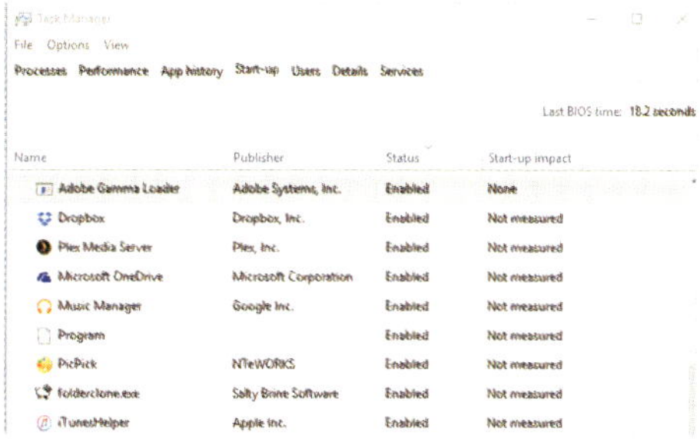

We recommend: Disable as needed

Not all the programs that get added to your start-up are as important as they think they are. Right-click the taskbar, then click Task Manager. Click 'More details' if shown, then click the Start-up tab and work through the list. Click any items you don't need, then click Disable. If you're not sure what an item does, right-click it and select 'Search online'.

9 Hibernate

Windows 10 default: Disabled

Hibernate is a way of shutting down your computer so it saves all your programs and files.

We recommend: Enabled

Hibernating can be a massive time-saver, as it lets you carry on working exactly where you left off when you restart your PC. To add Hibernate to the options available from the Start menu power button, right-click Start then select Power Options. Click 'Choose what the power buttons do', then click 'Change settings that are currently unavailable'.

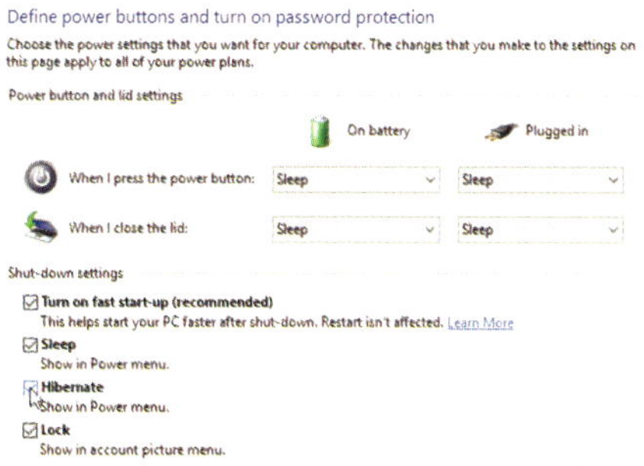

WHY DOES WINDOWS 10 HAVE SO MANY SETTINGS?

One of the reasons is that Windows 10 spreads them across so many different areas of the OS. Microsoft would argue that the new Settings app replaces many Control Panel items and simplifies them. But the Control Panel is still there and houses at least 41 items (sometimes more, depending on your system), compared with around 45 found in Windows 7. And this is in addition to more than 60 in the Settings app.

Next, tick the Hibernate box under 'Shut-down settings' (see screenshot below left). While you're there, check that 'Turn on fast start-up' is ticked, too. This is another time saver, though it's normally enabled by default. Click 'Save changes'.

10 Task View and Search bar

Windows 10 default: Enabled

Microsoft is so desperate for you to use the new features that it has stuck two of them – Task View and Cortana's search bar – permanently to the taskbar.

We recommend: Disabled (optional)

You can tidy up your taskbar by disabling both. To disable the Task View button, right-click the taskbar, then click 'Show Task View button' to untick it. To disable the Search bar, right-click the taskbar and select Cortana, then choose 'Show Cortana icon' to replace the Search bar with an icon, or choose Hidden to hide it altogether. Bear in mind that this won't disable features themselves – you'll still be able to use Task View by pressing Win+Tab, for example.

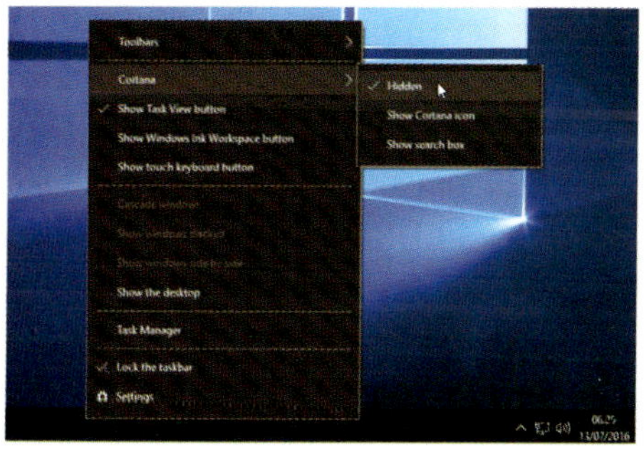

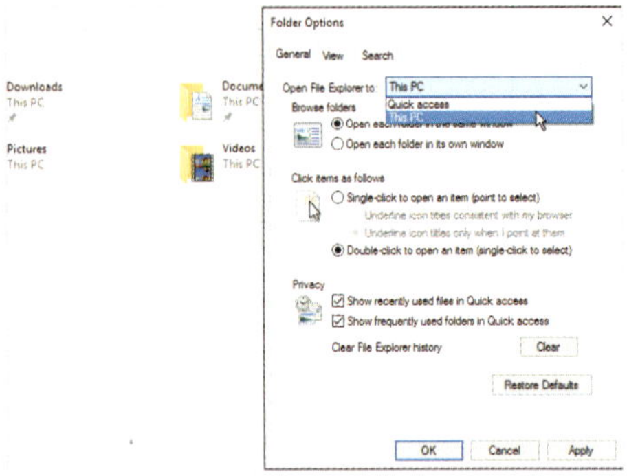

11 Quick Access view

Windows 10 default: Enabled

The new default view in File Explorer is intended to help you get to your most recently or frequently used files and folders quickly.

We recommend: Disable (optional)

This one's down to personal taste. Quick Access is actually quite useful, but takes some getting used to. If you don't like it, bring back the old My Computer-style view of all the drives on your computer by clicking the File Explorer icon on the taskbar. Make sure the ribbon is visible (click the down arrow in the top right if not), click the View tab, then click Options. On the General tab of the window that opens, choose This PC from the 'Open File Explorer to' dropdown menu and click OK.

NOTIFICATIONS AND ADVERTS

12 Get Office

Windows 10 default: Enabled

Microsoft wants you to buy Office, so it displays 'Get Office' messages in your Notifications.

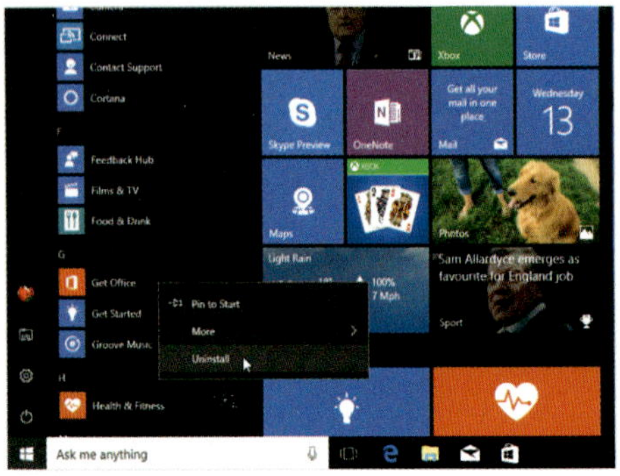

We recommend: Disable

These annoying notifications are essentially ads caused by a app that comes preinstalled with Windows 10. Uninstalling the app is an effective way of silencing them for good, so click Start, 'All apps', scroll to Get Office, right-click it and select Uninstall.

13 Get tips, tricks and suggestions as you use Windows

Windows 10 default: On

Your PC will deliver occasional 'helpful' tips to you via the Action Centre, in order to point you towards new features and tools.

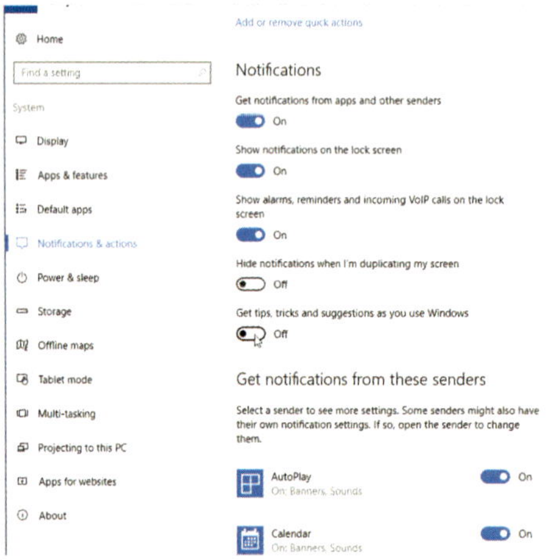

We recommend: Off

You don't have to put up with being hassled by unnecessary notifications. Some people have reported that disabling them dramatically boosts performance, too. Click Start, Settings, System, then 'Notifications & actions' on the left. Switch the setting (under the Notifications heading) to Off.

14 Get notifications from apps and other senders

Windows 10 default: On

Apps are allowed to send you notifications that appear as pop-ups near the notification area, as well as in the Action Centre and the lock screen.

We recommend: On, but Off for specific apps

Some notifications are useful but, with Windows 10's default settings, it's easy to end up drowning in annoying alerts.

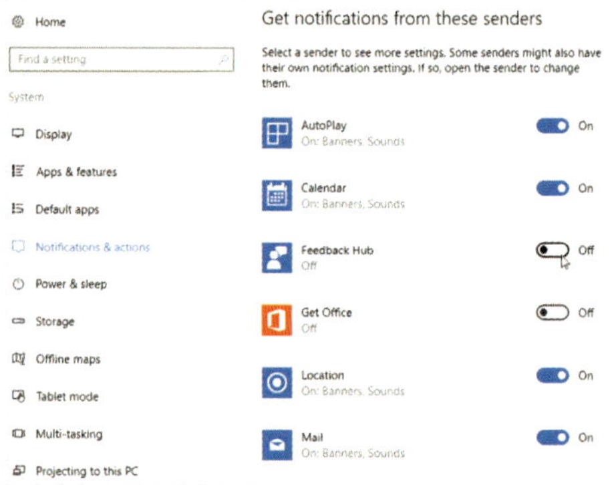

To fix this, click Start, Settings, System, then click 'Notifications & actions'. Leave the global 'Get notifications from apps and other senders' setting On, but scroll down and check the list of apps shown below, switching off any you don't need notifications from.

15 Show notifications on the lock screen

Windows 10 default: On

With this enabled, you can view notifications you've received without logging in.

We recommend: Off

The trouble with this setting and the one below it ('Show alarms, reminders, and incoming VOIP calls on the lock screen') is that other people can see the emails, calendar appointments, missed calls and other personal information that lock-screen notifications may contain. You may feel more comfortable switching these off, particularly if you use your PC at work or in public. Click Start, Settings, System, then click 'Notifications & actions' and scroll down to disable both settings.

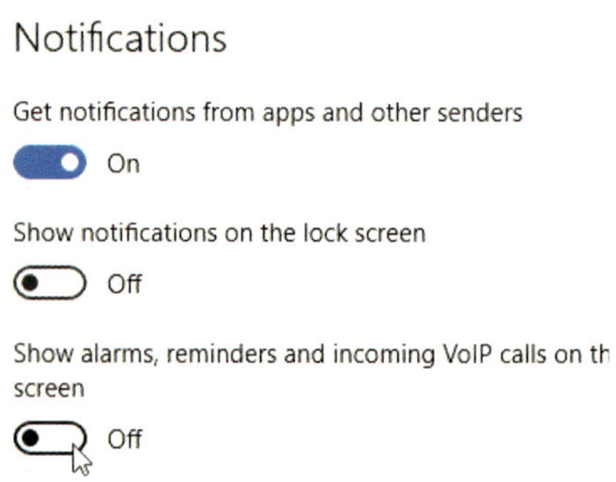

APPS AND PROGRAMS

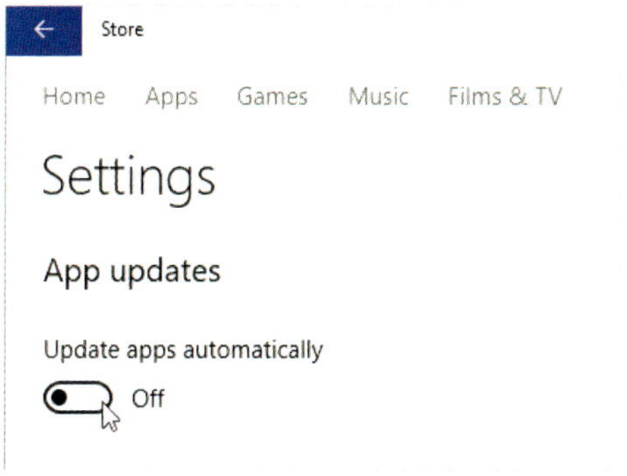

16 Windows Store App updates
Windows 10 default: On

The Windows Store app checks for and downloads any updates for your apps so that you don't need to think about it.

We recommend: Off

While this option may be convenient, it won't necessarily work for everyone. If you're on a capped or metered internet connection, for example, you may prefer to monitor or control the bandwidth these updates use up. Open the Windows Store from the taskbar icon, then click your account icon and select Settings. Switch 'Update apps automatically' to off.

17 Windows Store Live Tile
Windows 10 default: On

With this enabled, the Windows Store's Start menu Live Tile will display new or featured apps and games that you might be interested in.

We recommend: Off

This is another way for Microsoft to push Windows Store advertising at you. If you're fed up with this hard sell, open the Windows Store app and navigate to its settings as described in the previous tip, then switch 'Show products on tile' to Off.

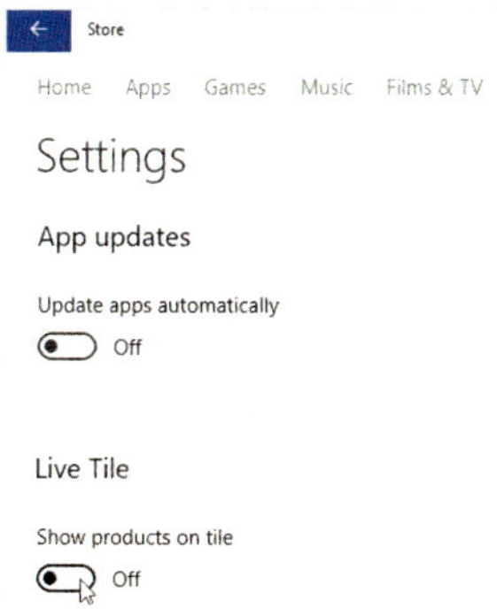

18 Default apps
Windows 10 default: Windows 10 apps

Unless you specify otherwise during setup, Windows 10 will set its new apps as the defaults for music, photos and more, while Edge will become your default browser.

We recommend: Your own favourite programs and tools

Getting you to use its own apps is another way that Microsoft will try to sell you stuff, because its Groove Music and Film & TV apps are tied directly into Microsoft's own online entertainment stores. To switch back to your preferred programs, click Start, Settings, System, then 'Default apps'. Now click each of the apps listed and choose the program you

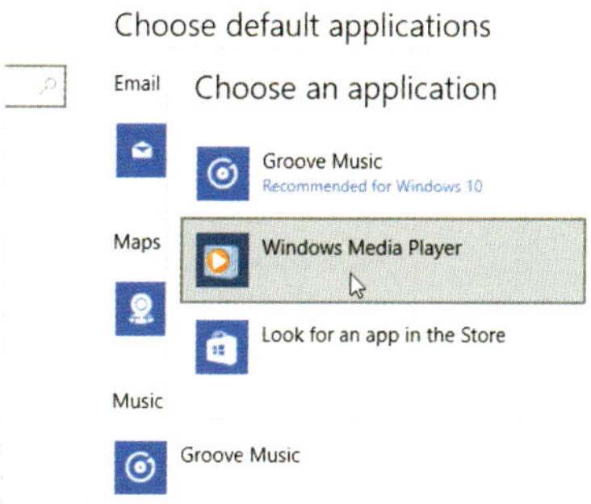

want instead. If the program you want isn't listed, you may need to install it. For even more control, scroll down and click 'Choose default applications by file type'. See page 34 for more on defaults.

19 Background apps
Windows 10 default: On

Windows 10 allows its built-in apps – plus many of those you download from the Windows Store – to run in the background all the time, so that they can remain connected and up to date.

We recommend: Off for certain apps

In some cases, it can be very useful to have an app running in the background. With News running, for example, you can get the latest headlines from your Start menu live tile without actually having to launch the app. But the more apps you run, the more memory you'll consume, as well as battery life if you're on a laptop. We'd suggest limiting background apps to a minimum, so click Start, Settings, Privacy, 'Background apps', then scroll through the list switching off any you don't need.

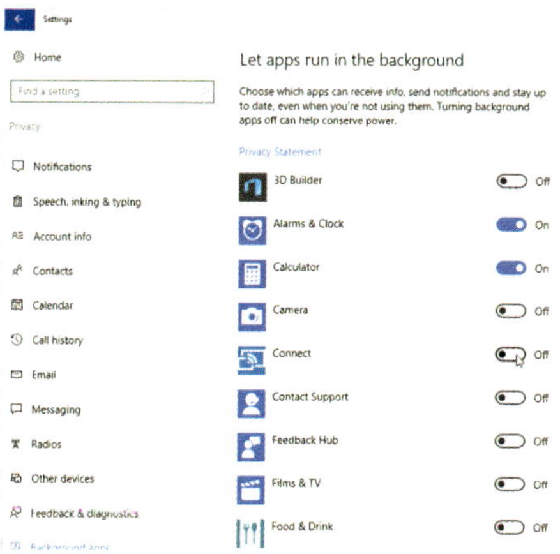

4 SETTINGS YOU SHOULD PROBABLY LEAVE ALONE

1 THE REGISTRY
Change the wrong thing in the Windows Registry and you could seriously mess up your PC. Best to leave it alone – at least until you've read our advice about using the Registry safely in Chapter 4.

2 SIDELOAD APPS
It's possible to install apps from sources other than the Windows Store: click Start, Settings, 'Update & security', then 'For developers' and enable 'Sideload apps'. But it isn't safe to do so.

3 WINDOWS DEFENDER
You can configure Windows 10's built-in antivirus protection by clicking Start, Settings, 'Update & security', then Windows Defender. But leaving these settings alone is safer.

4 START-UP SERVICES
You might be tempted to make your PC boot faster by disabling services that launch when it starts. But disable the wrong one and it may not start at all.

Chapter 3

Privacy & security

Windows 10 is safer than previous versions, but there's plenty of room for improvement… and its privacy defaults leave a lot to be desired

When it comes to using your computer, few things are more important than security and privacy. Windows 10 provides more protection from hackers and malware than any previous version of the operating system. But to keep your PC and your files safe, there are still many options you need to change and tools you need to add. Not only that, but one of Windows 10's chief flaws is that, unless you know which privacy settings to alter, the OS can play fast and loose with your personal data. In this chapter we'll explain everything you need to protect your PC… and your private info.

IN THIS SECTION

Change your privacy settings

Why is Microsoft watching everything you do in Windows 10? And what can you do to prevent it? We investigate

Microsoft's latest operating system has been celebrated for its speed, usability and design. But, as we mentioned back in Chapter 2, if there's one thing critics haven't been as keen on, it's the way Windows 10 treats its users' privacy.

Concealed within Windows 10 are numerous options that give the operating system permission to record a variety of information about you and the way you use your PC – including what you search for online and anything you type on your keyboard. All this is then sent back to Microsoft for analysis. What's worse is that most of these options are enabled by default. So, unless you take action, you could be unwittingly handing your private data to Microsoft on a plate.

Until recently, Microsoft has seemed to be relatively respectful of its users' privacy, so what has changed? What types of information is the company now gathering? And what does it do with your data once it has got it? We'll answer these questions and more, and show you what steps you need to take in order to keep your privacy safe.

What you can do

- Discover what personal info Microsoft is collecting
- Find out what Microsoft does with your personal data
- Protect your privacy by turning off Windows 10's hidden settings
- Disable Microsoft's tracking tools in Windows 10

YOUR PRIVACY QUESTIONS ANSWERED

What exactly is Microsoft doing?

It's using tracking tools built into Windows 10 to monitor users' activity. This data is then sent back to Microsoft. But that's not all. Windows 10 contains other privacy-eroding features that target you with adverts, log what buttons you press on your keyboard (your 'keystrokes'), and consume your internet bandwidth.

Microsoft provides ways to disable most of these, but they're scattered throughout the OS, making them difficult to find. And you will need to find them because most of Microsoft's snooping options are enabled by default. You'll need to opt out if you want to protect your privacy.

Don't worry, though. We'll be showing you exactly where to look and what to do from page 54.

Why is this so controversial?

While some of us now grudgingly accept that online services (Google, for example), and our mobile devices, collect our data, never before have we been in a situation where our own computers routinely spy on us and gather personal information on such a massive scale. It has made lots of people feel very uncomfortable.

To give Microsoft credit, it has been transparent about its data collection. But the company has made it unreasonably difficult for users to do anything about it. Not only that, but Microsoft also recently admitted that Windows continues to track PC activity, even when users have disabled the buried tracking options – more on this later.

What information is Microsoft collecting?

Microsoft can gather your name, demographic info (age, gender, language), interests, relationships and PC usage. But what's most unsettling is that Microsoft gathers something it ambiguously calls "content". This can refer to almost anything, including private files and emails.

By default, Windows 10 gathers data as you browse the web and use desktop apps. It uses this to build a profile of you that is then used by Microsoft and other third-party companies to target you with advertising. It also tracks your location, keeping a record of where you've been and gathering information about the networks you connect to. And, unless you tell it not to, it even connects you automatically to potentially unsafe Wi-Fi networks.

The OS gathers other info to make certain tools work. For example, Cortana records your keystrokes and spoken commands. It can also access your calendar and contacts as well as find out what you buy online. All this is stored online – or “in the cloud”, as Microsoft puts it.

Windows 10 automatically synchronises your settings and data with the cloud. This may not sound terrifying, but it does mean that you need to opt out if you don’t want information about you stored on Microsoft’s servers.

Should I be worried about it?

Some of Microsoft’s data-collection actions obviously pose more of a risk to your privacy than others, which is why we’ve given each of our tips (from over the page) their own urgency rating. In general, however, your level of concern is likely to fall roughly in line with the level of trust you have in Microsoft as a company.

In a lengthy Privacy Statement (www.snipca.com/19521, see screenshot), Microsoft states that it will “access, disclose and preserve personal data, including your content” – such as your emails or private files and folders – “when we have a good faith belief that doing so is necessary”. This effectively gives Microsoft the right to access and share your private files and data with anyone it likes, should it wish to.

To help reassure users, Microsoft gives some examples, such as when it may need to access or share your data in order to “comply with law enforcement or other government agencies” or “maintain the security of our services”. It’s somewhat perturbing to consider that “good faith” is the only thing standing between you and a situation where the contents of your personal files are being viewed, copied and handed over to unknown third parties.

There’s also the growing risk of hacking to consider. Even if Microsoft itself isn’t going to abuse your data, what’s to stop it being stolen from the company’s servers via a cyber-attack?

Why is Microsoft doing this?

In its Privacy Statement, Microsoft says that it collects data “to operate effectively and provide you the best experiences with our services”, as well as “to send communications, including promotional communications” and, finally, “to display advertising”. It admits that it uses some data to make adverts “more relevant” to you. One way this could work is by tracking which apps you use, then ‘recommending’ others that are similar.

It’s true that some aspects of the OS simply won’t work unless you’re prepared to put up with a certain amount of tracking. For example, you won’t be able to check your current whereabouts in the Maps app if you’ve turned off location tracking. And you won’t be able to get suggestions from Cortana if you block it from monitoring your activity.

What’s Microsoft really up to?

We’re not going to suggest that there’s anything profoundly sinister lurking behind Microsoft’s motivations. But

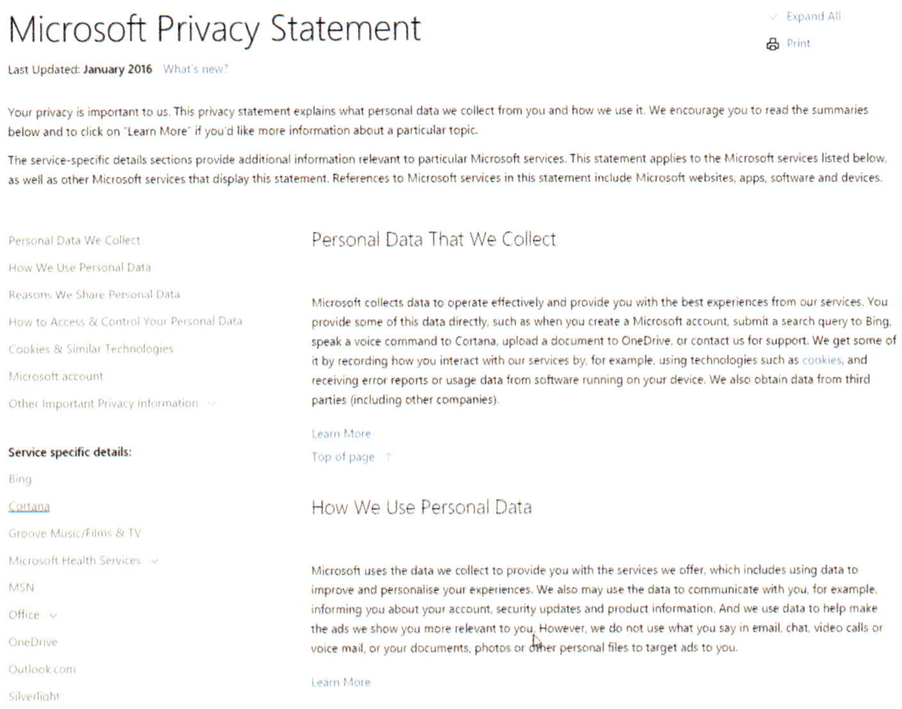

▲ Microsoft admits that it collects your data in order to show “more relevant” adverts

for all its talk about how “your privacy is important to us”, we’re convinced that its real motivation boils down to one thing: money.

By giving away Windows 10 for free for its first year, Microsoft has lost a very valuable source of revenue. It’s only natural that the company should look for alternative ways to make money. Google, which recently reported record profits, has proved that companies can generate vast amounts of revenue from advertising while providing free services to its users. Microsoft wants some of that action. That’s why every Windows 10 user is allotted a unique advertising profile and why there’s so much advertising

USE FREE PRIVACY TOOLS

As well as following our advice in this feature, you should try one of the many third-party privacy tools that have sprung up since Windows 10 launched. Though these rarely offer anything more than is already built into Windows 10, they do display all the major privacy options in one place, making your life easier. The problem is that some of the tools install unwanted software, which is actually worse for your privacy. However, Ashampoo's free AntiSpy for Windows 10 (www.snipca.com/19534) is safe to use. In fact, it's a portable program, which means you don't even need to install it. Just run the tool and choose which privacy options to disable or enable, based on our advice in this article.

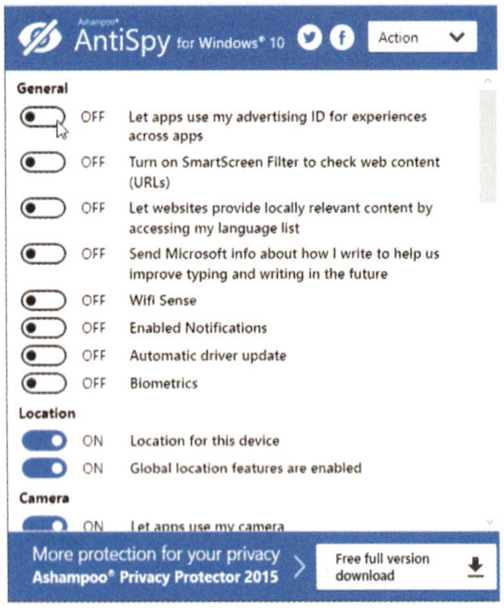

embedded within the OS and its related services. It would also explain why the company has been so pushy about getting everyone to upgrade to the new OS.

Collecting and using people's data is something that mobile operating systems – such as Apple's iOS and Google's Android – have been doing for years, so Microsoft is just catching up with other tech companies. But that doesn't make it any more palatable.

Microsoft has come under fire from all sides, with the campaign group European Digital Rights (EDRi) neatly summarising criticism of the company's privacy policies in a recent blog post: "Microsoft basically grants itself very broad rights to collect everything you do, say and write with and on your devices in order to sell more targeted advertising or to sell your data to third parties. The company appears to be granting itself the right to share your data either with your consent or 'as necessary'." Read the full post at www.snipca.com/19522.

Can I completely stop Microsoft snooping?

The tips we're about to provide will block most of Microsoft's data-collecting tricks. However, Microsoft's Corporate Vice President Joe Belfiore revealed in an interview last October that some data-collecting tools in Windows can't be disabled (read the full interview at www.snipca.com/19519).

Microsoft records something it calls 'telemetry' – diagnostic data about how you use your PC – though it's unclear what this data actually is. Belfiore claims it is only "to do with the health of the system" and doesn't contain personal information. But in an unrelated announcement in January trumpeting Windows 10's success (www.snipca.com/19520), Corporate Vice President of Microsoft's Windows and Devices Group Yusuf Mehdi revealed just how much the company knows about what its users have been doing with their PCs, including the number of photos viewed using the Windows 10 Photo app (82 billion) and how many hours of Xbox One games were streamed to Windows 10 PCs (6.6 million). This suggests that Microsoft may be collecting much more than merely how often your PC crashes.

Thanks to a backlash from its business customers, Microsoft recently provided a way for users of the Enterprise Edition of Windows 10 to disable telemetry collection but, sadly, the company has no plans to introduce a similar option for Windows 10 Home or Pro users.

PROTECT YOUR PRIVACY IN WINDOWS 10

Back in Chapter 3 we looked at the many ways you can change your operating system to suit your needs and tastes. Here, we'll be looking specifically at the settings you need to alter in order to stop Windows 10 from handing over your personal data to Microsoft.

1 Don't use Express settings

URGENCY LEVEL: Very high

During the Windows 10 upgrade (or set-up process, if you've bought a new PC), Microsoft sneakily glosses over a very important part in the procedure. It uses misleading wording to trick you into agreeing to a load of default settings – many of which potentially compromise your privacy. By choosing this 'Use

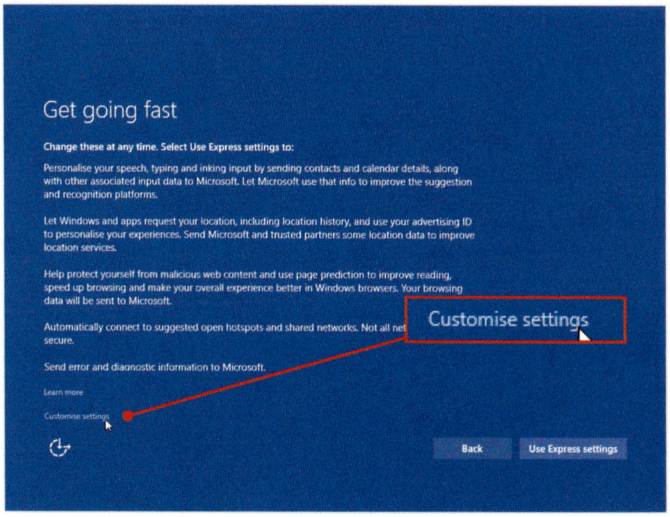

▲ Protect your privacy by clicking the tiny 'Customise settings' link

MICROSOFT ACCOUNTS: SHOULD YOU USE ONE?

The default user account type in Windows 10 (and 8) is a Microsoft account. You may already have one of these (from a Hotmail or Outlook.com email account, for example) or you may be prompted to create one when you first log in. The key benefits of using it include the ability to make purchases (and download free apps) from the Windows Store, synchronise your settings and passwords with other PCs, and sign into other Microsoft services. But because your account is online, Microsoft knows whenever you're using your PC. So one way to make Windows 10 more private is to use an offline-only Local account instead, similar to the user accounts used in Windows 7. This won't be ideal for everyone – you won't be able to use the Windows Store if you do this and, in truth, the privacy risks of sticking with a Microsoft account are relatively low. But if you're uncomfortable with your Microsoft account, switch to a Local one. In Windows 10, click Start, Settings, Account, then click 'Sign in with a local account instead' and follow the prompts (see screenshot). See Chapter 2 for more on accounts.

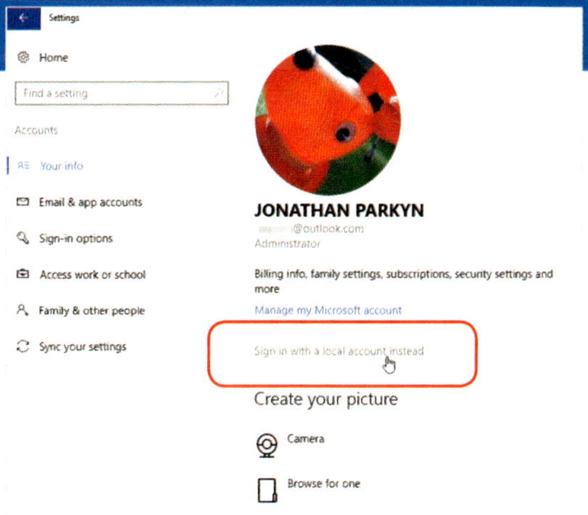

Express setup' option when prompted, you'll shave a few minutes off your setup time. But you'll also be allowing Microsoft to collect personal data from your contacts, calendar and more.

If you've already upgraded to Windows 10 or set up a new PC, then it's too late to change this. Instead, you'll need to switch off each tracking tool individually – follow our tips below. But if you've not upgraded, when you do so just click the tiny 'Customise settings' link on the 'Get going fast' screen to disable most of Windows 10's snooping features (see screenshot below left).

2 Disable targeted advertising

URGENCY LEVEL: High

Advertising has become an unavoidable part of modern computing, but Windows 10 goes much further than previous versions. You'll not only see adverts on web pages, but also within apps and even in your Start menu.

You can't turn off advertising completely, but you can stop advertisers from using information about you to target you with personalised ads. To do so, click Start, Settings, then Privacy. Click General on the left, then switch off 'Let apps use my advertising ID for experiences across apps'. While you're there, also switch off 'Let websites provide locally relevant content by accessing my language list'.

You'll need to change settings elsewhere too. Click 'Manage my Microsoft advertising and other personalisation info' to be taken to Microsoft's About Our Ads web page (www.snipca.com/19455). Sign in with your Microsoft account, then switch both 'Personalised ads in this browser' and 'Personalised ads whenever I use my Microsoft account' to Off (see screenshot above).

To block Start menu adverts, click Start, Settings, Personalisation, then Start and switch off 'Occasionally show suggestions in Start'. Finally, open the Windows Store app, click on your account and choose Settings. Here,

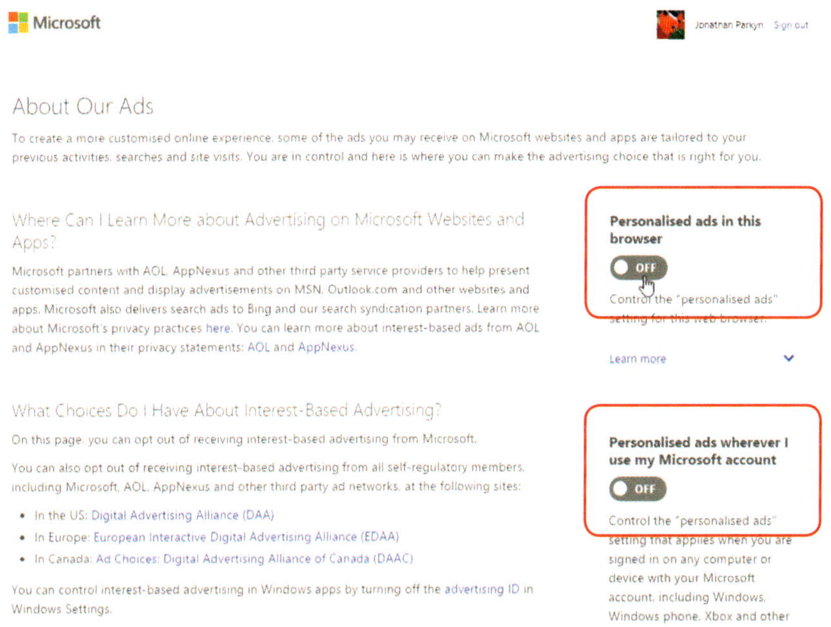

▲ Turn off these settings to stop Windows 10 targeting you with "personalised adverts"

switch off 'Show products on tile' if you'd rather not see adverts in the Store's Start menu Live tile.

3 Block location tracking

URGENCY LEVEL: Medium

If you don't like the idea of people knowing where you are and where you've been, click Start, Settings, Privacy, then Location. The settings you need to change here depend on what type of device you're using and the services you want to use. If you're using a standard desktop PC, for instance, there's no real benefit to having Location switched on at all, as the PC is fixed in one place. To plan journeys in the Maps app, you can always just use your postcode instead.

To disable Location altogether for anyone who uses the PC, click Change, then turn it off. To turn it off for individual user accounts, click the switch under Location to Off. To erase location data, click Clear under 'Clear history on this device'. If you're using a laptop – or a Windows phone or tablet – Location can be pretty useful for navigating, so you may wish to leave it on. But if you do, scroll down on the Location settings page and disable any apps you don't want tracking you under 'Choose apps that can use your location'. Almost all can be safely switched off.

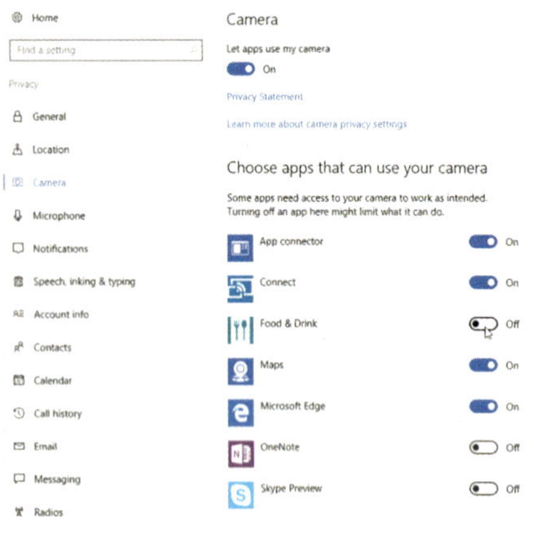

▲ Turn off apps that access to your camera

4 Stop apps watching and listening

URGENCY LEVEL: High

Giving apps permission to use your device's camera or microphone means that they could spy on you. They could even record your voice and take video footage of you. By default, Windows 10 lets apps use your camera and microphone, so to change this, click Start, Settings, Privacy, then either Camera or Microphone. The setting at the top of both pages turns off the camera and microphone for all apps, but you may not wish to do this – Skype, for example, won't work if it can't access the microphone or camera. Instead, turn off individual apps listed under 'Choose apps that can use your camera/microphone'.

5 Disable Windows 10's keylogger

URGENCY LEVEL: Very high

We've been warning people about the dangers of keyloggers – tools that record what you type on your keyboard – for years. So it's astonishing that Windows 10 should come with one built-in. Microsoft claims it's there to help improve services and provide you with a more personalised experience, but we think it's just plain creepy. First, click Start, Settings, Privacy, General, then switch off 'Send Microsoft info about how I write to help us improve typing and writing in the future'.

Once you've done that, click 'Speech, inking and typing' on the left, then click 'Stop getting to know me' on the right. This will stop Windows (and Cortana) collecting data from spoken commands and handwriting (on devices that support this), as well as from what you type. It'll also disable Cortana, and stop the voice-dictation tool from working. Click 'Turn off' in the warning message if you're happy with this.

6 Stop Cortana storing your data online

URGENCY LEVEL: High

For all of Microsoft's fanfare about Cortana, it's hard to ignore the fact that Windows 10's digital assistant is a privacy nightmare. Even if you disable it using the previous tip, Cortana will continue to store detailed personal information about you on Microsoft's servers unless you opt to delete it. To do so, click Start, Settings, Privacy, then click 'Speech, inking and typing'. Under 'Manage cloud info', click 'Go to Bing and manage personal info for all your devices'. This will open a web page – sign in with your Microsoft account, then scroll down to 'Other Cortana Data and Personalised Speech, Inking and Typing' and click Clear (see screenshot below).

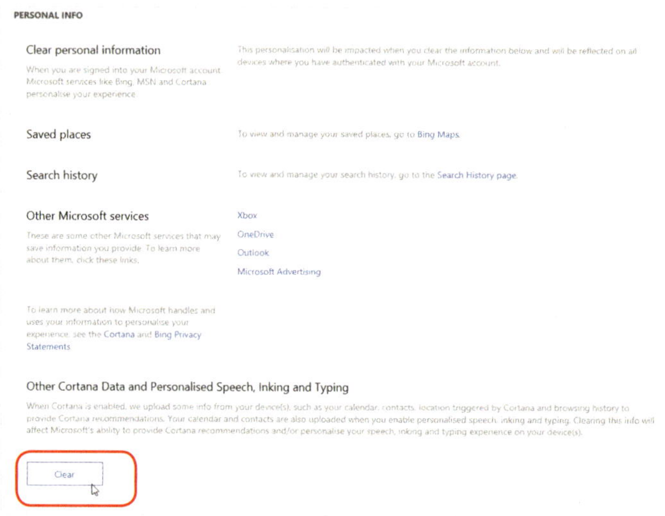

▲ Click 'Clear' to delete the data that Cortana stores on you

7 Block apps from accessing your private info

URGENCY LEVEL: Medium

Windows 10 allows apps to access a wide variety of different personal data – from your calendar and contacts to emails and text messages. To stop this, click Start, Settings, Privacy, then click 'Account info', Contacts, Calendar, 'Call history', Email and Messaging in turn. In each case (apart from Contacts) you'll see a main switch at the top of the page allowing you to turn off access completely.

However, as with Camera and Microphone, you may find that doing this prevents certain apps and tools from working properly. The Mail app, for example, needs to have access to your calendar, contacts and, of course, email. So, instead of disabling app access altogether, it's better to leave the top switch on in each case, then choose which apps to allow or disable from those listed below.

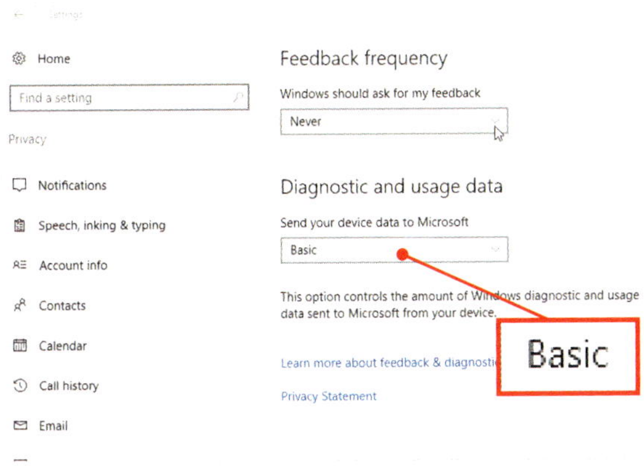

▲ Select 'Basic' to limit Microsoft's 'telemetry' tracking

8 Limit Microsoft's telemetry tracking

URGENCY LEVEL: Medium

It's not possible to turn off all of Microsoft telemetry tracking in Windows 10. But you can customise it to limit the amount of data you share, and to stop Windows nagging you for feedback. Click Start, Settings, Privacy, then click 'Feedback & diagnostics' on the left (you may need to scroll down if you can't see it). On the right, select Never from the 'Windows should ask for my feedback' dropdown menu, then select Basic from the dropdown menu under 'Send your device data to Microsoft' (see screenshot above).

9 Stop Windows 10 connecting you to insecure Wi-Fi networks

URGENCY LEVEL: High

Microsoft wants to make it easy for Windows 10 users to connect to Wi-Fi networks, so it automatically connects to "suggested" Wi-Fi hotspots. Not all Wi-Fi networks are secure – Microsoft admits as much just above the setting to turn Wi-Fi Sense off – which means that connecting to them automatically isn't always a good idea. Disabling Wi-Fi Sense doesn't stop you connecting to public wireless hotspots. You can still do this manually in the usual way (from the Notification area icon bottom right of your taskbar), but it will stop you automatically connecting to ones that potentially aren't safe. Click Start, Settings, 'Network & internet', then Wi-Fi. Under Wi-Fi Sense, switch 'Connect to suggested open hotspots' to Off.

10 Configure Edge's privacy options

URGENCY LEVEL: Medium

Microsoft's new web browser has its own set of privacy settings that need addressing. Click the menu (three dots) button in the top right and choose Settings, then 'View advanced settings'. Scroll to 'Privacy and services'. Leave 'Offer to save passwords' and 'Save form entries' enabled only if you are comfortable with the browser storing this information. We recommend enabling 'Send Do Not Track requests' to limit the amount your online activity is tracked (see screenshot below), and disabling 'Get Cortana to assist me in Microsoft Edge' (though this may already be disabled if you've switched Cortana off).

It's convenient to leave enabled 'Show search and site suggestions as I type' and 'Use page prediction to speed up browsing'. But it will mean data about your searches and browsing being sent to Microsoft. Under the Cookies section, we'd suggest selecting 'Block only third-party cookies', but bear in mind that this will stop some sites working properly.

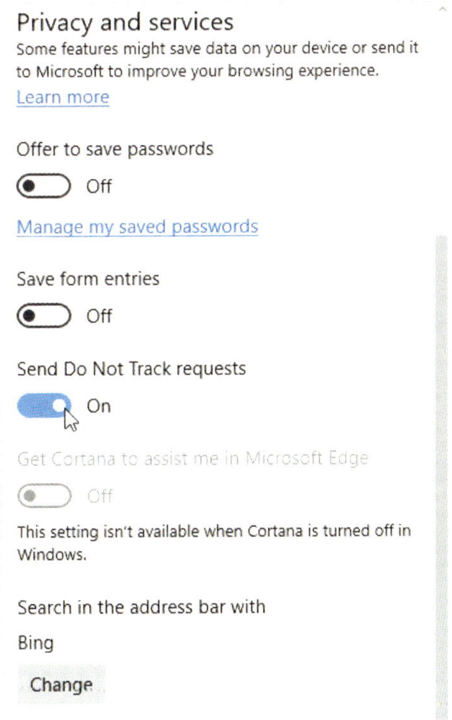

◀ Enable 'Send Do Not Track requests' to limit how much information Edge sends to Microsoft

CAN YOU REALLY BE ANONYMOUS IN EDGE?

Like most browsers Edge has a private mode. Called InPrivate (instructions at www.snipca.com/19559), it lets you browse the web anonymously, so you don't leave a trail containing your browsing history, image cache or cookies. This prevents other users of your PC from seeing what you've done online. In January, however, evidence was uncovered by researchers at website Forensic Focus (www.forensicfocus.com) suggesting that anyone with the right know-how and access to your computer could easily reconstruct your InPrivate browsing history via data stored in your user account's WebCache folder. Thankfully, Microsoft was quick to act and, in February, released an update that "fixed issue with Microsoft Edge browser caching visited URLs while using InPrivate browsing."

Protect your PC with Defender's new Anniversary Update features

Time required: 30 minutes

Windows 10 comes with built-in antivirus protection in the shape of Windows Defender. Up until now, Defender's main selling points have been that it's unobtrusive and doesn't require much intervention. But that's changed with the Anniversary Update.

Now, Defender offers a handy offline scanner for locating and removing hard-to-find malware. And even if you decide you don't want to rely on Defender for your day-to-day protection, you can still use it in tandem with your preferred security program as a second layer of protection, without causing conflicts. In this workshop, we'll explain how to make the most of the all-new Defender.

STEP 1 Click Start, Settings, 'Update & security', then click on Windows Defender on the left-hand side. Unless you've installed third-party anti-virus software, it's best to leave 'Real-time protection', 'Cloud-based protection' and 'Automatic sample submission' settings on. These improve protection for your PC while helping Microsoft stay on top of new malware. At the top of the screen, you'll see a link to Open Windows Defender **1**. Click this to launch Defender itself.

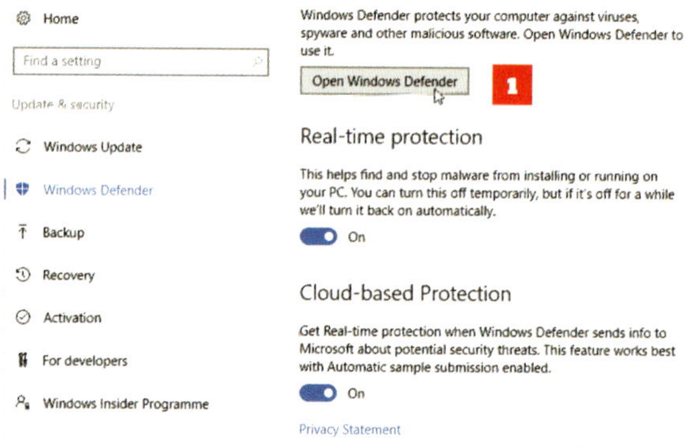

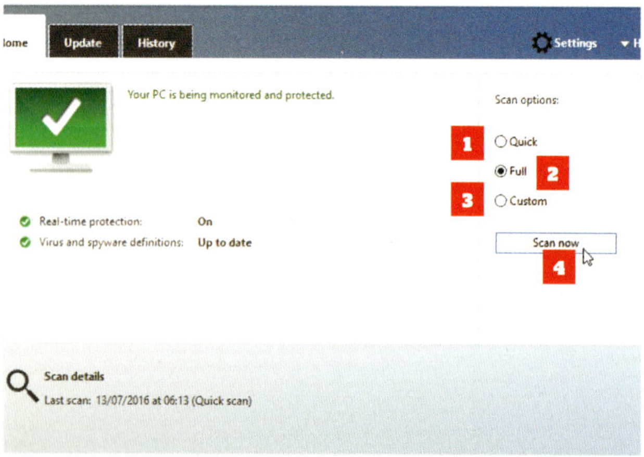

STEP 2 If this is the first time you've launched Defender (or the first time since installing the Anniversary Update) you'll see a brief message about what's new in the tool. Click 'Turn on', then click Close. To scan your PC for malware, choose either Quick **1** (for a fast but not 100 per cent comprehensive scan), Full **2** (for an in-depth but slow scan), or Custom **3** (to scan a specific drive or folder), then click 'Scan now' **4**. Virus definitions – the database of malware – will update automatically if you have Windows Update on. To update them manually, click the Update tab, then click 'Update definitions'.

STEP 3 Defender's History tab shows options for 'Quarantined items' **1** (malware that Defender has discovered and cordoned off for safety), 'Allowed items' **2** (items falsely identified as malware that you've allowed) and 'All detected items' **3**. Select one of these options, then click the View Details button to see the list. If there are any items in your list, you can click the tick box next to one, then click Remove or just click 'Remove all' **4** to delete them from your PC permanently. For falsely identified items, click them, then click Restore to take them out of quarantine and put them back where they were.

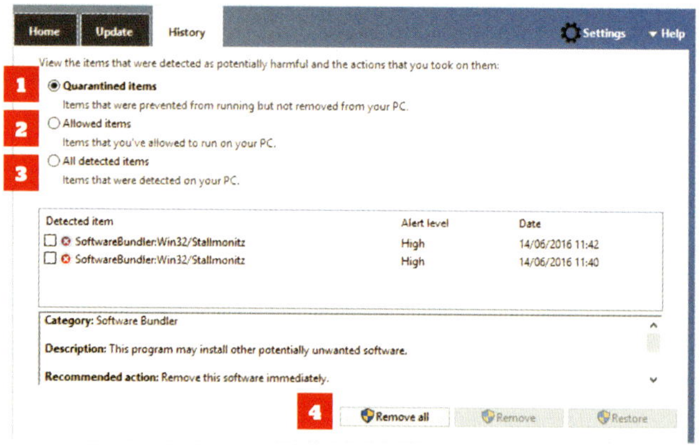

STEP 4 If Windows Defender keeps wrongly flagging files that are safe, you can exclude affected files or folders from its scanning. Just remember that every exclusion is a potential vulnerability to real malware. Click the Home tab, then Settings, then click 'Add an exclusion.' Click the plus button next to 'Exclude a file' **1**, 'Exclude a folder' **2**, or 'Exclude a .exe, .com or .scr process' **3**, depending on whether you want to exclude a specific file, folder or process (in other words, a program), then browse to item you want and double-click it. To exclude all files of a specific type, click the plus button next to 'Exclude a file extension' **4**, type the file extension you want to exclude, then click OK.

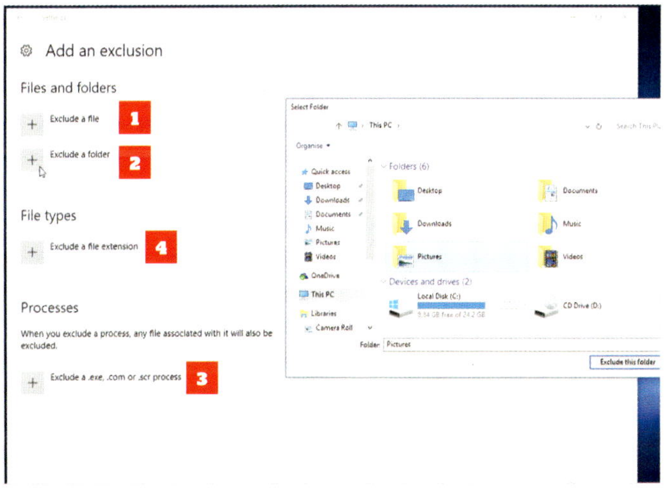

STEP 5 One of the new features in the Anniversary Update is the option to enable enhanced notifications for Defender. Prior to the update, Defender had remained virtually silent – only ever pipping up if it found something nasty in a scan. With enhanced notifications enabled, Defender will keep you up to speed on the health status of your PC by sending you regular notifications. These will pop up in the bottom right of your screen and in the Action Centre (click the speech bubble icon). If you'd rather not be bothered by these, though, click Start, Settings, 'Update & security', then Windows Defender **1**. Scroll down to 'Enhanced notifications' **2** and flip the switch off

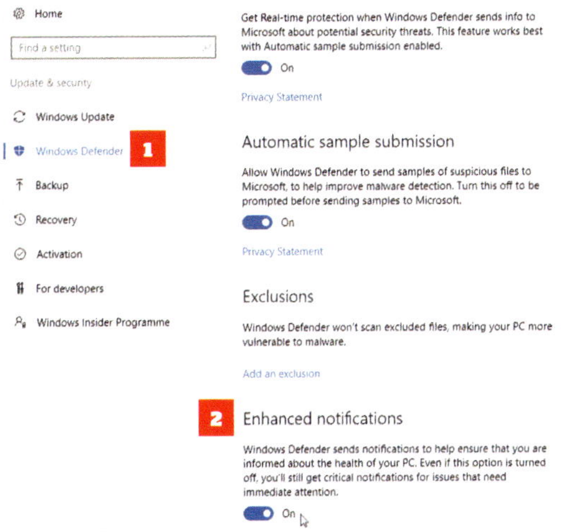

STEP 6 If you're having trouble removing malware, or if you suspect your PC is infected but can't get a normal scan to pick it up, you can try an 'offline' scan – a new feature in Windows Defender since the Anniversary Update, which restarts your PC in a special mode to check for and remove stubborn threats. To run this, click Start, Settings, 'Update & security', then Windows Defender. Scroll down to Windows Defender Offline, then click Scan Offline **1**. Leave your PC to reboot and complete the process. It should take around 15 minutes.

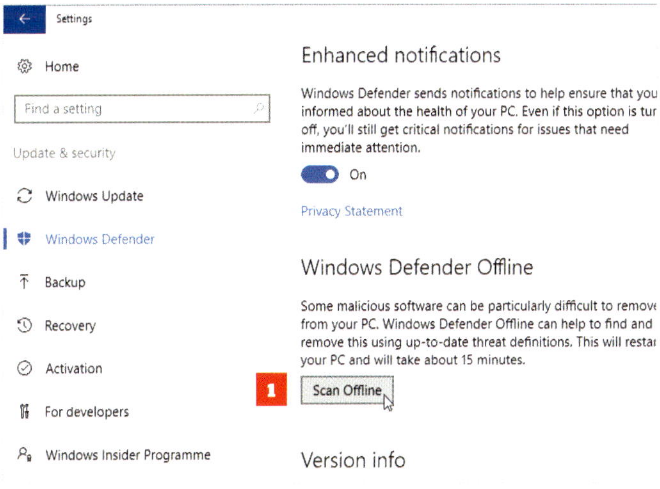

STEP 7 Previously, if you decided to install a separate third-party antivirus tool, Windows 10 would automatically disable Windows Defender, since running two anti-malware programs at the same time often causes conflicts. With the new version of Defender, though, it's possible to enable Defender too, providing you with dual-layer protection against malicious attacks. To do this, install another antivirus program, then click Start, Settings, 'Update & security', Windows Defender and switch on the Limited Periodic Scanning option **1**.

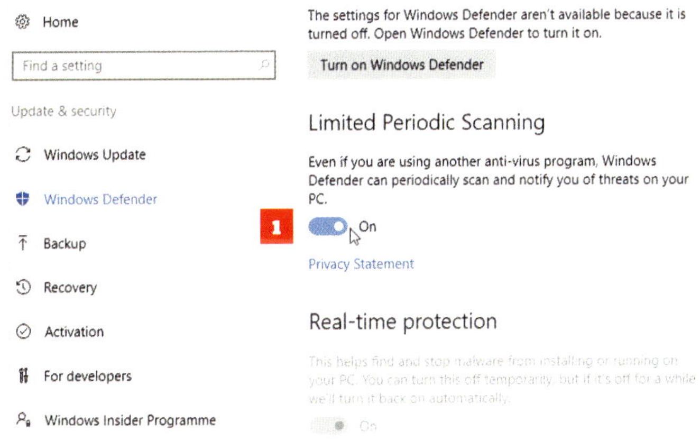

Take control of Windows 10's automatic updates

Time required: 30 minutes

In previous versions of Windows, you could let the OS update your PC automatically, or you could make your own choices about when and which updates were installed. With Windows 10, Microsoft decided to take that choice away, arguing that some silly people put themselves at serious risk by never updating. Unfortunately, this also means that those of us who are capable of making sensible choices have had the option taken away. Microsoft has made a small change to the Anniversary Update, which lets you choose a 12-hour period of time each day when you don't want updates to install. We'll take a look at how to set it up below. However, it's not really enough, so we'll also walk you through some other tweaks and hacks that let you do more. Remember that you must still regularly check for and install essential updates.

STEP 1 To explore the Anniversary Update's new settings, press Windows+I to open the Settings window and click the 'Update & security' icon. Click on Windows Update **1** if it isn't already selected, then click the 'Change active hours' link. **2**

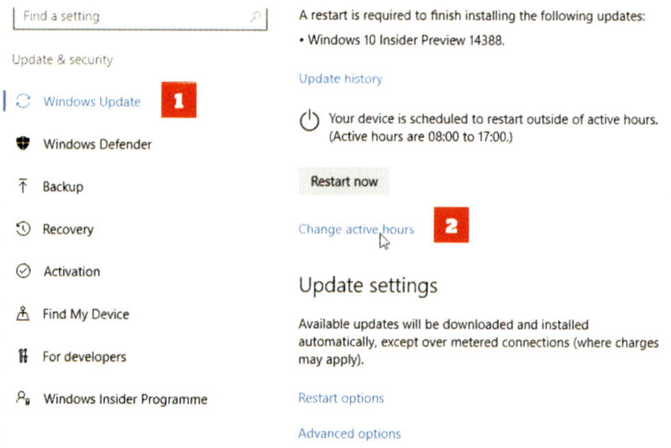

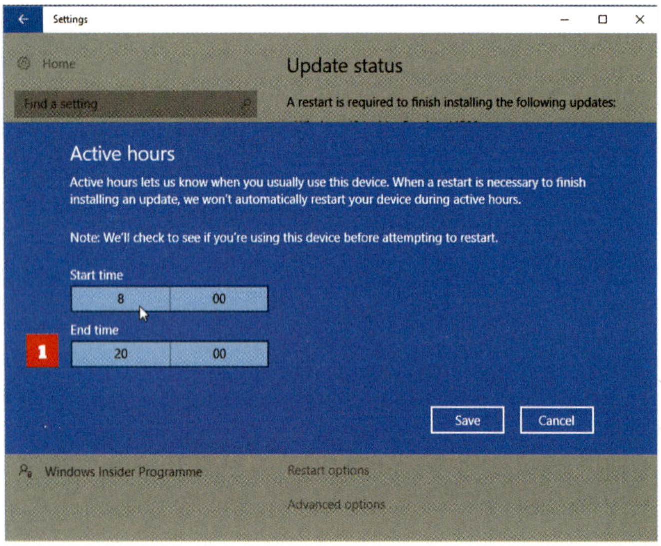

STEP 2 Annoyingly, you can only set a period of up to 12 hours during which you never want updates to install, so if you regularly use your PC for longer than that, you'll need to decide which 12-hour period within that is most important to avoid interruptions from updates. Click on the times below 'Start time' and 'End time' **1** to adjust them.

STEP 3 Scroll through the available hour slots using the up and down buttons. **1** You can only choose times on the hour – there's no option to break it down into half- or quarter-past the hour, for example. When you've chosen your time, click the tick button **2** to confirm and the Save button **3** when you've chosen both start and end times.

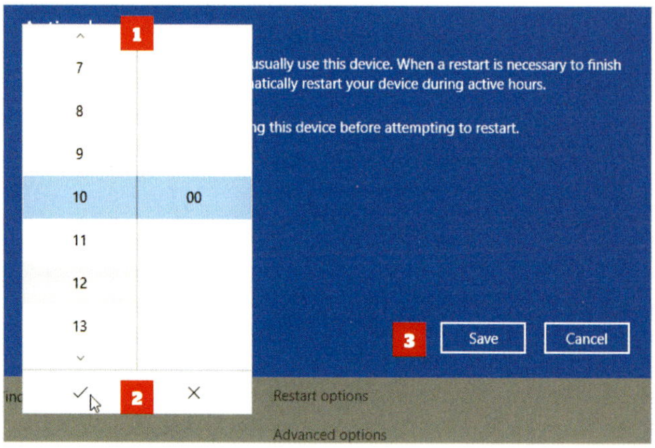

STEP 4 Often, Windows updates will require a restart to fully install them. If you have an update pending, waiting for a restart, you can reschedule when Windows will try and restart. Click the 'Restart options' link and flick the switch to On **1**. Choose a time **2** and day **3** for the restart to happen.

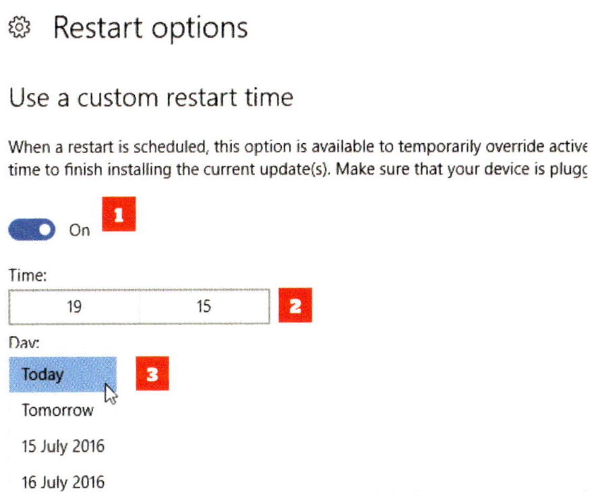

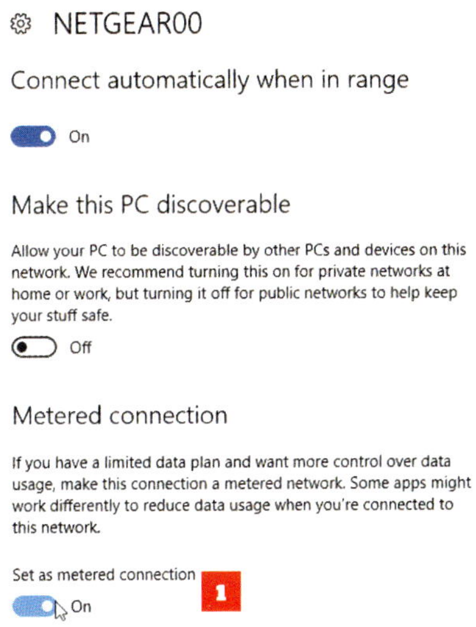

STEP 5 If you're on a Wi-Fi network, you can stop updates from downloading by setting your network connection to metered. From Settings choose 'Network & internet', 'Wi-Fi' then click on the current connection. Click the 'Set as metered connection' switch **1** to On. This might affect other programs and still lets essential security updates through.

STEP 6 Even if you don't want to turn updates off, there may still be occasions where you might still want to remove an update that's causing problems. In this case you can uninstall it. Go to Settings, 'Update & security', Windows Update, then 'Update history'. Click 'Uninstall updates', **1** click on the update you want to remove, **2** then click Uninstall. **3**

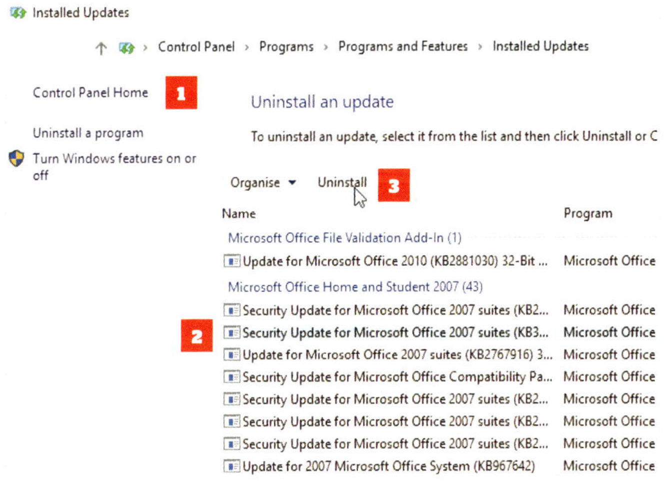

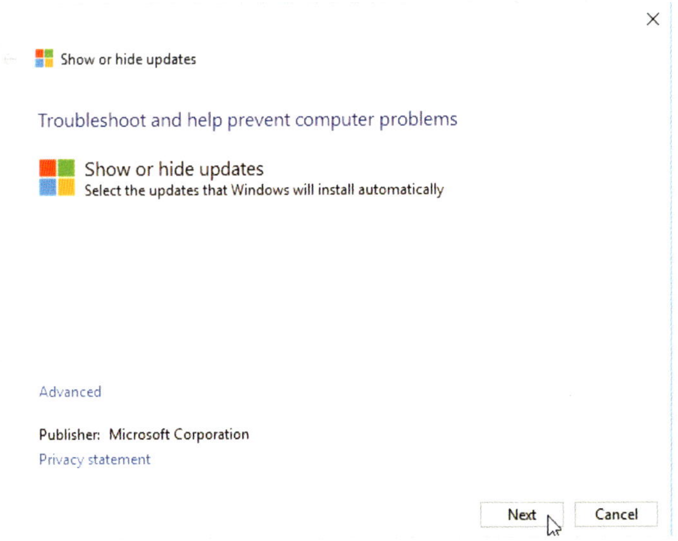

STEP 7 Once you've uninstalled a problematic update, you can then use a Microsoft troubleshooter tool to temporarily prevent the update from reinstalling. Go to bit.ly/show402 and scroll down the page until you see 'Download the "Show or hide updates" troubleshooter package now'. Click this to download the tool, then double-click the download to run it and follow the on-screen steps in the troubleshooter.

STEP 8 Windows 10 has a lot of apps built-in – but do you actually use them all? If you don't, there's no point automatically updating them. All app updates are set to download automatically, so to stop this from happening, open the Windows Store and click your account icon **1**. Select Settings **2** and click the 'Update apps automatically' switch to Off **3**.

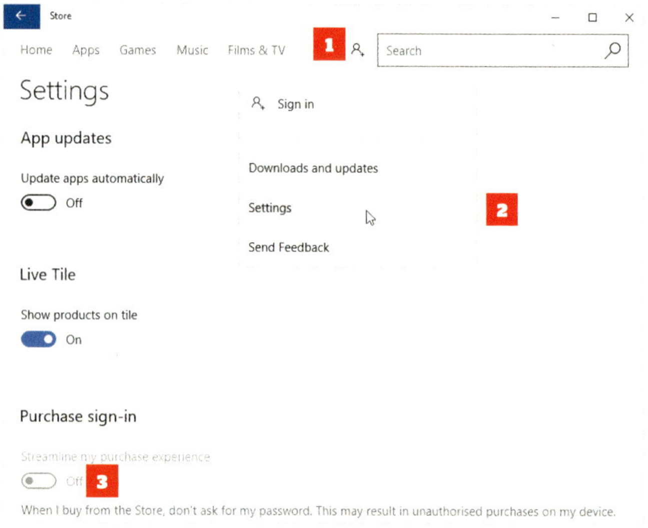

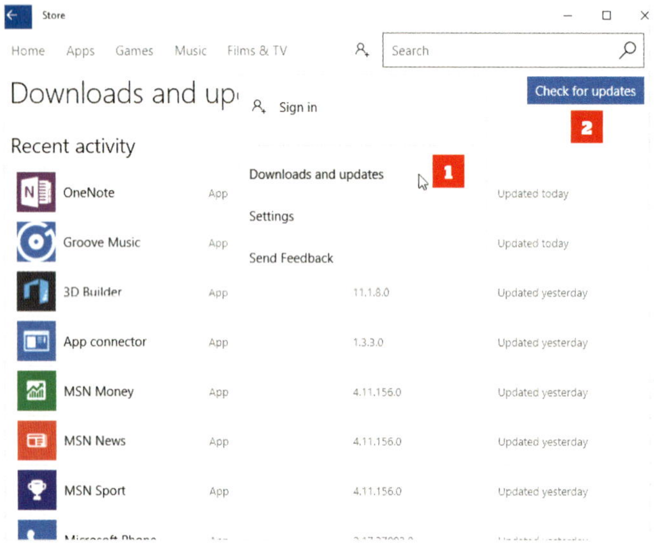

STEP 9 Once automatic updates have been disabled, you'll need to update apps manually. To do this, open the Windows Store and click the account icon again, then select 'Downloads and updates' **1**. Click the 'Check for updates' button **2**. It's worth doing this regularly if you use any of the built-in apps.

STEP 10 Most readers will have Windows 10 Home installed on their PCs, but if you have any other version, you can use something called the Group Policy Editor to make further tweaks to the operating system's update settings. We don't have space to explain it here, but visit bit.ly/pro402, which is Microsoft's page on the tool, which explains how to use it.

Expert Tip

Technically speaking, Windows Update is actually just a service that you can switch off, but this is a fairly drastic course of action. It'll stop any updates coming through to your PC – including ones that make it safer. Press Windows+R and type: **services.msc**

Scroll down the list to find Windows Update and right-click it. Choose Stop from the menu. Just remember to turn it back on again to get updates working again. It's best to treat this as a temporary fix for extreme cases where a lengthy update and restart process could really ruin your day.

Restore Safe Mode to Windows 10's boot menu

Time required: 10 minutes

Windows 10 starts up so much more quickly than older versions that tapping F8 is no longer a reliable way to access Safe Mode. You can still launch Safe Mode in a number of other ways, but they're clunky and, more importantly, are performed once Windows has already loaded, which isn't helpful if your PC won't start. In this Workshop, we show you how to configure your boot menu so that options for Safe Mode (or indeed 'Safe Mode with Networking' or 'Safe Mode with Command Prompt') are available whenever you start your PC. You add each boot entry using a simple command line in Command Prompt, then configure it using System Configuration. By default, your PC gives you 30 seconds to choose a boot option, but you can make it shorter to avoid slowing your PC's boot time. Adding a Safe Mode option also lets you access advanced tools such as Windows 10's troubleshooting menu when you start your PC.

STEP 1 Click the Start button and type cmd **1**. Right-click Command Prompt and select 'Run as administrator' **2** and Yes. In the console, type: bcdedit /copy {current} /d "Windows 10 Safe Mode" where "Windows 10 Safe Mode" is the name of your new boot entry. Then press Enter.

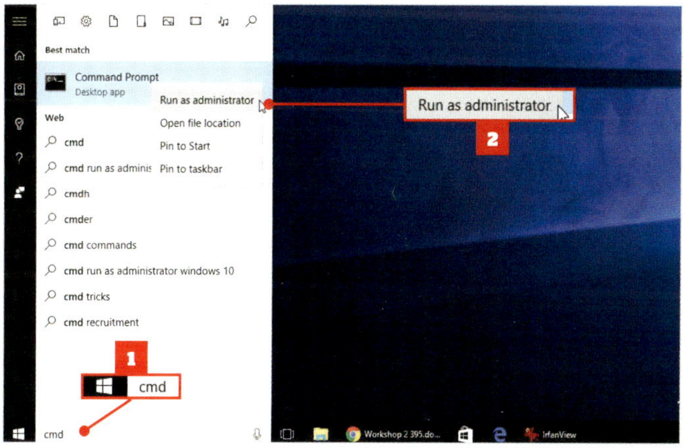

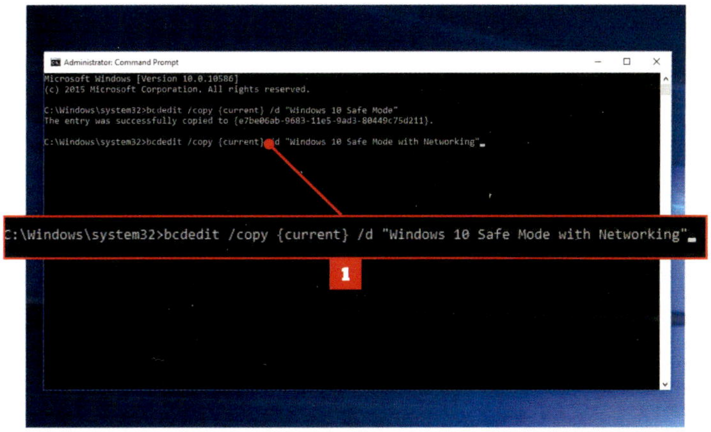

STEP 2 To add entries for 'Safe Mode with Networking' or 'Safe Mode with Command Prompt', repeat Step 1, changing only the title to describe these functions – so, for example: bcdedit /copy {current} /d "Windows 10 Safe Mode with Networking" **1**

STEP 3 To alter your new boot entries so they perform the appropriate function (instead of the standard boot procedure), click Start, type msconfig **1** and open System Configuration **2**. From the Boot tab, select the entry for 'Windows 10 Safe Mode' and tick the box for 'Safe boot'.

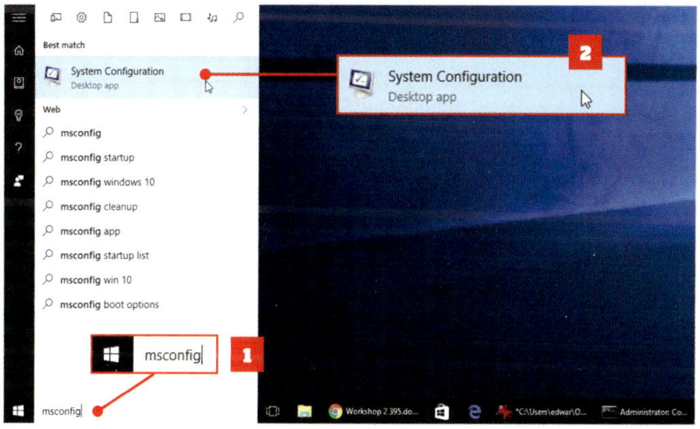

STEP 4 Leave the Minimal option selected for this entry **1** and tick the box for 'Make all boot settings permanent' **2** before clicking Apply **3** and Yes. Windows will warn you that the changes are permanent, but don't worry about this, because we show you how to undo them in Step 8.

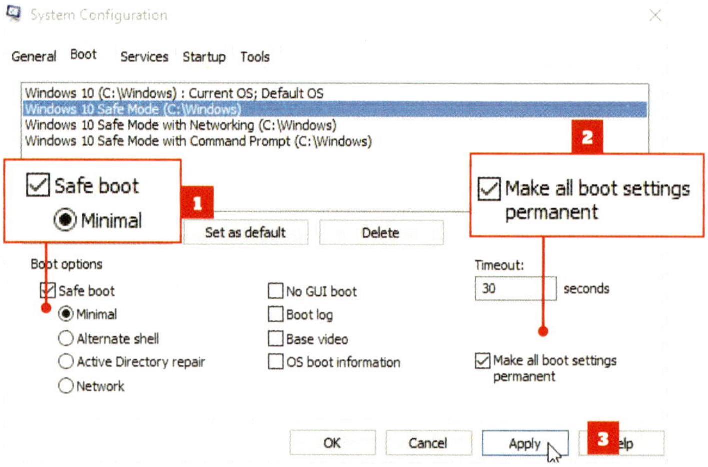

STEP 5 To set 'Safe Mode with Networking', follow the same steps, choosing Network instead of Minimal. To configure 'Safe Mode with Command Prompt', select its entry **1**, tick the box to 'Make all boot settings permanent' **2** and then select 'Safe boot' and 'Alternate shell' **3** before clicking Apply.

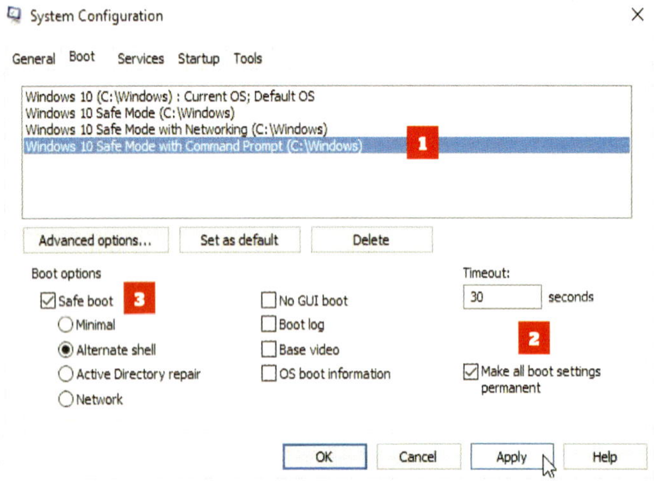

STEP 6 By default, you're given 30 seconds to choose one of your boot entries on startup. You can change this to a time of your choice by changing the Timeout figure **1** and then clicking Apply **2**. Setting Timeout to –1 keeps all the options on screen until you pick one.

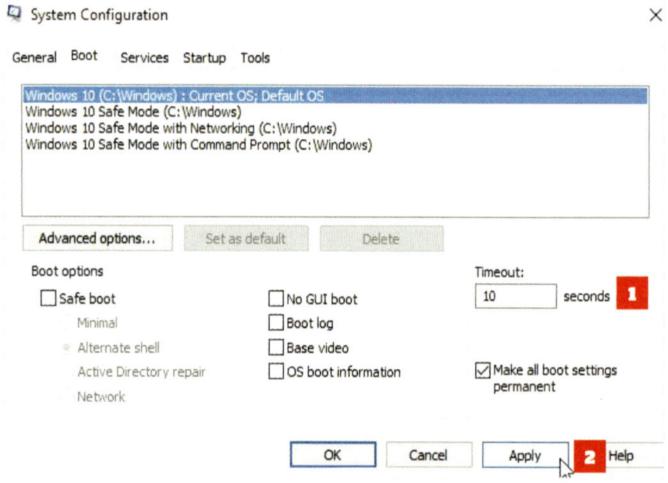

STEP 7 Once you've completed your configuration, click OK and you'll be asked if you're happy to restart your PC **1**. Select Restart **2** and your new boot menu will appear on screen. Use your mouse or the Tab key to select the option you want, then press Enter to proceed.

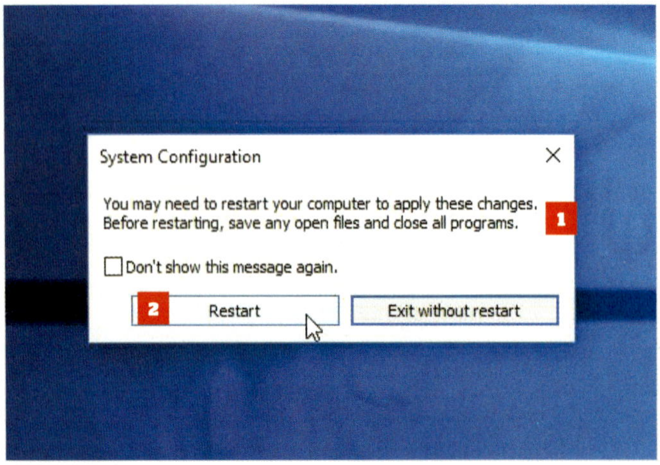

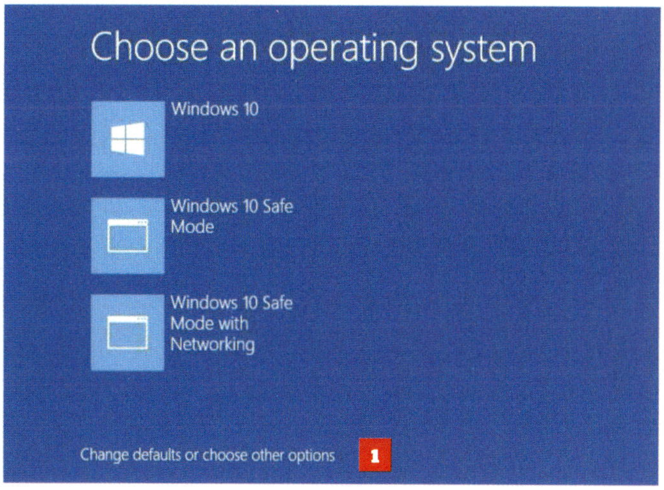

STEP 8 From the same menu, you can choose 'Change defaults or choose other options' **1**. Selecting this lets you change the timeout length and default boot entry. Clicking the 'Choose other options' button lets you access Windows 10's troubleshooting tools or boot from a USB device or DVD.

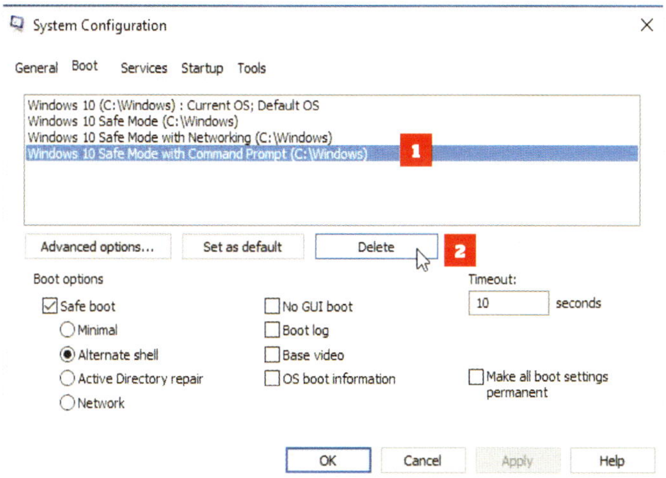

STEP 9 If you decide you want to delete your boot entries, type msconfig into the Start menu and run System Configuration again. From the boot menu, select the boot entry you want to remove **1** and click Delete **2**. When you click Apply and OK, Windows invites you to restart your PC again.

STEP 10 If you delete all your custom boot entries, your computer will boot straight to Windows 10, as before. Make sure you never delete the option marked 'Current OS' **1** because that would render your PC unable to boot into Windows.

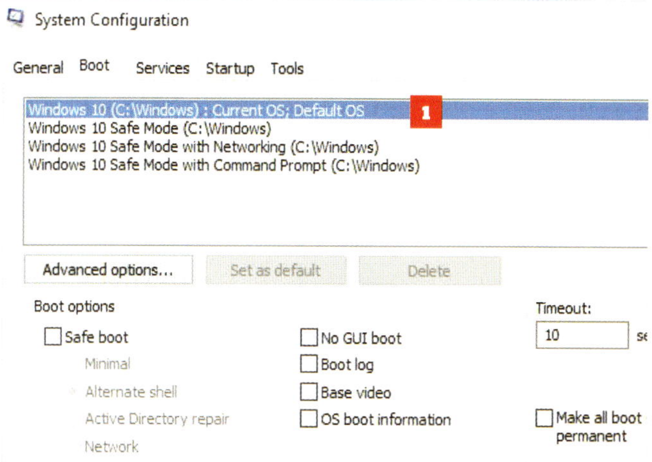

Expert Tip

If you run more than one operating system on your PC, you can access Safe Mode by reinstating the Windows 'legacy boot menu' (and tapping F8 when it loads). To do this, run the following command line in an elevated command prompt:

bcdedit /set {default} bootmenupolicy legacy

To undo the change, enter:

bcdedit /set {default} bootmenupolicy standard

Make restore points easier to set up

Time required: 30 minutes

Windows 10's System Restore feature can be a godsend if your PC isn't working properly. It lets you roll back any changes you've made to your computer and return Windows 10 to an earlier (functioning) state. In Chapter 2, we showed you how to enable System Restore, which isn't switched on by default in Windows 10. But it's also worth installing Restore Point Creator, a brilliant free alternative to Microsoft's built-in tool that lets you manage your restore points, create new ones and delete obsolete ones with just a few clicks. We'll also show you how to create automatic restore points.

STEP 1 Go to www.snipca.com/20103 and click the 'Download Restore Point Creator' link **1**. Don't bother with the 'ZIP File Package' link **2** – this is just for Windows XP users. Click the downloaded setup file, Run, then Yes. Some antivirus programs may detect the program as a false positive, but it's safe to run it. Next, accept the T&Cs, click Next three times, tick 'Create a desktop shortcut', Next, Install, then Finish. Open the program on your desktop.

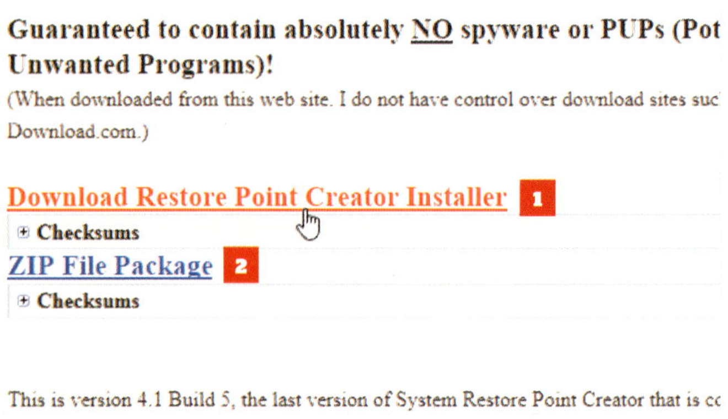

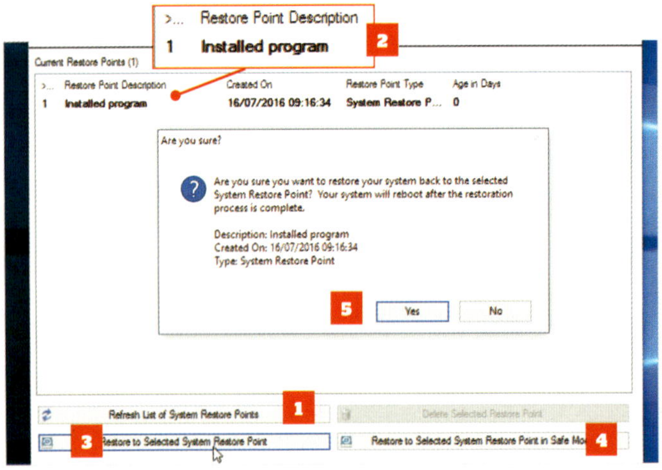

STEP 2 Click 'Refresh List of System Restore Points' **1** to see any restore points created on your PC **2**. To roll back your PC to one of those points, select it, then click 'Restore to Selected System Restore Point' **3**. If, for any reason, you're unable to do that, try restoring your PC i n Safe Mode **4**. You'll see a pop-up message confirming your action. Ensure you close all programs on your PC, then click Yes **5**. Your PC will reboot and roll back to the point you selected.

STEP 3 There are two ways to create a system restore point. One adds a default name, which is useful if you want to create a restore point quickly. To do this, click Create System Checkpoint **1**. You'll see a pop-up message when it's created and it will be added to your list **2**. The second method lets you name the restore point, which is handy if you're about to install a program that may cause problems, for example. To do this, click inside the field at the top, type the name you want to use **3**, then click Create Custom Named Restore Point **4**.

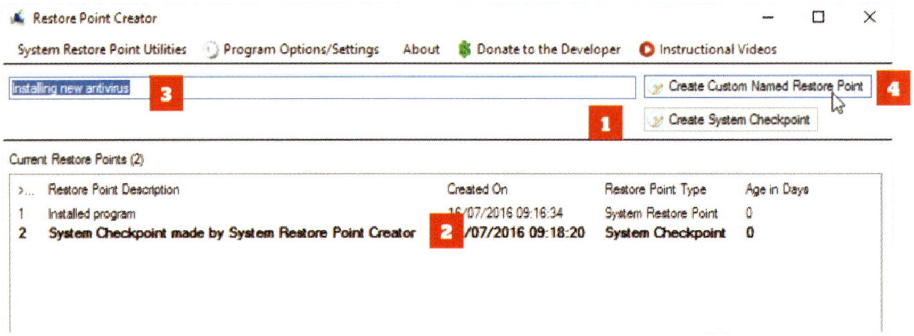

STEP 4 Each system restore point you create takes up space on your hard drive. Therefore, it's a good idea to delete older ones that you don't need. To do that, click System Restore Point Utilities 1 and move your cursor to Delete Restore Points 2. From here, you can delete all your restore points or only older ones 3. If you click the latter, you'll see the option to type a number of days (before which all restore points will be deleted) and click OK.

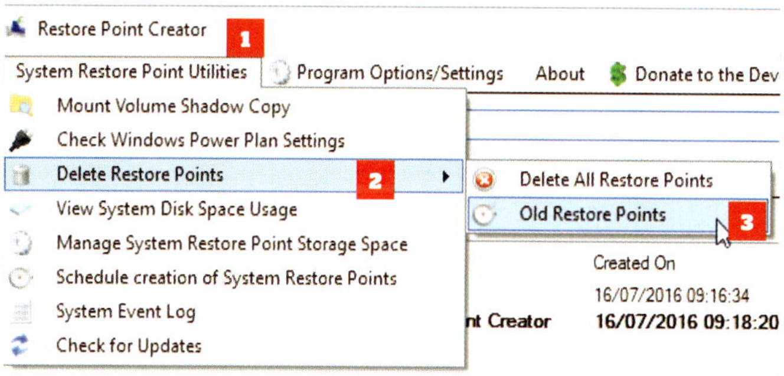

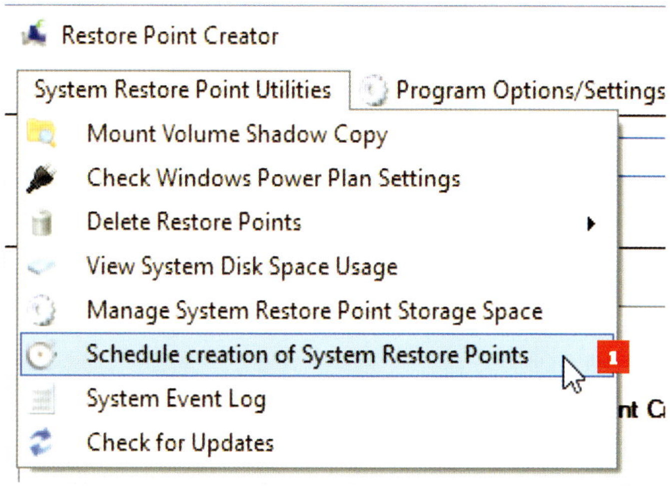

STEP 5 It's a good idea to set up automatic system restore points. Restore Point Creator has its own Task Scheduler that lets you do this in a few simple steps. To open it, click System Restore Point Utilities, then click 'Schedule creation of System Restore Points' 1. Click OK if you see a message about installing the program somewhere safe. Now select Weekly, then tick a day of the week that suits you.

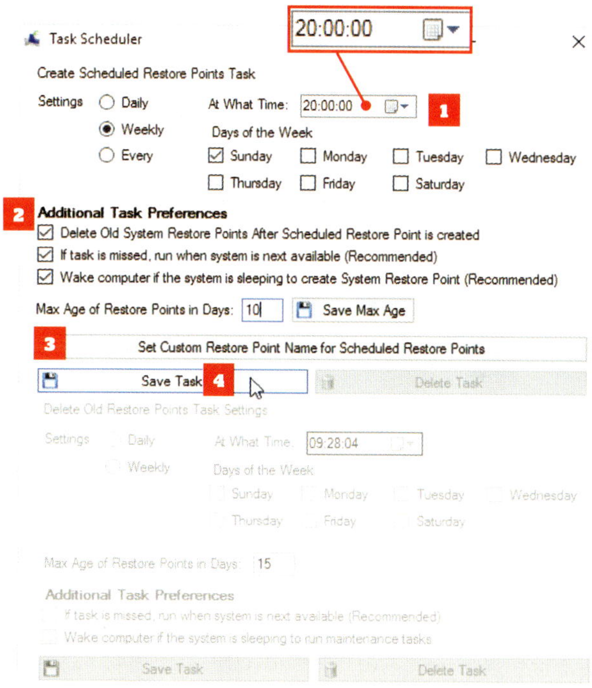

STEP 6 After doing that, select a time 1 when your PC is likely to be on. Next, tick the three boxes in the Additional Task Preferences section 2. The first box automatically deletes old restore points after creating the new one. If you PC is switched off at the time and date you set, the second box will ensure the restore point is created the next time you boot up. If your PC is in 'Sleep mode' when the restore-point creation is scheduled, the final box ensures your PC is switched on and the point is created. To set a name for your restore point, click the button near the bottom 3, type the name you want, then click OK. When you've finished, click Save Task 4.

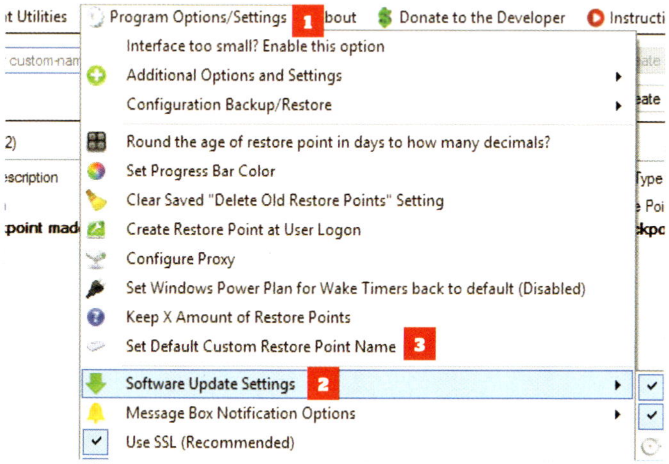

STEP 7 Now click Program Options/Settings 1. Here, you can check for updates to the program 2. Program Updates Channel lets you choose whether you want to use the beta version of the program. You can also set up notifications telling you when your restore points have been created. As we explained in Step 2, the program creates system restore points with a default name. You can change this name by clicking Set Default Custom Restore Point Name 3, typing the name you want, then clicking OK.

Uninstall junk using Kaspersky Cleaner

Time required: 20 minutes

Windows 10 has built-in tools for deleting junk files and cleaning your browser history but they're not great. They aren't very user-friendly and tend to leave lots of unwanted files and traces of your activity behind. That's where this brilliant free tool from Kaspersky comes in. It scans your PC for junk (including the cache, cookies, passwords and temporary internet files) and lets you delete it easily. The program is still in beta so its default settings are pretty basic, but we'll show you how to tweak these for a more comprehensive PC clean-up.

STEP 1 To download the program, go to www.free.kaspersky.com, scroll through the list of Kaspersky programs and click the green Download button beside Kaspersky Cleaner Beta. Open the downloaded setup file, click Install and wait until that's done. When the program launches, you'll see one big button **1** and four section icons below – System Cleanup, Restore System Settings, Private Browsing and Remote Activity Traces. Move your cursor over each icon **2** to see what that section does. Each section has a list of PC options (as tickboxes) that are divided into three categories – 'Important issues', 'Medium severity issues' and 'Minor problems'.

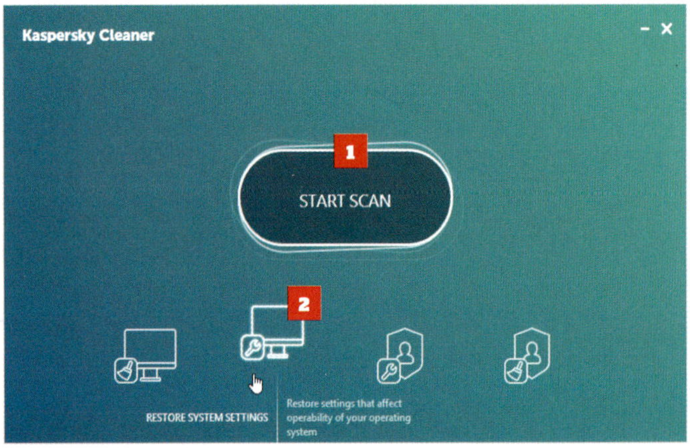

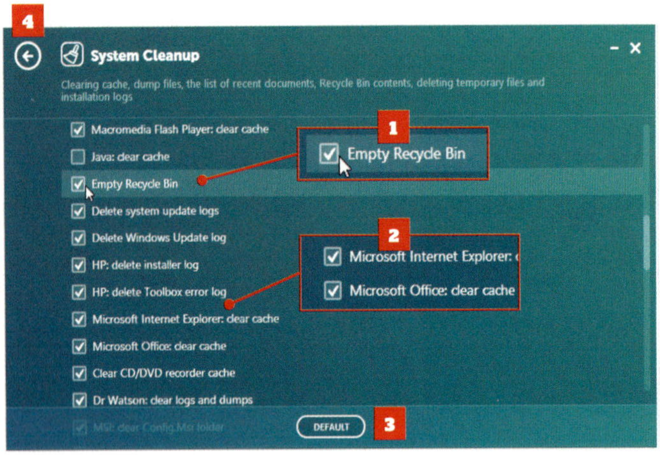

STEP 2 While going through each section, we found some important options that are not ticked by default. For example, click the first section System Cleanup and scroll to the 'Medium-severity issues' category. Here, you should tick Empty Recycle Bin **1** and the boxes to delete the cache from Internet Explorer and Microsoft Office **2**. Whenever you tick an option, you'll see a Default button **3**. If you ever want to revert to the program's default settings, click the Default button. If you use Google Earth, scroll to the bottom and tick the last box to delete its cache files. Finally, click the Back button **4** to return to the main screen.

STEP 3 Now click the second section 'Restore system settings', scroll to the bottom and tick the last box 'Windows Explorer: show extensions for known file types'. Go back and click the third section, Private Browsing. You'll see the option to Disable Cortana in the 'Important issues' category. In the 'Minor problems' section **1**, tick the second box **2**. This lets you automatically clean up Internet Explorer's cache whenever you close the browser. After doing this, go back **3** and click the last section – 'Remove activity traces'.

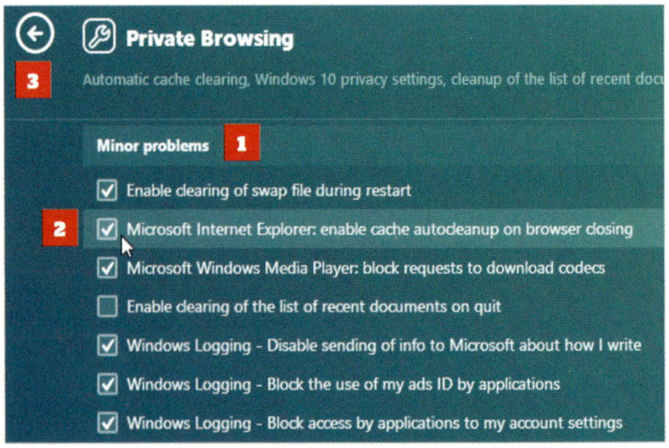

STEP 4 In the 'Important issues' category, you'll see the option to clear your browser history. If you use the popular remote-access program TeamViewer, then tick 'TeamViewer: clear logs' and 'TeamViewer: clear configurations' **1** if you want to delete those settings. Below, you'll see options to delete the cache, cookies and passwords for all your browsers (Chrome, Firefox, Opera and Internet Explorer). Select the options you want to delete for the browser(s) that you use **2**.

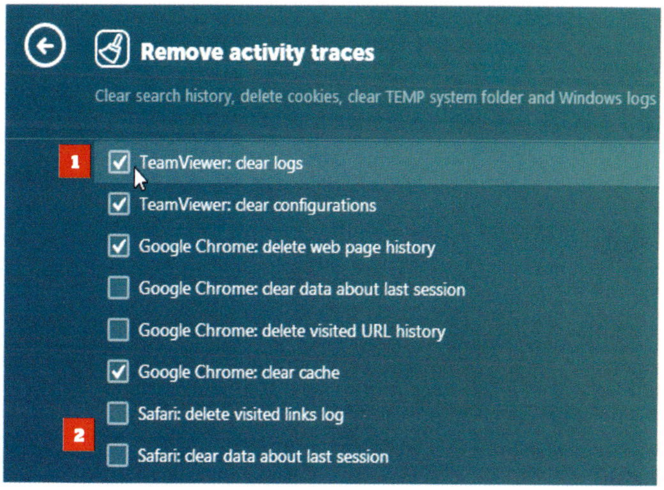

STEP 5 Scroll down to the 'Minor problems' category **1** where you'll see options to clear your File Explorer search history **2**, your Recent Documents list and even the option to clear any Run commands that you've typed (clearing them means they won't appear as part of your autosuggest options). You'll also see the option to clear your history in Paint and Windows Registry Editor. When you've ticked all the boxes that you want, go back and click the Start Scan button.

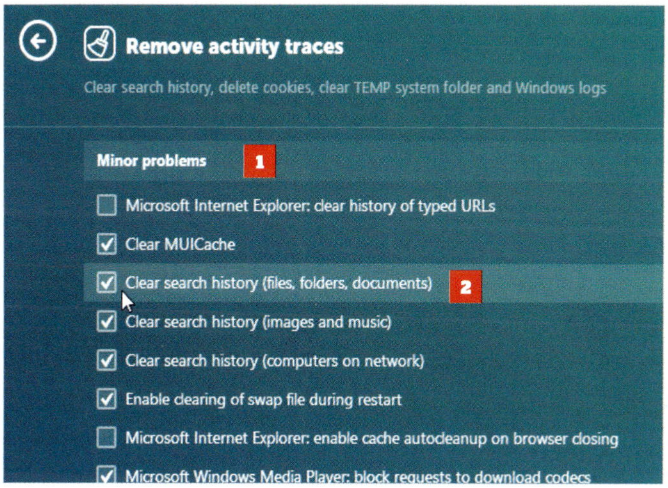

STEP 6 During the scan (which can take a few minutes), Kaspersky will check which of the ticked boxes require fixes. You'll see how many problems were detected on your PC **1**, a breakdown of the problems across each section and a Fix button. Click any of the sections **2** to see the problems in each (as red tickboxes). By default, all the boxes are ticked, meaning those problems will be solved when you apply the fix. Untick any boxes if you don't want to apply that particular fix. When you've finished, click the top-left Back button, then click the Fix button **3**.

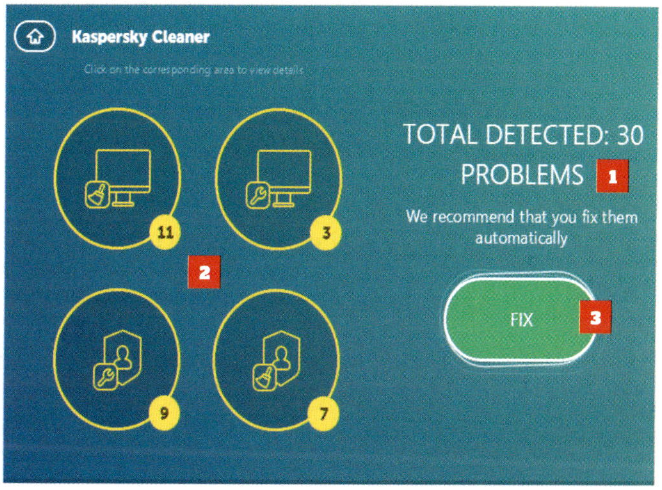

STEP 7 You'll now see a summary of how many problems were eliminated **1**. The fixes won't be applied until you reboot your PC, so close all your programs, then click Reboot Now **2**. If you're working on something important, you can postpone the reboot **3**. We noticed that our PC took longer to shut down, but booted much faster. If you notice any faults with your PC after rebooting, it's likely that Kaspersky Cleaner changed some of your default settings when you applied the one-click fix. Thankfully, it lets you reverse some of these (though it doesn't specify which ones). To do that, open Kaspersky Cleaner, click Roll Back Changes, click Start Reverting Changes and wait until that's finished.

Chapter 4

Master Windows 10

Take your Windows 10 knowledge to the next level with these advanced tips, tricks and hacks

Windows 10 makes it easy to learn the basics. In many ways it's a direct evolution of previous versions of the OS, meaning that it works mostly as you might expect it to; click Start, open a program, browse the web and so on. Except that's just the beginning. Dig a little deeper and you'll find that Microsoft offers countless ways to get more from your operating system, protect your data and take control of your PC. In this chapter we'll be looking at some of the advanced tasks you can carry out in Windows 10, from tweaking the Start menu to putting the entire OS onto a USB stick.

IN THIS SECTION

Expert tips for File Explorer

Become a File Explorer maestro with our guide to this essential component of Windows 10

Follow the breadcrumbs

At the top of the File Explorer window, you can see the path to the current folder: for example, This PC > Windows (C:) > Users > YourName > Documents > MyFolder. This is a breadcrumb navigation trail that shows where you are in the folder tree. You can jump to any folder in the trail by clicking it. Each folder is followed by a '>' symbol. Click that, and the subfolders it contains are displayed in a menu. Click one to jump straight to it. A surprising feature is that you can click a file or folder in the Explorer window and drag it to a folder in the breadcrumb trail to move it. As you hover the dragged item over a folder, the caption under the icon changes to 'Move to [folder name]'. Drop it and Explorer moves the item to the named folder.

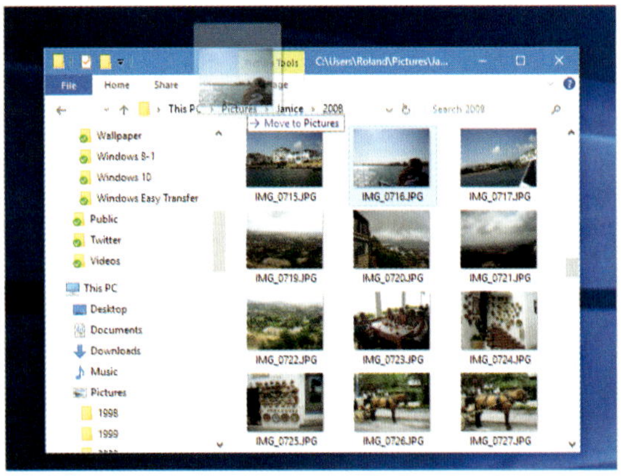

▶ Move files by dragging them to folders in the breadcrumb trail

Customise 'Quick access'

The 'Quick access' list at the top of the left panel lets you go to commonly used folders in one click. Drag any folder on the hard drive to the 'Quick access' list and drop it to add it. Once you've added your favourites, click and drag the folders to move them up or down in the list. Right-click folders and select 'Unpin from Quick access' to remove them from the list.

Strip files of their properties

Files contain extra information that isn't part of the file but tells you something about its contents. The obvious examples are music files, such as MP3s, which store the name of the artist and album, and photos taken on a phone or digital camera, which contain information such as shutter speed, aperture and metering modes.

This extra information can be stripped out, and it's sometimes useful to do this when sharing files on the internet. For example, you might want to remove GPS information that reveals where you live if you share a photo taken at home. Be careful with this tip, though, because the information you remove from the file is erased irreversibly.

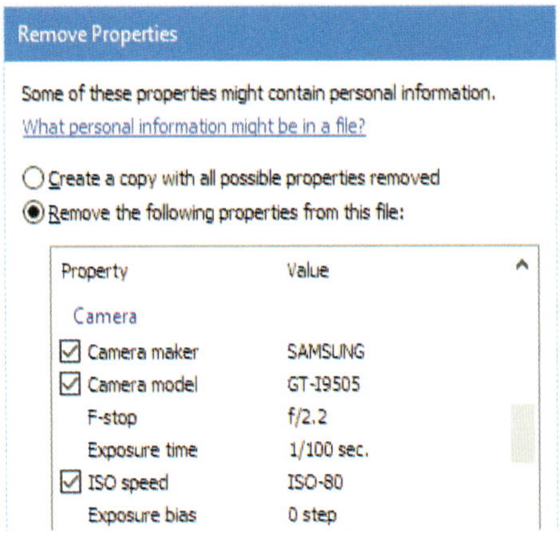

▲ Strip information from files before sharing them on the internet

Select a file in Explorer and click the Home tab. Click the arrow under the Properties icon and select 'Remove properties'. In the window that opens, select 'Remove the following properties from this file'. Use the Select All button to remove all the information, or tick the box next to each item you want to remove, such as a photo's GPS coordinates.

Alternatively, if you prefer to keep this information and want to make it easier to find, read our 'Optimise folders for content' tip (opposite).

Control your photos

Select one or more photos and a new Manage tab appears at the top of the Explorer window. Select a photo, click Manage and then 'Set as background' to make it the Desktop background image. There are also buttons to rotate images

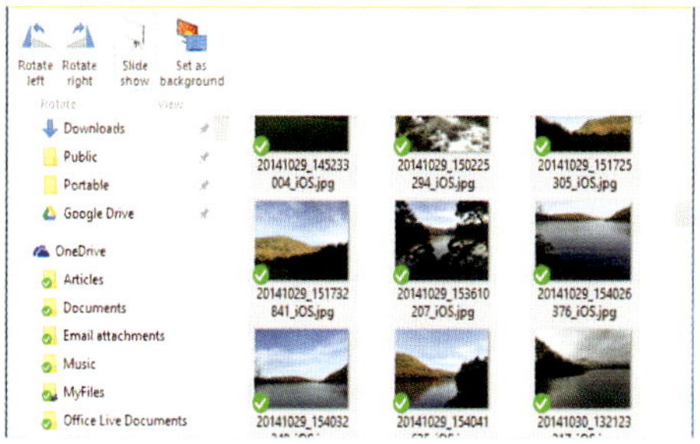

▲ Select one or more photos and then use the tools on the Manage tab

left and right, which you can use to rotate more than one image at a time. If you've just transferred photos from your camera, open the folder, hold down the Ctrl key while you click any images you want to rotate to portrait orientation, and then rotate them all in one go.

To show off your photos to friends, open Explorer and open the folder containing the images. Use your mouse to select the ones you want (or press Ctrl+A to select them all), then click Manage, 'Slide show'. Each image is displayed full-screen for five seconds.

Use the expanded 'Send to'

If you right-click a file in Explorer and select 'Send to' from the menu, you can send the file to the desktop, the Documents folder, a compressed Zip file and a few other places. Now hold down the Shift key, right-click a file and select 'Send to'. The menu now offers many more places to send the file, including Music, Videos, Downloads and so on.

Hide recent activity

When you open Explorer, you may see a list of recently used files and folders in the 'Quick access' area. You might not like the idea that anyone nearby can glance at the screen and see what you've been doing, but you can easily hide this recent history. From the File menu, click 'Change folder and search options' and select the General tab. In the privacy section near the bottom, you can choose between convenience or privacy. For privacy, clear the ticks against 'Show recently used files...' and 'Show frequently used folders...'

▲ Go to Folder options and clear the ticks in the Privacy section

Fix Explorer

If you're having problems with Explorer, Windows, the desktop, menus and other things, it can help to quit Explorer and restart it. Explorer runs in the background, not just in a File Explorer window, and the desktop is really just an Explorer view. Hold down Shift+Ctrl and right-click an empty part of the taskbar. Select Exit Explorer.

Bring back libraries

Libraries were introduced with Windows 7 and allowed Explorer to display the contents of two or more folders as if they were one. If you had three folders of photos, for example, you could add them to a library and then view all your photos by opening the library. Some people liked it, others didn't, but libraries seemed to disappear in Windows 10.

If you found them useful, you'll be pleased to hear that you can bring them back. Click File in any Explorer window and select 'Change folder and search options'. Select the View tab and scroll down to the bottom of the list of settings. Tick 'Show libraries'. There are now more libraries than there used to be, because Camera Roll and Saved Pictures have been added to the usual choice of Documents, Pictures, Music and Videos libraries.

Pin libraries to 'Quick access'

When libraries are enabled in Explorer, they appear at the bottom of the left-hand pane. For easier access, right-click Libraries and select 'Pin to Quick access'. The library is added to the bottom of the 'Quick access' list at top of the left panel. Click and drag it to the top, just under the 'Quick access' heading. Not only is it easier to find here, but it appears in the top-left corner in Explorer.

Keep libraries at the top

If you really love libraries and want to make them the default view in Explorer, right-click Libraries and select 'Send to', then 'Desktop (create shortcut)'. This places an Explorer icon on the desktop. Right-click it, select Rename and delete the word 'shortcut', leaving the name as Libraries. Now you can open Explorer with your libraries as the default view by clicking the desktop icon. Select your favourite view, such as Tiles or 'Large icons' in the View menu and Windows will remember your choice.

You can use the same technique to make any folder the default when Explorer is opened. Just right-click the folder and choose 'Send to' to create a desktop icon.

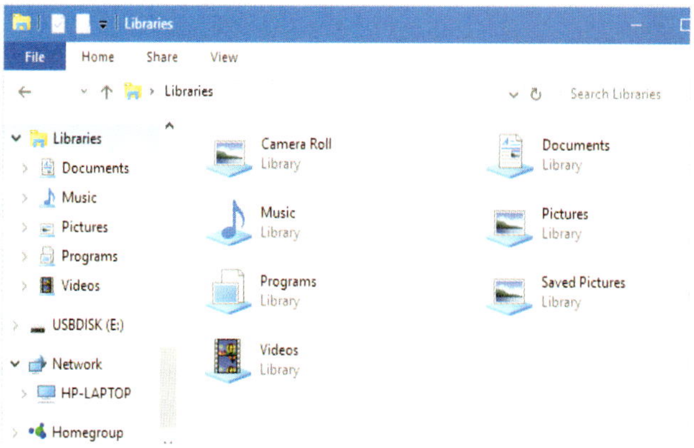

▲ Bring libraries back to Windows by enabling them in Folder options

Search speed vs thoroughness

The search box in the top-right corner of the Explorer windows is useful for finding files, and you can choose between speed or thoroughness. Go to File, click 'Change folder and search options' and select the Search tab. Remove the tick from every box for faster searches, or tick them all for more thorough but slower searches.

Optimise folders for content

If you prefer to see the extra information we mentioned in the 'Strip files of their properties' tip (opposite), you can tell Explorer which type of files you're keeping in a particular folder, and it will optimise the display to present the relevant information for that file type.

Right-click a folder, select Properties and click the Customise tab. Under 'Optimise this folder for', select Documents, Pictures, Music or Videos. This determines which information appears in the Details view for that folder. To refine this, open the folder and select Details on the View tab. Right-click the Name heading in the first column to see which information can be displayed, and tick the items you want.

Master the Start menu

We touched on customising the Start menu in Chapter 2 – here we'll go into more detail and show you how to make it faster and smarter

Choose between live and static tiles

The tiles on the Windows 10 Start menu can be either live or static. A static tile is a coloured box displaying an icon in the centre. If the tile is large enough, the name of the app or program is also displayed. Static tiles do the job required of them, but they're a bit boring.

Live tiles, as their name suggests, are more interesting. They can display specific information, but you don't have to run the tile's app to see this.

The Weather app is a good example; when the large tile is set to show live information, it displays today's weather along with a mini forecast for the next four days.

Right-click each tile on the Start menu and select 'Turn live tile on'. If you find a live tile too distracting, right-click it and select 'Turn live tile off'.

Resize the tiles

Start menu tiles can be set to a variety of different sizes. Not all apps support every possible size, but they all offer at least two. Some tiles – including Word, Excel and Edge – work well at the smallest size because they have instantly recognisable icons. If an icon is less easy to identify, it's better to use a medium tile because the app's name will also be displayed. Live tiles work best when they are sized wide and large. To change the size of a tile, right-click it, then select Resize and choose a size from the options.

Resize the menu

The width and height of the Start menu are adjustable, so if you want to display more tiles, to provide fast access to more of your favourite software, you can make the menu bigger. Hover your mouse over the right or top edges of the Start menu and, when the pointer becomes a double-headed arrow, click and drag the edge to the size you want.

Rearrange the tiles

The tiles on the Start menu are shortcuts to apps. When you add a new app, it's placed at the bottom of the menu, rather than grouped in a logical order, so it can become hard to find the app you want as the menu fills up. However, you can click and drag tiles to organise them. Drag your favourites to the top-left corner or wherever you find them convenient to access, and drag those you rarely use down to the bottom of the Start menu, off the screen.

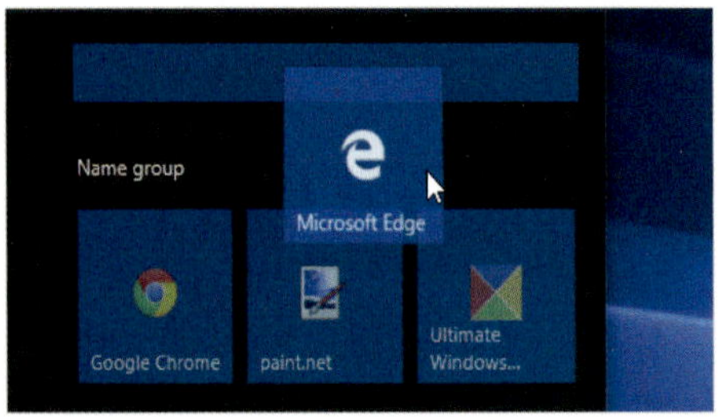

▲ Drag and drop a tile outside an existing group to start a new one

Rename groups of tiles

Start menu tiles are organised into groups and each group has a title. 'Life at a glance' and 'Play and explore' are provided, but you can rename them. Just click the title and type a new name.

To create a new group, click and drag a tile to the very bottom of the Start menu until a horizontal blue bar appears. Drop the tile under the bar to create a new group. Click the group title or the space where the title should be to name it.

Rearrange groups

You can also rearrange the groups. When your mouse is over the group title, a two-line icon appears at the right. Click and drag it to move the whole group. Other groups move out of the way to fit wherever you drop it.

Configure your Start menu's settings

Click Start, Settings, Personalisation, Start to customise the menu. For example, you can show or hide the list of most-used apps that appears on the left. When software is installed, it is highlighted on the Start menu to make it easy to find, but if you don't need this, then turn it off. In the unlikely event that you miss the Windows 8 Start screen, there is an option to enable it instead of using the Start menu.

Jump lists, which provide access to recent actions in applications on the 'Most used' list, can be switched on and off. For example, if Notepad is on the Start menu's 'Most used' list and jump lists are turned on, an arrow appears on the right. Clicking it displays recent actions, which in Notepad's case will be the files you've

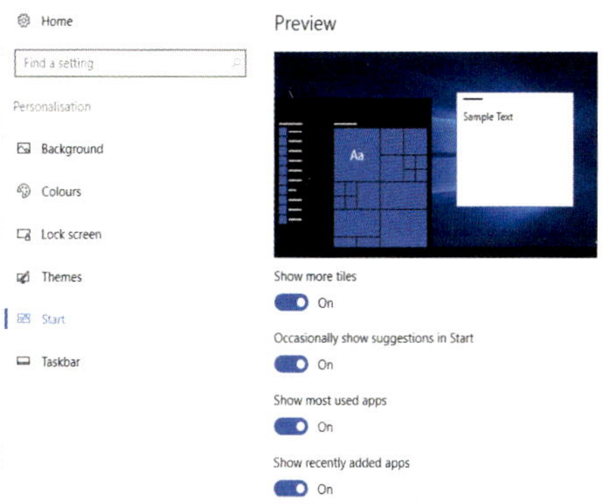

▲ Customise the Start menu in the Settings app

recently opened. Just click a file to open it again.

Click 'Choose which folders appear on Start' to pick from the 10 available options. These include Documents, Pictures, Videos, Downloads and others. They provide quick access to common folders without you having to open File Explorer first.

Pin and unpin apps

You can remove tiles from the Start menu that you don't use. This doesn't delete the app, which will still be available through the 'All apps' list, but it will make your Start menu less cluttered. Right-click a tile and select 'Unpin from Start'. If there is an app you use that doesn't have a Start menu tile, go to 'All apps' and find it, then right-click it and select 'Pin to Start'.

Run as administrator

Even if you are logged into Windows with an administrator account, most software is run in non-administrator mode by default. This improves security by preventing certain actions from happeneing, such as those that change system settings and the Registry. Sometimes, programs can only function properly if they are run in administrator mode. To do this, right-click a Start menu tile or program on the 'All apps' list, then select 'Run as administrator' on the menu that pops up.

Hide programs from the 'Most used' list

The top-left side of the Start menu shows a list of your most-used apps. It's designed so you can easily run your favourite programs without having to hunt for their tiles on the Start menu or in the 'All apps' list. However, it's not always the most convenient way to run software. For example, a program pinned to the taskbar can be launched in just one click, rather than the two clicks it takes to open the Start menu and then click a relevant tile.

For this reason, you might want to remove items from the 'Most used' list. Right-click any item and select 'Don't show this in list' to remove it.

Add a Run tile

If you've upgraded from Windows XP and miss the link to the Run tool on the Start menu, you can easily add it. Open Start, click 'All apps', scroll down the list to Windows System and expand the section. Right-click Run and select 'Pin to Start'. Find the tile on the Start menu and drag into your preferred position, then right-click it to set its size.

Pick your own colours

Windows selects the colour of the tiles on your Start menu depending on the desktop image used, which doesn't always look good. And if the desktop image changes, then the tile colour changes,

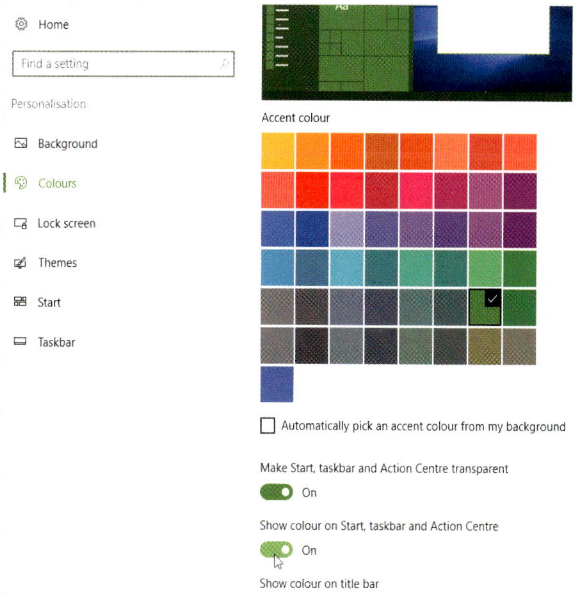

▲ Use the switches to stop Windows picking colours you don't like for your Start menu

too. In most cases, it's better to set a fixed colour.

Right-click the desktop and select Personalise. Select Colours on the left, and turn off the option to automatically pick a colour, then select a colour from the palette. Scroll down below the colour palette to see a switch to 'Show colour on Start, taskbar and action centre'. Switch this off to use black. The Start menu is slightly transparent and you can set a switch to turn this off if you prefer a solid background.

Uninstall software more quickly

The obvious way to uninstall software is to find the Control Panel in the Start menu (which isn't easy in Windows 10) and then open 'Programs and Features'. A quicker way is to right-click a tile or an item on the 'All apps' list and select Uninstall. If the item is a Windows Store app, it will be uninstalled directly, but with regular software, the 'Programs and Features' tool in the Control Panel will open. It's less effort and takes fewer mouse clicks.

Add advanced tools to your menu

Open Start, click 'All apps' and scroll down to Windows Administrative Tools. Expand the category and you'll find useful tools such as 'Defragment and Optimise Drives', Disk Cleanup and more. To make them easier to access, right-click and pin them to the Start menu.

Back up everything in Windows 10

Windows 10 has its own backup tools for keeping your PC and files safe. We show you how to find and use them

It's important to back up your PC on a regular basis. If disaster strikes – such as a hard-drive failure or a malware infection – you'll still be able to access to all your personal files and settings. Windows 10 comes with its own tools that you can use to back up your content, and there are plenty of other free programs available, too. Here, we're going to explain everything you need to do to make the perfect Windows 10 backup, from storing what you're working on now to creating complete local backups of your entire PC. Then, on page 78 we'll put it all into practice with a step-by-step guide.

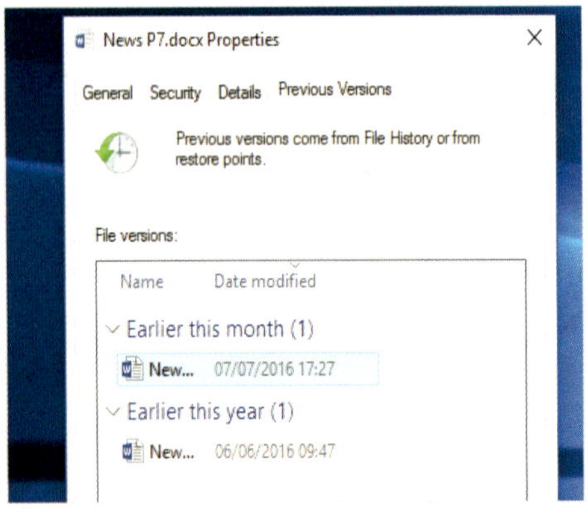

▲ Once you've got File History set up, you can access previous versions of your files

Keep old versions of files

File History is an incremental backup tool that was originally introduced in Windows 8. It saves multiple copies of your personal files to an external or networked hard drive, so if you accidentally delete a file – a document, photo or video, say – from your PC, you can use this tool to recover the missing item. More importantly, if you make a change to a file that you later regret, and need to revert to a previous version, you can use File History to restore it.

The tool is disabled by default in Windows 10, so you'll have to turn it on before you can use it. There are some limitations to be aware of, too. By default, File History only backs up copies of files that are in the Documents, Music, Pictures, Videos, Desktop and OneDrive folders. The OneDrive option only backs up the files that are synced locally, not everything that's saved in your cloud storage. If you want to back up files that are kept in a different location, you'll need add that folder yourself. We'll show you how to set up File History on page 79.

Restore a previous version from File History

Once you've set up File History and it's backing up your files, there are a couple of ways you can restore them. We'll be showing you how to do this from Windows' Backup Settings menu in our workshop but another option is to right-click the file you want to access a previous version of, then select Properties from the menu. Click the Previous Versions tab at the top, then select the version you want. You can either open the file or restore it. There are down arrows next to both buttons that let you 'Open in File History' or 'Restore To...' The latter lets you select a custom location.

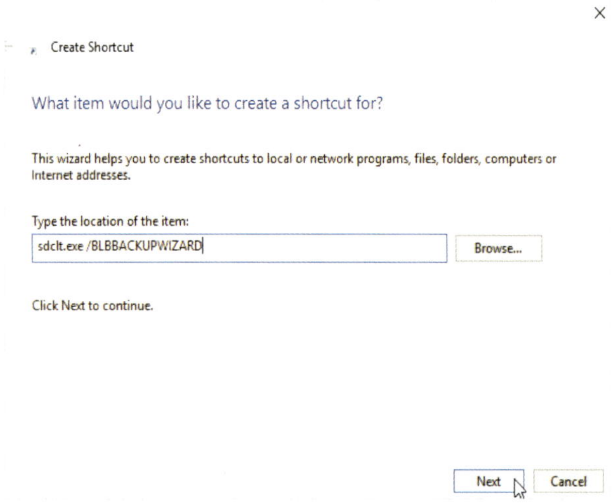

▲ Create a shortcut to get quick access to your backup tools

Create a backup of your files

File History is the primary way to back up and restore files in Windows 10, but it's not your only option. The backup tool that Microsoft introduced in Windows 7 is still available in Windows 10, and it's a capable option that works well. You can use this to back up your files to a local or networked drive, and choose exactly what to include.

The tool, called 'Back up and Restore (Windows 7)', is tucked away in the Windows Control Panel. Press Windows+X, choose Control Panel, 'System and Security', then 'Back up and Restore'. Once the tool is configured, you can use it to create new backups and restore files from previous ones. We show you how to use it in our Mini Workshop opposite.

Creating a desktop shortcut provides quick and convenient access to the tool.

Click 'System and Security' and right-click 'Back up and Restore (Windows 7)'. Select the option at the bottom to 'Create shortcut'. A message pops up announcing that Windows can't create a shortcut there, and offers you the chance to place it on the desktop instead. Click Yes. You can now launch the tool whenever you need to. Right-clicking the new shortcut will let you pin a copy to the 'Quick access' and Start menus.

Make a Windows 10 system image

You can create a backup image (an exact copy of everything on your drive) using the 'Back up and Restore (Windows 7)' tool. Open it and click the 'Create a system image' link on the left.

To create a shortcut to this option, right-click the Desktop and select New, Shortcut. The Create Shortcut wizard will launch. In the 'Type the location of the item' box, enter sdclt.exe / BLBBACKUPWIZARD. Click Next and name the shortcut 'Create System Image'. Click Finish to complete the wizard and the shortcut will appear on your Desktop.

You can save the image backup to an external hard drive, multiple DVDs or a networked drive. We'll explain how to create and restore an image from within Windows 10 in our workshop.

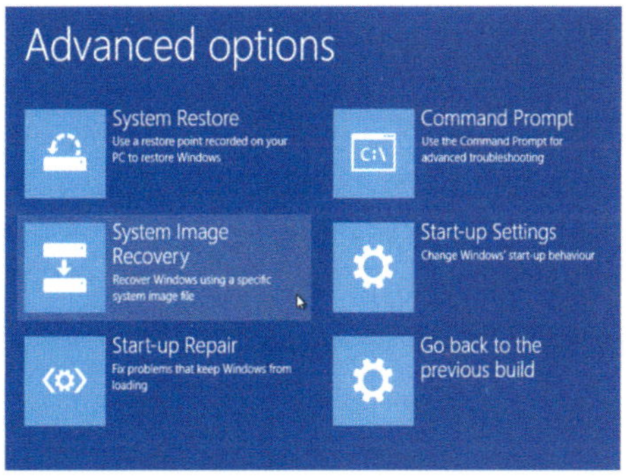

▲ Restore a system image via Advanced start-up

If you need to restore an image backup and you can't get into Windows, because the operating system won't load, the PC should automatically boot into the Advanced start-up menu. If this doesn't happen, because it hasn't worked out that you've got a problem, try rebooting the PC several times.

Try other backup tools

There's no shortage of free alternative backup programs available for Windows 10, such as FBackup 6 (www.fbackup.com), and AOMEI Backupper Standard (bit.ly/aomei391), which can back up everything and also clone drives and partitions.

Our favourite free backup tool is EaseUS Todo Backup Free (www.todo-backup.com). It backs up hard drives, partitions, your operating system and individual files or folders, and runs full, incremental or differential backups. Incremental backup saves only the files that have changed since the last backup, while differential backups target files that have changed since the last full backup.

To clone a hard drive, try using Macrium Reflect Free 6 (bit.ly/macrium391). It offers both drive imaging and cloning, and will let you reorder and resize partitions, and schedule, compress and browse backups.

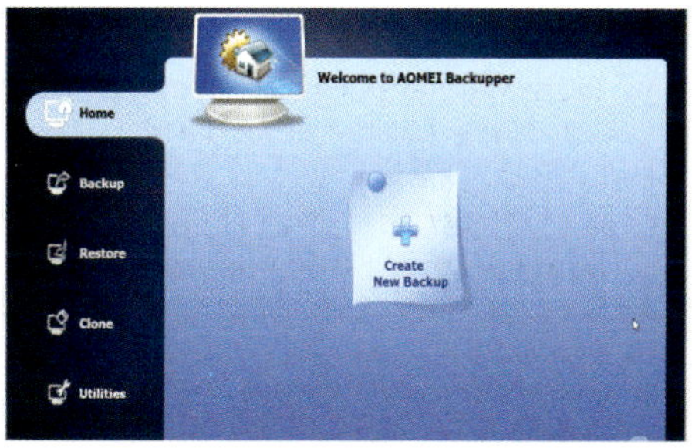

▲ AOMEI's Backupper can back up everything and clone drives and partitions

MINI WORKSHOP
Use Back up and Restore (Windows 7)

1 Launch the tool and a message will appear informing you that 'Windows Back-up has not been set up.' Click the 'Set up back-up' link **1** to launch Windows Backup. It may take a little while, so be patient. Choose the location to save your backup to **2**.

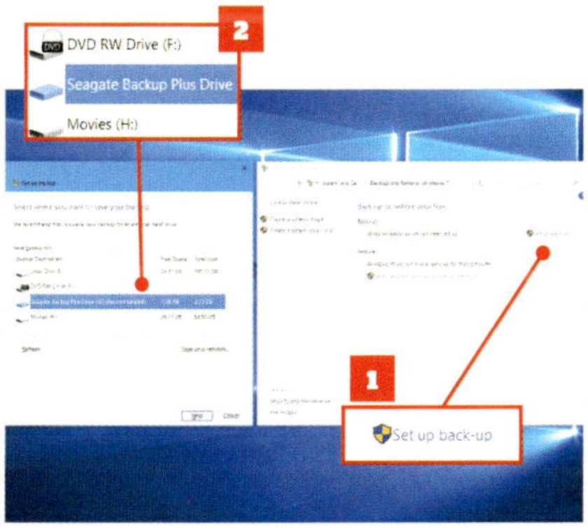

2 To select a location on your network, click the 'Save on a network' button, then enter the path and your network credentials. Once you've chosen your target location, click Next and either allow Windows to choose what to back up **1** (it will also create a system image) or make your own selection **2**.

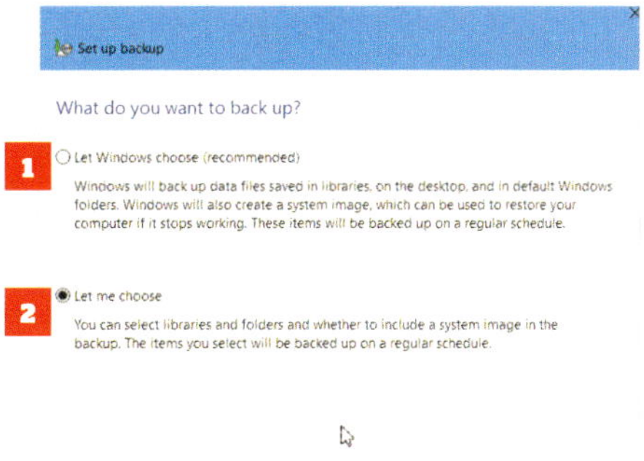

3 If you opt to customise your backup, the next window will let you browse your drives and select the folders you want to include. You can also add a system image. The final step is to review your settings. The backup will run at a set day and time but you can change the schedule **1**. Click 'Save settings and run backup' **2** to finish.

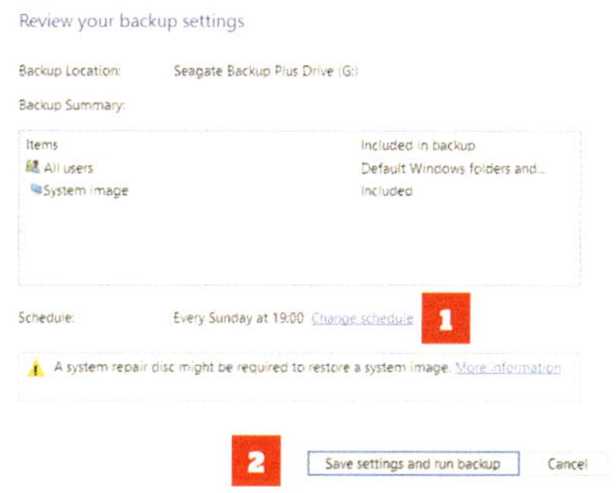

Back up Windows 10 automatically

Time required: 1 hour

In this age of constant online threats, it's extremely important that you back up your files on a regular basis. Thankfully, Windows 10 makes this easy with useful built-in tools that automatically back up all your important data (including documents, photos, music and videos).

In the steps below, we'll show you two different ways to do this, one that uses the File History feature, the other OneDrive. We'll also show you how to back up all your PC's settings and programs so you can easily restore them if something goes wrong.

STEP 1 First, we'll show you how to use Windows 10's File History feature. This lets you back up data to an external hard drive, then schedule automatic backups for that data. This is best used for larger files, because OneDrive offers limited free storage (see Step 6). First, connect an external hard drive to your PC. Now open your Start menu, click Settings, 'Update & Security', Backup, 'Add a drive' 1, then select your external hard drive 2.

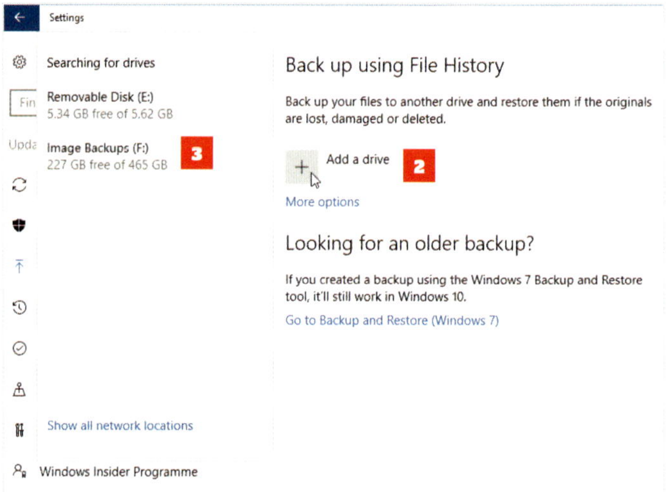

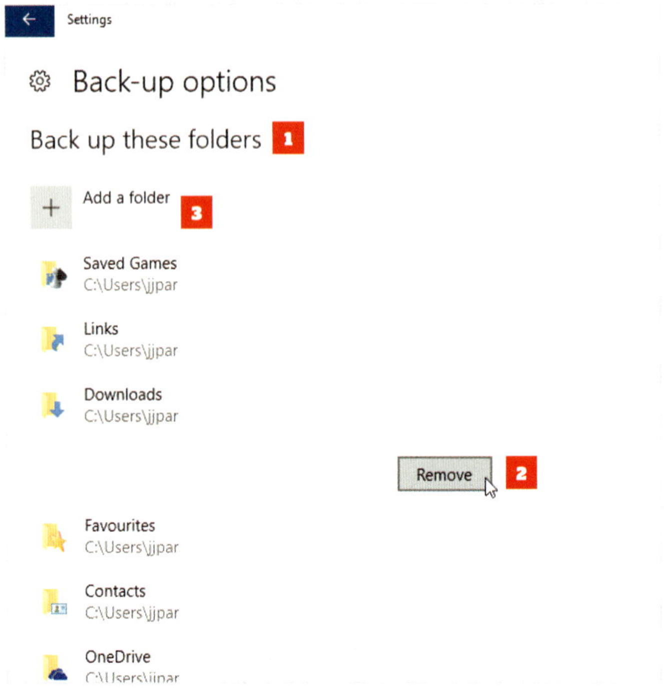

STEP 2 Next, switch the 'Automatically back up my files' slider on, then click the 'More options' link below that. Now scroll down to the 'Back up these folders' section 1. You'll see a list of folders that are set to be backed up by default. To remove folders from the list, click to select them, then click Remove 2. To add a folder you want to back up, click 'Add a folder' 3, navigate to the folder you want, then click 'Choose this folder'.

STEP 3 When you've finished amending your list, scroll to the top of the section. Click the 'Back up my files' dropdown menu **1** and select the regularity (from 'Every 10 minutes' to Daily). Next, click the 'Keep my backups' dropdown menu **2** and select how long you want to store your backups for (from '1 month' to Forever). When you've finished, click 'Back up now' **3**. The first time you do this, the process can take a while (depending on the amount of data involved), but you can continue using your PC because the backup takes place in the background.

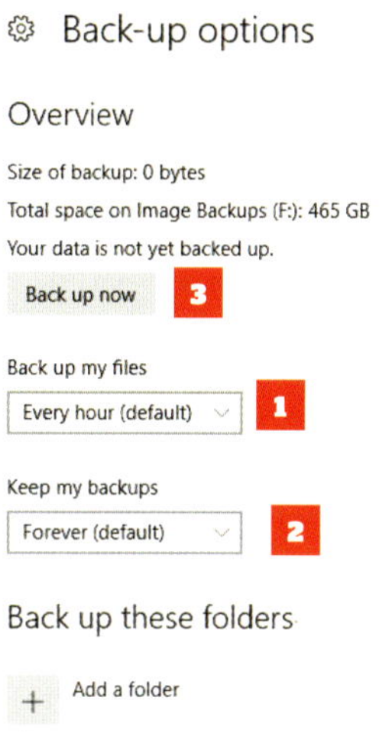

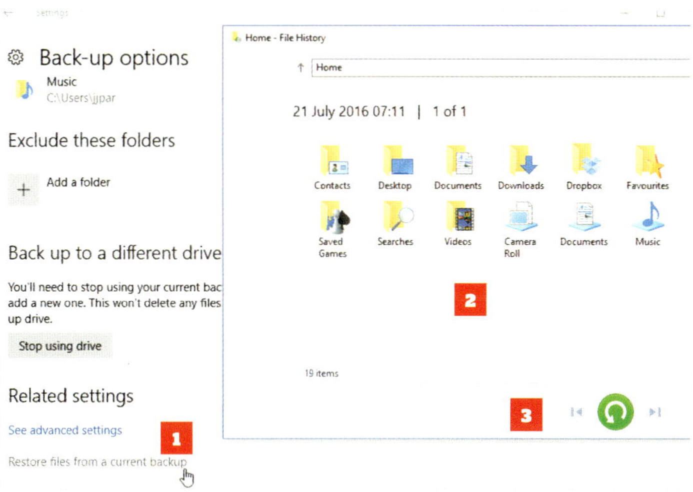

STEP 4 In future, changes you make to the files in the folders you've backed up will also be made to the files on your hard drive (as long as it's connected to your PC). If your PC or any of your folders become corrupted, you can easily restore the backed-up data from your hard drive. To do that, go to the Backup section (see Step 1) and click the 'More options' link below 'Back up using File History'. Scroll to the bottom, then click 'Restore files from a current backup' **1**. You'll now see your backed-up folders **2**. Press the Ctrl key on your keyboard, select the folders you want to restore, then click the Restore button **3**.

STEP 5 You'll now see three options. If you want to replace all the files in the folders on your PC with their backed-up versions, then select the first option **1**. If you only want to replace missing files with their backed-up versions, then select 'Skip these files' **2**. The third option **3** lets you tick boxes to decide which files you want to restore. Click Continue after selecting the option you want to use, then follow the prompts.

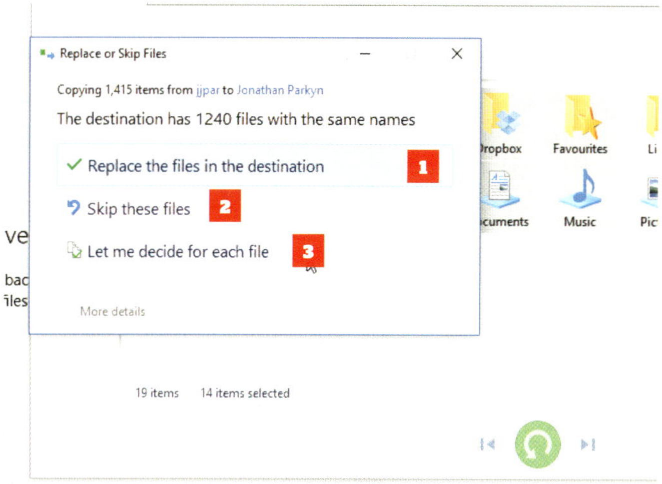

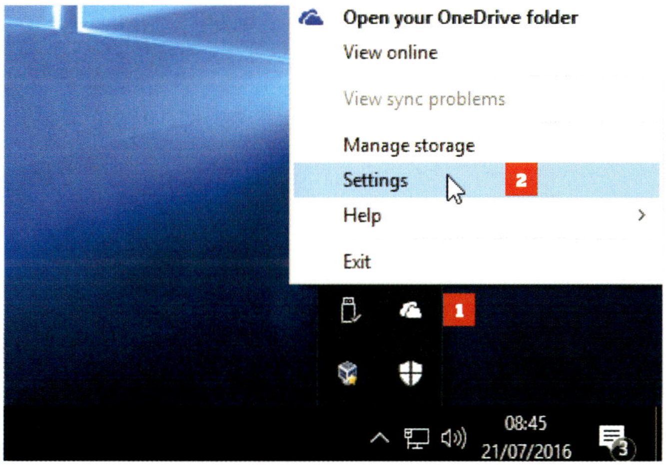

STEP 6 The second method of backing up your files involves using OneDrive – Microsoft's cloud storage service that comes with 5GB of free storage space and is a default program in Windows 10. Use this method to back up smaller files you access regularly, such as important photos and documents. If you've never used OneDrive before you'll need to sign in. Click the up arrow in the Notification area (bottom right of the screen), then click the OneDrive (cloud) icon. Enter your Microsoft account and click 'Sign in'. To set up OneDrive, click the up arrow in the Notification area, then right-click the OneDrive icon **1** and select Settings **2**.

STEP 7 On the Account tab, click 'Choose folders'. If you've used OneDrive previously, you'll see a list of your folders. By default, all these folders will start syncing with your PC, but you can untick any you don't want to sync 1. Ensure there's enough space on your selected drive to accommodate the synced folders 2. Click OK 3, then right-click the OneDrive Notification area icon and select 'Open my OneDrive folder'. All your OneDrive folders will now display small blue icons to indicate they are syncing. Once the sync is finished the icon turns green.

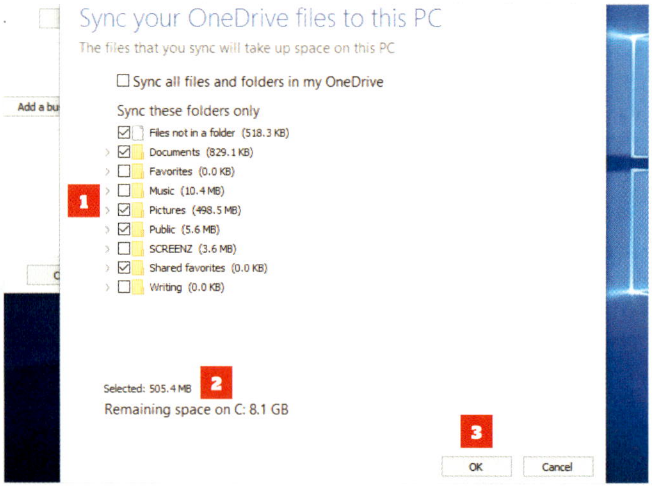

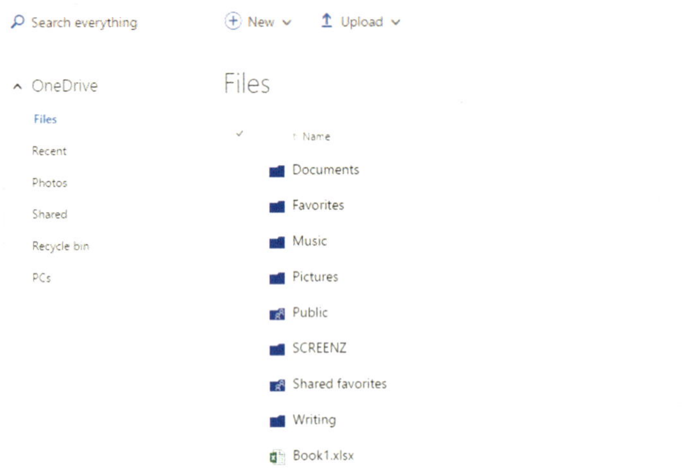

STEP 8 Select the files you want to back up to OneDrive then press Ctrl+C (or Ctrl+X to move them to free up space). Now open OneDrive on your PC, select the destination folder and press Ctrl+V. Any changes you make to these files in OneDrive will automatically be synced across all your devices. You can access OneDrive via www.onedrive.com (shown opposite) and its free mobile apps (Android www.snipca.com/20158; iOS www.snipca.com/20159).

STEP 9 Aside from File History and OneDrive, Windows 10 has a brilliant feature called System Image Backup. The 'system image' contains your PC's operating system, user settings and programs. It's great for restoring your PC if something goes wrong. First, connect your external hard drive to your PC. Now right-click your Start button, click Control Panel, ensure the 'View by' dropdown menu is set to 'Large icons' 1, then click File History 2. Next, click System Image Backup at the bottom right, then click 'Create a system image' link at the top left.

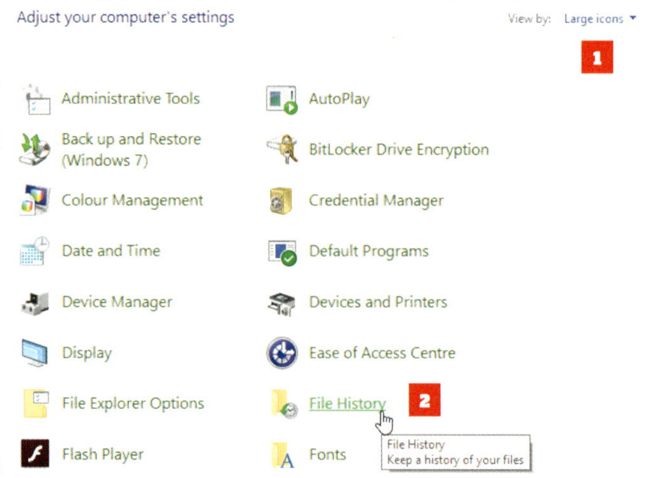

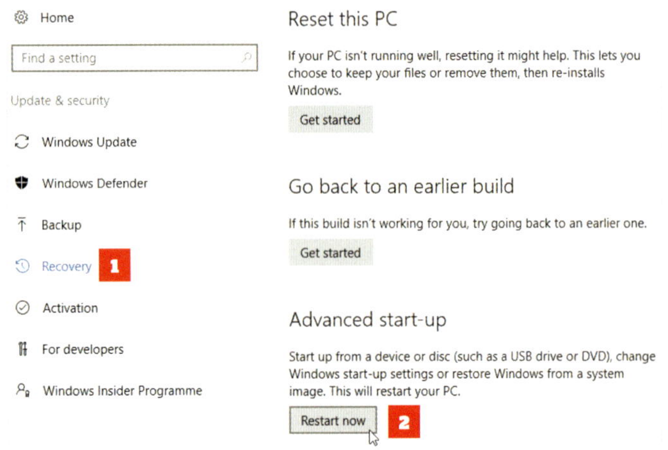

STEP 10 Next, select 'On a hard disk', click the dropdown menu below, select your external hard drive, click Next, then click 'Start backup'. The process can take a while, but you can continue using your PC. In future, if you have a problem with your PC, connect this external hard drive, open Settings, click Update & Security, Recovery 1, then click 'Restart now' 2. When your PC restarts, click Next, then click the 'Repair your computer' link at the bottom left. Now click Troubleshoot, Advanced Options, then choose 'System image recovery' to start restoring your PC's settings and programs to their backed-up state.

Create a bootable Windows 10 USB drive

Time required: 60 minutes

A bootable version of Windows 10 on a portable USB drive is a very handy tool to have around. It allows you to try the operating system on your own PC, before committing to installing and running it full-time, or you can simply use it as a personal version of Windows, containing your own software and settings, that you plug in and run from any other PC (such as at work or when visiting friends and family).

One of the quickest and easiest ways of doing this is to use AOMEI Partition Assistant's Windows To Go tool. You just need a disc or ISO image of Windows 10.

We'll also take a quick look at Partition Assistant's other bootable tool, called Make Bootable Media, which offers a stripped-back Windows PE-based console that lets you make a copy of your hard drive's contents.

STEP 1 You need a Windows ISO file to create a bootable version. Visit bit.ly/windows389 and click 'Download tool now' 1. Run the Windows 10 Media Creation Tool, accept its license terms and choose 'Create installation media for another PC'. Click Next and make sure the correct options are selected.

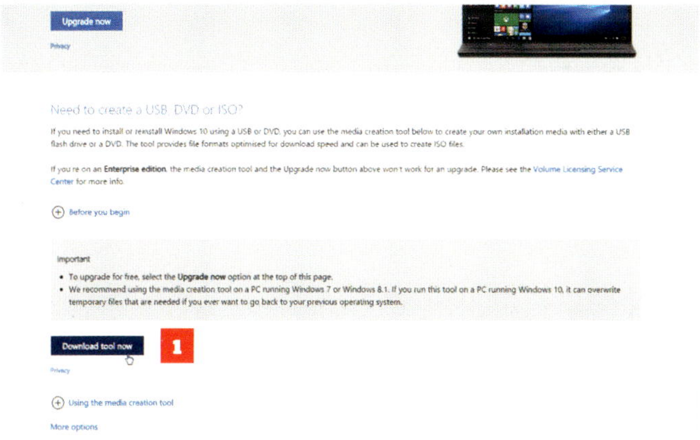

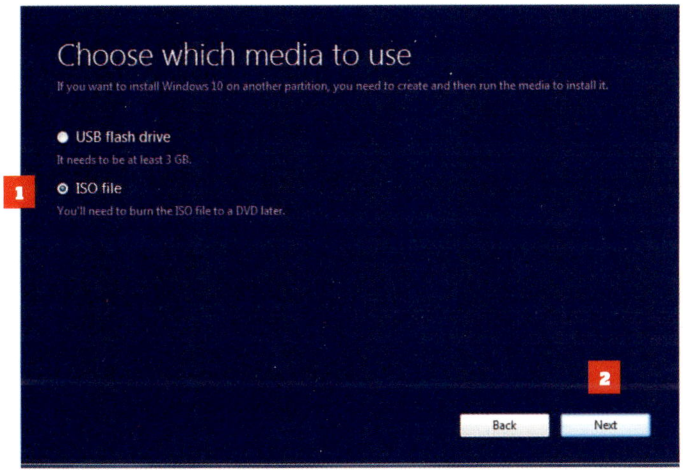

STEP 2 Click Next, then OK. The program asks how you want to save the operating system. Select 'ISO file' 1 and click Next 2, choose where you want to save it and select Save. You can carry on using your PC while the Media Creation Tool downloads Windows 10.

STEP 3 The final screen warns that you need a product key to install Windows 10 1. This is true if you want to use the OS without a watermark and access its Personalise settings, but you can skip the licence-key entry during installation and activate Windows later (if you decide you want to).

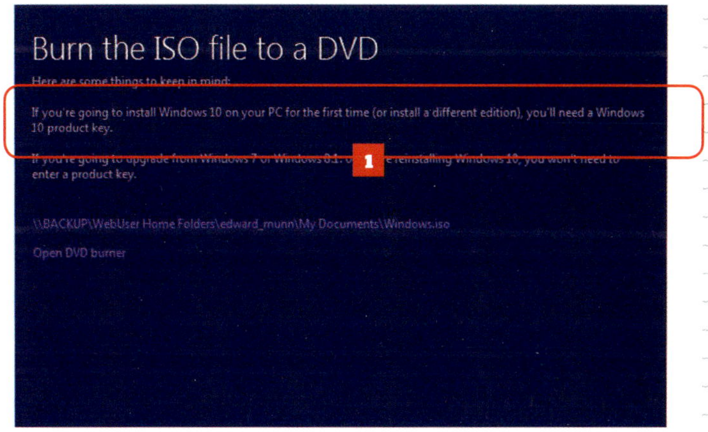

STEP 4 Click Finish, then download and install AOMEI Partition Assistant (bit.ly/partition389). Run the application and select Windows To Go Creator **1** in the Wizards sidebar. Insert a USB drive (see Expert Tip for size requirements), click Refresh **2** and select the drive from the drop-down menu **3**.

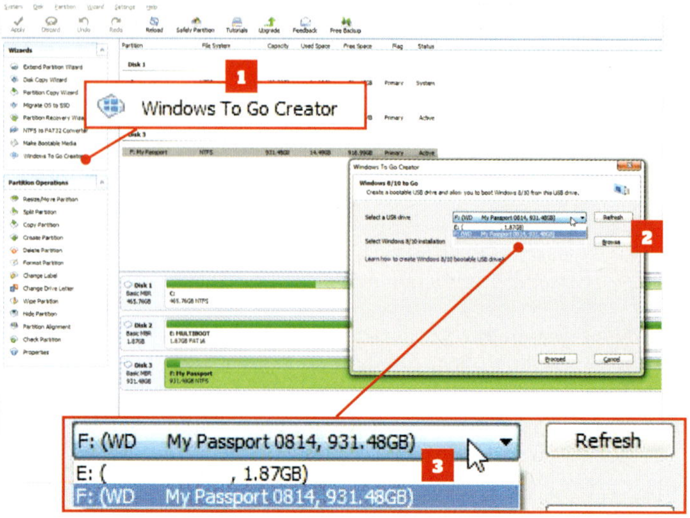

STEP 5 Click Browse, then Browse again, to navigate to the Windows 10 ISO file **1**. Select it and click Open **2**, then OK. Click Proceed and AOMEI warns that it will format your USB drive. Click Yes if you're happy that any important data you had on the drive is backed up elsewhere.

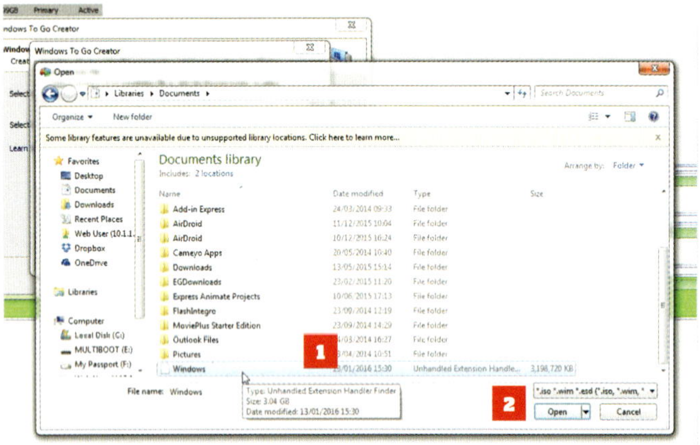

STEP 6 Once AOMEI has finished copying Windows to your USB drive, a window appears saying 'The operation completed successfully' **1**. Click OK **2**. The bootable USB drive is now ready to use. Restart your PC and enter its BIOS (you can normally do this by pressing F2 or F12).

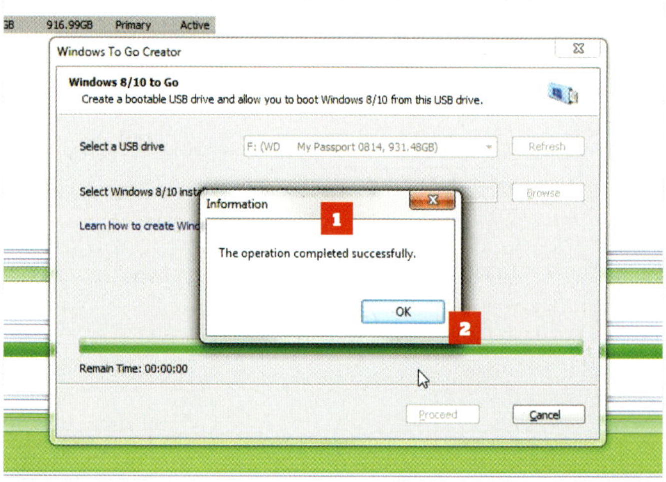

STEP 7 Navigate to the boot priority order page. If the USB isn't set as the primary option, change the settings accordingly, then save and exit the BIOS **1**. Your PC will boot from the USB drive and a Windows 10 setup screen appears. Follow the steps to finish preparing the OS on the drive.

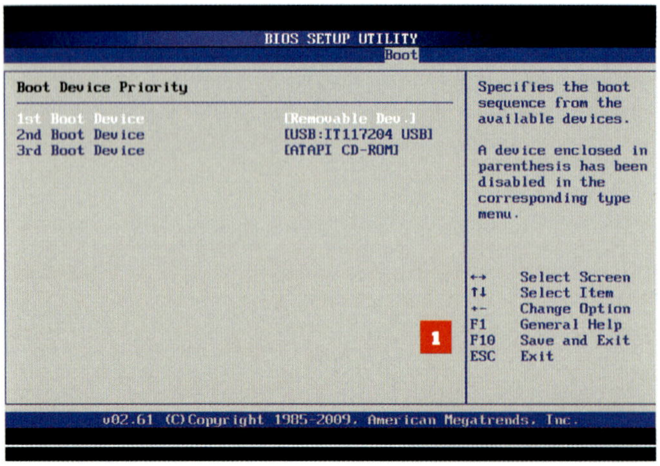

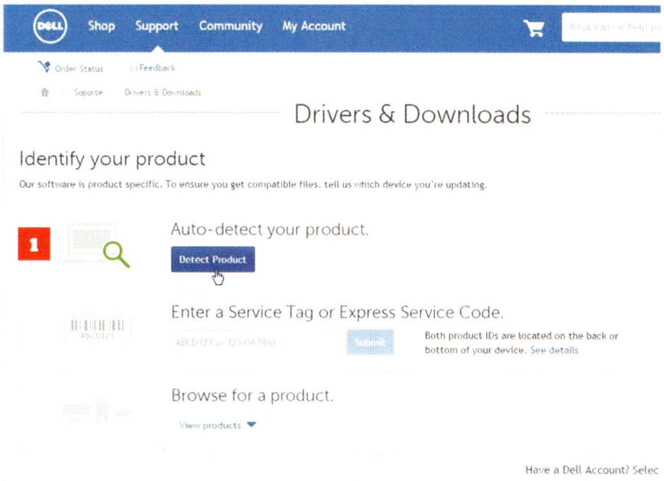

STEP 8 If you're mostly going to use the drive on a single PC, we recommend downloading and installing any necessary drivers for it by visiting the manufacturer's website and searching for the appropriate model **1**. All drivers will be installed as normal and saved to the USB drive.

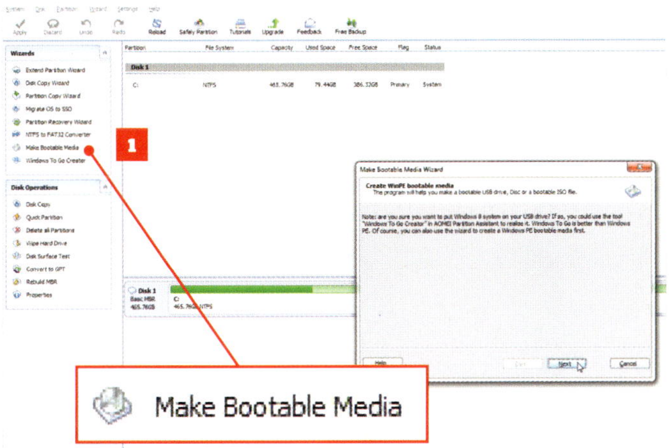

STEP 9 AOMEI Partition Wizard also lets you create a bootable Windows PE drive, which is invaluable if you need to rescue files from your hard drive when Windows won't start. To do this, insert an empty USB drive and click Make Bootable Media **1** in the Wizards sidebar.

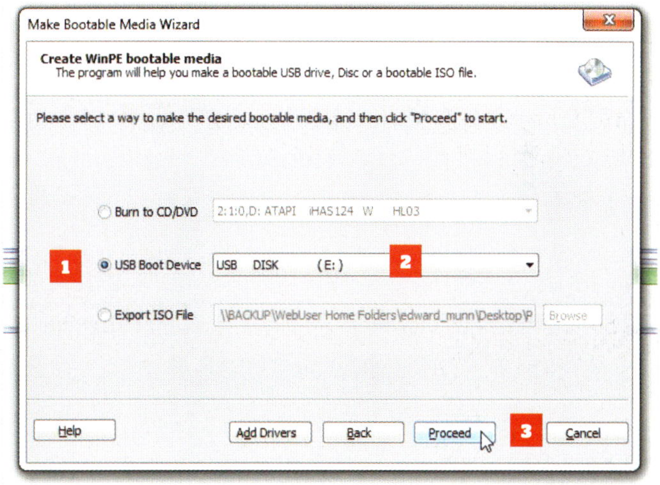

STEP 10 From the pop-up screen, click Next, select USB Boot Device **1** and choose the drive on which you want to install Windows PE **2**. Click Proceed **3** and, once the wizard has finished, you can boot from the USB drive to run a light version of the AOMEI Partition Assistant.

Expert Tip

To create a Windows To Go bootable drive with AOMEI Partition Assistant, you need a USB drive with a capacity of at least 13GB. However, we found the tool extremely slow when we used a 16GB flash drive (indicating it would take more than 24 hours to complete!), so we recommend using a larger drive. With a 1TB WD My Passport Slim, the same process only took about 10 minutes.

Edit PDFs in Windows 10

Time required: 20 minutes

Adobe Reader is the software most people use to view PDFs, but it's bulky and lacks editing tools. A good, free alternative is Xodo. It offers a range of platforms, including a web app (which works on any device and doesn't need installing), a browser add-on for Chrome (works in any version of Windows), and mobile apps for iOS and Android. Here we're using Xodo's excellent Windows 10 Desktop app, which you can download for free from the Windows Store.

STEP 1 Go to the Windows Store and search for Xodo, then click 'Xodo PDF Reader & Editor' and click the 'Get the app' button. The app will download and you can access it by typing xodo in the search box. Right-click Xodo and pin it to your Start menu for easy access. When it's loaded, click the hamburger button **1**, you can choose to Browse existing PDFs **2** select from Recent Documents **3** or create a new document, either from a blank file or a photo. For now, click Browse and open any PDF file to test out Xodo's features.

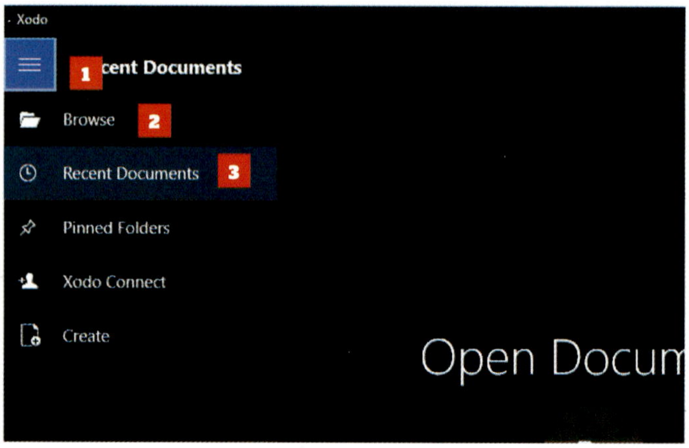

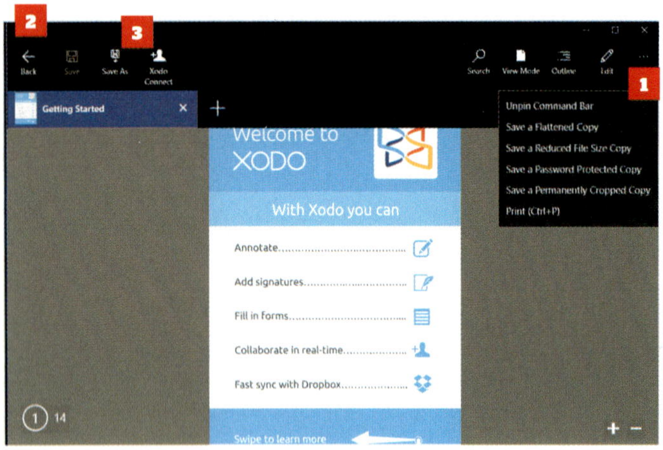

STEP 2 Click the Menu (three dots) button **1** to access Print and Share tools, and right-click anywhere on the screen to reveal the command options. The Back arrow **2** takes you back to the screen in Step 1, and there are options to save changes and collaborate **3**. On the right you'll see options to Search, change the View Mode, see an Outline and Edit.

STEP 3 Right-click the screen and click the Edit button. A selection of editing tools will appear at the top of the screen. Whenever you make changes you'll be prompted to save them as a new file. You can't overwrite an original document, so click Save As. You can add annotations (as speech balloons) **1**, make style changes to the text **2**, add your own signature **3**, insert new text **4** or add a variety of shapes and freehand drawings **5**. Click the cross to close the Edit bar.

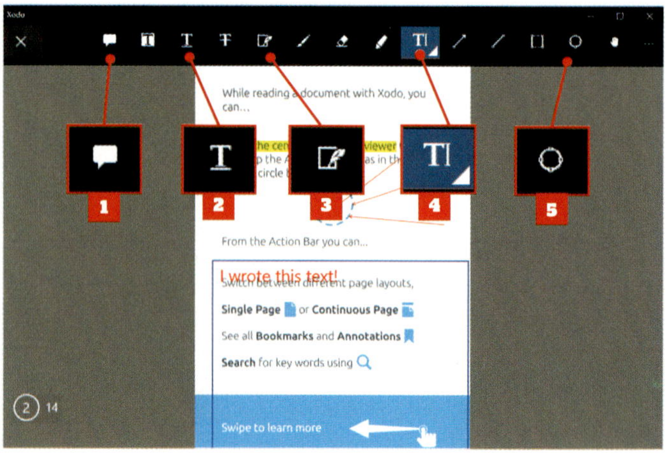

STEP 4 Assuming a PDF has been set up correctly, you can use Xodo to fill it out. Click a text box 1 and type the text you want. Click anywhere outside the box, and your text will be saved. You can also enter answers by clicking option buttons 2 and dropdown menus 3, and insert your signature 4.

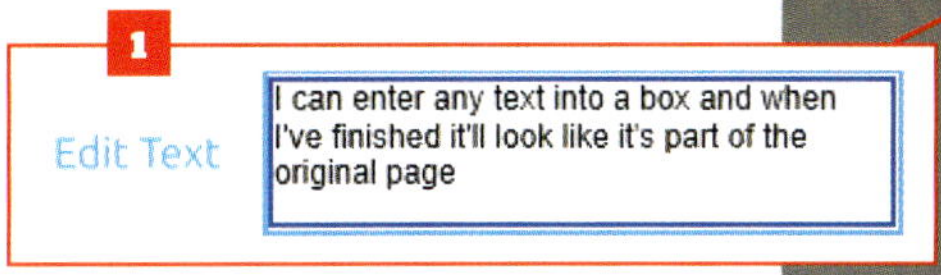

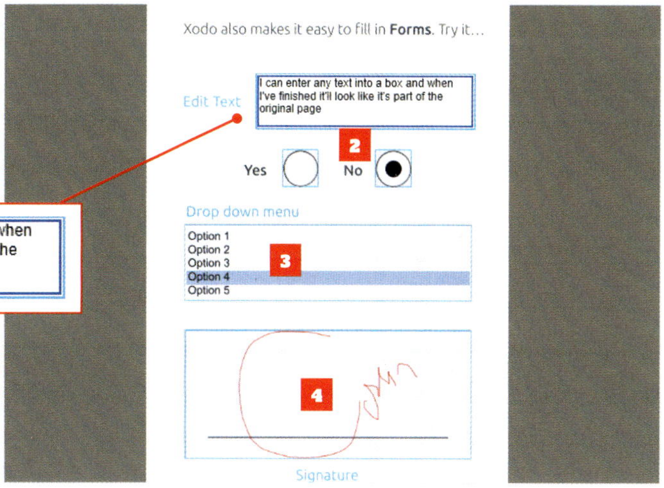

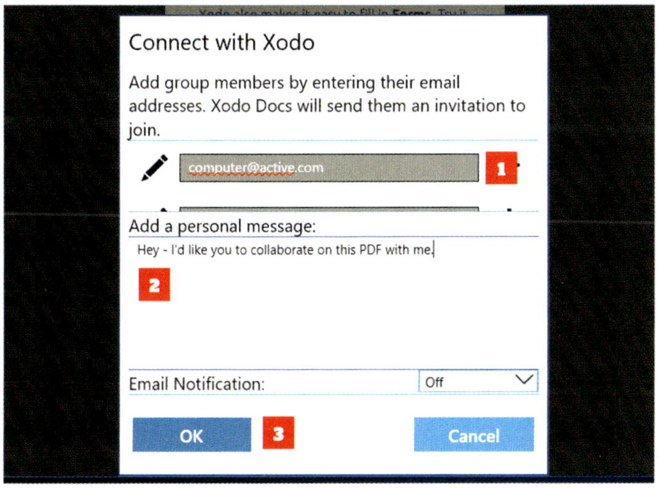

STEP 5 To collaborate on a PDF with other people click Xodo Connect at the top. Your collaborators can work via the web interface without having to sign in. Xodo will ask you for your name and email address the first time you do click Xodo Connect, then you'll need to enter the email addresses of your collaborators 1. Type a message if you like 2, then click OK 3. They'll receive an email with a web link to the PDF. To view the changes they make you need to view the PDF online. To do this, right-click the screen, select Xodo Connect and choose the file you're sharing. You may need to right-click again and select 'Open in Web Browser' – this will open the document in the web app.

STEP 6 To create a new PDF from scratch, click the back arrow to return to the first screen (see Step 1). Click the hamburger icon, then click Create and choose Blank Document. Give the document a name 1, select its print size 2, the orientation 3 and the number of pages 4. Click the Create PDF button 5 and you'll see a blank page. You can use the editing tools outlined in Step 3 to create your PDF.

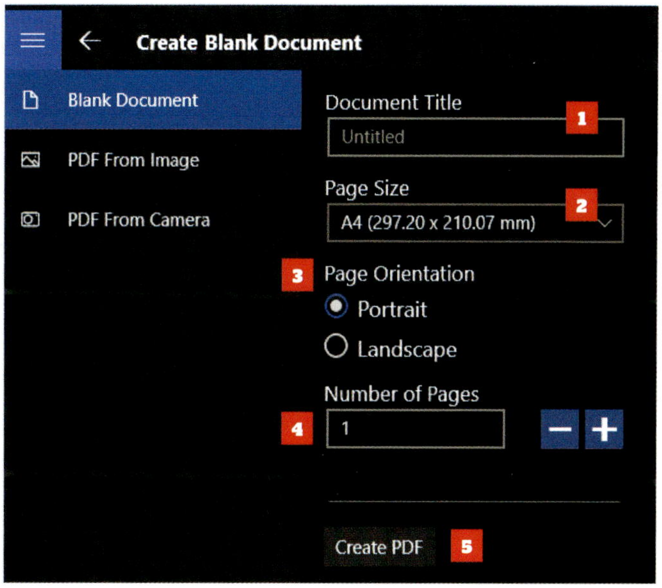

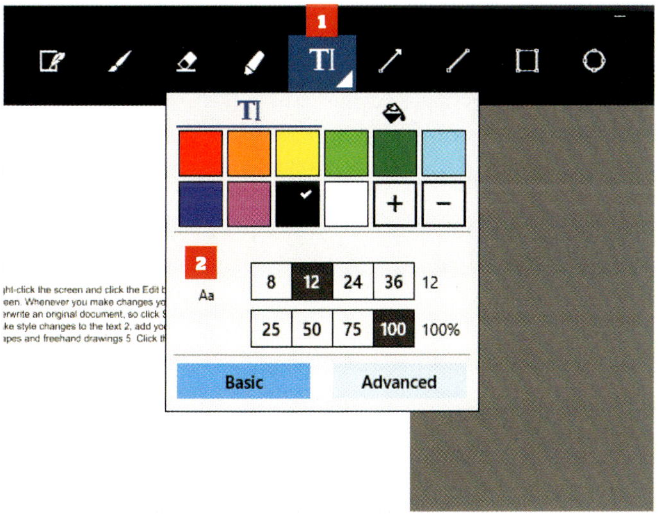

STEP 7 The easiest way to add text and images to a new PDF is to cut and paste them from other programs. To do this, find the text or image you want to include and copy it by selecting it and pressing Ctrl+C. Return to your PDF and click the text-cursor button 1, choose your font size and colour 2, then click on the document where you want the top-left corner of the pasted section to sit. Press Ctrl+V to paste your copied content into the PDF.

Master Windows 10's right-click menu

We show you some new tricks for customising your Windows right-click 'context' menu

Turbo-charge your right-click menu

When you right-click a file or folder, a menu of useful options pops up. FileMenu Tools (www.snipca.com/21257) gives this 'context' menu a massive power boost, adding over 30 useful commands such as Run With Parameters, Copy To, Move To, Copy Name, Copy Path, Attributes, Delete Locked File, Copy Content and many more. They all appear on the FileMenu Tools sub-menu.

Download the portable version of FileMenu Tools to avoid adware, run it and save it to the Downloads folder. Open the folder and double-click Register FileMenu Tools. Right-click any file and explore the new menu. Run the FileMenu Tools program to view the commands, modify them or add your own, though you should only try the latter option if you're an expert. The Help menu provides individual descriptions of all the commands.

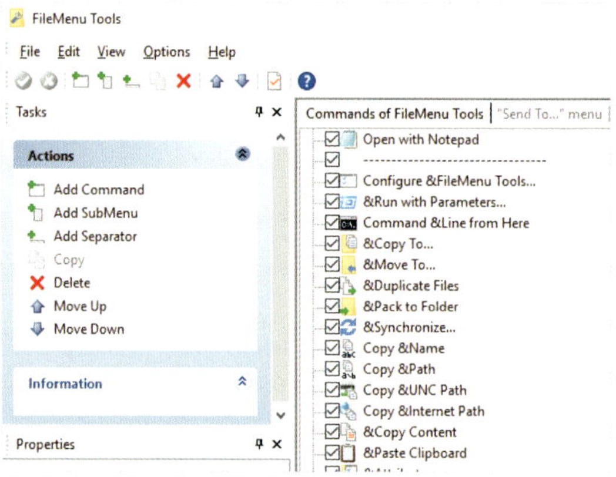

Add, remove and clean up right-click options

Easy Context Menu (bit.ly/easy381) is one of the best editors and clean-up tools for the right-click menu that we've found. It's a brilliant free tool that adds many useful commands to the right-click menu on the Desktop and in Explorer windows. It offers different sets of commands that depend on the object that is right-clicked, including the Desktop, computer, drives, folders, files and executable files.

Unzip the download and run EcMenu (for 32-bit versions of Windows) or EcMenu_x64 (for 64-bit versions). It displays a long list of commands that are grouped together. Show or hide commands by clicking the plus or minus boxes, and use the tick boxes to select the commands you want. Click the first icon in the toolbar to apply the changes. Most of the commands are obvious, such as Delete Temporary Files, Log Off, Defrag and Permanently Delete. If you want to put everything back as it was, click the second icon in the toolbar to uninstall everything.

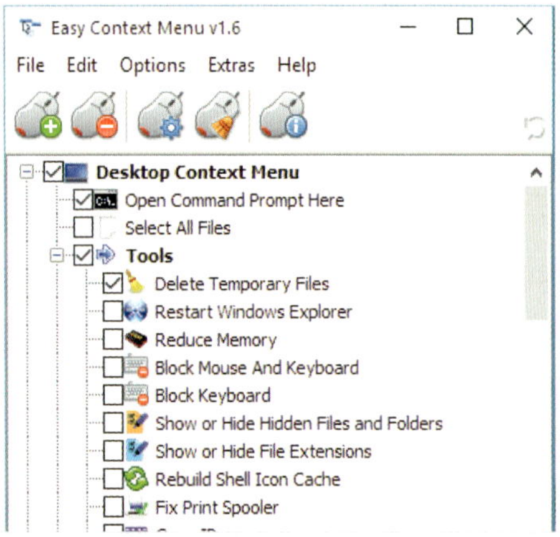

▲ Add lots of useful commands to the right-click menu with easy context menu

There is an extra tool, called the ContextMenu Cleaner, which can be used to clean the right-click menu. Click the fourth toolbar button to see a simple list of right-click menu items, then use the tick boxes to make menu items active or inactive. Select one or more items and use the buttons on the left to enable, disable or delete them. Click 'Jump to registry key' to open the Registry Editor and show the item's key and values.

View shell extensions

When software is installed into Windows, it can add its own extra items to the right-click menu. For example, anti-virus software often adds a 'Scan this' option to the menu when you right-click a file. Many other programs also add extra items, which can make the menu grow significantly and become unwieldy.

These extras are often called shell extensions and the free tool ShellExView (search for 'shellexview' at nirsoft.net) lets you view, enable or disable them. The program doesn't need installing, so just unzip it and double-click the program. After a few seconds, it displays a very long list of items. Go to the Options menu and select Hide All Microsoft Extensions. This hides the ones built into Windows, which will make the list shorter and more manageable.

Right-click an item to bring up a menu with options to enable or disable it. This can be used to remove troublesome items or to tidy up a long right-click menu. Select Properties to view useful information about the menu item, such as the developer, product name, filename, and so on.

Customise the 'Send to' menu

Right-click a file on the desktop or in an Explorer window and you'll see a 'Send to' menu option. Hover your mouse over it and you'll see items including 'Compressed (zipped) folder', Desktop and Documents. Send To Toys (bit.ly/send381) lets you modify the 'Send to' menu and adds a number of useful extras.

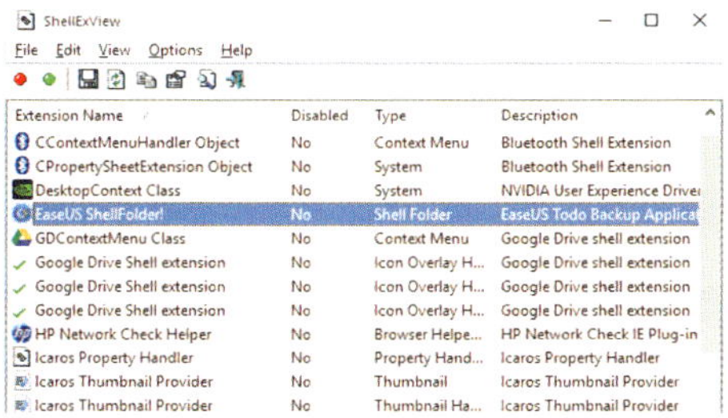

▲ Use ShellExView to enable or disable right-click items added by programs

Download and run the program. During installation, you can choose which items to add. All the options are ticked by default, and it's fine to leave it like this while you experiment with the tool. In the configuration window that appears, you'll be able to customise some of the commands. For example, in the Folder option, you can select the Folder tab and choose a destination for your files. The 'Clipboard (as content)' option copies the contents of a file, such as a document, to the clipboard, and the 'Clipboard (as name)' item copies the filename and path to the clipboard. Recycle Bin deletes a file; Folder copies or moves it to your last folder or whatever folder you specify; and Run adds it to the Run window.

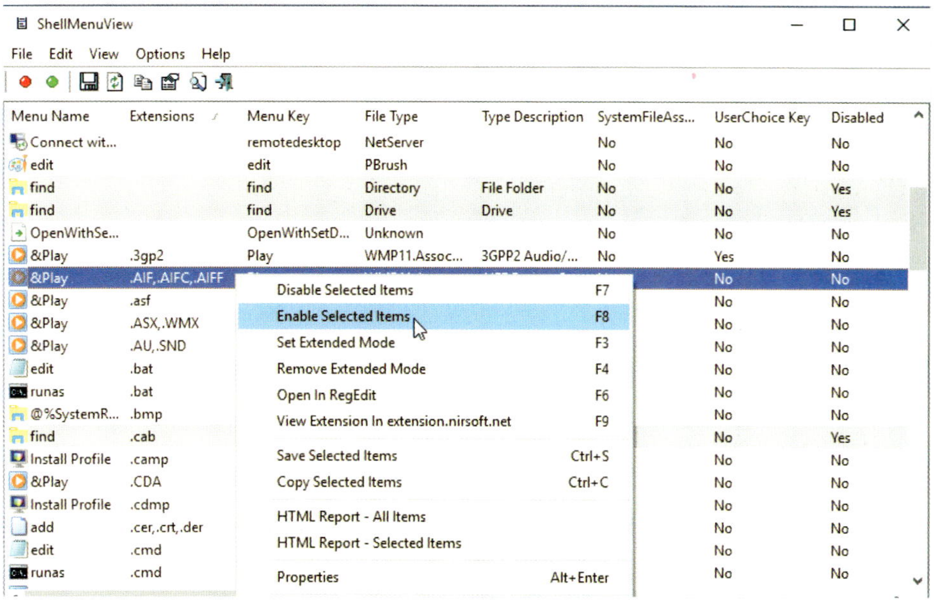

▲ Use ShellMenuView to enable or disable commands on the right-click menu

Add any program to your right-click menu

Have you ever wished it was easier to launch your favourite programs on your PC? Instead of hunting around in the Start menu, you can put the programs you use regularly on the right-click menu, where they can be accessed with two clicks. And it only takes a few Registry tweaks.

Press Windows+R to open the Run box and type regedit then Enter. The Registry Editor opens. In the left-hand pane, expand the keys and select: HKEY_CLASSES_ROOT\directory\background\shell.

Right-click it and select New, Key. When asked to name it, give it the name of the program you want to add to the right-click menu. For example, name it WordPad.

Right-click the key you just made and select New, Key. Call this one command. Select it and, on the right, double-click '(Default)'. The full path to the program must be typed in quotes. There is an easy way to do this using Explorer.

Find the program, such as Write.exe in the C:\Windows folder, hold down Shift and right-click it. Select 'Copy as path', switch back to the Registry Editor and press Ctrl+V to paste it into the (Default) value. Close the Registry Editor and right-click an empty part of the desktop or an Explorer window to see the new menu item that you've added. Click it to run the program.

Manage shell menus

ShellMenuView (search for 'shellmenuview' at nirsoft.net) is a small tool that lets you view, enable or disable items on the right-click menu. It doesn't need installing – just unzip the file and double-click the program to run it. It produces a very long list of items that look confusing at first, because it contains multiple entries for some items, such as Edit and Open. The key to distinguishing them is to look at the Extension column. When you right-click a .docx file in Explorer, the entry listed in ShellMenuView for .doc files is used, but if you right-click a .xlsx file, the entry for .xlsx files is used.

Right-click items in ShellMenuView and select Properties to see which program will open a particular file type. Right-click an item and select Disable to remove it from Explorer's right-click menus or select Enable to add it again. You should only disable items if they don't work, for example, because the software has been uninstalled.

DIY context menus

One final tool that's worth looking at is Right-click Context Menu Adder (bit.ly/rcma381), which lets you create right-click menu items that will run a program, go to a folder, open a web address in a browser or access any type of file. The tool downloads as a .rar file and you will need to use 7-zip (7-zip.org) to extract it from the archive.

Access all Windows 10's settings in one place

Time required: 20 minutes

It's easy to get lost in Windows 10, particularly when you're trying to configure your PC's settings for optimum performance. With tools split across the Settings window and the Control Panel, it's tricky enough to even know where to look. And the more complex settings sometimes need Registry access to work properly.

Ultimate Windows Tweaker 4 (UWT) solves this problem by bringing over 200 tweaks into one handy interface. It's portable, so you don't have to install it, and it takes up just 495KB of hard drive space. Download it from bit.ly/tweaker381, open the Zip file and copy the enclosed folder to a safe place, such as the Program Files folder. The program needs to run in administrator mode (which it will do automatically) and it will create a restore point for you before you start.

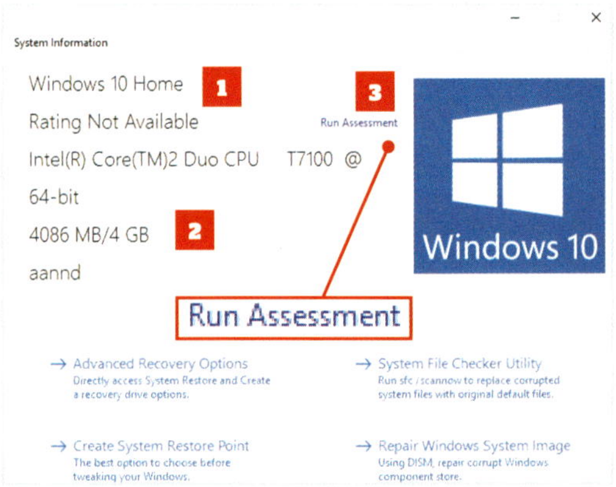

STEP 1 The main System Information screen displays information about your PC, including the version of Windows you're running **1** and the amount of installed memory **2**. You can test your PC using the Windows Experience Index (this isn't in Windows 10). Click Run Assessment **3** to find your score.

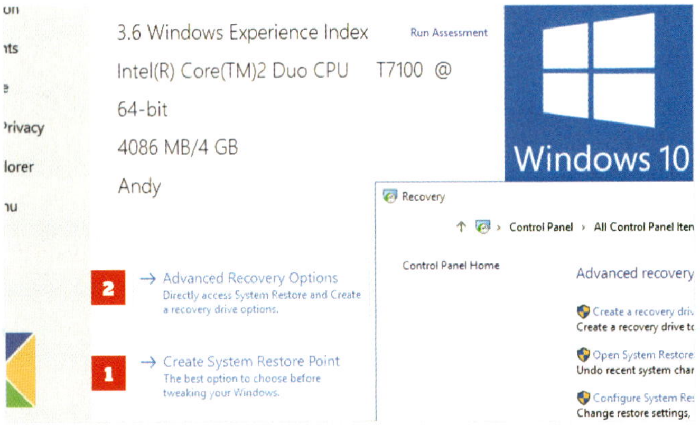

STEP 2 UWT creates a System Restore point the first time it runs but this is worth doing every time you launch the software. You can do it from the System Information page by clicking Create System Restore Point **1** or get more control by using the Advanced Recovery Options **2**.

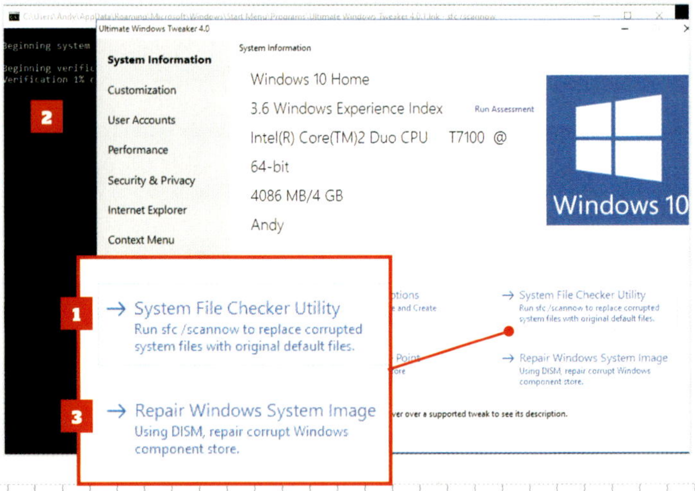

STEP 3 You can also run the System File Checker Utility **1** from here – normally you'd have to use the command prompt, which the software opens for you **2**. If it doesn't work, an extra tool can help fix problems with your Windows files, which you can run by clicking Repair Windows System Image **3**.

STEP 4 Click Security & Privacy 1, then select the Privacy tab 2. This has new settings for Windows 10. If you want to shut down Windows' communication with Microsoft, tick all the boxes. Otherwise, tick the ones that bother you or that you don't use, such as Cortana 3 or the Password Reveal Button 4.

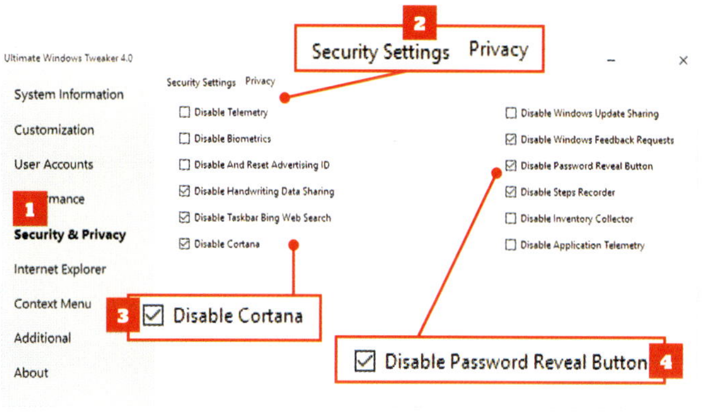

STEP 5 You can add some of Windows 10's new apps directly to the right-click context menu, so that they can be quickly launched from the desktop. Select Context Menu 1, then go to the Modern Apps tab 2. Tick any apps you want to access and click the Apply button 3.

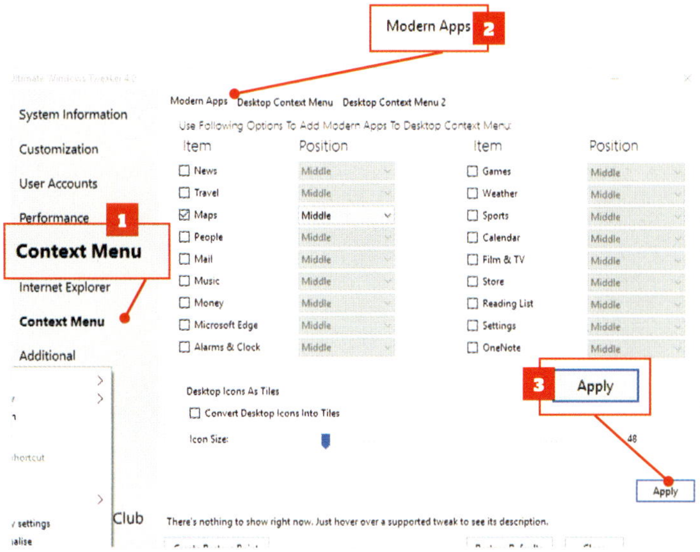

STEP 6 Select the Desktop Context Menu 2 tab 1. A new Drives section lets you add shortcuts to individual drives to your right-click menu. Choose the drive and its position on the menu, then click Add 2. Click Apply at the bottom of the page. To remove a drive, select it again and click Remove 3.

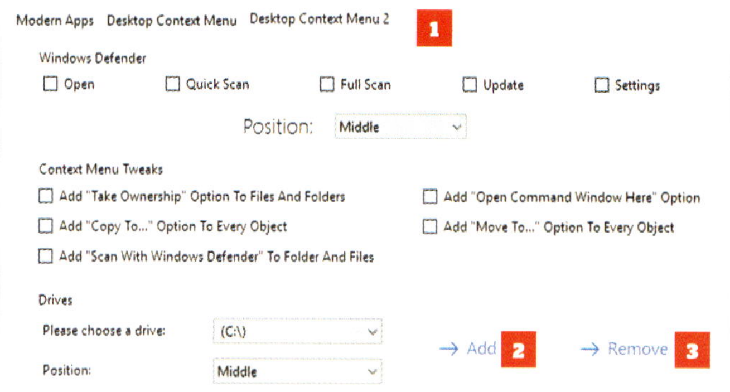

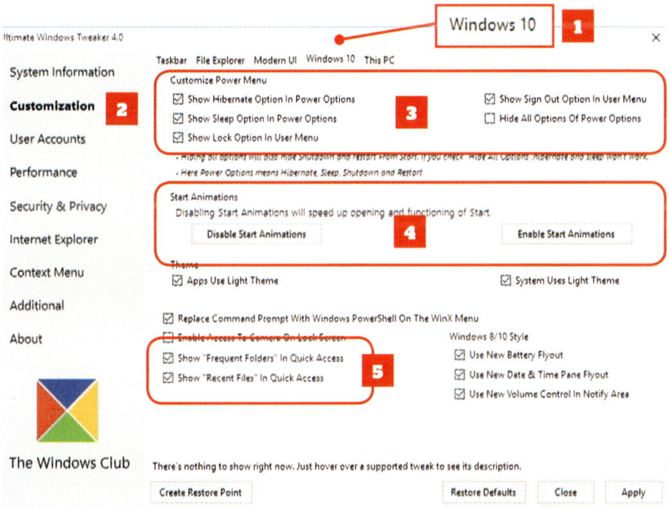

STEP 7 There's a new Windows 10 tab 1 in the Customization section 2. You can make changes to the Power Menu 3, remove animations from the Start menu 4 (to speed it up), and tweak the items that appear in the Quick Access section of Explorer 5.

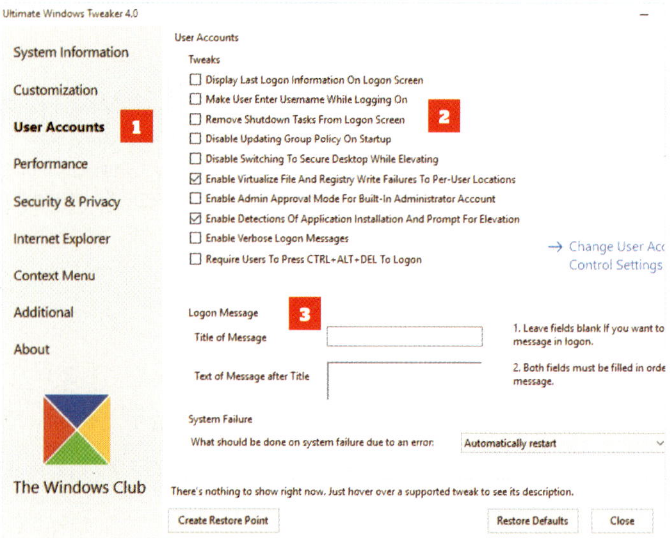

STEP 8 The User Accounts section **1** contains tools you can use to change the logon screen, where you select which user account to load. The list of Tweaks **2** lets you set options, such as forcing users to type in their names for added security, and you can add a message to the logon screen **3**.

STEP 9 The Additional section **1** is worth taking a look at. You can change how the icons display in the Notification Area **2**, adjust the width of scroll bars **3**, and make changes to hide your PC and its files from your local network **4**.

STEP 10 If you like to regularly tweak your settings, look under the Ultimate Windows Tweaker Options and tick Automatically Start When Windows Starts **1**. Alternatively, add it to your right-click menu **2** to launch it from there. We've got more right-click tricks earlier in this chapter.

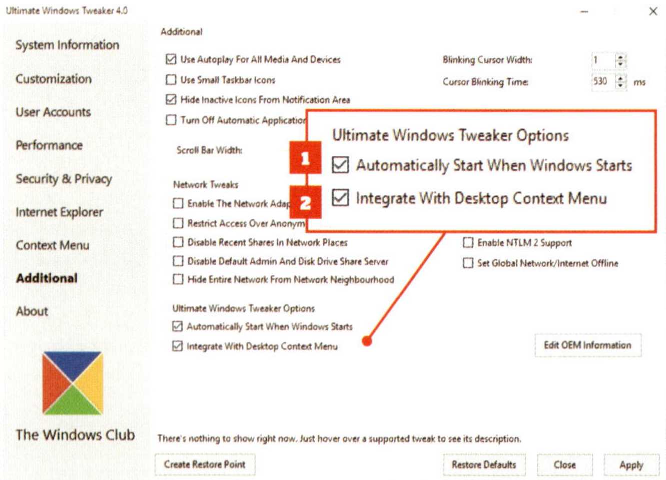

Expert Tip

If you're not sure what a tweak does, hover your mouse over it. The section at the bottom, which usually says 'There's nothing to show right now' should change into a tool tip explaining what the tweak will do, although it isn't available for all the tips. If something goes wrong, use your restore point to go back or click the Restore Defaults button, then click Apply.

Computer act!ve WebUser

READ ALL OF 2015's COMPUTERACTIVE & WEB USER ISSUES ON CD!

These easy-to-use CDs contain every issue of Computeractive and Web User published in 2015. They have a searchable index that gives you one-click access to thousands of tips, workshops, apps, product reviews, free programs, security updates and problems solved. You can also print and keep every article.

BUY THE

COMPUTERACTIVE 2015 CD

from Amazon at www.snipca.com/19124, or by typing 'computeractive cd' into Amazon's search box.

BUY THE

WEB USER 2015 CD

from Amazon at bit.ly/webusercd15 or by typing 'webuser cd' into Amazon's search box.

Use Windows 10 keyboard shortcuts

Mastering keyboard shortcuts adds an extra level of convenience when using your PC, and Windows 10 has more than ever. We reveal the best new key combinations

Keyboard shortcuts don't begin with Ctrl+C and end with Ctrl+V – those handy hotkeys for copying and pasting text. In fact, there are literally hundreds of key combinations in Windows, each designed to give your mouse arm a rest and let your fingers do the work.

Windows 10 introduces even more shortcuts to help you navigate your system, organise open windows and customise your desktop. Here, we reveal all the best shortcuts in Microsoft's new operating system to speed up everything you do on your PC.

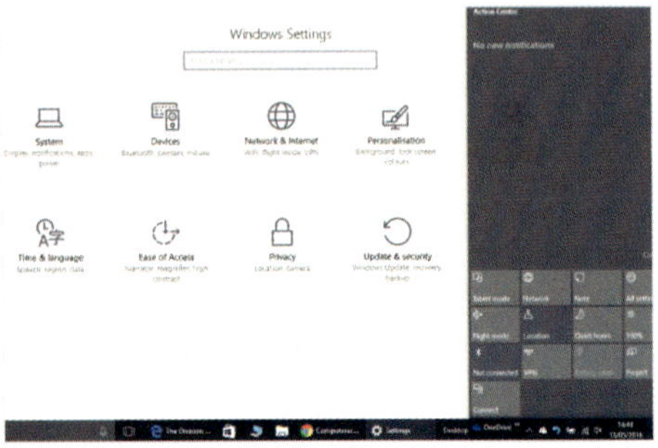

▲ Press ⊞+I to open Windows 10' s Settings app (left) or ⊞+A to open the Action Centre (right)

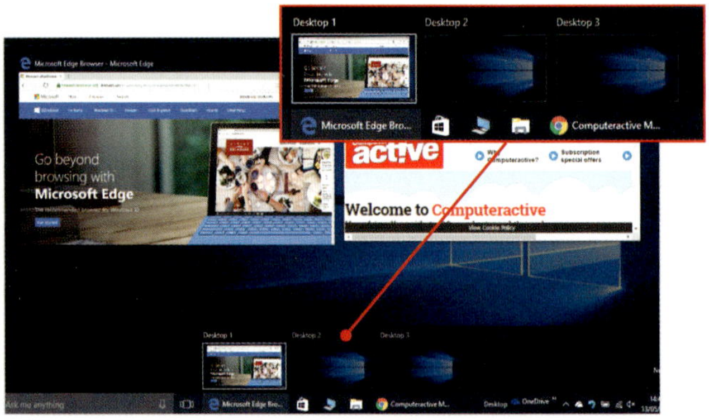

▲ Press ⊞+Tab to see all open virtual desktops

Access settings menus and apps

Each new version of Windows introduces new features, and Windows 10 has more than most. But did you know you can summon some of its most popular features (Action Centre, the Settings app, the Connect panel and Cortana) with simple key combinations?

The key you'll use most in the majority of the new shortcuts is the Windows key (⊞). For example, ⊞+A, opens the Action Centre, where you can access your notifications, while ⊞+I launches Windows 10's new Settings app (see screenshot below left). Then there's ⊞+K, which opens the Connect panel for when you want to link your PC to other devices on your network (such as your TV). Meanwhile, ⊞+X brings up the alternative Start menu (usually accessed by right-clicking the Start button), where you can launch the likes of Control Panel and Device Manager.

Press ⊞+E and a File Explorer window will open with the 'Quick access' tab selected, giving you instant access to anything you may have pinned to it. Try tapping ⊞+H and the Share Charm will slide into view. This handy Windows 8 throwback lets you share websites, videos and photos via email, Windows 10's Messaging app or social media.

Windows 10's accessibility settings can be triggered by shortcuts too. Struggling to make out what's on your screen? Pressing ⊞+Enter launches the Narrator app, which reads aloud any text displayed on screen. Alternatively, ⊞+U opens the 'Ease of Access' panel and ⊞+plus symbol will open the Magnifier. Still can't quite read something? Press ⊞+plus symbol again to zoom in even closer, ⊞+minus symbol to zoom out and ⊞+Escape to close the Magnifier.

Speed up Cortana

Microsoft's digital assistant Cortana isn't proving very popular, but a few handy shortcuts might convert some disbelievers. Pressing ⊞+C opens Cortana in 'listening mode'. This instantly activates your laptop's microphone so all you have to do is speak your search terms and reminder requests. Saying 'money news', for example, will search the internet for the latest financial headlines. Bear in mind, Cortana uses Windows 10's Edge browser instead of a browser of your choice. You might also notice the musical-note icon at the top right in listening mode. Clicking it triggers Cortana's music-recognition mode, which identifies any music playing nearby (much like the app Shazam).

If you don't relish the idea of talking to your computer, then try ⊞+S. This opens Cortana without activating the microphone, so you can search your computer or the internet by typing.

Organise open windows

Microsoft added a function to Windows 10 called Snap Assist that lets you arrange your open windows into four quadrants of equal size (see screenshot above right). Using your mouse involves grabbing an

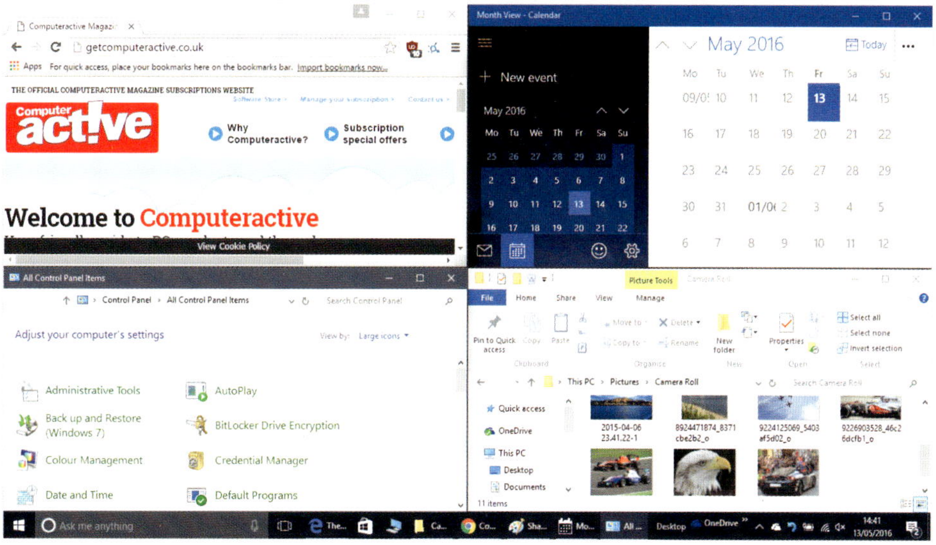

▲ 'Snap' a program or open folder and using the windows key along with your keyboard's cursor keys

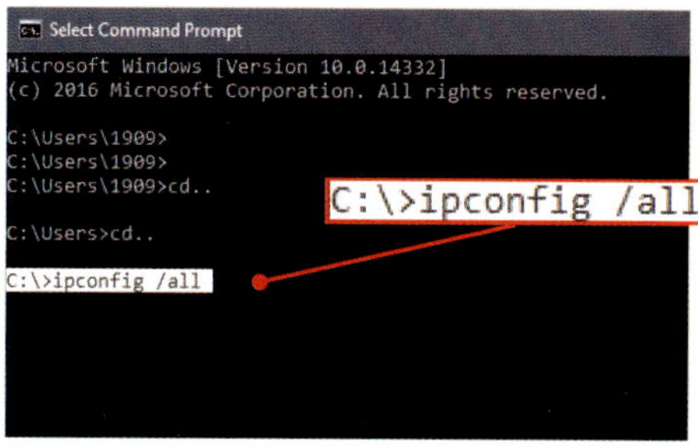

▲ Enable Mark Mode to select text you want to copy with your mouse

open window and dragging it to one of the corners of the screen to 'snap' it into position, but you can accomplish this with your keyboard.

To position a window simply hold down the Windows key and press the left or right arrow key to move it to one side or the other. Then, with the Windows key still held down, press the up or down arrow to move it into one of the four quadrants. You can also press ⊞+up arrow again to maximise it, or ⊞+down arrow to minimise it. Another clever shortcut is W+Shift+up arrow, which maximises the window while retaining its current width.

⊞+Tab opens Windows 10's new Task View, which gives you a neat view of every window you have open (just click one using your mouse to move to it). If you then have any notes pinned to your desktop that you want to quickly refer to, hold down ⊞+,(comma key) for a quick look at your desktop without minimising any open windows.

Customise virtual desktops

One of Windows 10's best new features is virtual desktops, which let you have open programs and windows across multiple workspaces. This is useful if you use your PC for home and work tasks and want to keep the two apart.

To create a new virtual desktop, hold down ⊞+Ctrl+D and your desktop will shift slightly to the right. Now press ⊞+Ctrl+left arrow (or right arrow) to cycle between virtual desktops. To quickly see a preview of any open virtual desktops, hold ⊞+Tab to open Task View – the thumbnails are shown along the bottom of the screen (see screenshot left). You can also hold ⊞+Ctrl+F4 to close the current virtual desktop and clone its contents to the next desktop in the sequence.

Command Prompt shortcuts

The Command Prompt has been overhauled in Windows 10 to make it much easier to use. The overhaul includes a number of new keyboard shortcuts you can use to edit text within the Command Prompt window.

Old shortcut favourites, Ctrl+C and Ctrl+V, now work exactly as they do in Word and – as anyone who has had to type a tortuously lengthy line of computer code into Command Prompt will tell you – the ability to copy and paste text is a huge time-saver.

Likewise, Ctrl+A selects all the text in Command Prompt's window (which is useful, for example, if you want to post a broken command line online to seek help). And Ctrl+F lets you search within Command Prompt for a specific word or phrase.

The Windows 10 Command Prompt also has a new feature, called Mark Mode (activated by pressing Ctrl+M). Mark Mode lets you select text you want to copy by clicking and dragging with your mouse (see screenshot above). Or you can highlight text with a little more control using other shortcuts: Shift+left or right arrow selects one character at a time; Ctrl+Shift+left or right arrow selects text one word at a time; or Shift+Home or End selects one line at a time.

THE RETURN OF SOME OLD FRIENDS

Here are five more vintage Windows shortcuts that are as useful as ever when it comes to adding some much-needed convenience to your desktop...

⊞+1, ⊞+2, ⊞+3 and so on: launches the corresponding program shortcut in your taskbar (for example, ⊞+1 would open Edge in the screenshot below)

⊞+D: minimises all open windows and returns you to the desktop (tapping the same combination again will re-open all closed windows).

⊞+L: locks the PC so it requires a password to be unlocked (assuming you have a password set up on your computer).

⊞+R: displays the Run dialogue box from where you can search for and open programs, settings menus, files and websites.

⊞+Home: minimises all non-active windows, but leaves the one you're currently using open. Press ⊞+Home again to undo the process.

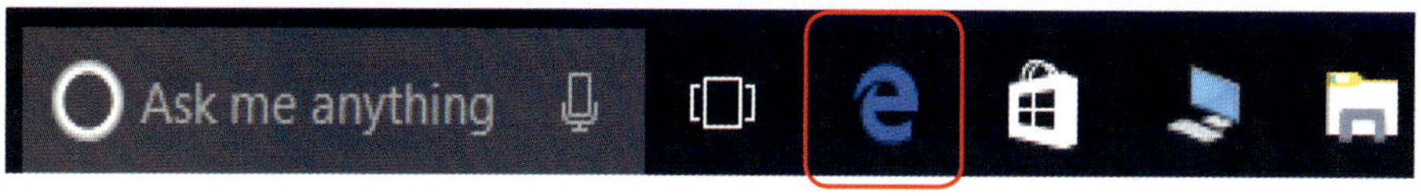

Clone a hard drive in Windows 10

Time required: 1 hour

Looking for a great way to back up your data? Then you should try AOMEI Partition Assistant – a fantastic free program that lets you clone all the partitions on your PC's hard drive, and more besides. You can then copy this to another partition on your PC or to an external drive. The program also makes it easy to move data to a new PC and lets you create a bootable drive so that you can rescue your PC even if Windows 10 won't start.

STEP 1 To install AOMEI Partition Assistant Standard Edition (APASE), go to www.snipca.com/19442 and click the green Download Freeware button. Click the downloaded setup file, Run, Yes, then OK. Now click Next, accept the agreement, then keep clicking Next until you see an option to click Install. Click Install, then Finish to run the program. You'll see a breakdown of all your PC's hard drives (including any external ones you've connected) and their partitions. Disk 1 **1** represents partitions on your PC and Disk 2 **2** represents external ones.

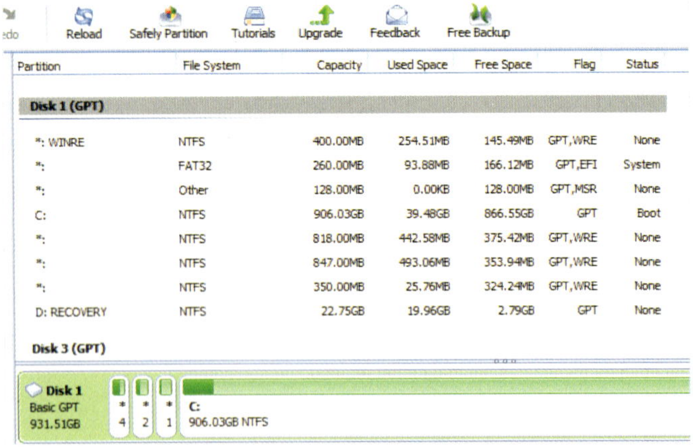

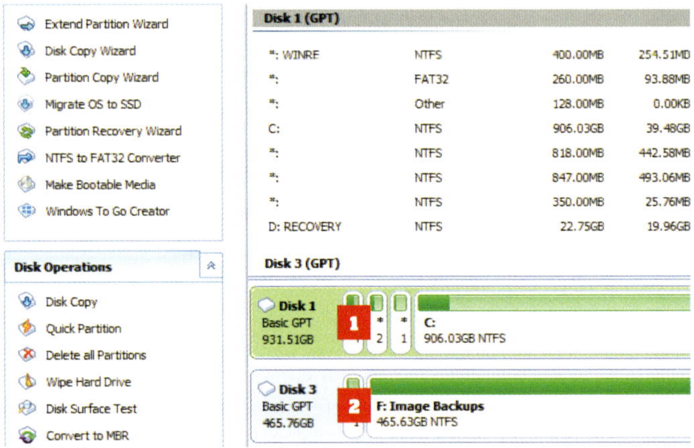

STEP 2 Any partitions listed as Primary contain data. Before cloning any of these, you need to create a new empty partition by borrowing unallocated (free) space from one of your Primary partitions. You can then clone all the data from whichever partition you want to this new one. Before creating this new partition, check in the Free Space column to see which partition has the most unallocated space. For this example, we'll create a new partition using around 150GB of the 866.55GB of free space on our C: partition.

STEP 3 Right-click the C: partition, then click Resize Partition. Now click and drag the slider to the left **1** until you see the amount of space you want **2**, then click OK **3**. After doing this, you'll see a new Unallocated partition added to your hard drive within APASE. This partition will be represented by an asterisk (*), not a letter. You won't be able to access it at this point because it hasn't been created yet.

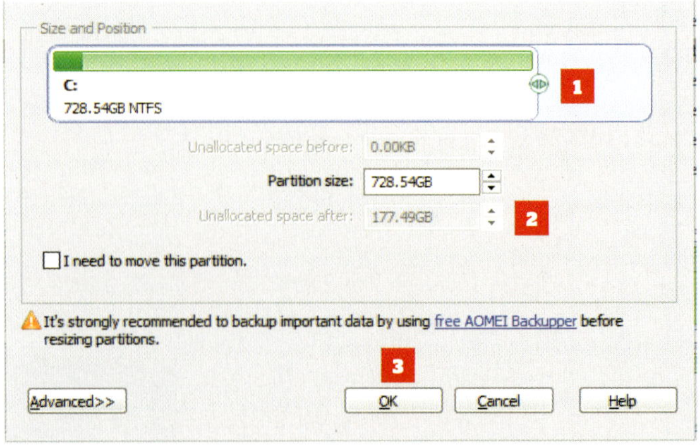

STEP 4 Now right-click the partition on your PC that you want to clone 1, then click Copy Partition. You'll see two options. Copy Partition Quickly 2 is faster because it only copies data to the new partition. 'Sector-by-Sector Copy' 3 copies the entire partition (including any unused space) and therefore takes longer. Select the method you want, then click Next 4. Now select your new, unallocated partition (with an asterisk), then click Next.

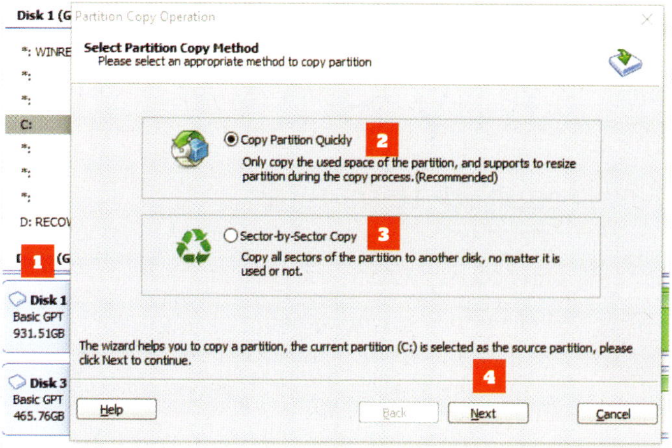

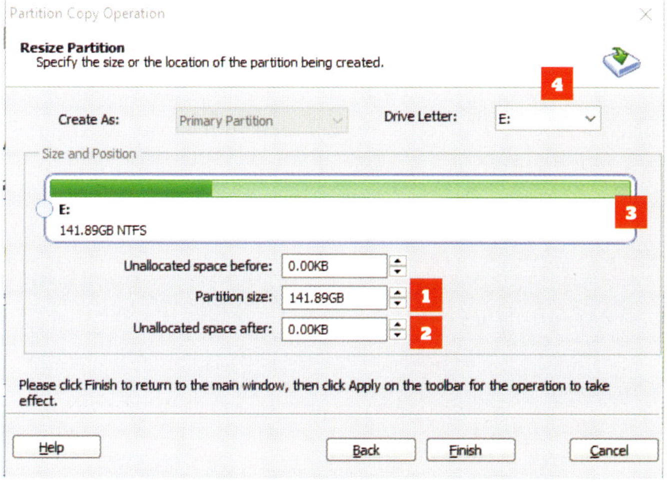

STEP 5 You'll see a breakdown of your new partition size 1 and how much unallocated space you'll have after cloning your selected partition to it 2. Drag the partition size slider to the extreme right 3. Use the Drive Letter dropdown menu to assign a letter to your new partition 4, then click Finish. You'll be taken to the main screen of APASE. Click Apply at the top left, then Proceed, and Yes to begin cloning. Click OK when that's done.

STEP 6 Another useful APASE feature is the ability to create a bootable rescue disc. This can be a life-saver if your PC crashes or gets corrupted and you can't boot it. If this happens, you can then boot your PC using the rescue disc, retrieve any precious data and reformat your PC. To create a bootable disc, you'll need a blank CD, DVD or USB stick. Insert your chosen media into your PC, click Make Bootable Media , then click Next. Now select the device you inserted 1, then click Proceed 2. After that's done, click Finish. Now whenever your PC fails to boot, insert your bootable disc/USB stick.

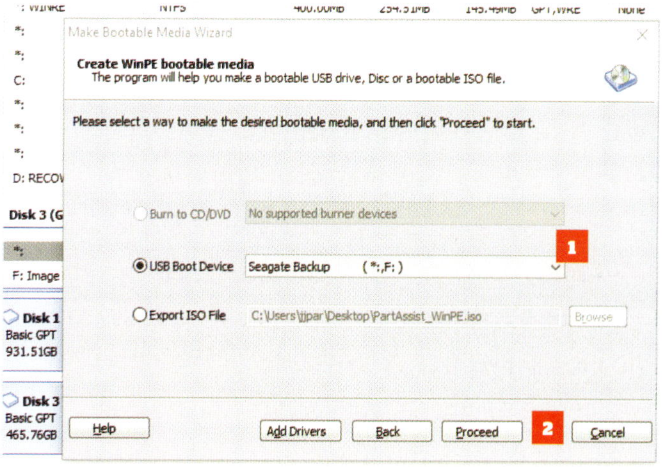

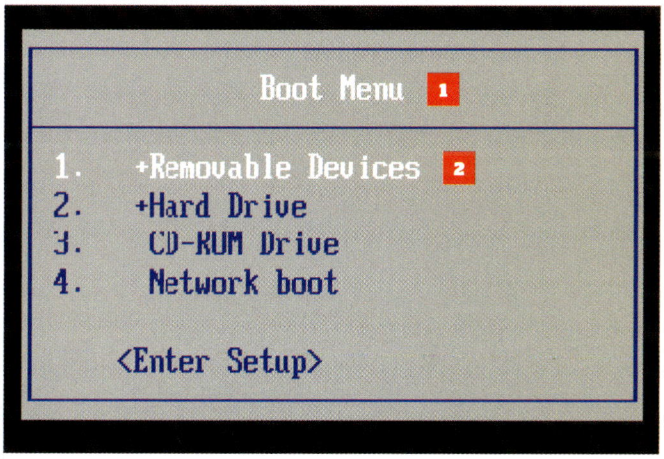

STEP 7 Switch on your PC, then look for the screen that tells you which key to repeatedly press to enter your PC's BIOS (it's F2 or Del on most PCs) and press that key as your PC launches. Once in the BIOS, navigate to the 'Boot menu' 1 using the arrow keys. It's usually set to Hard Drive by default. Using the arrow and Enter keys, set it to CD-Rom Drive or Removable Devices (depending on what device you used) 2. Now exit the Boot menu and restart your PC. You'll now be able to boot into your PC and access your files.

Hack Windows 10's Registry in only a few clicks

Time required: 15 minutes

Windows 10 has some irritating qualities, particularly with regard to privacy and advertising. Some of these can easily be resolved from the Settings menu, but others are more complex and require you to make tweaks to the Registry. If you're not comfortable doing this, Win10 Wizard (free from bit.ly/wizard399) lets you tweak many of Windows 10's Registry settings from one, user-friendly interface, with only a few clicks. It has separate menus for privacy, security and location services, from which you can disable various features including targeted advertising, feedback notifications and app reminders. You can make changes to the OS's appearance by disabling tools such as the Battery Indicator and Action Centre. It also includes useful tools for scanning your PC for hardware-compatibility problems and reclaiming precious drive space.

STEP 1 On launch, Win10 Wizard shows any compatibility problems that may have cropped up since you upgraded. Click Device & App Compatibility **1** to review them. Drivers that have not successfully installed are listed under Drivers and removed applications are shown in the Applications drop-down menu.

STEP 2 Click Done to return to Win10 Wizard's main menu, then click Privacy to browse Windows 10's privacy settings. To stop Windows 10 showing you targeted ads, tick the box to 'Disable and reset Advertising ID and Info' **1**.

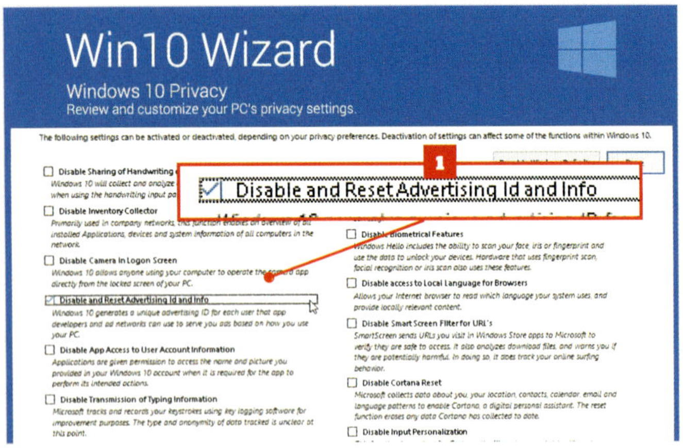

STEP 3 You can stop Microsoft tracking your keystrokes by ticking the box for 'Disable Transmission of Typing Information' **1**. If you find the Action Centre's notifications irritating, you can stop them by ticking the box for Disable App Notifications **2**.

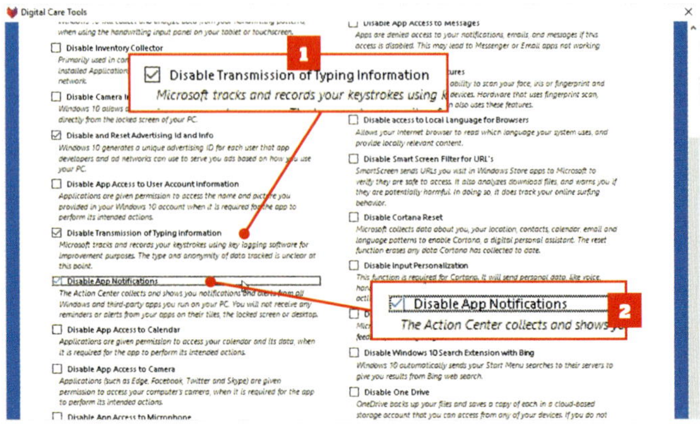

STEP 4 The SmartScreen tool tracks the URLs you click in Windows apps (along with some files you download) to make sure that they are safe. To disable it, tick the box to Disable Smart Screen Filter for URLs **1**.

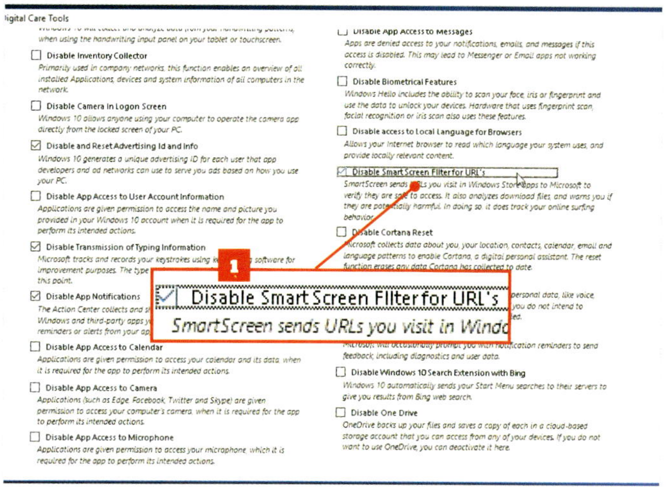

STEP 5 To stop Windows 10 asking for feedback with diagnostics and user data, tick Disable Feedback Reminders **1**. You can also disable Bing in the Start Menu **2** and turn off OneDrive **3**. Click Done and No (for the time being) when asked if you want to restart your PC now to implement the changes.

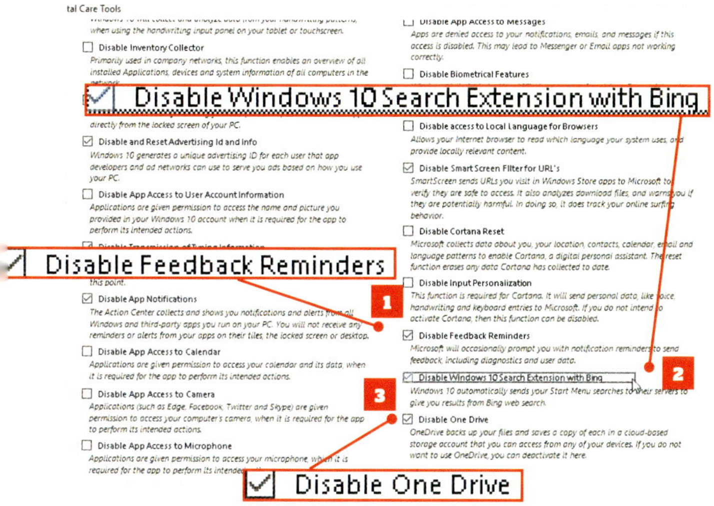

STEP 6 Click the Location Services button. To stop Windows 10 and its apps using your location, tick all the appropriate boxes **1**, then select Done **2**. Bear in mind that disabling these settings can affect some of Windows 10's functionality. If you find something isn't working, just switch it back on.

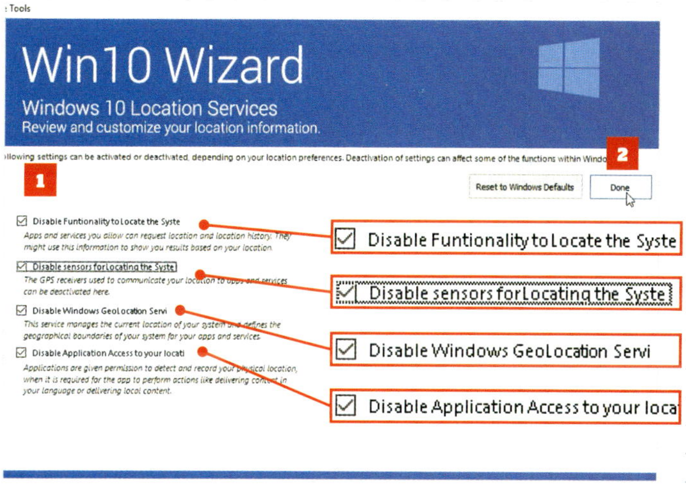

STEP 7 Windows 10 automatically shares information with Microsoft about how it is functioning. To disable this, open Win10 Wizard's Security menu and tick Disable Telemetry **1**. While you're here, you can also turn off Wifi Sense **2** – a tool that automatically connects you to available Wi-Fi networks.

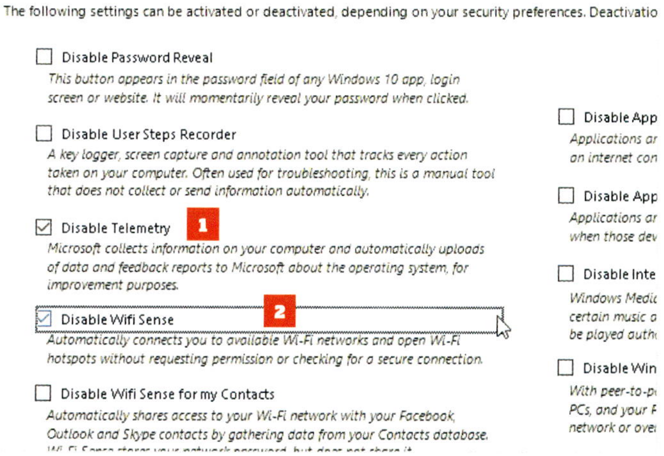

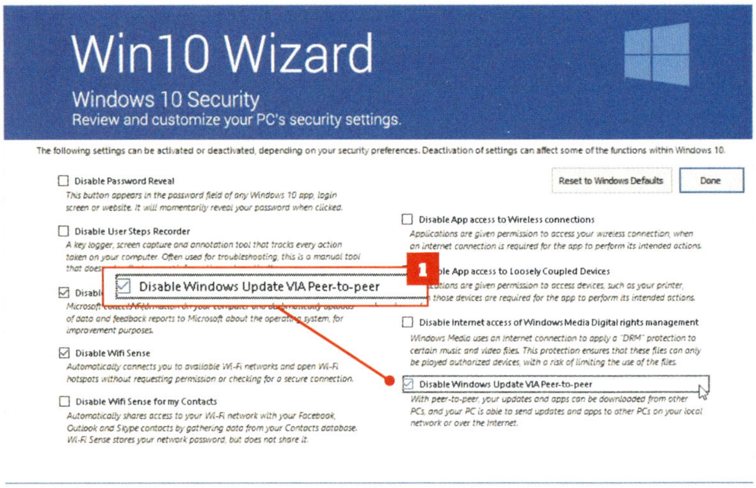

STEP 8 Windows 10 is set to share Windows Updates with other PCs on your local network (and over the internet). To deactivate this feature so you can only download updates directly from Microsoft's servers, tick the box for 'Disable Windows Update via Peer-to-Peer' **1**.

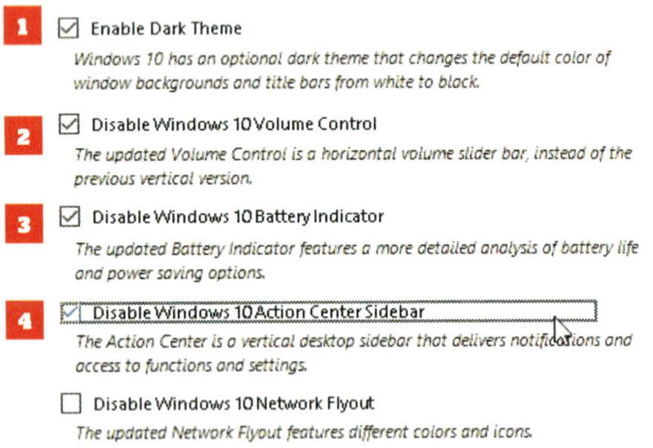

STEP 9 In Win10 Wizard's Themes menu, you can enable the dark theme **1** and deactivate features such as the Volume Control **2** and Battery Indicator **3**. You can also remove the Action Centre **4**. To implement your changes, click Done and select Yes when prompted to restart the computer.

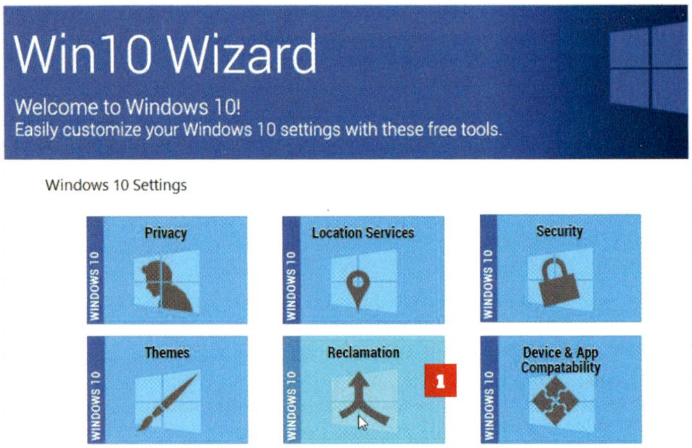

STEP 10 To reclaim hard-drive space lost by upgrading to Windows 10, click Reclamation **1**. Selecting 'Clean my System now' performs a clean-up scan that removes the option to roll back to Windows 7 or 8, so make sure you're happy with Windows 10 before activating it.

Expert Tip

If you change your mind about any of the tweaks you've made to Windows 10, you can undo them by simply unticking the boxes you've selected. If you've made a lot of changes that you now want to undo, there's a 'Reset to Windows Defaults' button in each section that you can use to make the process even quicker.

Become a Windows Insider

Time required: 1 hour

If you want to try out all the latest Windows 10 features before they're released, you could consider joining the Windows Insider Programme. Doing this provides you with access to preview builds of the OS that Microsoft, many of which include new tools and options. Be warned, though – pre-release software is often unstable, particularly for Insiders on the Fast ring (see step 3), so it's best not to install preview builds on your main PC. If you're a technology enthusiast, though, it's a fun to try out the latest Windows 10 features on a second PC – or even a virtual one.

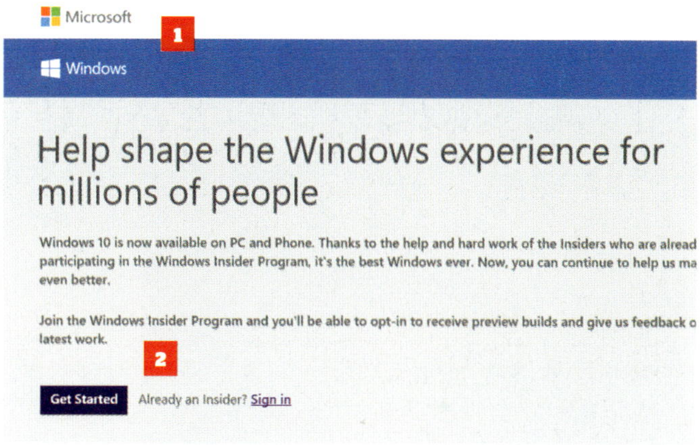

STEP 1 To join the Windows 10 Insider Program, open the Microsoft Edge browser on your PC, go to insider.windows.com **1**, click Get Started **2**, log in with your Microsoft account, then click Join and accept any prompts. You can now download and install the Windows Insider Preview build on your PC. To do that, go to Settings, click 'Update & security', select Windows Update at the top left then click the 'Advanced options' link at the bottom.

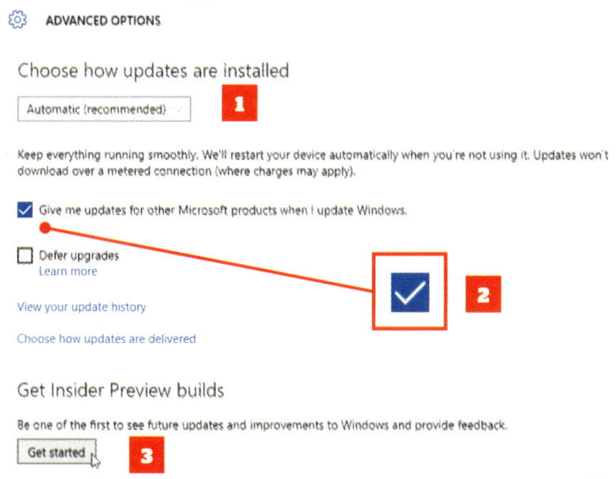

STEP 2 Ensure the drop-down menu at the top is set to 'Automatic (recommended)' **1**, then tick 'Give me updates for other Microsoft products when I update Windows' **2**. Depending on which version of Windows 10 you're running, either click 'Get started' **3** on this screen (shown), or if you've already installed the Anniversary Update and you see Windows Insider Programme on the left, click this, then click 'Get started'. In both cases, follow the remaining on-screen instructions and restart your PC when prompted.

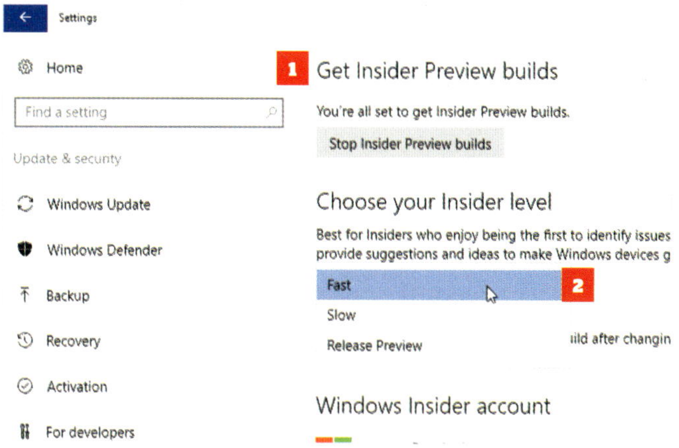

STEP 3 When your PC restarts, navigate back to 'Update & security' settings and either click the 'Advanced options' link or Windows Insider Programme on the left, depending on your version of Windows 10. Under 'Get Insider Preview builds' **1** use the dropdown menu **2** (or the slider in pre-Anniversary Update Windows 10) to choose your Insider level. The programme is comprised of three 'Rings'. Users on the Fast Ring get new features earliest, but these may be unstable and prone to crashes. Once any flaws at this stage are fixed, the features are released to users on the Slow Ring for further testing. After further refinement, they're released to users on the Release Preview Ring.

Chapter 5

Improve Windows 10

Make Microsoft's operating system faster, smoother and easier to use with our expert improvements

By its very nature, the latest version of Microsoft's OS is already much faster than Windows 7 and much easier to use than Windows 8, but it's possible to get even more from Windows 10, in terms of both boosting raw performance and making everyday tasks simpler and quicker. In this chapter, we'll be exploring ways you can optimise the OS for speed, as well as how you can increase your PC's performance by upgrading its hardware – adding a lightning-fast SSD, for example. We'll also examine ways you can streamline both the tasks you carry out on your PC and the OS itself.

IN THIS SECTION

Speed up tasks in Windows 10

We explain the best tweaks and speedy shortcuts to make Microsoft's operating system easier to use and get it working faster than ever

Windows 10 is built for speed. It's a lean, streamlined OS that starts up quickly and runs at a jaunty pace. Well that's the theory. In practice, chances are you've upgraded an older, slower PC, or you haven't got round to discovering Windows 10's brand new navigational shortcuts yet.

As in any version of Windows, you can improve its speed by uninstalling programs you don't use, disabling startup items you don't need and clearing out junk you never wanted in the first place. But Windows 10 also offers new settings and approaches to speed up familiar tasks. These will give you quicker access to your favourite files and programs, while drastically improving startup times, system performance and more besides.

Windows 10 doesn't always make these settings easy to find, meaning some serious digging is required to unlock the full potential of the OS. But don't worry – we've done the spadework for you.

So, whether you want to print photos quickly, access the most important settings in a flash, open programs faster, or speed up Windows 10 on an older PC, it's all explained here. Read on as we reveal 15 brilliant ways to speed up Microsoft's operating system, and give you before-and-after examples to show you what a difference each tip can make to Windows 10.

What you can do

- Uncover hidden ways to perform everyday tasks at lightning speed
- Optimise Windows 10's startup and overall performance
- Add shortcuts to the Start menu, taskbar and File Explorer
- Enable GodMode to access all your PC's settings in one place

FIVE-MINUTE FIXES

1 Access your favourite files and folders

THE SLOW WAY

Most of us have specific folders on our computers that we return to time after time. Maybe it's a specific folder of cherished photos, or a sub-folder within your Documents folder where you store important letters. Either way, if you laboriously click Start, File Explorer, and then navigate to the relevant folder every time you want to access the files it contains, you're wasting valuable time.

THE FAST WAY

In previous versions of Windows, you had the option of creating shortcuts for your frequently used folders by dragging them to your desktop. You can do this in Windows 10, but doing so for multiple items will soon clutter up your desktop. Windows 10 offers a much neater system called 'Quick access', which is the default view in File Explorer.

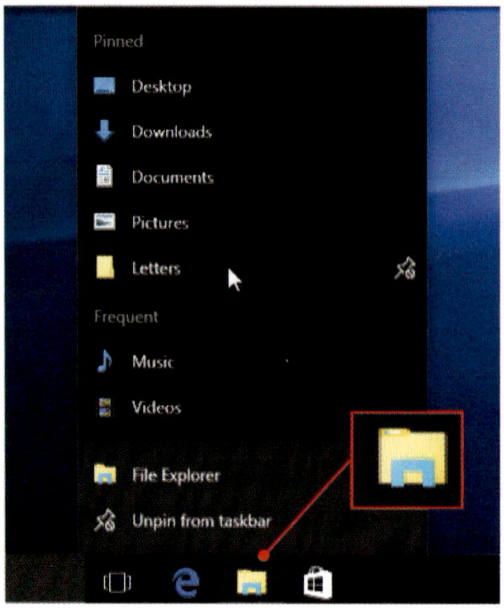

▲ Right-click File Explorer for 'Quick access' folders

Whenever you open an Explorer window 'Quick access' will automatically display shortcuts to any folders and files you've recently used. But you can customise it to display any folders you choose. Simply navigate to the relevant folder, right-click it and select 'Pin to Quick access'.

Better still, you can now bypass File Explorer altogether when opening your favourite folders. For example, if you've already pinned a folder called 'Letters' to 'Quick access', simply right-click the File Explorer icon on your taskbar and you'll see a shortcut to the folder listed in the Pinned section. Click this and you'll be taken straight there (see screenshot below left).

2 Disable notification sounds

THE SLOW WAY

Notifications are useful, but there are times – at night, for example – when you might not want to be disturbed. You could click Start, then click Settings, System, 'Notifications & actions', then switch off each individual option you require. Or you could use 'Quiet hours'.

THE FAST WAY

'Quiet hours' is a setting in Windows 10 that instantly silences all notifications. You can reach it via the 'Quick actions' panel at the bottom of the Action Centre. This is a collection of handy shortcuts that you access by clicking the speech-bubble icon to the right of your taskbar (see screenshot below). You'll see only four 'Quick action' icons by default, so

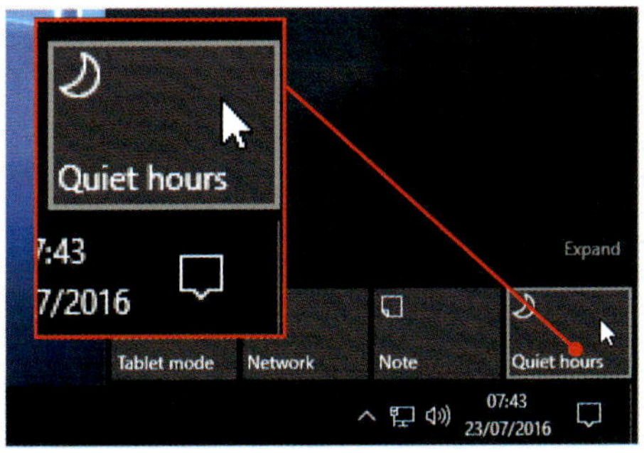

▲ 'Quiet hours' quickly silences notifications

click Expand if you don't see the 'Quiet hours' icon. And if that isn't quick enough for you, simply right-click the speech-bubble icon and select 'Turn on quiet hours'.

You can customise the 'Quick actions' panel to include other tasks. For example, it might be handy to have two-click access to Tablet mode if you're using a touchscreen device, or to Flight mode if you regularly need to disable or enable all wireless connections. To choose which four 'Quick actions' you want shown when you open the Action Centre, click Start, Settings, System, 'Notifications & actions', then select your preferred options.

3 Instantly zoom in on hard-to-read text

THE SLOW WAY

You'll need to click your way through

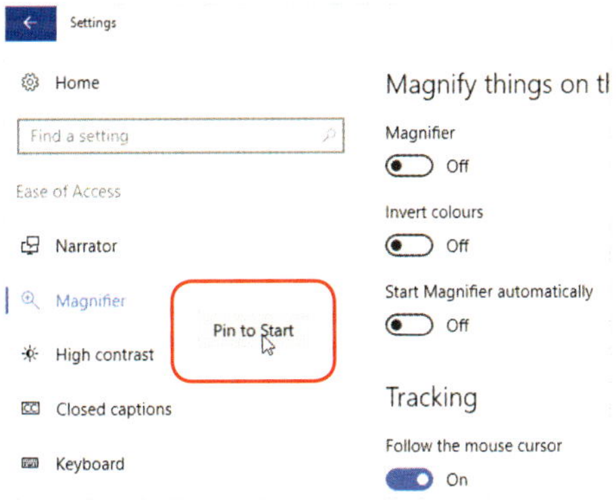

▲ Pin any setting to the Start menu with a right-click

Windows 10's Settings app to carry out many everyday tasks. For example, to switch on the Magnifier so you can zoom in on a piece of text, you'll need to click Start, Settings, Ease of Access, Magnifier, then click the switch to enable the tool. The Magnifier is something you'll probably only want switched on when you want to read small text, so wouldn't it be good if you could quickly switch it on and off without this rigmarole?

THE FAST WAY

Well, as it happens, Windows 10 lets you add any setting in the Settings app to the Start menu as a tile. To add the Magnifier to the Start menu, navigate to it in the Settings app (as described above), then right-click Magnifier in the left-hand column and select 'Pin to Start' (see screenshot left), then click Yes. The same method can be used to pin other settings.

4 Open programs faster every time

THE SLOW WAY

Looking for a program that begins with the letter 'W'? Such as Word 2016, for example? Well, it'll be lurking at the bottom of your alphabetically arranged Apps list. Unless you've added a shortcut tile to your Start menu (see previous tip), you'll need to click Start, 'All apps', then scroll through a lengthy list of all your installed programs to get to the one you want.

THE FAST WAY

Windows 10's 'All apps' list offers a clever, albeit hidden, way to navigate to a specific program quickly. Click Start, 'All apps', then click the letter 'A'. The list of programs changes to a grid of letters (see screenshot below). Clicking the letter 'W', for example, will take you directly to all the programs whose name begins with that letter, including Word 2016. Greyed-out letters in the grid (such as 'B' in our screenshot below) mean there are no programs installed beginning with that letter. Click the clock icon at the top left to return to the 'All apps' list.

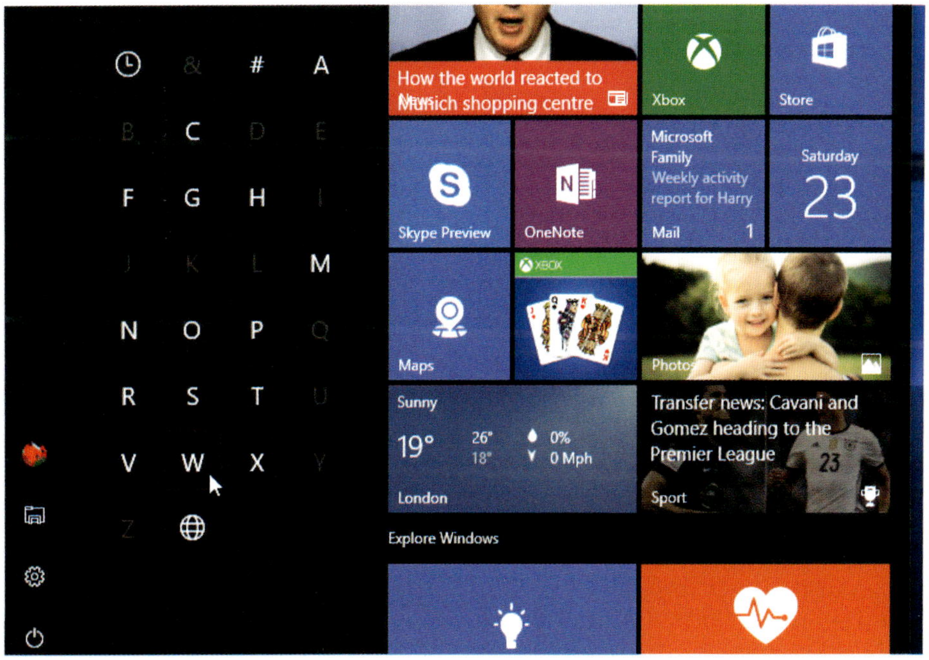

▲ Find programs quickly by clicking the first letter of a program's name in this alternative to the 'All apps' list

5 Launch Windows tools you use most often

THE SLOW WAY

Device Manager, System Properties and Control Panel have always been among the most used tools in Windows. Many of their core functions and options are now accessible via the Settings app in Windows 10, which many people find easier to use. However, there are still crucial tasks that can only be carried out using these older tools. For example, if you need to roll back to an earlier hardware driver or check whether a device is working you'll still need to rely on Device Manager. But to open it, you'll have to delve deep into the 'All apps' list, find Computer Management (under Windows Administrative Tools), then select Device Manager from the left-hand pane of the window that opens.

THE FAST WAY

Thankfully, there's a much quicker way to launch Device Manager and many of the other useful tools that Windows 10 tries to bury. Right-click the Start button to reveal a handy hidden menu of shortcuts to important management tools, including Device Manager, Control Panel, System, Disk Management and the Command Prompt (see screenshot below).

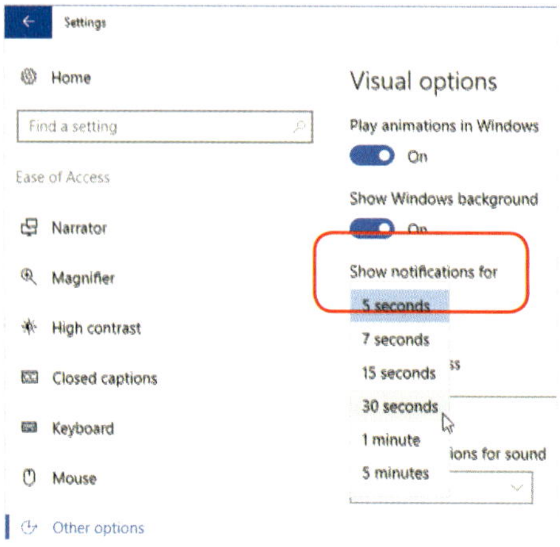

▲ Make sure notifications remain on screen longer

6 Read important notifications before they disappear

THE SLOW WAY

While most of this feature is concerned with speeding up tasks in Windows 10, some aspects would be more convenient and save you time if they were slowed down. Notifications, for example, flash up in the bottom-right of the taskbar, then disappear before you get a chance to read them. Missing a notification can have serious consequences, particularly if it is alerting you to security problems or an urgent email. You can always visit the Action Centre to review your recent notifications after the event. But you wouldn't have to waste time doing this, if the notification stayed on-screen long enough for you to read it in the first place.

THE FAST WAY

A quick tweak to your Windows 10 settings will make this happen. Click Start, Settings, 'Ease of Access', then 'Other options'. Under 'Visual options' on the right, choose a longer period (anything up to a minute) from the 'Show notifications for' dropdown menu (see screenshot left).

7 Navigate between open windows

THE SLOW WAY

If you tend to work with multiple programs, browsers and File Explorer windows all open at the same time, you can easily get bogged down in an endless loop of clicking taskbar icons and dragging windows around the screen to see the one you want.

THE FAST WAY

If you prefer using the Alt+Tab keyboard shortcut to cycle through taskbar thumbnails of all your open windows, you'll be pleased to hear you can still do this in Windows 10. But there's

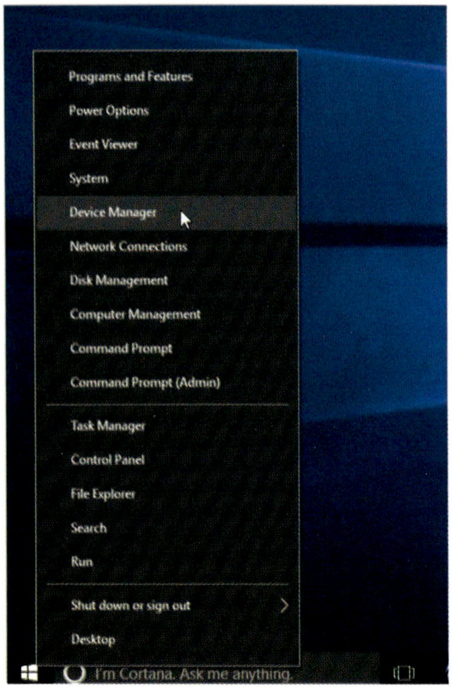

▲ Access a menu of shortcuts by right-clicking Start

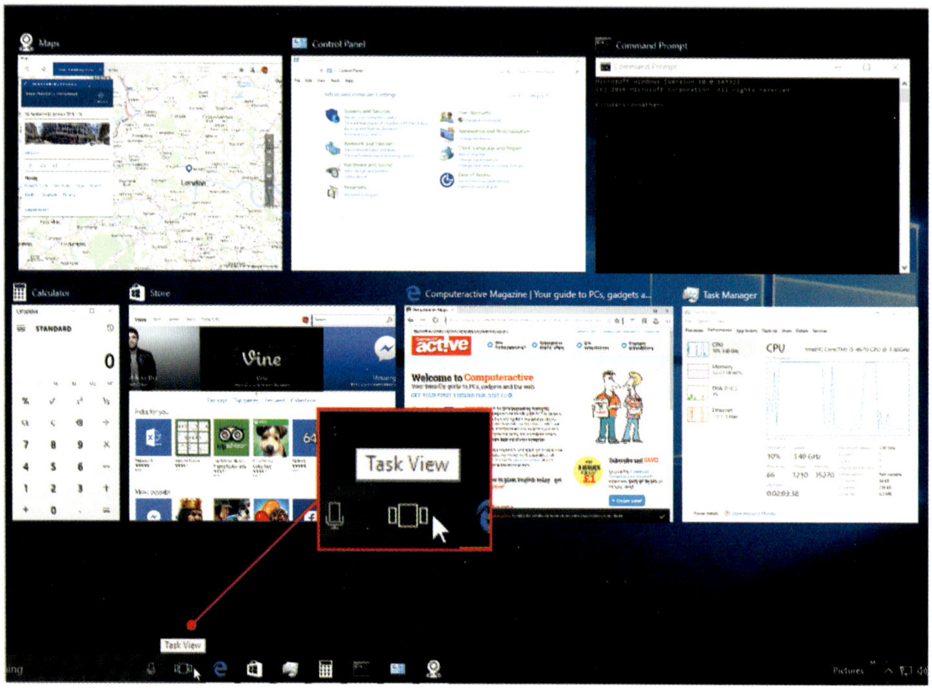

▲ Click Task View to see all open programs as thumbnails so you can quickly switch between them

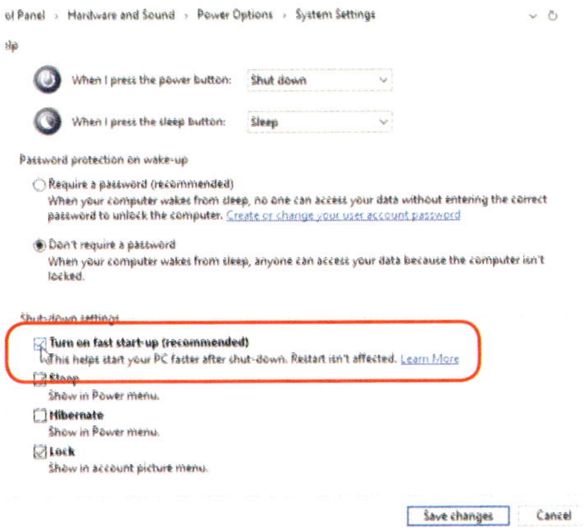

▲ Get your PC up and running more quickly

another, potentially quicker method too. To the left of your taskbar you'll see the Task View button (an icon with two overlapping rectangles). Click this and your screen will fill up with larger thumbnails representing all your open programs (see screenshot left). Simply click the one you want to switch to it.

8 Start up your PC faster

THE SLOW WAY

Windows 10 already starts up quicker than many of its predecessors, but if you stick with its default settings, you may be missing out on even shorter boot times.

THE FAST WAY

To enable Windows 10's 'fast start-up' option, click Start, type power, then click Power Options. In the window that opens, click 'Choose what the power buttons do', then 'Change settings that are currently unavailable'. Under 'Shut-down settings' check whether the 'Turn on fast start-up (recommended)' option is available. If so, make sure it's ticked (see screenshot above) and click 'Save changes'. If 'Turn on fast start-up (recommended)' is greyed-out, click 'Change settings that are currently unavailable' so you can access the tickbox. To make Windows 10 load even faster you can also use hibernation mode in combination with 'fast start-up'. To put your computer into hibernation mode, first click Start, then click the power button and choose Hibernate (rather than 'Shut down'). This will put your PC into a very low power-usage mode, the benefit of which is much faster load times the next time you switch on your computer.

20 MINUTE TWEAKS

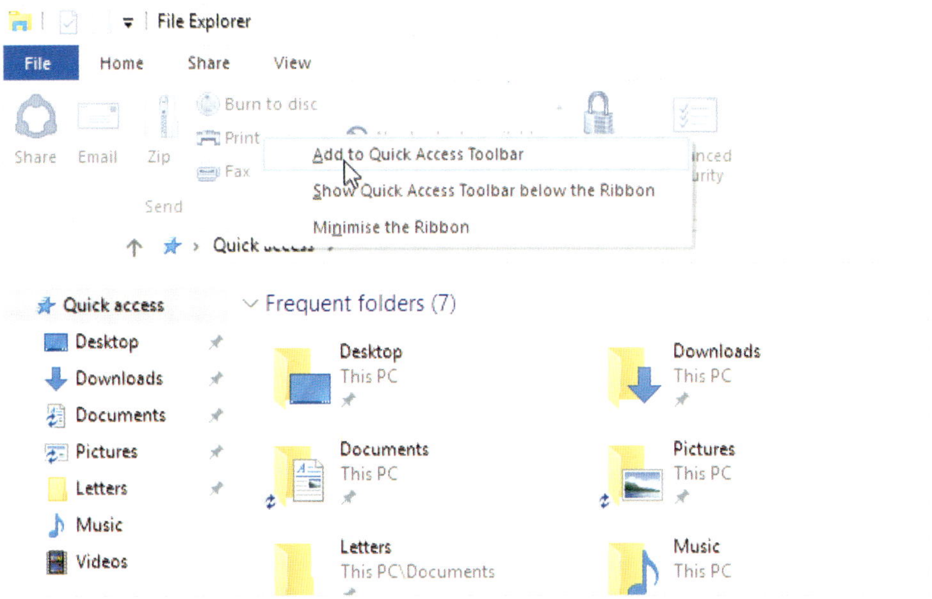

▲ Print any file or photo with a single click by adding the Print button to the Quick Access Toolbar

9 Print photos and files faster

THE SLOW WAY

To print a photo or a document, the conventional method is to navigate to the file you want, open it in a dedicated program, click File, then Print. It's the logical way to do it, but it's also the most long-winded.

THE FAST WAY

Windows 10's File Explorer includes a tabbed ribbon toolbar at the top, which contains shortcuts for a number of useful tasks – including printing. So rather than opening the file you want to print, you could just locate it in File Explorer, then click the Share tab, followed by Print. But there is an even faster way.

File Explorer has a hidden toolbar called the Quick Access Toolbar. You'll find it, by default, just above the ribbon in the top-left corner of the File Explorer window. The Quick Access Toolbar only contains two shortcuts – Properties and 'New folder' – but you can add others, including Print. Click the Share tab, then right-click the Print command and select 'Add to Quick Access Toolbar' (see screenshot above right). You'll now see the Print icon in the top-left corner whenever you open a File Explorer window, letting you print a selected file or photo with a single click.

You can customise the Quick Access Toolbar further, according to your needs. For example, you may want to add the 'Burn to disc' or Email shortcuts. In fact, you can add any command in any ribbon tab to the Quick Access Toolbar. Click the down arrow to the right of the toolbar's icons to add even more icons (Undo, Redo, Delete and Rename) or select 'Show below the Ribbon' to give the toolbar more prominence.

10 Access all your important items from one place

THE SLOW WAY

You can waste a lot of time tracking down Windows' hidden tools, files and settings. Thankfully, Windows 10 makes the process faster by letting you search for almost anything via the taskbar's search field. However, this still requires you to type the name of whatever you're looking for. A better solution would be to have a dedicated place for all your most frequently used folders, programs and settings so they are only ever a click away. Windows 10 can provide exactly that.

THE FAST WAY

With a little customising and re-organising, Windows 10's Start menu will provide super-fast access to just about everything you need.

The first thing to do is unpin any tiles you don't use from the right-hand section of the Start menu. Simply, right-click each and select 'Unpin from Start'. Now, pin all the items you want. These can include folders, programs listed in the 'All apps' list, and individual settings from the Settings app. To add any of these to the Start menu, right-click the program, folder or setting and select 'Pin to Start'.

Next, click and drag the tiles to reposition them. It's a good idea to arrange tiles into groups. You can create a new group by clicking and dragging a tile to the bottom of the menu until you see a solid coloured strip appear above it. Release the tile and you'll see it sitting below the other groups. Click above the tile and type your chosen name for this new group. So, for example, you could create groups for your programs, folders and settings – all available simply by clicking Start. You can also extend the Start menu by clicking and dragging outwards from its top and right-hand edges.

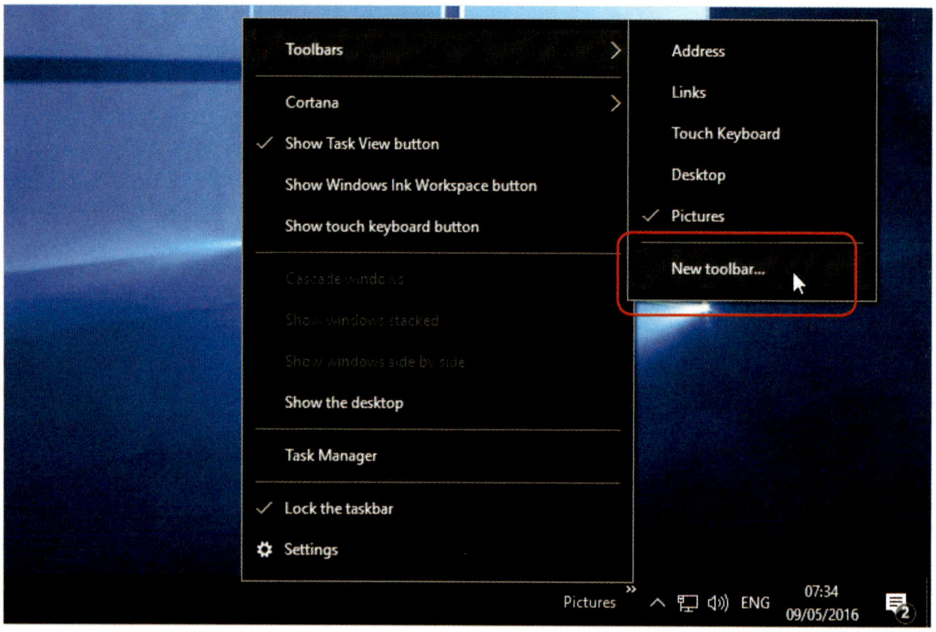

▲ Access any folder from the taskbar by creating a new toolbar for it

11 Access all your photos from the taskbar

THE SLOW WAY

Earlier, we explained how to pin folders to 'Quick access' for... well, quick access. And that's a great way to get to a specific folder in no time. But what if you want a fast way to access the files and sub-folders stored within a particular folder, such as your Pictures folder? Of course, you could open File Explorer and navigate to the folder you want. Or you could turn the folder into a toolbar and access its files directly from your taskbar.

THE FAST WAY

Right-click a blank space on your taskbar and select Toolbars. Here, you'll see a small selection of default toolbars that you can add to the right-hand side of the taskbar to speed up certain activities.

For example, you can select Address here to add an address bar to the taskbar, which lets you access any web page directly from your desktop by typing its URL into the address bar and pressing return; the page will open in your default browser. The Links toolbar lets you navigate directly to a list of your bookmarked websites, but this currently only works with Microsoft's Edge browser.

There will be other toolbars listed here that you can enable, depending on your PC and the programs you have installed.

MONITOR YOUR PC'S PERFORMANCE

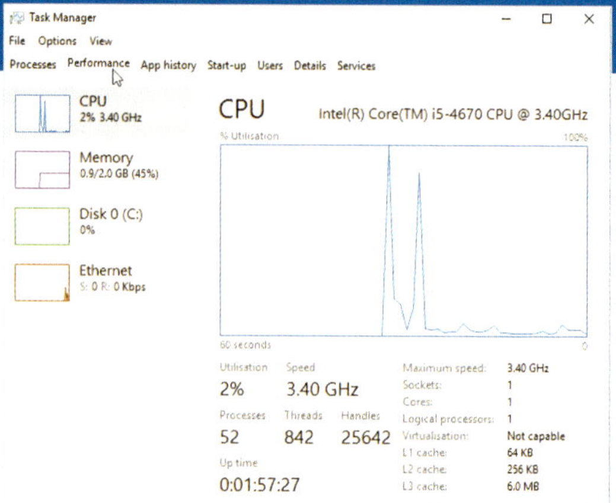

Do you suspect that something might be slowing your Windows 10 PC down? If so, there are tools built into the operating system that let you monitor and analyse your PC's performance and help identify the causes of its sluggishness.

First, right-click the taskbar and select Task Manager. Click 'More details' at the bottom of the window that opens, then click the Performance tab. Here you'll see a real-time graphical representation of your CPU, Memory, Disk (hard drive) and Wi-Fi or Ethernet, depending on what type of network connection you're using (see screenshot).

Click the thumbnails on the left to see more details in the main section on the right. If any of these graphs indicate constant high levels of activity on your hard drive, it could mean that your PC is struggling to cope with a program or process that's running. To find the culprit, click the Processes tab, then the column heading (CPU, Memory, Disk or Network) that corresponds to the graph showing excessive activity. For example, if the CPU graph on the Performance tab is showing high usage, click Processes, then click the CPU column until you see a small down-arrow next to the percentage figure. This will sort the list of processes so that those using the most processing power will be at the top. Similarly, if Task Manager indicates that your memory is near to its limit, click the Memory column to find out which programs or tasks are hogging your RAM. To stop a resource-hungry program from running, right-click it and choose 'End task'.

Alternatively, click 'New toolbar' (see screenshot on the left), then navigate to the folder you want (Pictures, for example), then highlight it and click 'Select folder'. The name of the folder will appear on the taskbar. Click the pair of arrows (>>) next to the folder's name for immediate access to any files or folders contained within it.

12 Log into Windows without a password

THE SLOW WAY

By default, you can't log into Windows 10 without typing your password first. In many situations, this is a security feature that should be left enabled – if you use a laptop, for example, or share your PC with others. But if you are the only person who has access to your PC, then the login process could be costing you unnecessary time. Still, you should only carry out this tweak if you are absolutely certain no one can take advantage.

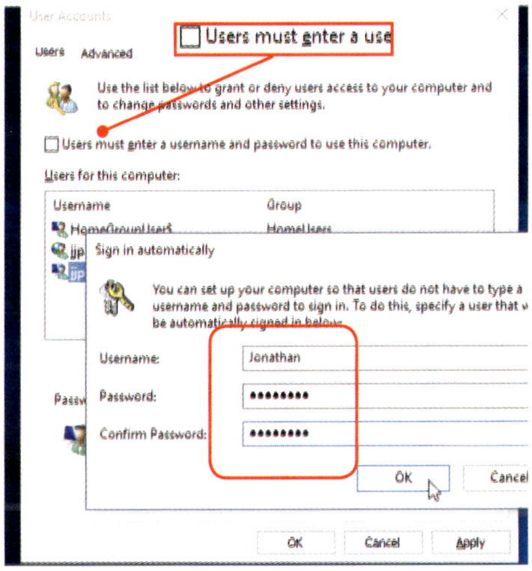

▲Bypass Windows 10's sign-in screen

THE FAST WAY

To skip the Windows login screen and move straight to the desktop, press Windows key+R to open the Run dialogue box, then type netplwiz into the box and press Enter. In the window that opens, click to highlight your user account, then untick the box next to 'Users must enter a user name and password to use this computer' and click Apply. A new window will open, asking you to confirm this action by typing your password twice (see screenshot above). Once you've done this, click OK.

EXPERT HACKS FOR A FASTER PC

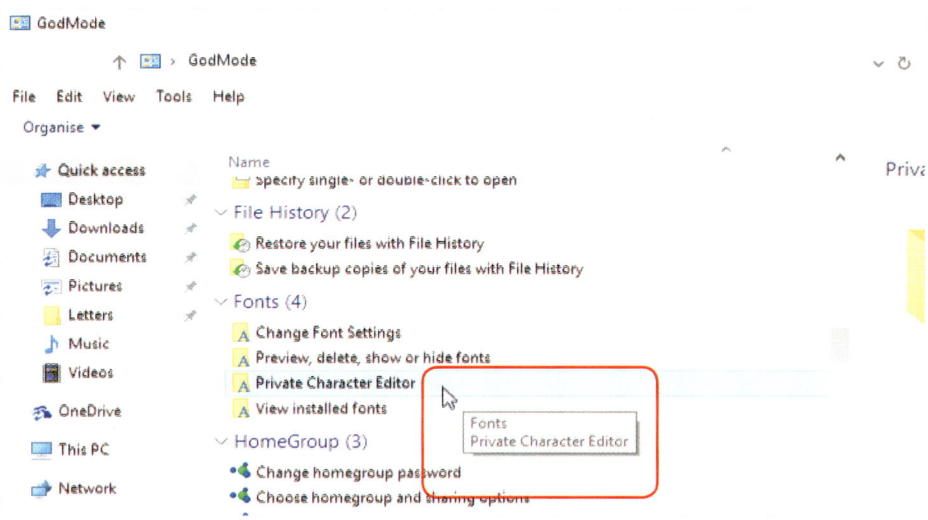

13 Find hidden settings by unlocking GodMode

THE SLOW WAY

Windows 10's Settings app is much easier to navigate than Windows 7's Control Panel and easier to access than Windows 8's PC Settings. But if you're not sure what you're looking for or where the setting you want might be, then it can still be time-consuming to trawl through the various pages of settings to find the one you want. This isn't helped by the fact that some settings can only be found in the Control Panel, which can be a palaver to access. Luckily, there's a way to view all of Windows 10's configuration options in one place.

THE FAST WAY

GodMode is a hidden folder that makes a wide range of useful PC customisations available in one place. GodMode isn't new to Windows 10. In fact, it's available in Windows 7 and 8.

But it's particularly useful in Windows 10, whose settings are spread across two different environments (Control Panel and the Settings app).

Enabling GodMode requires a hack, but it's a very simple one. Right-click anywhere on your desktop and select New, then Folder. The folder's name will be highlighted – rename it with the following command and press Enter when you've finished typing:

GodMode.{ED7BA470-8E54-465E-825C-99712043E01C}

A GodMode shortcut will appear, displaying a Control Panel-type icon. You don't have to call it GodMode – you can type whatever you like before the full stop, and this will become the shortcut's name.

Once you've created the shortcut, double-click it to view its contents. You'll find more than 220 settings listed, all of which are grouped by type – Fonts, Troubleshooting, User Accounts and so on – and you can use the top-right search box to look for settings by keyword.

Now, if you ever find yourself trying to track down an obscure setting or tool, such as Windows' hidden program for creating custom characters for your fonts – the mysteriously named Private Character Editor (see screenshot above) – you know where to go.

GodMode recently came in for some bad press, when security firm McAfee revealed it had detected a new strain of malware that used GodMode-like techniques to make it difficult to detect or remove. But this doesn't mean enabling or using GodMode on your PC is dangerous.

14 Remove preinstalled junk

THE SLOW WAY

Almost all new PCs these days come crammed with preinstalled junk software that you'll never use, and that's especially true for Windows 10 PCs. Not only will your PC have all those unwanted programs from your PC's manufacturer, but you'll also find a load of Windows 10 apps that Microsoft has added. Many

SPEED UP TASKS WITH KEYBOARD SHORTCUTS

As with all previous versions of the OS, Windows 10 can feel much faster if you use keyboard shortcuts to carry out tasks, rather than laboriously moving your mouse to a menu and clicking to select the option you want. Those who already use keyboard shortcuts will be pleased to hear that many familiar key combinations – including Ctrl+C for copying and Ctrl+V for pasting – can be used in Windows 10, too. But the latest OS also brings with it a selection of handy new shortcuts. Turn back to Chapter 4 for more on these.

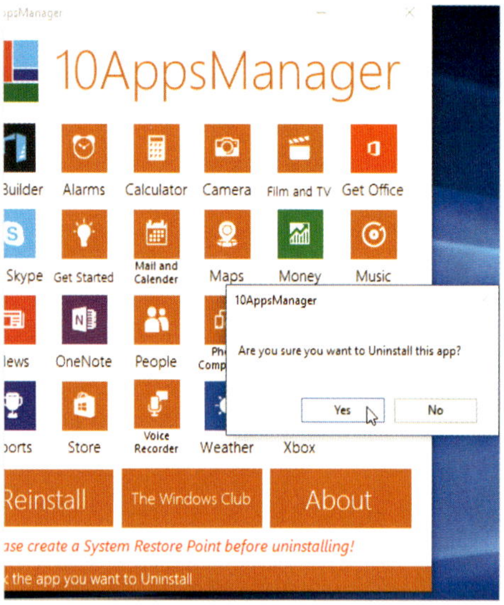

▲ Remove preinstalled apps in just a few clicks

of these do little more than sit there consuming space and system resources. Windows 10's junk doesn't just affect new PCs. Upgrade an older computer to the new OS and you'll be importing a large number of useless tools in the process.

You can ditch the manufacturer's junk fairly quickly using 'Uninstall a program' in the Control Panel, but removing Microsoft's apps is a lengthy process that involves scrolling through the 'All apps' list, right-clicking any apps you don't want, then selecting Uninstall. Worse still, some won't even let you uninstall them.

THE FAST WAY

There's a Powershell command that lets you uninstall all of Windows 10's built-in apps in one go. And, while this is certainly fast, we recommend taking care, as it removes certain apps that are essential for Windows to function correctly, including the Windows Store. The procedure can also make it difficult to reinstall any apps you later realise you want back.

Instead, we'd recommend using a free tool called 10AppsManager (www.snipca.com/19259), which can safely remove many of Windows 10's more pointless apps (3D Builder, we're looking at you). Before you start, it's worth creating a system restore point so you can rewind your PC to this point in time in the unlikely event that installing apps causes problems in the future. Once you've done that, unzip and run the tool, then click a tile to remove its associated app (see screenshot above). You can also click Reinstall to see instructions on how to et back the apps you uninstall (though you can also use the system restore point you created earlier). For more advice about uninstalling Windows 10 apps, refer to Chapter 7.

15 Speed up Windows 10 on an older PC

THE SLOW WAY

Windows 10 should feel snappy and responsive. But, on some older or lower-powered PCs, the operating system may not run quite as speedily as you would hope.

THE FAST WAY

First, try disabling animations by clicking Start, Settings, 'Ease of access', then 'Other options' and switching off the 'Play animations in Windows' option. Now click the Back arrow (in the top left of the Settings app window), and click Personalisation. Here, click Colours and switch off 'Make Start, taskbar and Action Centre transparent'. This will save valuable system resources.

Finally, there's a Registry hack that lets you reduce the time it takes for menus, such as the Start menu, to appear when you click – another way to make your system feel more responsive.

Make sure you set a system restore point before you start, then click Start, type regedit and press Enter. In the Registry Editor, navigate to HKEY_ CURRENT_ USER\Control Panel\ Desktop. In the right-hand pane, double-click MenuShowDelay, then change the number shown from 400 to something significantly lower – 20, for example (see screenshot below) – then click OK and restart your PC.

We'll be looking at further Windows 10 optimisation techniques later on in this chapter.

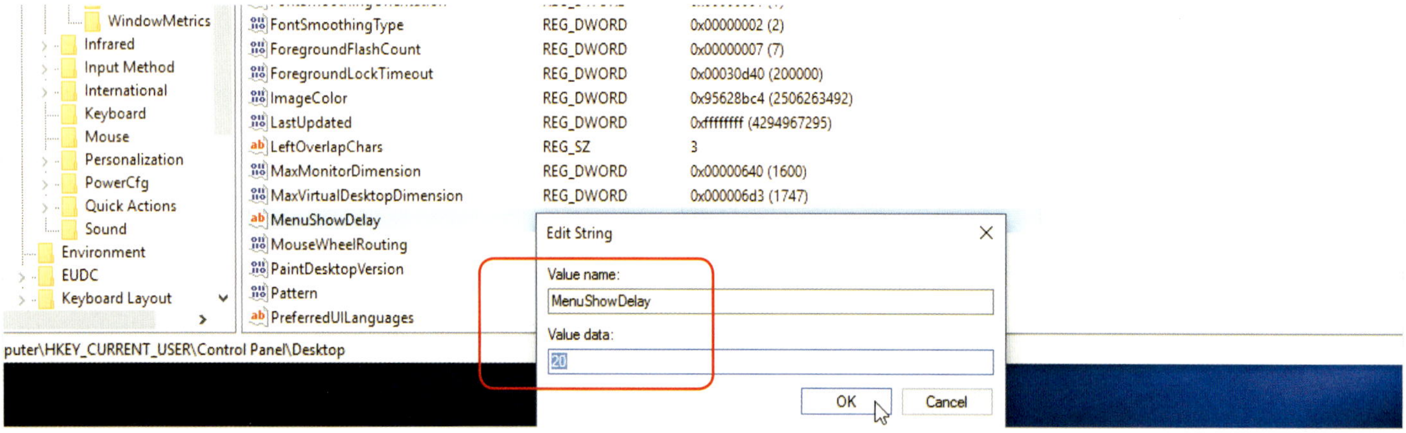

▲ Use this Registry hack to change the MenuShowDelay value and make menus open faster in Windows 10

Improve your Windows 10 System Tray

Time required: 10 minutes

Your PC's System Tray – also known as the Notification area – is the section on your taskbar at the bottom right of your screen that informs you of any pending notifications or system updates. It also shows indicators for audio volume, battery life and internet connection. TrayStatus is a brilliant tool that adds all kinds of useful icons to your System Tray. It has indicators for Caps Lock and Num Lock, and you can add icons that tell you when your Control, Alt and Shift keys are pressed.

STEP 1 To install TrayStatus, go to www.snipca.com/19507 and click the blue Download Now button. Click the downloaded setup file, Yes, Next, accept the licence agreement, then keep clicking Next until you reach Install. Click this, then click Finish to launch the program. You'll see two new icons (a 1 and an A) **1** in your System Tray. If you don't see these icons, click the 'Show hidden icons' (up arrow) **2** button to reveal them.

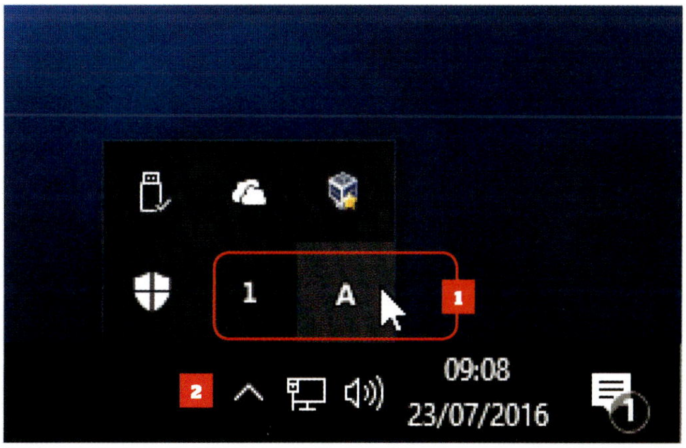

STEP 2 1 and A tell you respectively whether your Number Lock and Caps Lock keys are on. Click and drag the 1 and A icons from the 'hidden menu' to your System Tray to see them. If your Caps Lock or Number Lock key is on, the relevant icon will appear in a green box **1**. You can add five other icons to your TrayStatus System Tray. To do this, right-click an icon, then click TrayStatus Settings **2**.

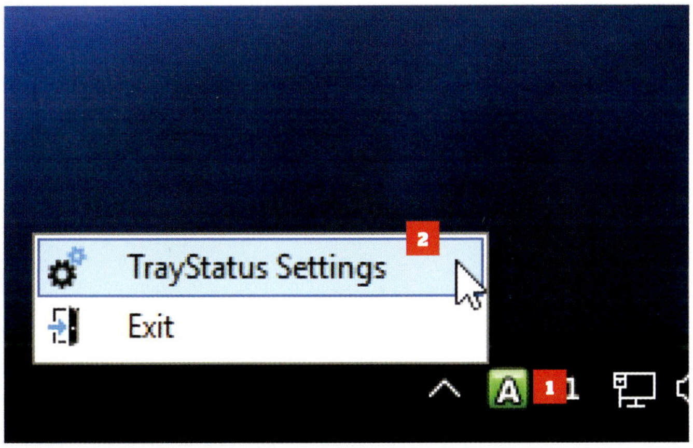

STEP 3 In the settings, you'll see options to enable/disable all eight TrayStatus icons. Select those you want by ticking/unticking the relevant options **1**. After doing that, click Apply, then OK. The Alt, Control, Shift and Windows keys will only be indicated as being switched on if you keep them pressed for a few seconds.

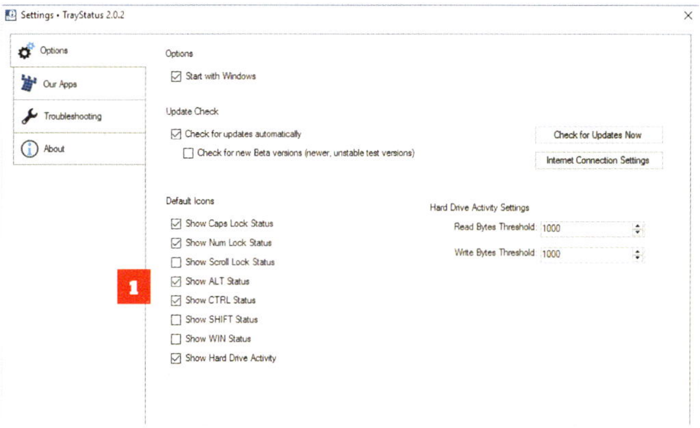

Use a great alternative to W10's File Explorer

Time required: 20 mins

File Explorer is one of the most used tools that comes with Windows 10. It's used for essential tasks, like organising files or navigating your hard drive. However, there are free alternatives that are better, such as the brilliant XYplorerFree. It has lots of extra options and can be run alongside Explorer, so you can switch between the two as and when you want. However, once you've given it a try, we doubt you'll look back.

STEP 1 Go to www.xyplorer.com/free.php and scroll down to the Download section. Click the Download Now button 1 to download the installer. Open the zip file and save the .exe file to your Desktop. Double-click the file to start the installation. By default, it installs to the Program Files folder (you can choose an alternative location). You have the option to create a Desktop icon 2.

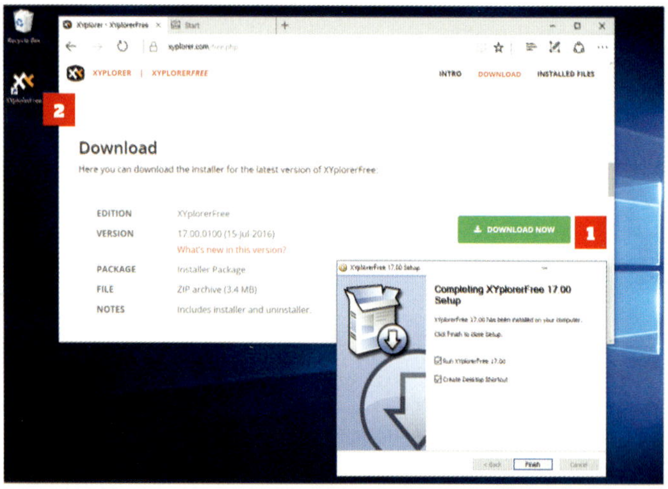

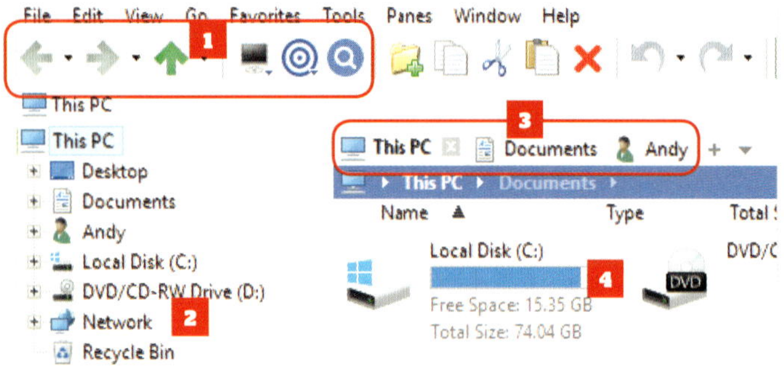

STEP 2 When you first open the program, you'll see it looks similar to Windows Explorer. There is a menu under the title bar and a row of icons below that 1. A tree structure on the left helps you navigate around your PC. Click a location to open it in the main screen on the right, or click on the '+' symbols to see sub-folders 2. The main window has tabs at the top, a breadcrumb trail that shows you where you are in the folder hierarchy 3, and a view of the current folder's contents 4.

STEP 3 Handily, you can have multiple tabs open within the same window. Click a tab to switch to it and click its 'x' symbol to close it **1**. The '+' symbol **2** lets you open a new tab. The dropdown menu at the end displays a list of open tabs **3**. On your keyboard you can press the number of the tab you want to jump to. One of the best things about the tabs is that they are saved from one session to the next, so you can return to where you left off, even if you've shut down and restarted Windows in the meantime.

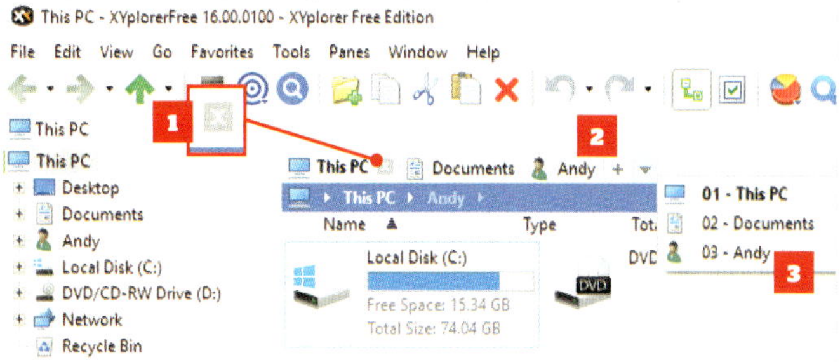

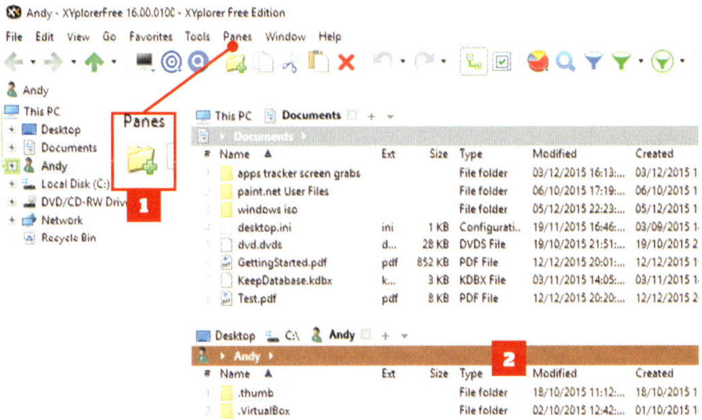

STEP 4 Open the Panes menu **1** and select Dual Pane (or press the F10 button on your keyboard). This splits the main window into two, opening new tabs in the one below **2**. This is extremely useful when you need to copy files from one place to another by simply dragging and dropping them to the other pane. You can also drag and drop tabs, repositioning them in the same pane or dragging them across to the new pane.

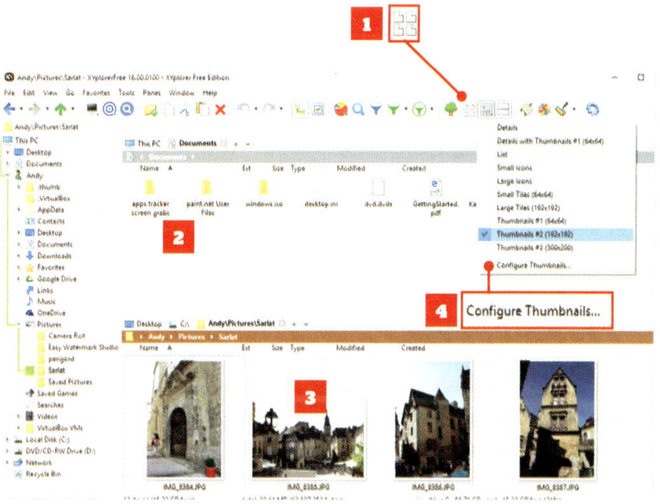

STEP 5 You can change the way the contents of each panel and tab are displayed, with lots more options than are available in Explorer. Click the Views button **1** and choose an option from the dropdown menu. In our screenshot the top panel shows Large Icons **2** and the lower panel shows Thumbnails #2 **3**. Click the Configure Thumbnails option **4** and you'll see a screen where you can define the size of the thumbnails and set further options, such as whether you want thumbnails to be cached (saved) to the hard drive for speed, or created each time you visit a folder to save space. Selecting the former will make thumbnails appear faster.

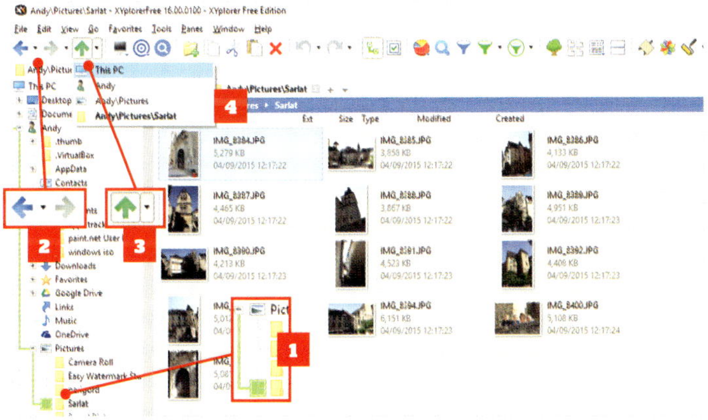

STEP 6 The tree-menu column on the left shows exactly where you are in the map of folders and storage devices. The green line **1** follows the trail you've taken through your folders, representing the one you're currently viewing with a green square. The left and right arrows **2** will take you back and forwards through your file-browsing history, while the up arrow **3** takes you back through your folders in the drive you're navigating, (all the way back to This PC). You can use the drop-down arrows to skip straight to a folder in the list **4**.

STEP 7 Right-click a file, folder or blank space in the main window and you'll see a context menu, which is far more comprehensive than Windows Explorer's version. You can change how you view and sort items **1**, compare two files **2** and select items using special filters **3**. The Paste Special menu **4** lets you do interesting things with the last item you copied to the clipboard, such as making a new file from a clipped image, inserting an item into a new folder and sending it straight to an editing program.

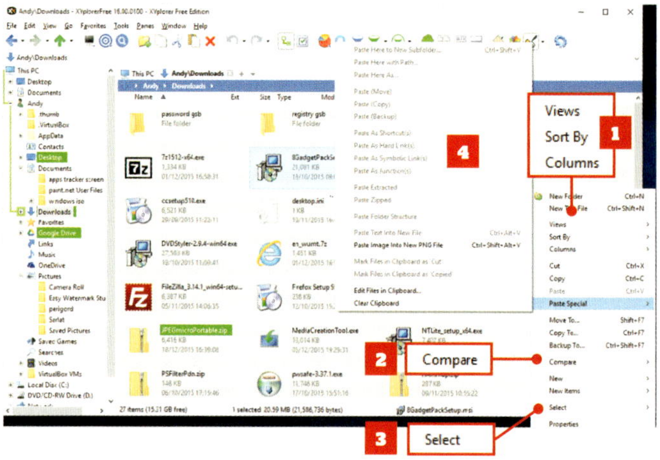

STEP 8 The Floating Preview button **1** opens a large preview window, which is great for browsing through a folder of photos (use your left and right cursor keys to flick through them). The Enable Color Filters button **2** will highlight certain files and folders in green **3**. By default, this is set to files and folders that have changed today, but you can choose a different option from the dropdown menu next to the Toggle Instant Color Filter button **4**.

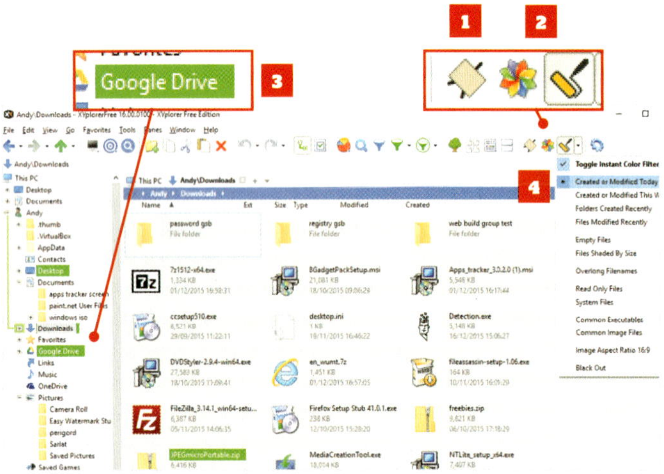

STEP 9 Click the Toggle Info Panel button **1**, which sits in the bottom right corner of the screen when the panel is closed. Select a file in the window above and the Info Panel will display a wealth of information about it. If you're flicking through images the Preview tab **2** is useful, as it doesn't just show you a larger thumbnail of the image, but also has size, date taken and other useful information. Properties, Version and Meta **3** hold more information about the file, while Tags **4** lets you add your own tags, which you can use to organise and filter your files.

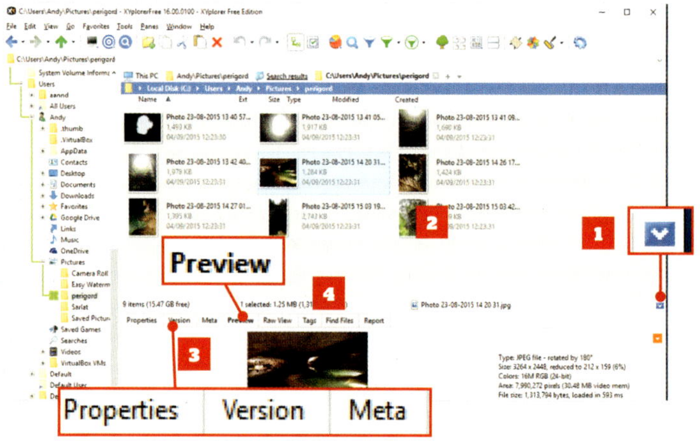

STEP 10 Click the Find Files tab **1** to access XYplorer's powerful search tool. A number of extra tabs are created below this so you can carry out the relevant type of search, based on what you know about the file you're looking for. Under Name & Location **2** XYplorer will look for any files containing the text you type in their names. You can limit the location if you know where things are, and tick the box to include subfolders **3**. For more nuanced searches, try the Contents tab or the Tags tabs **4** if you know what's in the file or have labelled it previously.

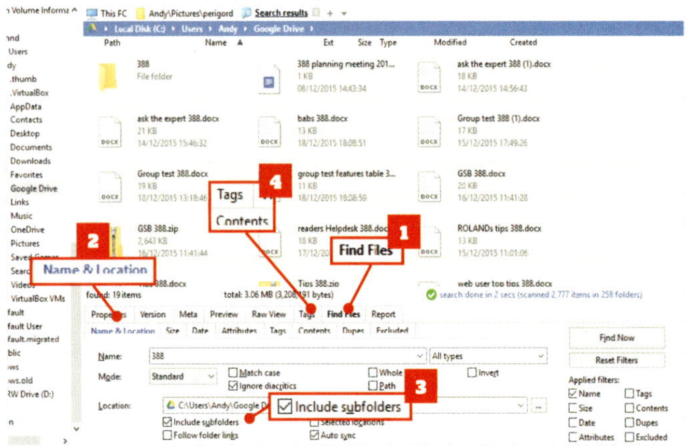

Add new tools to Windows 10's clipboard

Time required: 10 minutes

ArsClip is a handy little program that makes the Windows clipboard more powerful. It lets you go back through your clipboard's history and find previous copied items (clips), even if you've copied other items since. You can then use quick and simple keyboard shortcuts to paste these into your documents or programs. There are lots of ways you can customise the program to make it easier to use. We'll explain how to add extra tools and create keyboard shortcuts.

STEP 1 Download the portable version of ArsClip from www.snipca.com/19297 (double-click the green download zip link). Ignoring the setup program in the zip folder, extract the .exe file and put it somewhere safe, from where you can run the program. We found it wouldn't run from the Desktop so we made an ArsClip folder within the Program Files folder and ran it from there **1**. An icon **2** is added to your taskbar's Notification area. Hover over it and you'll see the contents of the clipboard in a pop-out box.

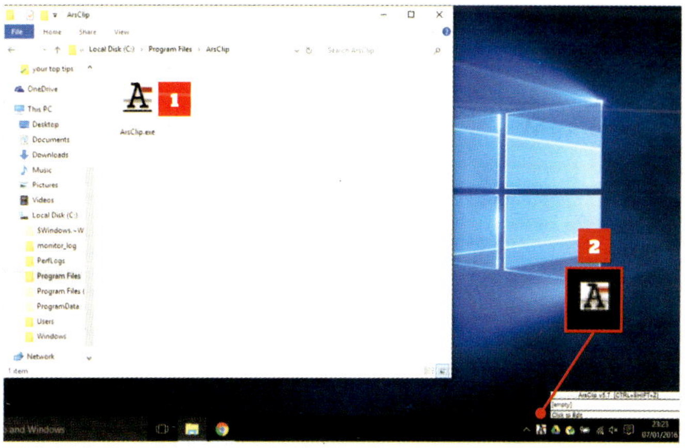

STEP 2 Press Shift+Ctrl+Z to bring up a window listing previous clips **1**. Click a clip to select it, then paste it into any program using the standard Ctrl+V shortcut. Alternatively, if you press the number or letter next to a clip **2**, it will automatically paste into the program you were using before you pressed Shift+Ctrl+Z. Click the magnifying-glass icon **3** to search the clips for specific words or letters. You can also rearrange the order of the clips by clicking and dragging the icons in the left-hand column of the window.

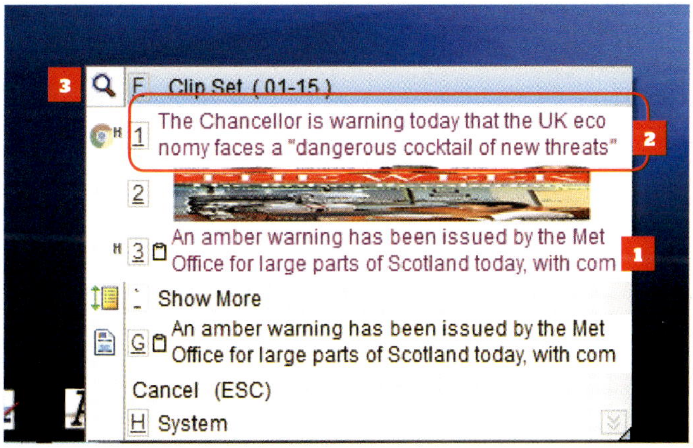

STEP 3 Right-click the icon in the Notification area to bring up its menu **1**. The Configure option launches the program's settings window **2**, where you can select and change a range of options, such as the keyboard shortcut used to open its pop-up window. The right-click menu also has a selection of other tools you can choose from, such as Edit Clipboard **3**. This opens a text editor that lets you make changes to copied text before pasting it elsewhere.

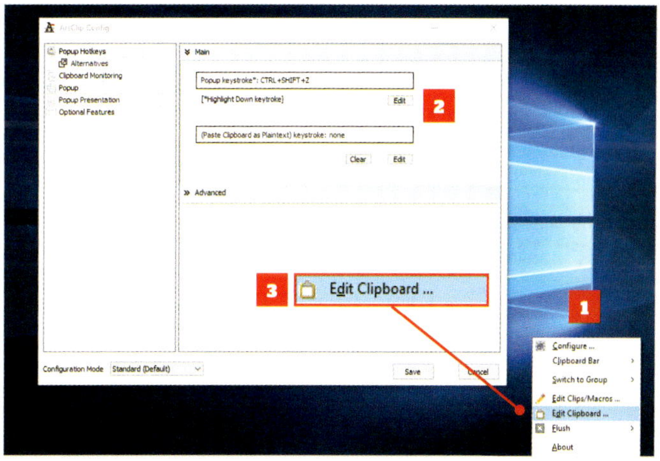

Upgrade your Windows 10 PC

You don't have to spend a fortune to improve your PC's performance. We show you the best components to buy and explain how to install them

There's no need to spend hundreds of pounds on a new PC, just because your old one is slowing down. If you upgrade one or more of its internal components, you can give your PC a significant boost without any major expense. The biggest problem is deciding which components to upgrade and what to replace them with. To help you, we've tested dozens of products you could use to upgrade your PC, including processors available from both Intel and AMD. Rather than fill these pages with tables and charts, however, we'll present you with our recommendations in each category, to help you choose the most suitable products.

We'll also show you how to install the upgrades or, if it's beyond the scope of this article, point you in the right direction for reliable advice online.

Memory

Your PC's memory (or RAM) is the super-fast temporary storage that keeps everything you're working on easily accessible. We've tested memory modules before in our labs and have come to the conclusion that the only real differences between modules with the same specifications are price and capacity.

There are two types of memory available nowadays. DDR3 is the most common and is used by all PCs with AMD, Intel Haswell or Intel Devil's Canyon processors. The latest Intel Skylake processors, however, use DDR4 memory.

▲ The more memory, the better the performance

▲ Faster memory will provide a performance boost

At current prices, we think that DDR3 1,866MHz is the best value memory and it suits everything from entry-level PCs to high-end models. For DDR4, 2,400MHz memory is the best value, but 3,200MHz will provide a further performance boost.

A Windows 10 PC should have at least 8GB RAM installed – if you have less than that, it's definitely worth upgrading. If you carry out a lot of resource-hungry tasks, such as video and audio editing, or just have a lot of programs and browsers running simultaneously, you might want to consider going to 16 or 32GB – you won't notice much overall speed improvement, but it will let you keep more software open and use bigger files without slowing down. Check the maximum amount of memory your motherboard supports and make sure you don't exceed it.

▲ Samsung's 850 Evo SSD is good value for money

Memory is generally best fitted in pairs. In our experience, it's best to buy branded memory from well-known manufacturers such as Corsair (www.corsair.com), Crucial (uk.crucial.com) and Kingston (www.kingston.com).

We show you how to install memory in our Mini Workshop opposite.

Hard drives and SSDs

Replacing a mechanical hard drive with an SSD is one of the most effective upgrades you can carry out on a PC. We've devoted an entire section to it over the page, so it's worth having a l ook at this if you want to install one.

Of the four SSDs we tested, our

▲ Traditional hard drives are slower than SSDs

favourite is the Samsung 850 Evo, which offers great value for money (£66 for a 250GB model, www.ebuyer.com) and a standard SATA3 interface. For fastest performance, look to the Samsung 950 Pro M.2 (£146 for 256GB, www.ebuyer.com) but make sure your motherboard has an M.2 slot to connect it to.

Hard drives are installed in exactly the same way. If you want a standard drive that performs well, we rate the Western Digital Green, which provides the best price per GB – a 2TB hard drive costs just £64 (www.scan.co.uk). We'll explain how to install an SSD later in this chapter.

Graphics cards

Upgrading your graphics card won't make much difference to Windows but it can significantly improve how games look and run on your PC. You first need to check that your power supply will be up to powering your new card, particularly if your PC currently uses your processor's built-in graphics. You can find out what you need for your particular graphics chipset at bit.ly/calc392 – you'll need to know a lot of details about your PC, though.

If you need a new power supply unit up to 550W, we recommend the Super Flower Leadex Platinum 550W (£88, www.overclockers.co.uk). For more power, the EVGA Supernova G2 750W (£93, www.scan.co.uk) will take you up to the 750W mark.

▲ Nvidia's GeForce GTX 980Ti is expensive but fast

▲ The GeForce GTX 950 offers a great-value boost

If you're upgrading your graphics, it's worth spending a bit of money. In our tests, the make and manufacturer of a graphics card was less important than the type of graphics processor that was running on it. Cards with the Nvidia GeForce GTX 950 chip offered the best value, costing around £128 and getting more than 25fps (frames per second) out of the latest games at high graphical settings. If you can afford another £50, a card with the Nvidia GeForce GTX 960 is a good buy for around £177. For the best performance we tested, the Nvidia GeForce GTX 980Ti offers frame rates in modern games of up to 156fps but the card alone will cost you £545.

We show you how to install a graphics

MINI WORKSHOP
Install extra memory in a desktop PC

1 Switch off the computer at the wall socket and earth yourself (by touching a radiator), then open the PC's case and lay it flat. Locate the memory sockets **1** and ensure you have clear access to them. You may need to move or unplug any cables or devices that are in the way **2**.

2 Open a memory slot by pressing down on each locking tab in turn. If you're replacing existing memory, pull out the chip and set it aside. Insert your new module, making sure the notches align. With a thumb on each end, press down firmly until there's an audible click and the locking tabs pop up **1**.

3 Add any other modules, then reassemble your PC and switch it on. The new memory should be listed on the boot-up screen. You can check how much is available to Windows **1** by going to Settings, System, About **2**.

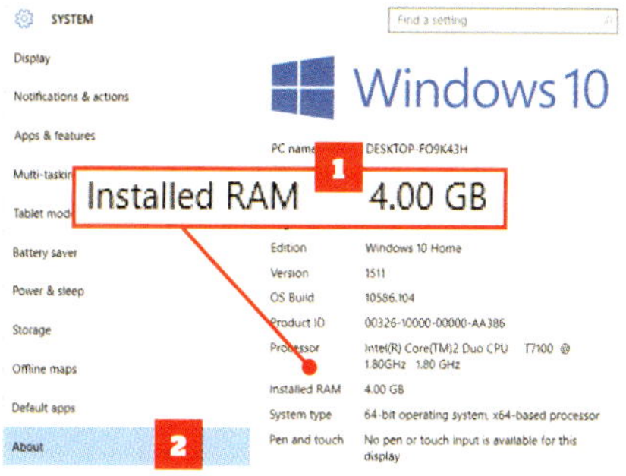

card in our Mini Workshop below.

Processors and motherboards

Upgrading your processor is trickier than most upgrade jobs. If you want a brand new type of chip, you'll have to upgrade your motherboard, too. This is more akin to building a new PC from your old parts than performing an upgrade of your existing machine, so don't attempt this unless you're confident that you know what you're doing.

There are two processor manufacturers to choose from: Intel and AMD. AMD's chips tend to be better value, and you can get an AMD A6-7400K for just £48 that has enough built-in graphics power to run Dirt Showdown at 37.3fps at HD resolution with high detail, though its Windows benchmark score was a low 27. If on-board graphics aren't important or you're thinking of a separate graphics card, the FX-8350 is £137 but achieved a Windows benchmark score of 98.

▲ You can upgrade your processor, but it's a big job

By comparison, our favourite budget Intel processor is the £66 Pentium G4500, which scored 45 in our Windows benchmark and ran Dirt Showdown at 45.3fps. If you can stretch to £198, the Core i5-6600K scored 113 in our Windows tests but only matches 45.3fps in Dirt Showdown because it has the same on-board graphics.

Both the Intel chips use the latest Skylake technology so you'll need a motherboard with an LGA1151 socket to use them. Our favourite is the ASUS Z170-A (£113, www.scan.co.uk), which includes lots of expansion options, a legacy PCI slot (which is a rarity) and six USB 3 ports.

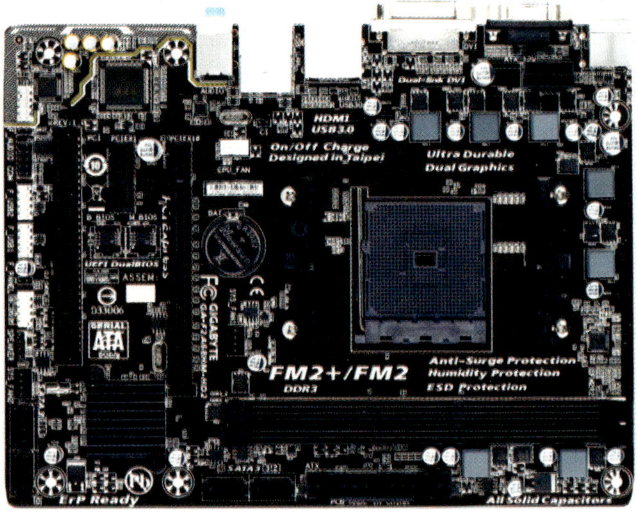

▲ Fitting a new motherboard isn't a simple upgrade

As with the chips, AMD motherboards are also better value. For the A6-7400K, you'll need an FM2+ board and we'd recommend the Gigabyte GA-F2A68HM-HD2 (£42, www.ebuyer.com). The FX-8350 needs an AM3+ board – we like the MSI 970A-G43 (£51, www.box.co.uk).

HP provides a comprehensive guide to upgrading a processor at bit.ly/hpproc392. For advice on upgrading a motherboard, try bit.ly/mother392.

MINI WORKSHOP
Install a graphics card

1 Turn off your PC at the mains but leave it plugged in and earth yourself. Open the case and remove your existing graphics card. If you're currently using onboard graphics, locate a free PCI Express slot **1**. Modern cards can be large so make sure there's enough space in the case for it to fit.

2 Connect the power to your new card. This might involve plugging a single white four-pin Molex connector or connecting two Molex to a six-pin PCI Express cable and plugging that in **1**. If you fail to attach the power or there's another problem, the PC will issue a loud beep when it's switched on.

3 Insert your graphics card into the spare slot and make sure it clicks firmly into place **1**. Secure it, put the case back together and connect your monitor cable. Turn on the computer. You'll need to install the supplied graphics drivers, then download the latest ones from Nvidia (bit.ly/nvid392) or AMD (bit.ly/amdg392).

Speed up Windows 10 by using an SSD

Upgrading your Windows 10 PC with an SSD can dramatically boost its speed. We show you how to install one and set it up

There are a lot of simple upgrades you can perform to boost the speed of your PC. In the past, the most popular (and cheapest) option was to pack your computer with more memory, although this was restricted by the number of available slots on your PC's motherboard and the operating system you were running. These days, transferring Windows onto an SSD (solid-state drive) will yield far greater speed improvements, and dramatically reduce the length of time it takes your PC to start up. In this section of our guide, we'll show you how to install an SSD and get Windows 10 to run as speedily as possible.

Most of the advice we've provided also applies to previous versions of Windows, which similarly benefit from being run from an SSD.

Why choose an SSD?

Like USB sticks and camera memory cards, SSDs use flash memory. This means they are significantly faster than traditional hard drives because they store their data on memory chips, which provide almost instant access to any section of the drive. Traditional hard drives use a movable mechanical arm with a read/write head to access information from a spinning platter, which is a much slower process.

If you move Windows 10 and your installed programs from a hard drive to an SSD, your computer will feel like it's been turbo-charged. Instead of waiting minutes for your PC to boot up, you'll be able to use Windows in seconds. Your applications will load significantly quicker, and the drive's read and write speeds will also improve.

▲ Choose an SSD from a manufacturer you trust

Windows 10 is a speedy operating system as it is, but if you install it on an SSD, you'll really notice the difference.

What to buy

SSDs have some drawbacks. In theory, they have a shorter lifespan than hard drives because the MLC (Multi-Level Cells) memory chips that make up an SSD can only be written to a set number of times. They're also more expensive: while a 2TB hard drive might set you back £60, the SSD equivalent is likely to cost upwards of £500.

Unless you've got enough money to splash out on a huge capacity SSD and not worry about its shorter lifespan, it's worth considering a combination of the two: an SSD for Windows and your installed programs; and a hard drive for storing your personal data, such as

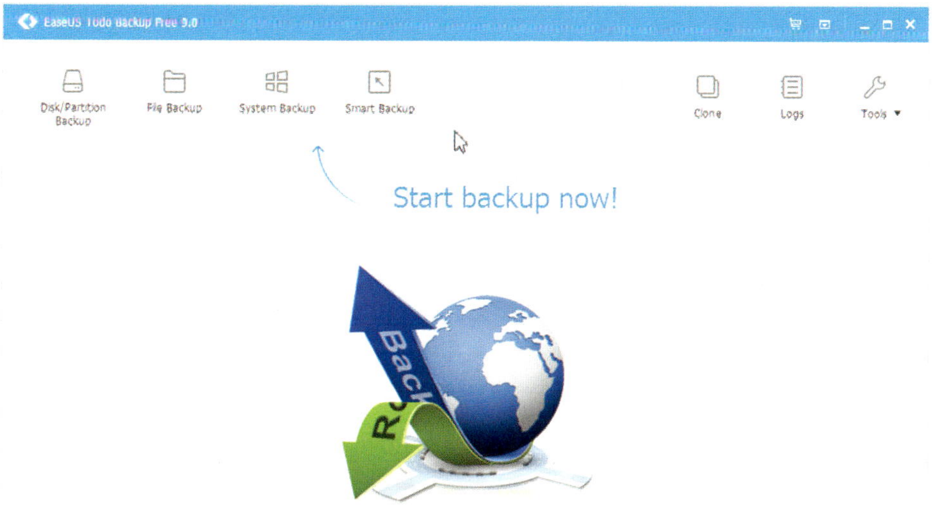

▲ Use Todo Backup Free to make a backup of your old drive and install it on the new one

documents, photos, videos, music and downloads.

A 120GB SSD might just suffice but a 240GB or 480GB model, which will set you back around £60 or £115 respectively, is a safer bet. As with buying memory or USB sticks, it's worth spending a little extra to buy an SSD from a brand you trust, such as Crucial (bit.ly/crucial389) or Kingston (bit.ly/king389), so you can be sure you're getting a reliable component.

Back up your data

Before you do anything, back up all your personal data with a purpose-built program such as EaseUS Todo Backup Free (www.todo-backup.com). The beauty of this software is it can also be used to migrate Windows 10 from your existing hard drive to a new SSD.

After you've created your backup, you'll need to install the SSD in your PC. We show you how to do this in our Mini Workshop, below.

Copy or install Windows 10 onto the drive

Once you've fitted the new SSD into your computer, the next step is to install Windows 10 on it. If you already had the operating system installed on your PC, you can transfer this and any software to the SSD using a clone tool. Your drive may have come with software that does this but, if not, EaseUS Todo Backup Free is ideal for the job. This is the quickest approach and will have you up and running in no time at all, with all your existing software ready to use.

However, if you want to get Windows 10 running as fast as possible on your PC, the best option is to perform a fresh install. This ensures that no errors or junk files make their way on to your new drive, taking up unnecessary space (which is an important factor considering the reduced size of the SSD) or causing problems down the line. Bear in mind, though, that carrying out a fresh install is also more time-consuming, because you'll need to install all your programs and configure them from scratch. That said, it's important to remember that installing anything on an SSD, including a new operating system, will take much less time than installing it on a slower mechanical hard drive.

To perform a clean install of Windows 10 on an SSD, you will either need a Windows 10 licence (which you have to pay for) or you'll need to have previously upgraded Windows on your old hard drive. Microsoft recently updated Windows 10 to allow users to activate the license using a valid Windows 7 or 8 product key. So, one way to carry out a clean install would be to use the Media Creation Tool program from Microsoft at bit.ly/mct389 to download and install a fresh copy of Windows 10, then enter your Windows 7 or 8 product key when prompted.

▲ Some SSDs come with software and extra connection equipment

MINI WORKSHOP
Install an SSD in your PC

1 Laptop hard drives are the same size as SSDs, so you simply swap one for the other. Remove the battery from the laptop, ground yourself on a radiator or similar, and remove the back of the case. Take out the old hard drive and replace it with the new SSD, then attach the power and SATA connectors and reassemble everything.

2 To install an SSD in a desktop PC, you'll need a 2.5in to 3.5in adapter. Your new drive may come with one but, if it doesn't, you can pick one up for around £7 from the likes of Amazon. Ground yourself to disperse any static electricity, as in Step 1, then insert the SSD into the adapter and screw it in **1**.

3 Turn off and unplug your PC, then remove the case. If necessary, unscrew and remove the existing drive. Insert the adapter (with the drive in) into a spare drive bay and secure it in place **1**. Once done, attach the power and SATA cables and you're ready to install an operating system or clone a drive.

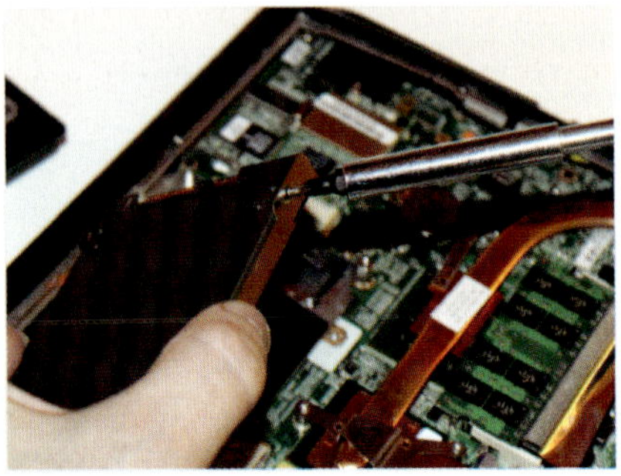

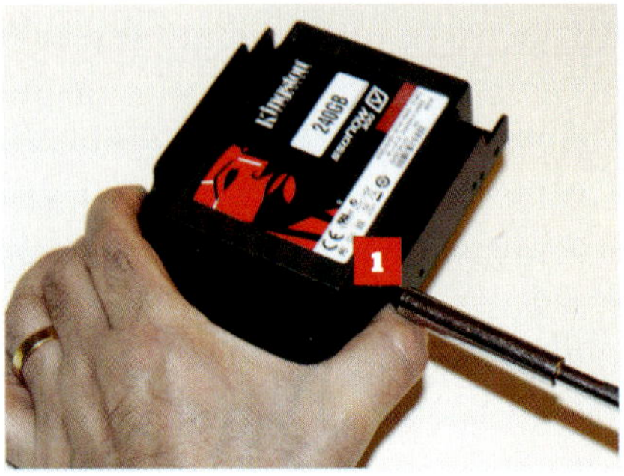

MINI WORKSHOP
Clean up your SSD after a Windows 10 upgrade

1 When you upgrade to Windows 10, a lot of temp files get left behind. This is to allow you to roll everything back to the previous OS if it turns out that you don't like it. However, this just wastes space on an SSD. To remove these leftovers, click Start and type Disk Clean-up **1**. Click to launch the application **2**.

2 Select the drive you want to clean up (this will be the SSD with Windows on, probably C:) and click OK. The tool will calculate how much space can be saved and then present you with a list of items that can be cleaned **1**. Ignore this and instead click the 'Clean up system files' button **2**.

3 Select your SSD again, and the tool will repeat the process, but this time a new option is displayed – 'Previous Windows installation(s)'. Tick this box **1** and the box for 'Temporary Windows installation files', **2** then click OK to remove those files and regain your missing hard-drive space.

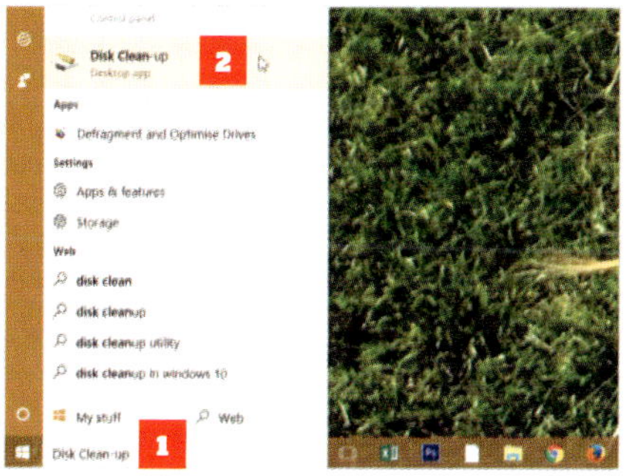

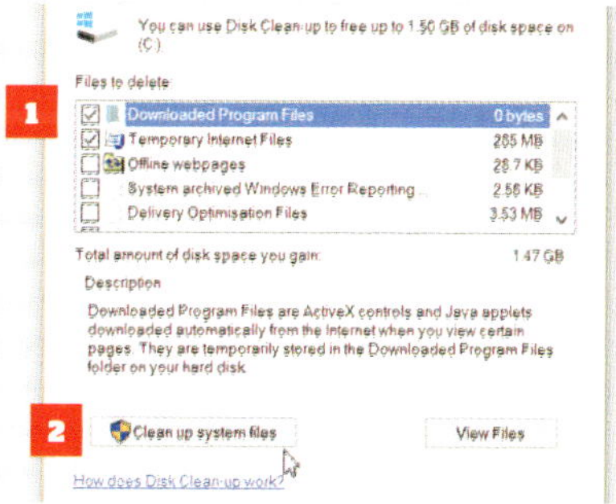

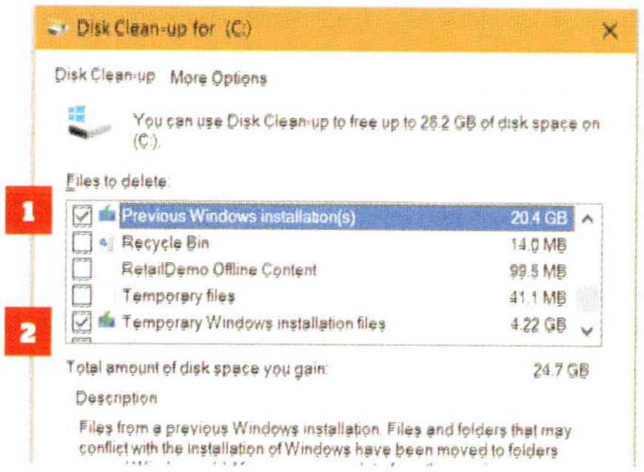

Look after your SSD

Unlike mechanical hard drives, SSDs don't need to be defragmented. In fact, defragging an SSD regularly can significantly shorten its lifespan.

Windows 10 automatically recognises when it's installed on an SSD and can perform an optimisation known as TRIM. This tells the SSD which blocks of data are no longer considered to be in use so they can be wiped. Click Start and type defrag, then launch the Defrag function. Your system drive should be listed as a Solid State Drive under Media Type. Select it and click the Optimise button.

Personally, we don't think Windows needs to index your SSD's contents, as it does little more than contribute to wear and tear.

To turn off this feature, press Win+R and type services.msc into the Run box. Press the Enter key.

In the Services window, scroll down to Windows Search, then right-click it and select Properties. Change the Startup type to Disabled and click OK. Close the window, and open File Explorer, then right-click your SSD and select Properties, making sure 'Allow files on this drive to have contents indexed in addition to file properties' is unticked. Click OK when you have finished.

Windows 10 is automatically optimised for SSDs but if you want to check this on your PC, right-click the Start button and select Command Prompt (Admin) from the menu. In the window that opens, type Winsat formal -V (note that's 'formal', not 'format').

This will test your computer and make any changes required to ensure that Windows works as intended with your SSD.

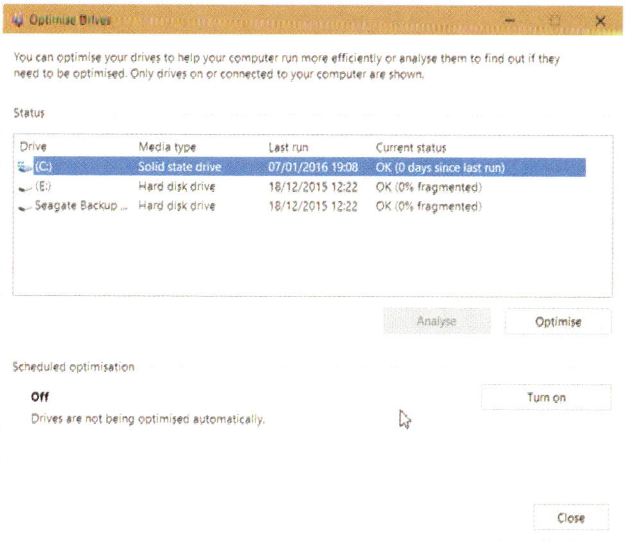

▲ You shouldn't defrag an SSD but you can optimise it using W10's tools

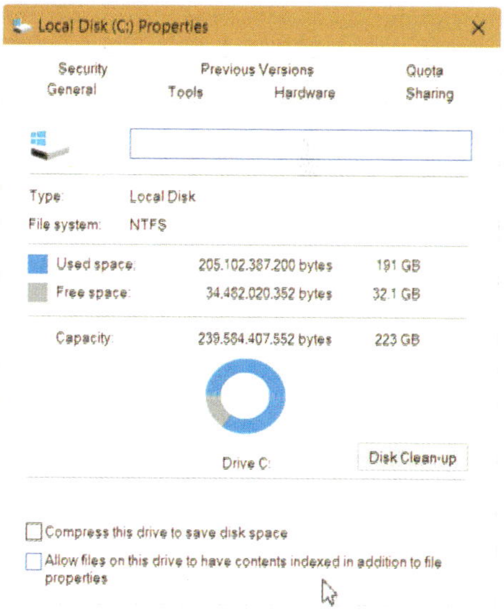

▲ SSDs won't get a big boost from being indexed

Expert tips for optimising Windows 10

We demonstrate advanced tips and tricks designed to keep Windows 10 running smoothly and speedily

Defragment your hard drive

When you upgrade to Windows 10, thousands of files are installed, moved and deleted. This causes files to fragment, which can affect performance. Windows has a built-in disk defragmenter that runs to its own schedule, but you can give it a helping hand by launching it yourself or setting a different schedule.

Open an Explorer window and select This PC on the left. Right-click the drive and select Properties, then click Optimise on the Tools tab. Click the Optimise button to defragment the disk immediately or click the Change Settings button and set the frequency to Daily. It will then start when the computer is idle for a few minutes. Remember that disk defragmenting only improves the performance of traditional hard drives, not solid state ones (SSDs). Turn back to the previous article for more on this.

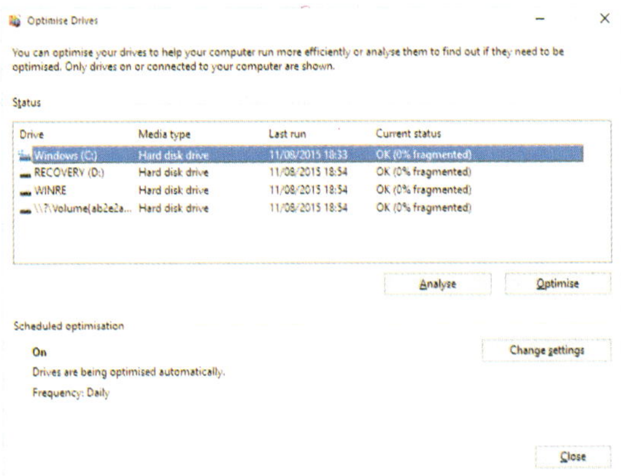

Check for problems

After writing and moving so many files on the hard drive, it's a good idea to check the structure. Minor problems occasionally occur and they can affect your PC's performance and reliability. Open an Explorer window and select This PC in the left panel. Right click the hard drive, select Properties and then the Tools tab. Click the Check button and then click 'Scan drive', even if it says that you do not need to. If problems are detected, then an option to fix them becomes available.

Update your software

Whenever a new version of Windows is released, developers update their software. Sometimes this is to fix bugs, but it might also be to change how a program operates, so it fits better with how the operating system works. For example, Windows Store apps now run in a window on the Desktop instead of full screen, which affects how you use the app. Software might be updated to take advantage of new features that were not in previous versions of Windows, too.

Go to an application's Help, About menu to find the company and website, then check if there is a newer version. Some applications have a menu option to check for updates, which is even easier to use.

Update your drivers

Windows 10 may be running on your computer, but is it running as well as it could be? Hardware components such as the hard drive, graphics card, Wi-Fi, printer, webcam, motherboard and so on, all require drivers to work properly, and many manufacturers of these components have released updated drivers that work better in Windows 10 than the old ones, so you should make sure your drivers are up to date to ensure optimum performance.

If you're not sure what components are inside your computer, click the search box in the taskbar and type system information. Click it in the results and, in the window that opens, expand the Components section and select each item. The name can be found among the information. Go to the manufacturer's website and search for drivers. Drivers

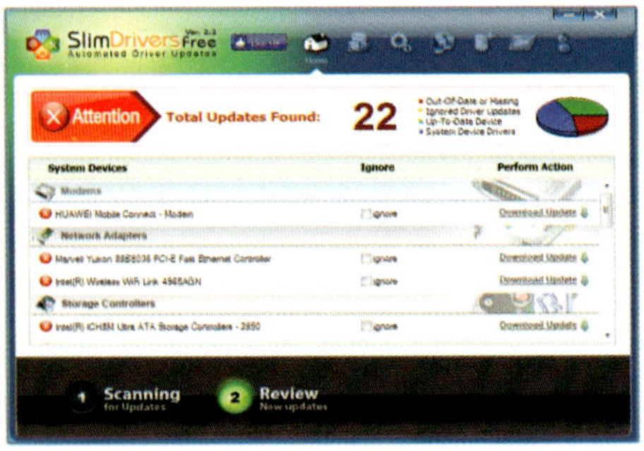

▲ SlimDrivers can check if drivers need updating

released just before or after the launch of Windows 10 should be downloaded and installed.

There are a couple of free tools that can find and install updated drivers, of which our favourites are SlimDrivers (www.slimwareutilities.com) and IObit Driver Booster (www.iobit.com). Use these to check for outdated drivers, but don't try to update them all at once. Update one driver, then check that the PC is running properly. You can then update another driver.

Get double the protection

Windows Defender, which comes built into Windows 10, provides protection from viruses, spyware and other malware. The latest version is an improvement on previous releases, but it might be safer to use a free third-party anti-virus tool and use Windows Defender only as a secondary layer of protection. As long as you've updated to Windows 10's Anniversary Update, this won't cause any conflicts.

Take your pick from Avast (www.avast.com), AVG (www.avg.com), Avira (www.avira.com) and Panda (www.pandasecurity.com). After installing one of these security programs, click the search box in the taskbar, type Windows Defender, then click Defender in the results and switch on Limited Periodic Scanning.

Turn off fancy features

Windows 10 looks great, but fancy appearances can hog your PC's power. It can be made to run slightly faster by turning off unnecessary Windows features such as animations that launch when windows are opened and closed, moving icons on the taskbar, objects fading and sliding into view, and translucent items. Click the search box and enter Performance. In the results, click 'Adjust the appearance and performance of Windows'. In the Performance Options window, you can manually select or deselect items in the list, or select either

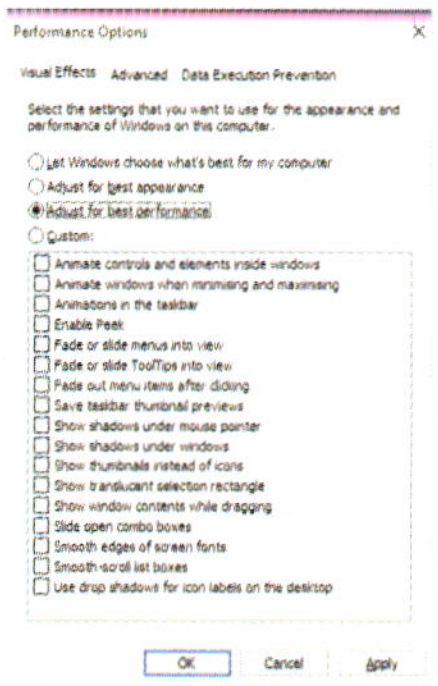

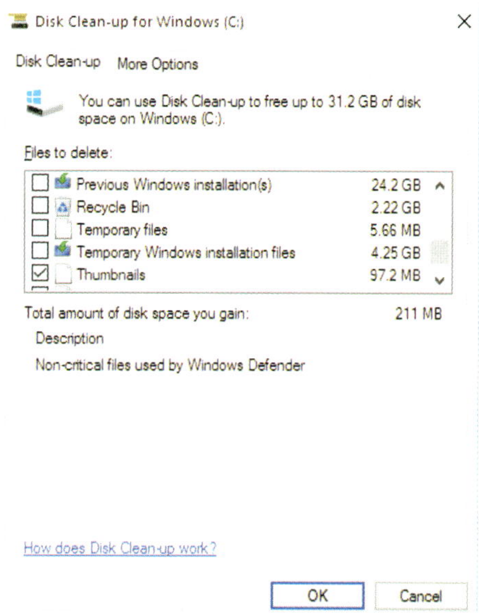

▲ Free up space, but not if you want to downgrade

'Adjust for best appearance' or 'Adjust for best performance'. It's your choice and you can either have Windows 10 look amazingly good or run terrifically fast.

Clean up your hard drive

A Windows 10 upgrade can leave behind junk and temporary files on your hard drive, and these can be cleaned to free up space. If the drive is nearly full then the extra space will also improve the performance. Click in the taskbar's search box and type disk cleanup then click the link that appears above. Now follow the Mini Workshop on page 119 to clean up all the files the upgrade left behind.

Only if you are sure you will never want to return to the previous version of Windows should you select all the items in the list and delete them. Tens of gigabytes of drive space will be made free – a whopping 31.2GB on our test PC (see above). That could make a big difference to a drive that is short of space.

Defrag your PC on boot

Windows can defragment files on the hard drive, but only if they are not currently being used. The problem is that system files are always in use, so they are never defragmented. After upgrading to Windows 10, fragmented system files can slow down your computer a little. Some disk defragmenters get around this problem by offering boot time defragmentation, which runs before Windows launches. This is able to defragment system files, which results in better performance. IObit Smart Defrag (www.iobit.com) is one of the few free tools that can do this.

Open the program and, on the home screen, select the Boot Time Defrag option on the C: drive. Select the Boot Time Defrag tab and tick all the options. Click Configure, expand Automatic Service on the left and select Boot Time Defrag. Select 'Every 7 day first boot' in the Method list. It runs once a week and adds about 30 seconds to the computer's startup time.

Block bad updates

You have less control over Windows Update in Windows 10 than with previous versions, and the updates run automatically, so you can't choose what is installed. In rare circumstances, an update such as a driver might not be compatible with your PC. What can you do?

If a driver is causing problems, click the search box in the taskbar. Enter 'device manager' and click it in the results. Find the device, right click it and select Properties. On the Driver tab are two useful buttons: Roll Back Driver and Uninstall. Try rolling back and if that does not work, uninstall it.

Unfortunately, Windows Update will detect the old or missing driver and download the new, faulty one again. The solution is Microsoft's 'Show or hide updates' troubleshooter (bit.ly/updates379). Click the Next button on the first screen and then 'Hide updates' on the next to see a list of updates that are available. Tick the ones you don't want to install.

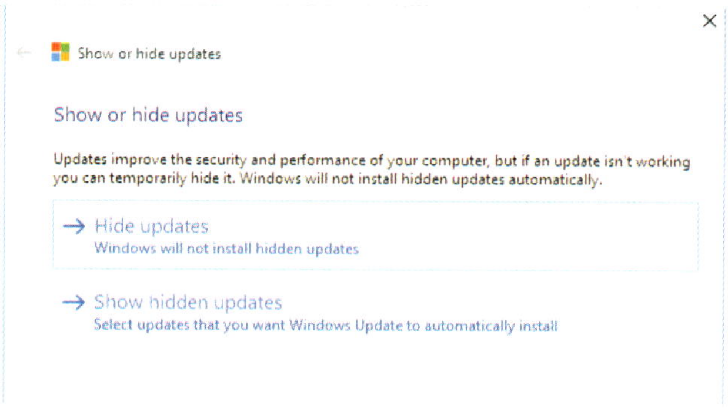

▲ Use this free troubleshooter to choose which updates to install

Chapter 6

Troubleshoot Windows 10

If you're having problems with Windows 10, don't worry – our expert fixes have got you covered

Computer problems can be frustrating and worrying at the best of times. But when you've just upgraded to an unfamiliar operating system or bought a new PC, solutions can be even harder to find. That's why we've devoted a large chunk of this guide to troubleshooting Windows 10 problems. Whether you're suffering from an upgrade that's gone wrong, or you're trying to get a favourite program to run properly, we'll have all the solutions you need. And in our bumper Q&A section from page 140, we'll be providing fixes for dozens more Windows 10 woes.

IN THIS SECTION

Solve problems installing Windows 10

We explain how to fix infuriating problems that can occur before, during or after a Windows 10 installation or upgrade

Though Microsoft's free upgrade offer is now over, there are still ways to install Windows 10 on your PC. The official route is to buy the OS from www.snipca.com/21365 for £99. Alternatively, you can download a copy of the ISO free from www.snipca.com/21366 to try out, then pay for a licence later if you want to keep it. There's even a sneaky way to upgrade completely free of charge by visiting www.snipca.com/21364 and clicking 'Upgrade now'. Technically, this offer is only for customers who use assistive technologies but Microsoft isn't asking for proof, meaning anyone can still install the OS for free (see page 127). Whichever route you take, there's no guarantee the installation will go smoothly. So we're going to provide solutions to many of the errors you may encounter when trying to install Windows 10, as well as problems that can occur during or immediately after installation.

What you can do

- Fix problems that are preventing you from carrying out a Windows 10 upgrade
- Troubleshoot errors that occur during the process of installing Windows 10
- Diagnose and solve problems that happen as a result of an upgrade being carried out

DOWNLOADING & INSTALLING

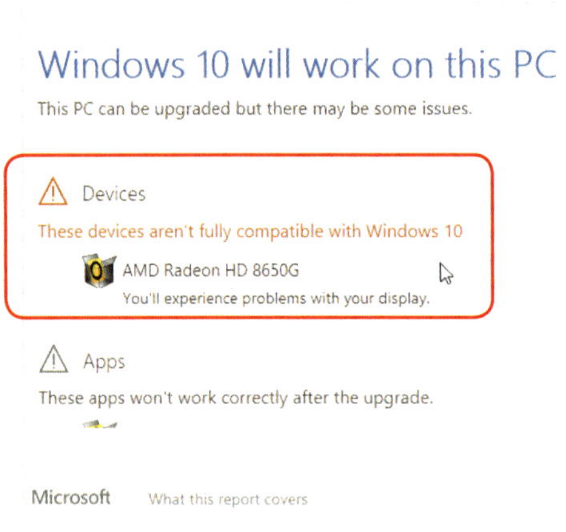

1 'These devices aren't fully compatible with Windows 10'

When you launch the Windows 10 upgrade tool, it automatically runs a compatibility test on your PC to check whether you have any hardware that may not work with Windows 10. This includes anything from your graphics card to your network adapter. You may see a 'These devices aren't fully compatible with Windows 10' alert, but this won't actually prevent you from installing Windows 10.

The problem can usually be fixed by installing the latest driver for the affected device. Make a note of the devices listed, then visit the manufacturer's website for each component and look for the most recent driver for your current OS (Windows 7 or 8.1). Next, reboot your PC, run the Windows 10 upgrade tool again – your computer should pass the compatibility test this time.

2 'This PC will have problems running Windows 10'

If the Windows 10 upgrade tool's compatibility message says 'This PC will have problems running Windows 10', the chances are you can carry out the upgrade, but certain components, such as graphics cards and processors, may cause problems afterwards.

This could be because the manufacturer of a device in your PC hasn't yet released a Windows 10-compatible driver for it. First, visit the manufacturer's site to see if an updated driver is available (see above). If a Windows 10 driver doesn't exist, it may be possible to manually install a Windows 7 or 8 driver using Windows 10's compatibility mode after you've upgraded the OS (we'll explain how to do this in the next section). If that doesn't work, then unfortunately you will need to consider replacing the incompatible component.

3 'Windows 10 will not run on this PC'

If, after checking your computer,

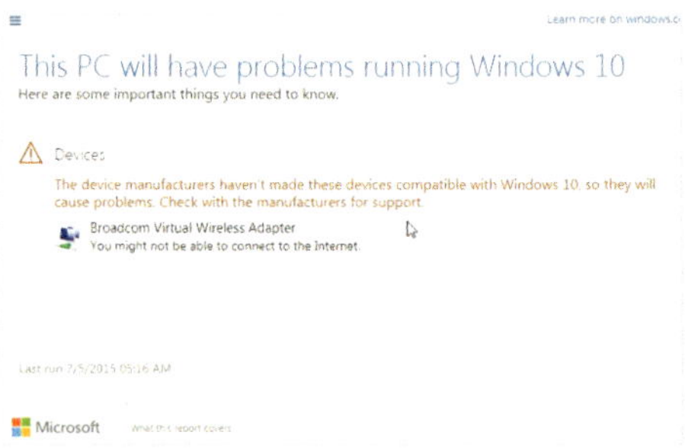

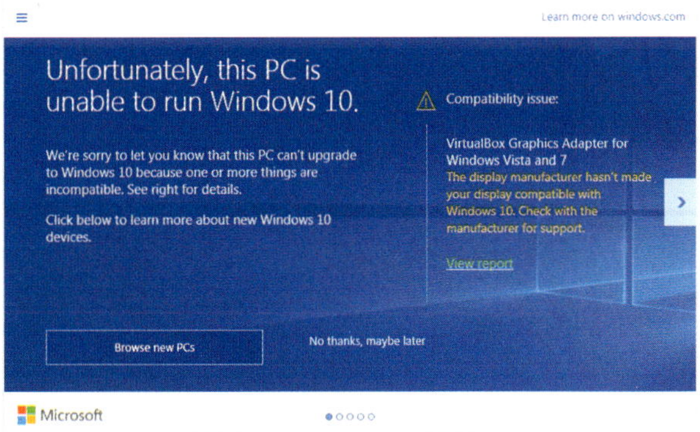

the Windows 10 upgrade tool says 'Windows 10 will not run on this PC' or 'Unfortunately, this PC is unable to run Windows 10', then it's likely to be bad news. In many cases you won't be able to resolve this by updating a driver. You can buy a new component to replace the incompatible one, but doing so could prove to be almost as expensive as buying a brand new computer – certainly if you need a new graphics card or processor.

4 'These apps won't work correctly after the upgrade'

As well as hardware incompatibilities, the Windows 10 upgrade tool will flag up any programs that will struggle to work with the new operating system. Again, this won't stop you upgrading, but you may find that the programs in question are unreliable or don't work at all. Visit the program developer's website in each instance, to see whether there's an update available that is compatible with Windows 10.

If there's no Windows 10 fix for the program you're using, or you'd need to pay to upgrade to a newer version of the tool, then it could be time to consider an alternative program. However, bear in mind that many software problems can be resolved using Windows 10's compatibility mode (see later in this chapter for more on this).

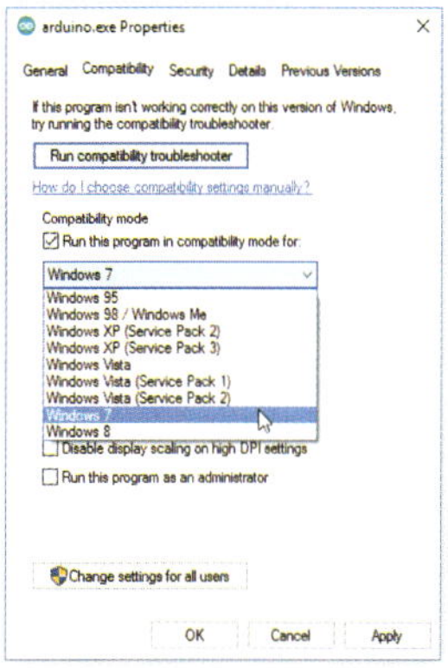

5 'Windows needs more space'

To carry out the upgrade, the Windows 10 installer needs a certain amount of

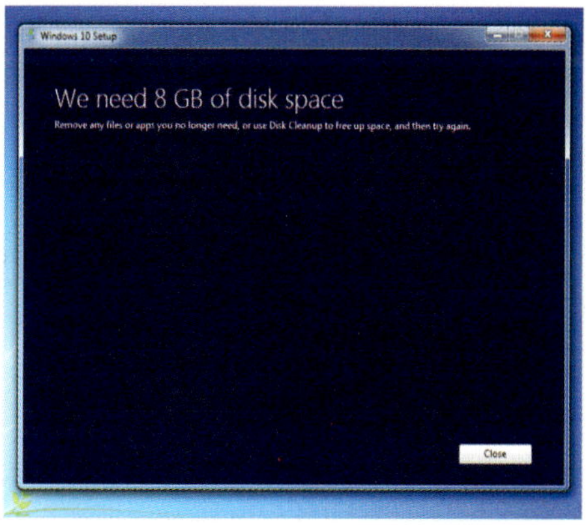

free hard drive space – anything up to 16GB (depending on the version you're installing). If you see a 'Windows needs more space' (or similar) error message at any point when upgrading, you should make more room before attempting the installation again.

The warning will tell you how much space is needed. Make a note of this, then click Start, type cleanup and click Disk Cleanup to remove any junk that may be hogging space.

If this doesn't free up sufficient space, consider uninstalling programs you don't need (via 'Uninstall a program' in Control Panel) or moving files to an external drive to make room on the installation drive.

DURING & AFTER INSTALLATION

1 Installation hangs with no notification

If the Windows 10 installer appears to freeze mid-installation, don't panic. The installation process can take several hours depending on the processing power of your PC, so it's worth waiting to see if it continues.

If you're sure the installation is permanently stuck, cancel the upgrade, unplug any external devices (such as printers and hard drives), disable your Wi-Fi and disconnect any wired network cables, before running the upgrade again.

If the same thing happens, you might be installing the wrong edition of Windows 10 for your PC. For example, if you're upgrading a 32bit Windows 7 Home Premium PC, you need to install a 32bit version of Windows 10 Home, not a 64bit or Pro edition. This can be a particular problem if you're upgrading

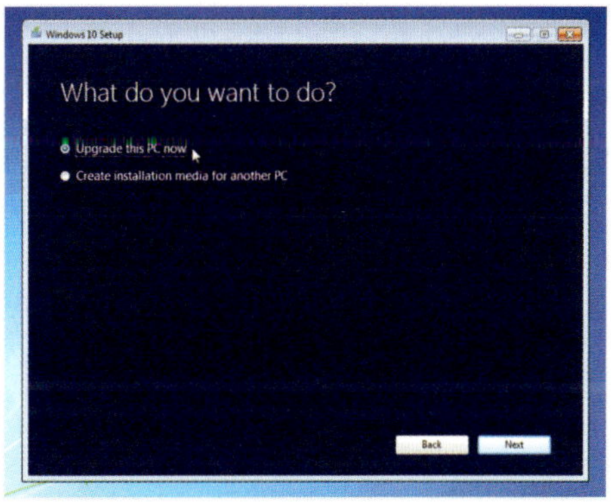

from an installation DVD or USB stick that you created when downloading the operating system from Microsoft's Windows 10 ISO download page at www.snipca.com/21366.

If you're unsure which version you require, you should upgrade via the direct download method because this will automatically install the correct version for your PC.

2 Your PC endlessly reboots during the upgrade

The dreaded 'reboot loop' affected many early upgraders, but Microsoft fixed this via Windows Update. If, however, you experience the same problem it may be that you never received the required update. Cancel the upgrade, then run Windows Update (several times if necessary to make sure you have all the latest updates installed).

If Windows Update doesn't seem to be working properly, open Windows Update on your Windows 7 or 8 PC and make sure it's set to install updates automatically (click 'Change settings' and select 'Install updates automatically' if not), then navigate to the C:\Windows\SoftwareDistribution\Download folder

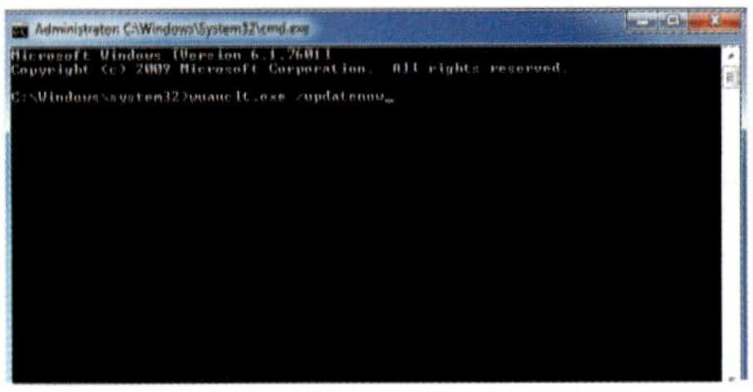

and delete everything you find in there. Next, click Start, type cmd but don't press Enter – instead right-click the cmd link and select 'Run as administrator'.

At the command prompt, type the following line and press Enter to see if this fixes the problem:

wuauclt.exe /updatenow

3 You see a 'Something happened' error message

If you receive this infuriatingly vague error message when upgrading to Windows 10 it could be down to a conflict within your PC's language settings. Open Control Panel, click 'Clock, Language and Region', then 'Region and Language'.

Make sure English (United Kingdom) is selected on the Formats tab (see screenshot below), as well as on the Location tab, and on the Administrative tab where it says 'Current language for non-Unicode programs'.

Once you have made the changes, click OK and retry the upgrade.

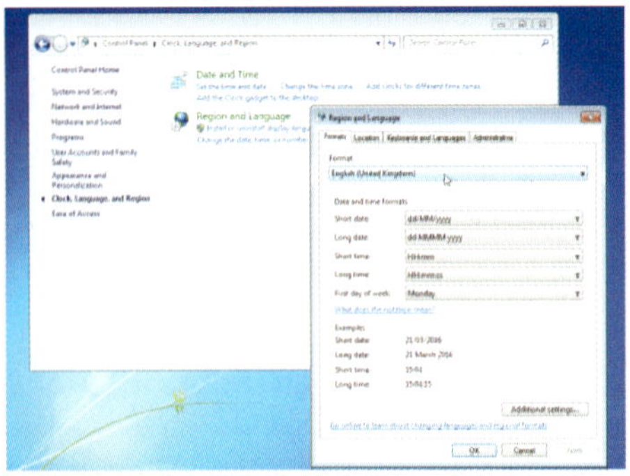

4 'Windows 10 couldn't be installed' / 'We couldn't install Windows 10'

These vague error messages usually come with an error code, such as 80070008 in the screen above right.

You can find out what this and other error codes mean at www.snipca.com/20144, along with possible fixes.

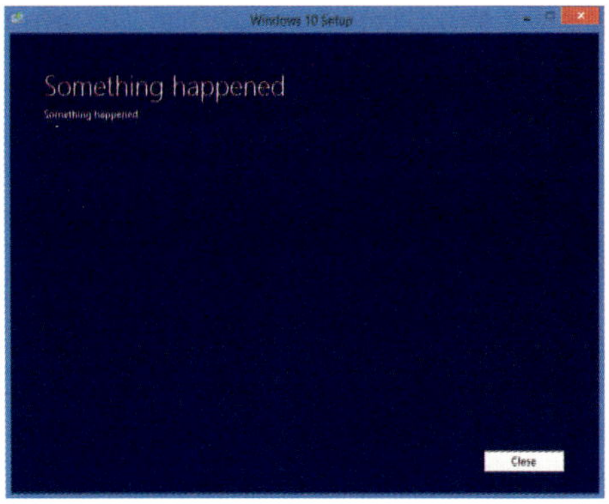

Problems like these can be caused by your antivirus program, so you could try temporarily disabling your security software before attempting the upgrade again (but do remember to turn it back on as soon as possible).

Windows Update glitches may also be to blame, so one solution is to bypass it altogether by downloading and installing the Windows 10 download tool (see the box opposite).

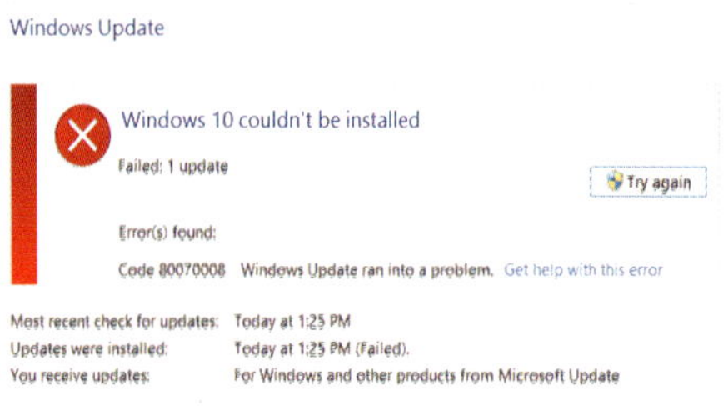

5 You see a black screen after the upgrade completes

If you're upgrading a desktop PC, first make sure the cables connecting your monitor and PC are securely connected. Next, see whether your cursor is visible on screen by slowly moving your mouse. If you don't see it, the install may have caused Windows 10 to switch to a virtual monitor instead of your actual one. Try pressing the Windows key+P to see if this switches your screen back on. You may need to press this key combination three or four times to go through the screens.

If this doesn't work, you could try updating the screen's driver by booting into Safe Mode using a Windows 10 installation DVD or USB stick. You can make one by going to www.snipca.com/20069 on another PC and clicking 'Download tool now'. Run the tool, select 'Create installation media for another PC' when prompted, and follow the onscreen steps, making sure you choose the correct edition of Windows 10 for your PC when prompted.

Boot the PC with the black screen from your DVD or USB drive, then click 'Repair your computer' when prompted. Click Troubleshoot, Advanced Options, Start-up Settings, then Restart and choose the 'Safe Mode with Networking' option. Once your PC starts, right-click Start, select Device Manager, then click the arrow next to 'Display adapters'. Right-click your display adapter and select Properties, then click the Driver tab and click Update Driver.

If none of these solutions work, you may need to upgrade your PC's BIOS. Visit your computer manufacturer's

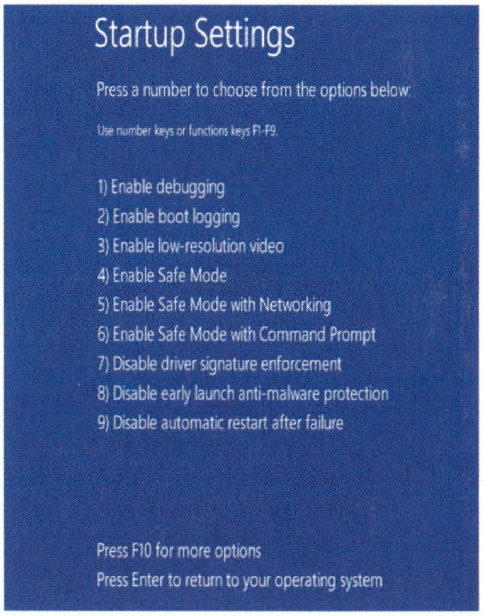

support website (on a working PC) to see if there's a newer BIOS available – if so, follow the manufacturer's instructions for installing the update. This usually involves booting from a USB stick.

6 You can't activate Windows 10 after upgrading

As part of the upgrade process, Windows 10 checks that you have a genuine Windows 7 or 8.1 installation on your PC, then automatically activates your copy of Windows 10. Sometimes activation fails, but this is supposed to happen only when the copy of Windows 7 or 8.1 wasn't genuine. Unfortunately, many people have experienced activation problems on upgrades that are completely valid.

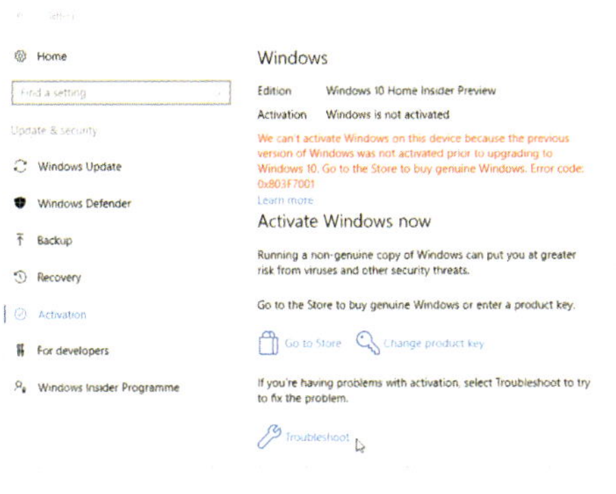

Now, though, a new troubleshooting tool introduced in the Anniversary Update allows you to identify and fix many activation problems automatically. Click Start, Settings, 'Update & security', then Activation and click the Troubleshoot icon if it's present. Follow any remaining on-screen prompts to complete the process.

Activation problems can also happen when you inadvertently carry out a 'clean' installation, which wipes all traces of your existing copy of Windows. However, another recent update to Windows 10 allows you to activate the OS by typing a Windows 7 or 8.1 product key.

So, if you have the Windows 7/8.1 product key that came with your PC, first make sure all the latest Windows 10 updates are installed, then click Start, Settings, 'Update & security', then Activation. Click 'Change product key' and enter the key.

If it still doesn't activate or you don't have the original Windows 7/8.1 product key, you could try calling Microsoft's Licensing Activation centre on 0800 018 8354 and explaining your problem to see if they can help.

7 A program doesn't work properly after upgrading

If you're having problems with a particular program in Windows 10, try running it in compatibility mode. You'll need to locate the program's exe file, which is usually stored in the program's folder in C:\Program Files or C:\Program Files (x86). Right-click the exe file then select 'Troubleshoot compatibility' (see screenshot above right). First, click 'Try recommended settings' to see if this fixes the problem. If not, run the troubleshooter again and this time click 'Troubleshoot program', then follow the on-screen steps.

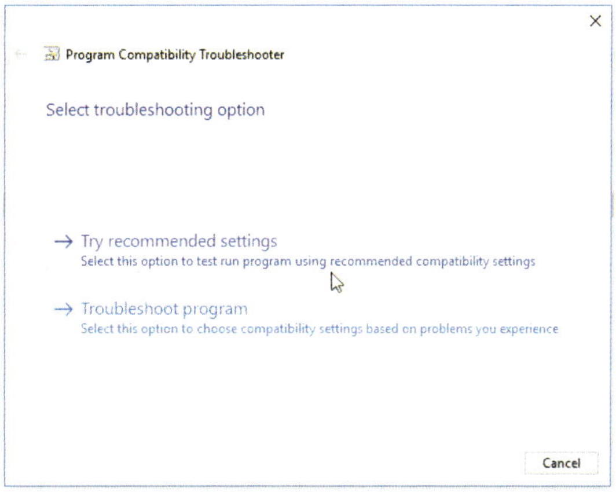

If the program still doesn't work, right-click the exe file again and select Properties. Click the Compatibility tab and try the various options to configure compatibility mode. A good rule of thumb is to select the operating system you previously used the program on. We'll be covering compatibility in more detail later in this chapter.

8 A component fails to work after upgrading

If a PC component – a wireless adapter or sound card, for example – isn't working properly after you install Windows 10, first try running Windows Update several times. If it still doesn't work it's probably because its manufacturer hasn't released a Windows 10-compatible driver. This can usually be fixed by downloading the latest drivers and installing them. Your PC manufacturer may provide driver downloads for all your model's hardware on its website, so try there first. Otherwise, have a look on the component manufacturer's website.

In some cases, if the driver was designed for Windows 7 or 8, you might have problems getting the installer to run in Windows 10. If this is the case, run the installer in 'Compatibility mode'. Locate the driver's setup (.exe) file that you downloaded, then right-click it and follow the instructions in the previous tip to try different compatibility-mode options, starting with Windows 7, until you find a setting that allows the installer to run.

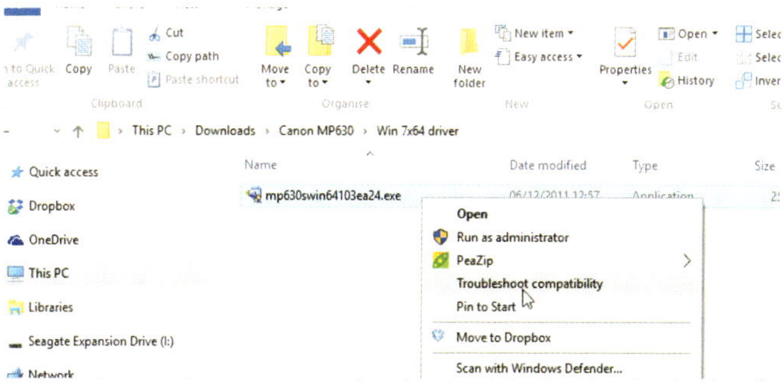

WHY IS MICROSOFT STILL LETTING PEOPLE INSTALL WINDOWS 10 FOR FREE?

As mentioned, Microsoft seems to have intentionally left a loophole for those wanting to avoid paying for Windows 10, thanks to the 'hidden' assistive technologies free upgrade offer at www.snipca.com/21364. It might seem strange that the company has done this, but it makes a strange sort of sense. Microsoft is desperate to get Windows 7 and 8 users onto Windows 10 and will have been hoping for a last minute surge prior to the cut-off date on 29 July. But by leaving a back door open, it's also allowing a semi-unofficial opportunity for many more people who wouldn't normally pay £99 to upgrade. Back doors can suddenly slam shut, though, so if you haven't already grabbed your copy, we'd recommend getting it soon!

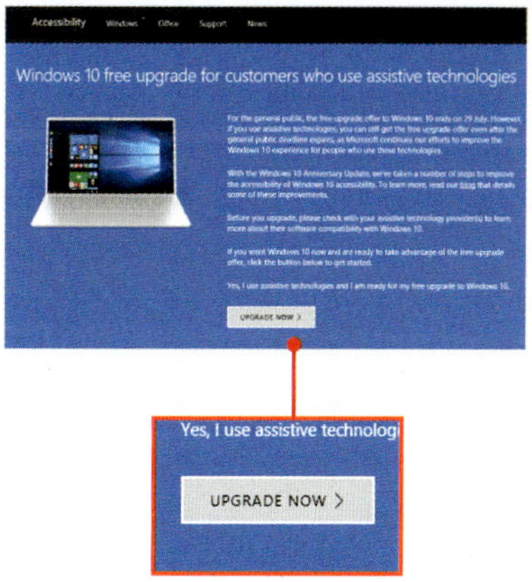

Recover lost files after upgrading to Windows 10

Time required: 40 minutes

In the previous pages, we explained how to fix some of the things that go wrong with Windows 10 during an upgrade. But some people are discovering that the upgrade appears to go fine – until they realise they can no longer find their files. There are a number of ways to recover these files, as Microsoft explains (www.snipca.com/20348). We'll take you through each of Microsoft's suggestions in more detail, as well as provide alternative solutions. If you've backed up your files to an external hard drive or cloud storage before upgrading, then you can easily restore these files to your PC.

STEP 1 If you recently upgraded to Windows 10 and can't see any of your files it may be because Windows has logged you in with a temporary profile. This is an additional user account that Microsoft creates during the upgrade process. To check whether you're logged in with such a profile, go to Settings, Accounts, then click 'Sync your settings' 1. If you see a message at the top saying 'You are logged in with a temporary profile. Roaming options are currently unavailable' 2, go to Step 2. If not go to Step 3.

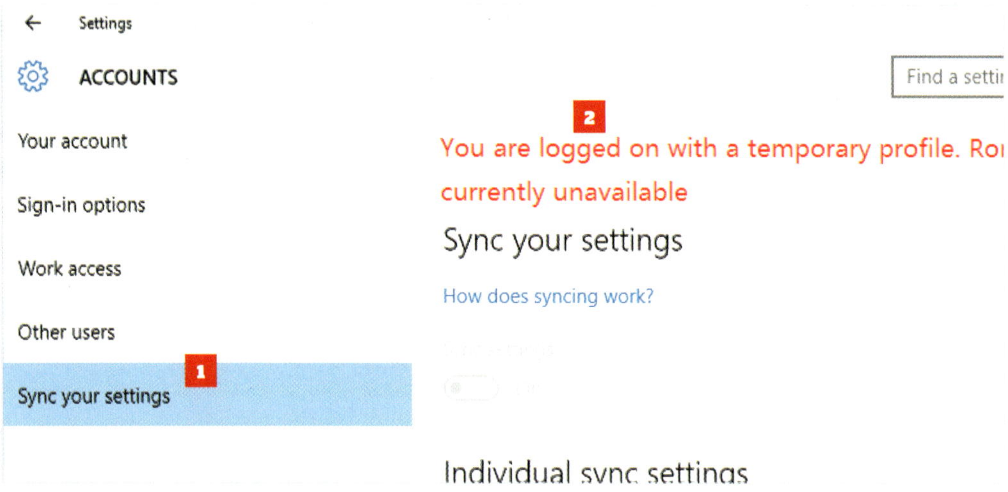

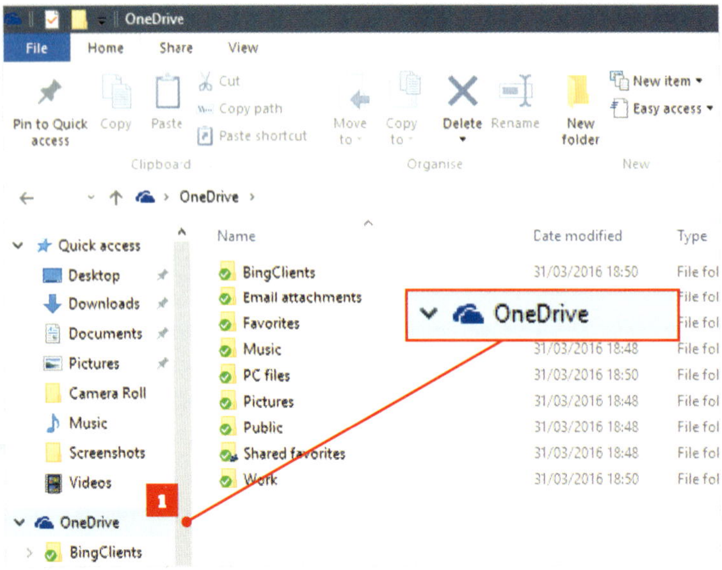

STEP 2 If you've created any new files before realising you're using a temporary profile, ensure you back these up to an external hard drive or a cloud-storage account (such as OneDrive 1, Google Drive or Dropbox) because you won't be able to access these files when you sign in with your normal user profile. To log into this, restart your PC, select your user account from the login page and sign in. You should see all your files, settings and programs exactly as they were on your previous Windows version.

STEP 3 This step only works if you've upgraded your PC within the past 30 days (skip to the next step if not). Windows saves a copy of your previous operating system and all its files for 30 days in case you want to revert to it. To access these files, open Computer, click Local Disk (C:) 1, then open the 'Windows.old' folder 2. Now click Users, then click your PC user name. You'll now see all your files in their correct folders. Copy and move them to your upgraded PC. Windows automatically deletes the 'Windows.old' folder after 30 days.

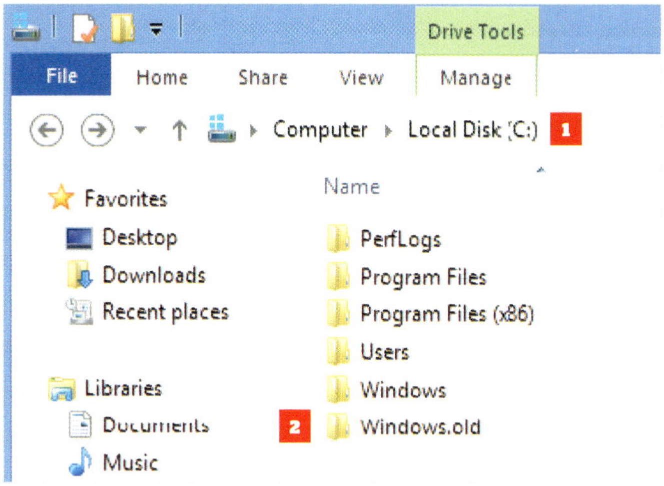

STEP 4 If you logged in using your Microsoft (Hotmail or Outlook) account when Windows 10 first booted, Windows might have disabled your old Administrator account, thereby locking your files. In this case, you need to re-enable your old Administrator account and log in to access your files. To do that, type computer management in the search field on your taskbar, then click 'Desktop app'. Once it's opened, click the dropdown menu beside 'Local Users and Groups' 1, then click the Users folder 2.

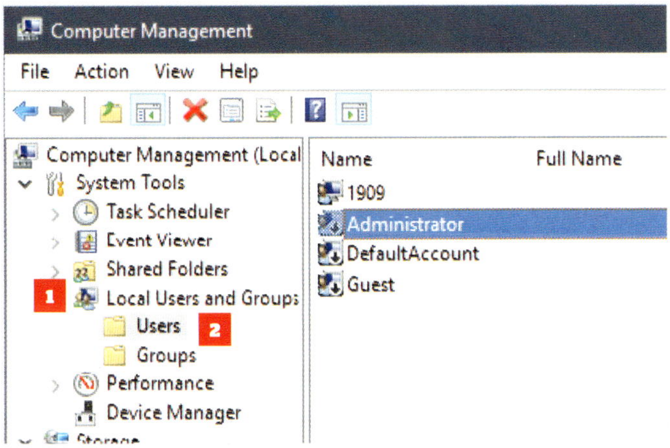

STEP 5 You'll see all your user accounts listed (including those from previous Windows versions). If the Administrator account icon has a down arrow on it 1, your account was disabled during the upgrade. To enable it, double-click the Administrator icon. In the Properties box that opens, untick 'Account is disabled' 2, then click Apply 3 and OK. Now restart your PC. When it boots, choose your previous Administrator account and log in to access your files.

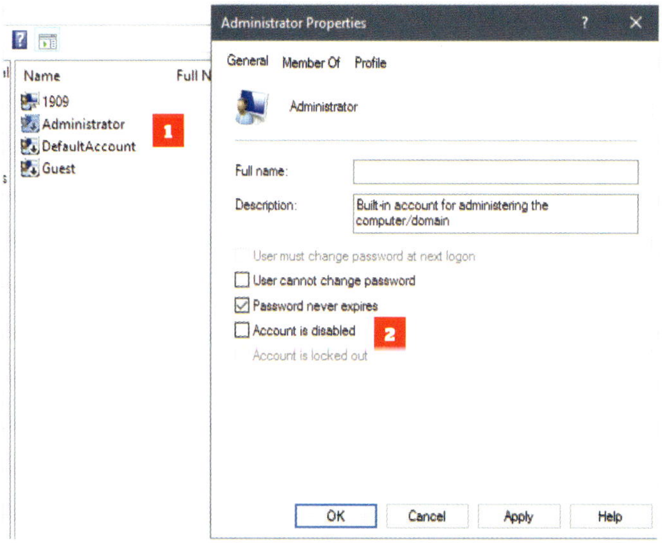

STEP 6 If you still can't find your files, it's likely that Windows moved them to a different location during the upgrade process. In that case, simply search for one of the files. You can search for a file name (such as paris holiday) or a file type (*.doc 1, *.jpg or *.mp3). If you see your file in the search results, right-click its entry 2, then click 'Open file location'. Now move the file to where you want it on your computer.

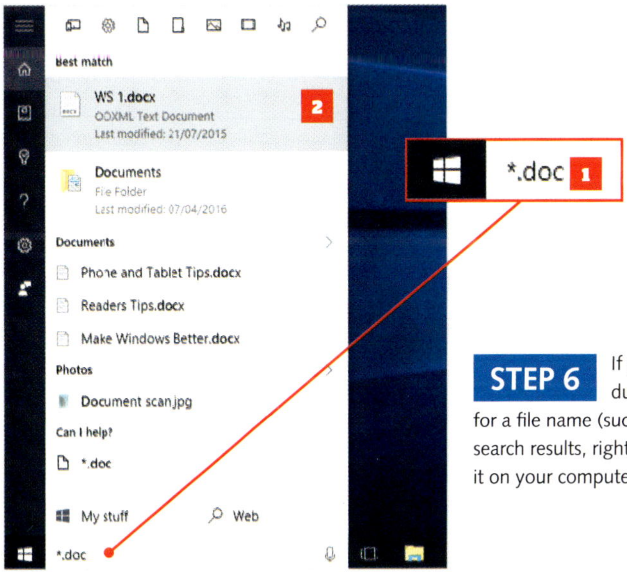

STEP 7 If you still can't find the file(s) you want, they may have been moved to a hidden folder on your PC and won't appear in your search results unless you choose to reveal them. To do that, type show hidden files and folders in the search bar and click the first result. Now select 'Show hidden files, folders and drives' **1**, click Apply **2**, then OK **3**. Find your file, then copy it to your PC (see Step 6).

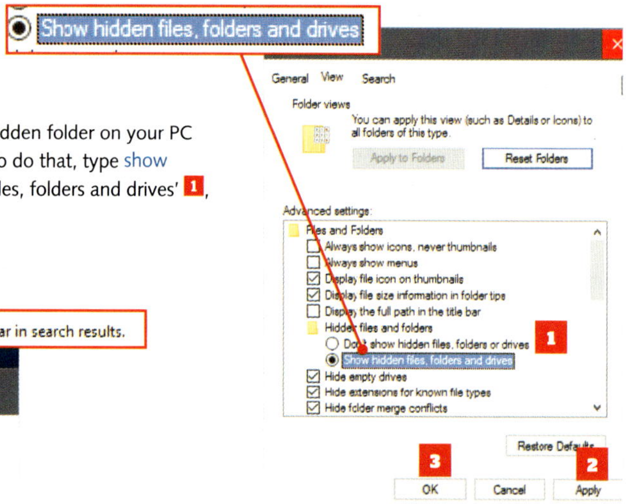

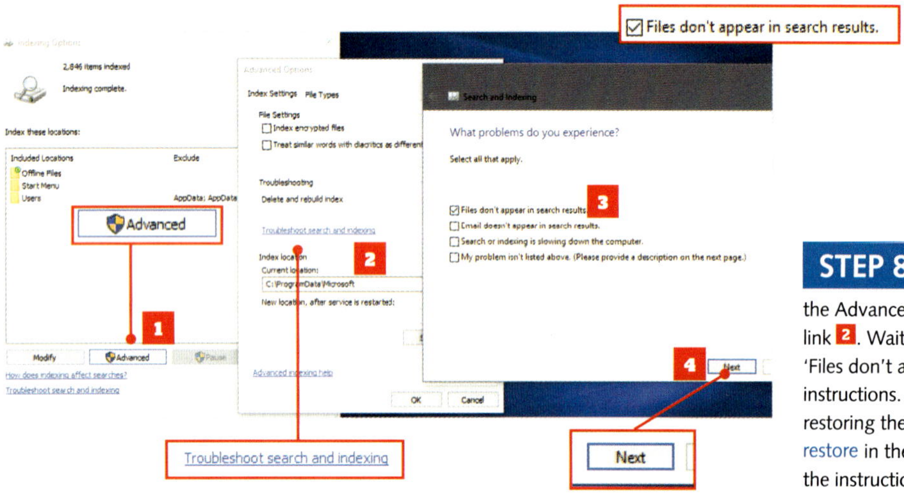

STEP 8 If that doesn't work, type indexing options in the search bar and click the first search result. Now click the Advanced button **1**, then the 'Troubleshoot search and indexing' link **2**. Wait for Windows to detect what the problem is, then select 'Files don't appear in search results' **3** click Next **4** and follow the instructions. If you still can't find your files, then you should try restoring them from a previous backup version. Type backup and restore in the search field, then click 'Restore my files' and follow the instructions.

STEP 9 This final method is useful if you can't find a particular missing file, such as a document, spreadsheet or photo. Windows saves a copy of your files at regular intervals as 'Previous Versions'. Simply right-click any Word or Excel file, click Properties, then click the Previous Versions tab **1** to view them. You can then easily revert to these earlier versions by clicking the version you want **2**, then clicking Restore **3**.

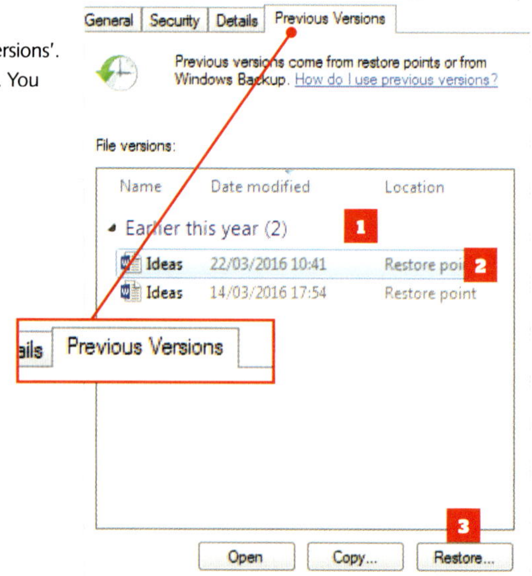

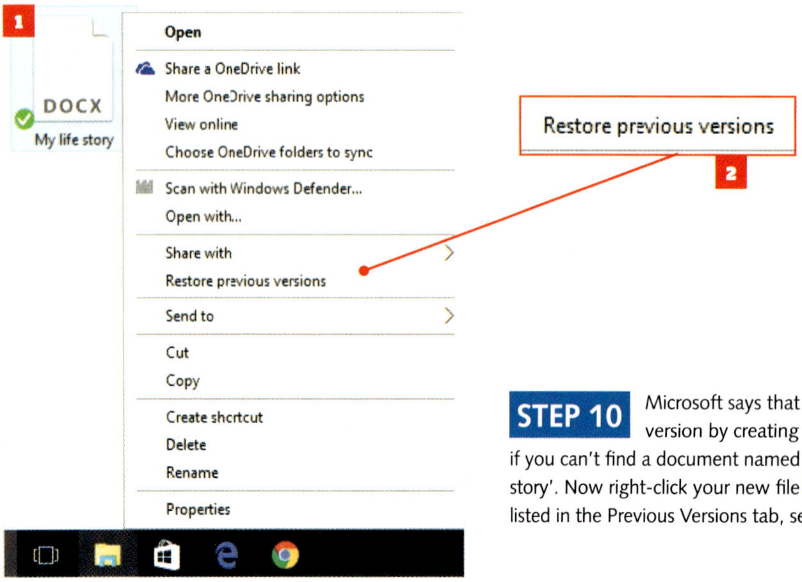

STEP 10 Microsoft says that you can sometimes deceive Windows into recovering an earlier version by creating a new file with the same file name and format. So, for example, if you can't find a document named 'My life story', simply create a new Word file and name it 'My life story'. Now right-click your new file **1**, then click 'Restore previous versions' **2**. If you see any items listed in the Previous Versions tab, select the one you want, then click Restore **3**.

Fix Windows 10 problems in one click

Time required: 30 minutes

FixWin for Windows 10 is a brilliant free tool that's specifically designed to resolve problems with Microsoft's latest operating system. So if your PC keeps crashing, you struggle connecting to the internet, your printer doesn't work or you're running out of storage space, FixWin for Windows 10 will help you fix any of these problems (and around 70 others) – all within a quick click of a button. Here we'll demonstrate how to get and use the tool.

STEP 1 The download process for FixWin 10 differs slightly depending on which browser you use. We're using Windows 10's new browser Edge, but it's just as easy in Chrome, Firefox and Internet Explorer. Go to www.snipca.com/18705, scroll down and click the blue Download File button 1. You'll see a message at the bottom of your browser window 2 when the download is completed. Click Open 3 to see four files, double-click the FixWin 10 setup file, then click 'Extract all'.

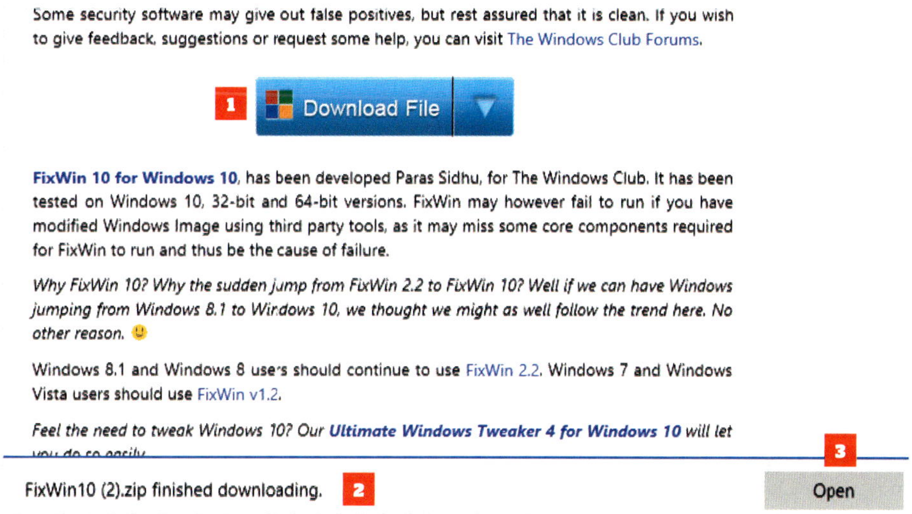

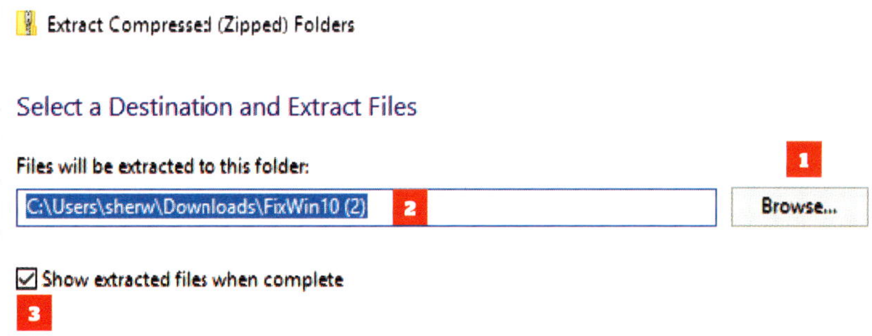

STEP 2 Next, click Browse 1, select a location for the folder's contents on your PC (your Downloads folder 2, for example), ensure 'Show extracted files when complete' is ticked 3, then click the Extract button. When the folder opens, launch the FixWin 10 setup file 4, then click Yes to open the program. FixWin doesn't create a Desktop shortcut, so you'll need to launch this setup file every time you want to use it. The program opens on a Welcome screen providing basic information about your PC (version of Windows 10, processor, hard drive and so on).

STEP 3 Before using FixWin, it's a good idea to create a system restore point so you can undo any changes you make if you're unhappy with them. Click that option **1**. After a few seconds, you'll see a 'Restore point has been created successfully' message. Click OK, then click System File Checker Utility **2**. This will scan your PC and fix any corrupted files. You'll see a message informing you the scan is taking place in the background. Click OK to see a Command Prompt window showing the progress of the scan. It takes about 10 minutes and you'll need to restart your PC if any problems are detected.

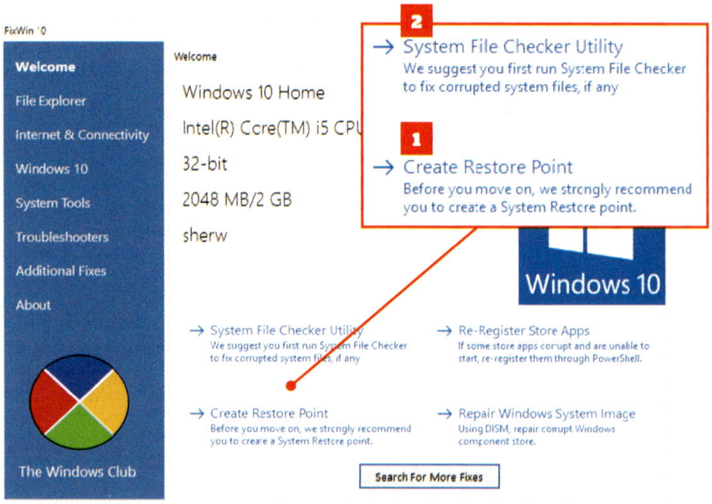

STEP 4 FixWin 10 contains six sections **1**, each containing a number of fixes **2**. Every fix has two buttons **3**. The question mark (?) button describes the problem in more detail and explains what FixWin will do if you click the Fix button. In most cases, clicking Fix will simply change a value in your PC's Registry or add a command to your PC's Command Prompt. First, click the Windows 10 section to see a list of common problems reported by users after upgrading their operating system.

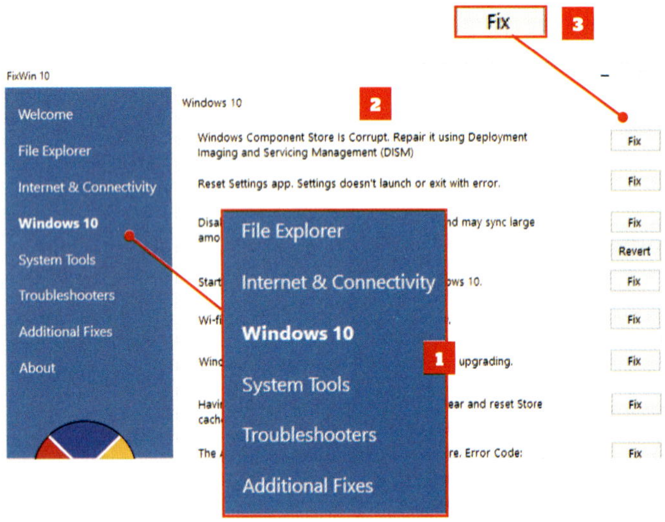

STEP 5 Windows 10 hogs a lot of your hard drive, but syncing OneDrive can slow your PC further. If you don't use Microsoft's cloud-storage service, click the 'Disable OneDrive…' Fix button **1**, then click OK **2** to confirm your changes upon reboot. Some options (like OneDrive) also have a Revert button **3**, letting you undo the action. If your Wi-Fi doesn't work in Windows 10, then simply click the 'Wi-Fi doesn't work after upgrading to Windows 10' fix **4**. Work through the list in this section to fix any other problems you have with Windows 10.

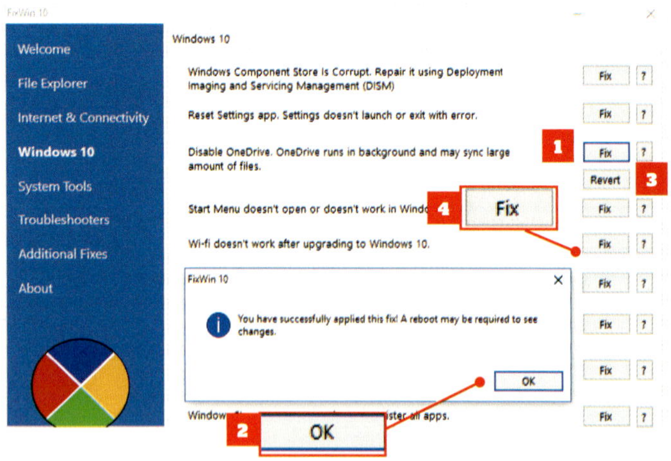

STEP 6 Next, click File Explorer **1** to see fixes for problems associated with File Explorer, Recycle Bin and your folders. Some options include a choice of two fixes, so click the question mark button **2** to see what each fix does **3**. In this section you can recover a missing Recycle Bin icon, fix a problematic DVD drive and restore folder thumbnails in File Explorer. Don't worry if your problems aren't resolved instantly because many fixes require you to restart your PC before coming into effect.

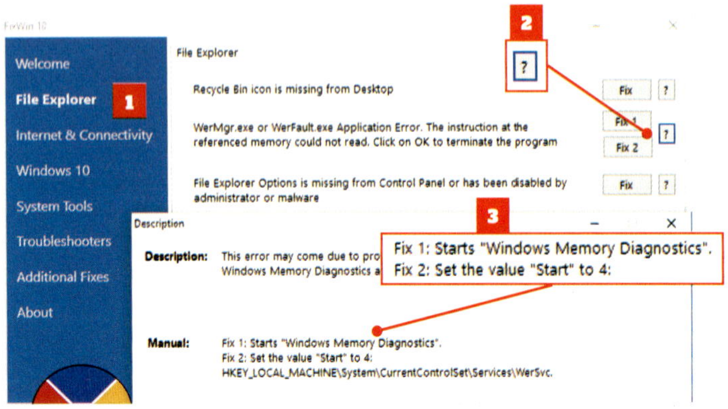

STEP 7 Internet & Connectivity 1 addresses glitches with your broadband, Wi-Fi and firewall, which may be blocking certain content. If you use Internet Explorer, you can apply a fix that lets you download two files simultaneously (third fix from the bottom). System Tools 2 contains two tabs. The System Tools tab 3 offers fixes for your PC's Administrator, Command Prompt, Registry Editor, Device Manager and Windows Defender. The Advanced System Information tab 4 provides detailed information about your PC, including RAM and screen resolution.

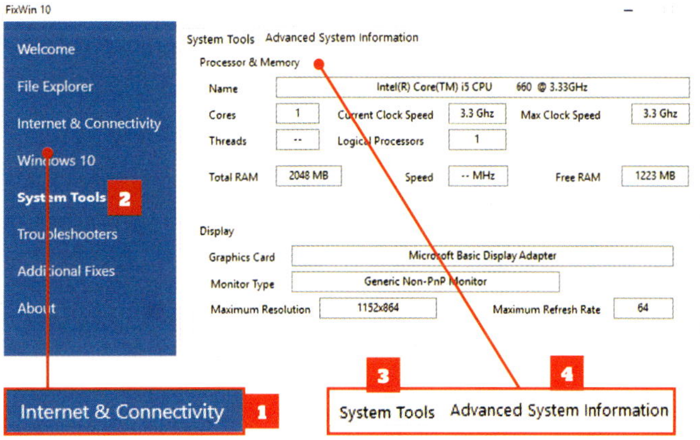

STEP 8 If you don't find a fix elsewhere, you should check the Additional Fixes section 1. This includes, for example, the time-saving option of adding Hibernate to the 'Shut down' button 2. You can also fix disabled Windows 10 notifications 3, corrupted desktop icons and Office files that won't open 4.

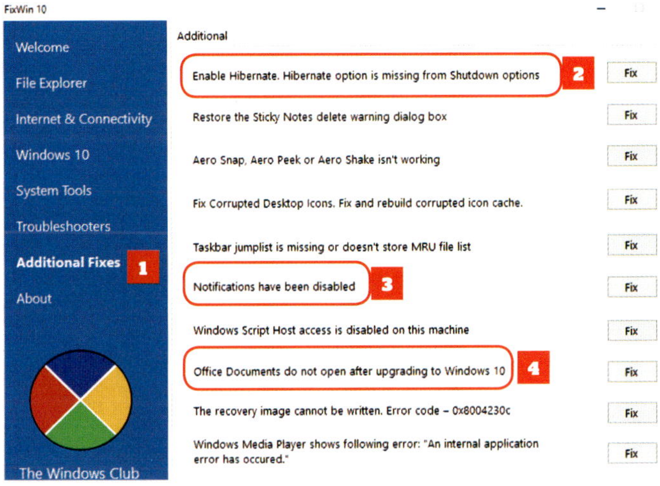

STEP 9 The Troubleshooters section 1 doesn't contain Fix buttons. Instead, it uses Windows' built-in Troubleshooter to address common hardware, software and network problems (including those relating to printers, audio recording/playback and Windows Update). For example, if you can't connect to the internet after applying some of the fixes above, click Internet Connections Troubleshooter 2, then click Next 3. Windows will begin scanning your PC for possible causes. If it's a driver-related problem, for example, you'll be taken to a website, where you can download and install the appropriate driver.

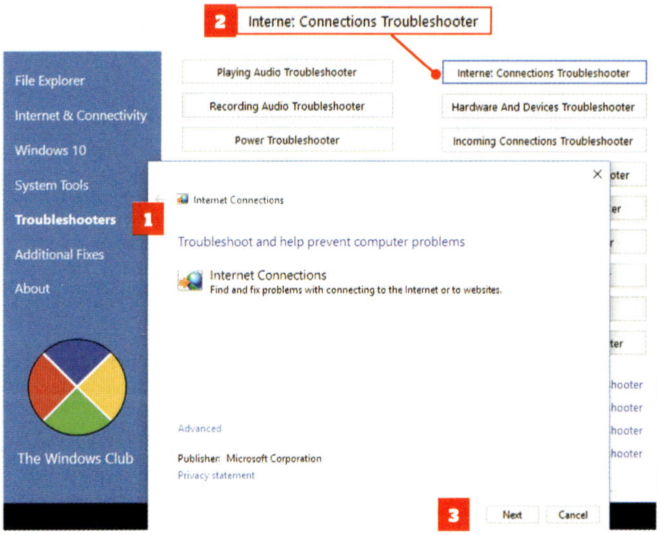

STEP 10 The Troubleshooters section also has four options at the bottom 1. These deal with problems relating to printers and misbehaving apps (Mail, Calendar, Settings and Windows Store). To fix any of these, click the relevant Download Troubleshooter link 2. This will either open a web page containing information about how to resolve the problem, or direct you to a web page from where you can download a relevant file that will fix the problem. Finally, click the Start button 3, Power, then Restart to apply any pending changes.

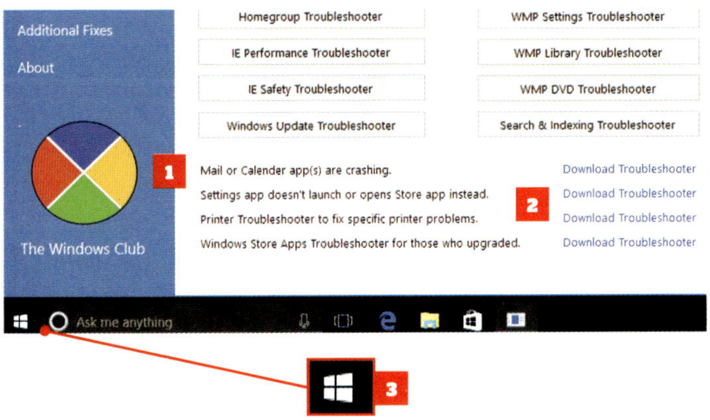

Get old programs running in Windows 10

Solve compatibility problems and get older tools, applications and games working smoothly again

Run as administrator

Some old programs that don't work in Windows 10 can be fixed by running them in administrator mode. This is because, over the years, Microsoft has changed the way Windows works to tighten security loopholes, which older software was sometimes programmed to take advantage of.

There are two types of user account in Windows: standard and administrator. It seems counter-intuitive, but programs are always run in standard mode, even if you are logged in with an administrator account. To run a program in administrator mode, you have to specifically instruct it to do so. Find the program's tile on the Start menu (go to 'All apps' if you can't find it anywhere else), right-click it and select More, then click 'Run as administrator'. Click Yes in the User Account Control window and the program will run.

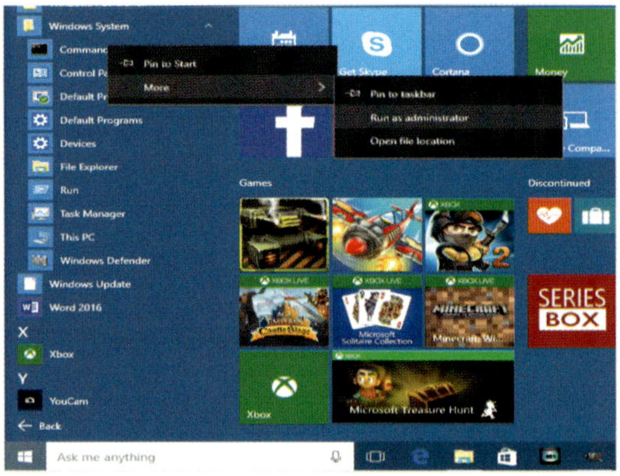

Always run in admin mode

If you find that an old program only works in administrator mode – and you have tested it by right-clicking it and selecting 'Run as administrator' – you can set it to always run in this mode.

If you usually launch the software via a desktop shortcut, right-click this and select Properties. Alternatively, go to Start, 'All apps' and find the program. Right-click it and select More, 'Open file location', then right-click the shortcut to the program in the Explorer window that opens. Select Properties, then the Compatibility tab. Tick the box next to 'Run this program as an administrator' and click OK to apply the setting.

Set the compatibility mode

An old program that won't run might work if you run it in Compatibility Mode. Windows 10 is able to fool programs into thinking they are running in an older version of the operating system. If a program only works in Windows XP, for example, it is possible to set the compatibility mode for that program to Windows XP.

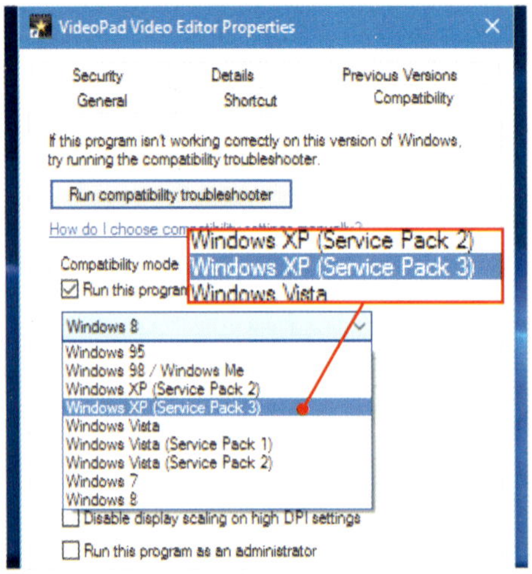

Go to Start, 'All apps' and find the program. Right-click it and select More, 'Open file location'. Right-click the shortcut and select Properties, then the Compatibility tab. Tick 'Run this program in compatibility mode for' and select an earlier version of Windows, such as Windows 7. Click OK and run the program. If it doesn't work, return to the Properties window and try an earlier version, such as Vista or XP, and try it again.

Reduce the colours

High resolutions, 32-bit colour and other advanced capabilities in modern PCs can prevent old programs from running properly, and disabling these elements can fix the problem. Find the icon on the desktop – or go to Start, 'All apps' – then right-click the menu item and select More, 'Open file location'. Right-click the icon, select Properties, then select the

Compatibility tab. In the Settings section, you'll find options to reduce the colour mode, run in 640 x 480 screen resolution and disable display scaling. One or all of these settings may need to be selected for the software to run. Set them and try running the program again.

Use 32-bit Windows

Your PC will either be running the 32-bit or 64-bit version of Windows and, if you upgrade, the corresponding version of Windows 10 will be installed. However, you can switch from one version to another by performing a clean install.

All modern software is designed to run in the 64-bit version of Windows, but if you still use programs designed for Windows XP or Vista, you may encounter compatibility issues by upgrading to the 64-bit version of Windows 10. If this is the case, you may prefer to use the 32-bit version, which ensures maximum compatibility with older software.

If you use any 16-bit software, which was common in the days of Windows XP, you will have to use 32-bit Windows 10 to run it, because the 64-bit version doesn't support 16-bit software.

Troubleshoot compatibility problems

If old software isn't running properly, you can sometimes fix the problem by using a troubleshooter. Right-click the Start button and select Control Panel. Click Troubleshooting, then click 'Run programs made for previous versions of Windows'. When the troubleshooter opens, click Next. It will search the computer (very slowly, so be patient!) for programs that might cause problems. If it finds solutions, simply follow the prompts to put them into action.

Try DRM solutions

SafeDisc and SecureROM DRM (digital rights management) were used on some CDs (usually games) in the early 2000s to protect them from piracy. Windows 10 won't allow them to run but you may be able to make them work in a virtual machine, such as VirtualBox, with Windows XP or Vista installed. Or you could buy the game again, but without DRM. Go to GOG (www.gog.com) and see if the game is listed. Lots of classic games are available at reasonable prices, many for less than £5.

Use VirtualBox

VirtualBox can solve several compatibility problems. It lets you use any version of Windows from within your current version, running the entire OS in a Window within your existing Windows software. If you have software that only works in Windows XP, you can run XP in VirtualBox, then install and run the software in the virtual machine.

Running two versions of Windows, such as Windows 10 and Windows XP, requires a lot of memory. It is just about possible with 4GB, but it will run better with more. Get the VirtualBox software from www.virtualbox.org and download the extension pack, too. Install VirtualBox, then go to File, Preferences, Extensions and click the button on the right to add the extensions.

Click New in the toolbar and select the Windows version you want to install from the Version list. It has them all from Windows 3.1 to Windows 10, in 32- and 64-bit versions where available. You can run a 32-bit version of Windows inside a 64-bit version of Windows 10. To install XP, Vista or 7, just follow the prompts. Increase the memory and hard-drive space settings if you need more, though.

Windows can be installed from a CD or an ISO file created from a CD. Versions up to and including Windows 7 can be installed and run for 30 days without a licence key but, if you plan on keeping it longer, you will need to purchase the full version. Full Windows XP, Vista and 7 discs are still available from a few suppliers. Do not buy the upgrade versions because they can't be installed in this way. Start the virtual machine with the CD or DVD in the drive to install it into VirtualBox.

Run DOS programs

You might want to run old MS-DOS programs on Windows 10, just for fun. There were some great games and applications that have long gone, but you can still find them by searching the internet. Go to DOSBox (www.dosbox.com) and click the Downloads link. Double-click the file to install it, then double-

▲ Revive old DOS games, thanks to DOSBox

click the Desktop shortcut to run it.

Once DOSBox starts, you can't access your PC's hard drive. To get around this, open Explorer, click This PC, then the drive you want to view as C:\. Create a folder called 'dosbox' and put your DOS programs in it. In DOSBox, type mount c c:\dosbox.

Typing c: in DOSBox will now take you straight to that folder. Type dir to list the contents and type the name of the program to run it. To access the CD or DVD drive, type mount d f:\ -t cdrom at the command prompt.

Disable driver signing

Driver signing is a security system that helps to block malware but, because old software often uses unsigned drivers, it will stop it installing. This security measure can be disabled, but it makes the PC less secure, so it's not recommended. Click Start, Power, hold down the Shift key and click Restart.

When the PC restarts, click Troubleshoot, 'Advanced options', Startup Settings, Restart. A number of options are displayed and pressing F7 restarts your PC with driver signing disabled.

▲ Run older versions of Windows within Windows 10 using VirtualBox

Use Windows 10's hidden recovery tools

Time required: 20 minutes

In previous versions of Windows, if you were having problems with your computer, you could get to Safe Mode by booting up the PC and pressing one of the function keys.

Although this no longer works in Windows 10, the OS still has a Safe Mode, along with a range of other handy troubleshooting options – including automatic startup repair and system restore tools – it's just not obvious how you get to them. In this workshop, we'll show you what recovery tools are available and how to find them.

STEP 1 To get to Windows 10's recovery options – including Safe Mode – open the Start menu and click Settings, then 'Update & security'. Click Recovery 1 and, under the 'Advanced start-up' section, click the 'Restart now' button 2. Alternatively, you can click Start, Power, then hold down the Shift key and click Restart. Your computer will reboot and, instead of the usual lock screen, you'll be presented with a blue screen of options. See steps 6 and 7 for how to get to the recovery options if Windows won't start.

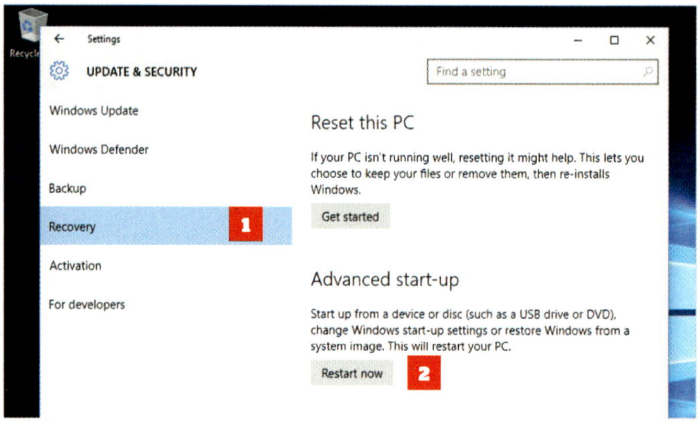

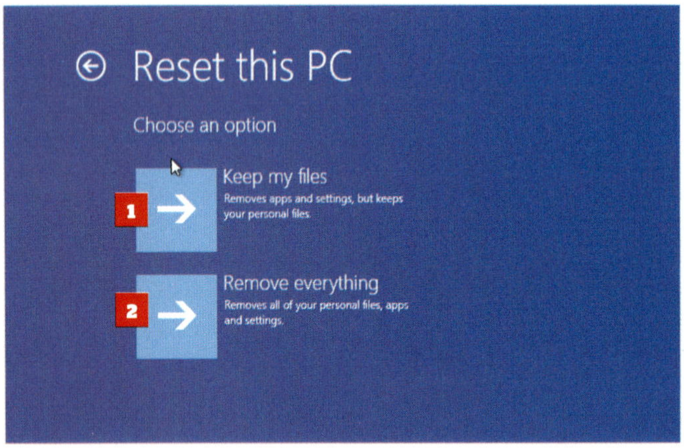

STEP 2 On the 'Choose an option' screen, there are three choices available. Clicking Continue will start your PC as normal. Clicking 'Turn off your PC' will just switch your computer off. So, instead, click Troubleshoot. Now there are two more options to choose from. You can either click 'Reset this PC' or select 'Advanced options'. 'Reset this PC' refreshes your Windows installation but removes apps and settings. Use 'Keep my files' 1 or 'Remove everything' 2, but use both options with caution. Resetting your PC is very much a last resort.

STEP 3 Less drastic tools are available in the 'Advanced options' menu. If you've made a backup of your entire PC using the system image option in Windows' Backup & Restore tools, you can use the System Image Recovery option here 1 to restore your PC. Make sure the external hard drive you backed up to is plugged in, then click this option and follow the steps. If you're having problems starting Windows, click Start-up Repair 2. This is an automatic process that can scan and fix any problems Windows is having when loading.

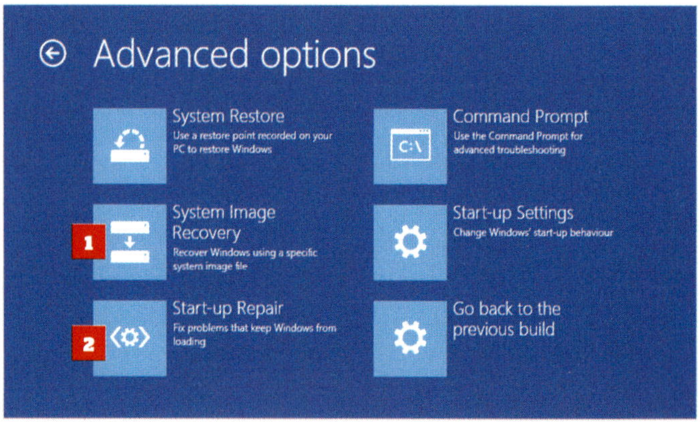

STEP 4 Click System Restore **1** to access your recent restore points – snapshots of your system settings – which might be enough to roll back your PC if you've installed something and you're having trouble reversing it. The 'Go back to the previous build' **2** may or may not be of use, depending on when you installed Windows 10 and when it was last updated. Within 30 days of upgrading, this option will allow you to roll back to your previous OS. If you've installed the Anniversary Update, clicking this will allow you to roll back to the pre-updated version of Windows 10. If you've cleaned previous Windows installations from your hard drive, though, 'Go back to the previous build' won't work at all.

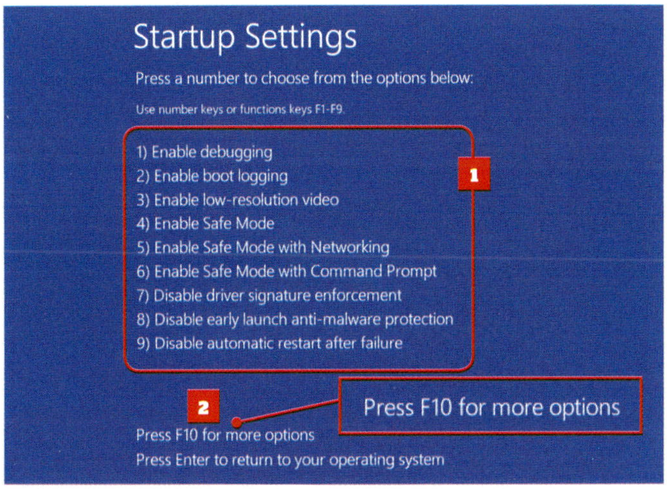

STEP 6 If your problem is so bad that you can't boot into Windows, then you won't be able to access these recovery tools using the instructions in Step 1. In theory, Windows 10 is supposed to understand when you're having a problem starting the OS and automatically boot to the recovery options. If you don't see them straight away, though, try rebooting a few more times – eventually, you should see the blue the 'Choose an option' screen. If not, then using another PC, download a Windows ISO from bit.ly/winiso3821 and burn it to a DVD, then try booting to the disc. You should be able to reach the recovery tools this way.

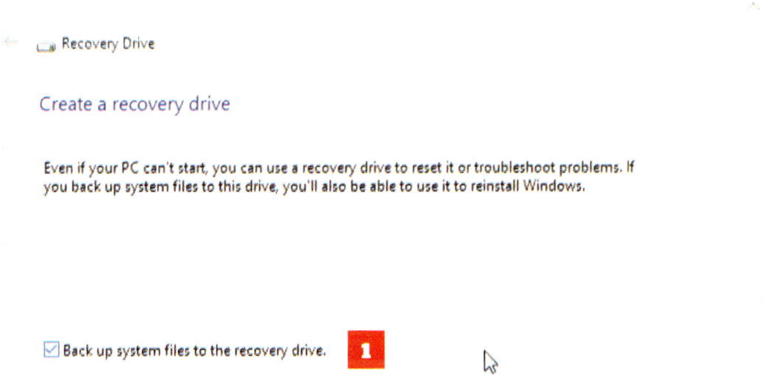

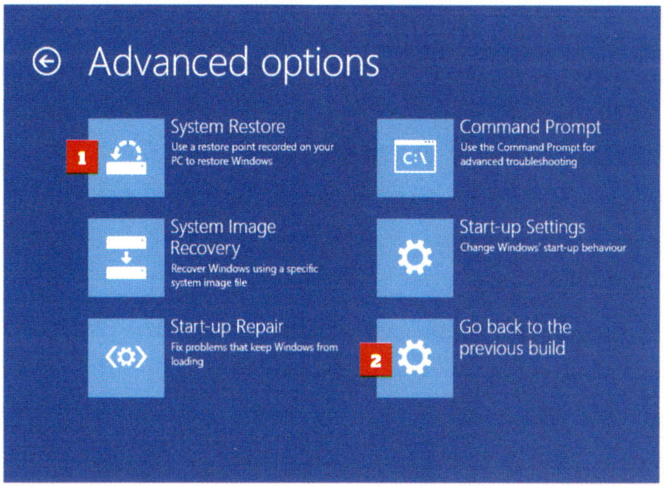

STEP 5 Start-up Settings provides a selection of options that can help you get Windows going, even if there's something wrong with it. Select the option from the Advanced menu, then click Restart to boot your PC to another blue screen with a new list of options. These include various types of Safe Mode **1**. Use the F1 to F9 keys to select an option – 'Enable Safe Mode with Networking' is the most useful for troubleshooting – or press F10 to see even more options **2**.

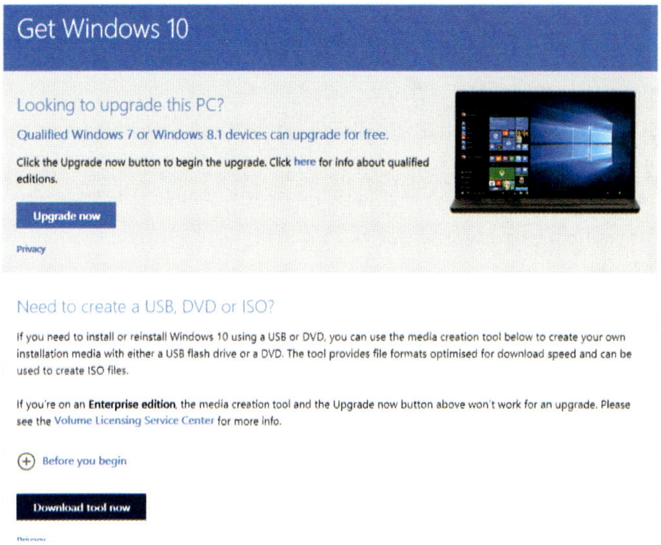

STEP 7 In case Windows can't automatically boot to the recovery options, it's a good idea to create a USB recovery drive to ensure you can always access the recovery tools when you need to. Insert a USB flash drive, then right-click Start and select Control Panel. Click 'System and Security', then 'Security and Maintenance', then Recovery, then click 'Create a recovery drive' and follow the remaining on-screen steps. If you want to back up system files as well **1**, you'll need a larger (16GB) drive. Keep your drive safe and use it to boot your PC in emergencies.

Computer act!ve Reader Offer

Kaspersky Internet Security – half price!

We're big fans of Kaspersky Internet Security.

It has won the past SEVEN Computeractive Antivirus tests, regularly hitting 100% protection.

It keeps you safe from all the threats that lurk online – viruses, Trojans, worms and more.

We want our readers to use the best security programs, so we run a Software Store selling Kaspersky at incredible discounts.

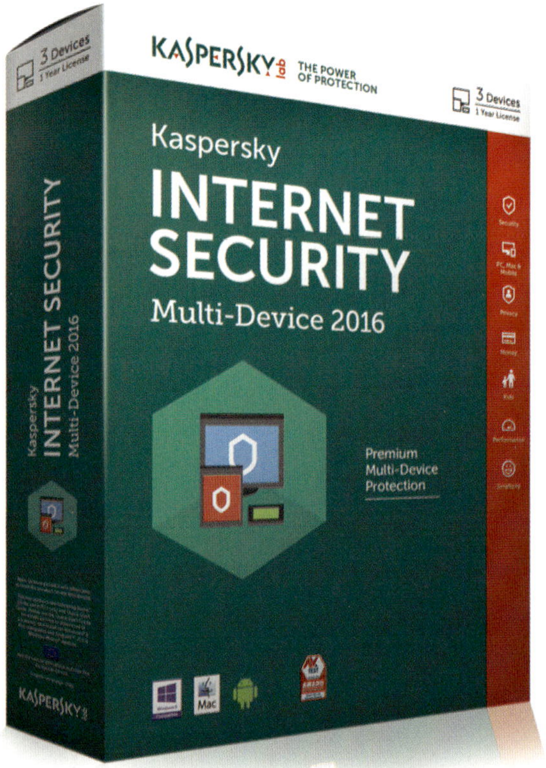

Prices on our Software Store vary, but you can usually find a reader offer that slashes Kaspersky by 50 per cent.

To see which Kaspersky discounts we're currently offering visit:

www.snipca.com/21305

KASPERSKY: WINNER OF THE PAST SEVEN
COMPUTERACTIVE ANTIVIRUS TESTS

Fix problems with Windows 10's Start menu

Time required: 10 minutes

Most people welcomed the return of the Start menu in Windows 10, but many have also had problems with it. And it seems Microsoft is listening, because it recently released a free tool that automatically identifies and fixes Windows Start menu problems. It checks whether apps are installed correctly, analyses your registry and addresses problems that may have occurred. These steps will also fix any problems with Microsoft's personal assistant, Cortana.

STEP 1 First, Microsoft recommends that you update your PC to the latest version. To do that, open Settings in your Start menu (if you can't open your Start menu, right-click your taskbar, click Settings at the bottom, Home at the top left). Next, click 'Update & security', then 'Check for updates' 1. Wait for any pending updates to install, then click the 'Restart now' button. After restarting, check whether your Start menu problems have been fixed.

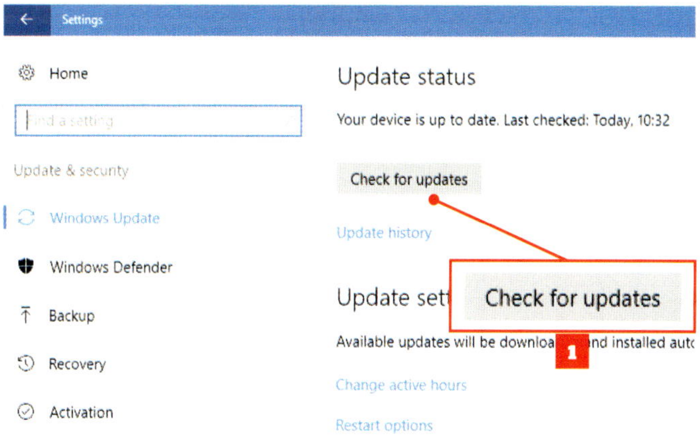

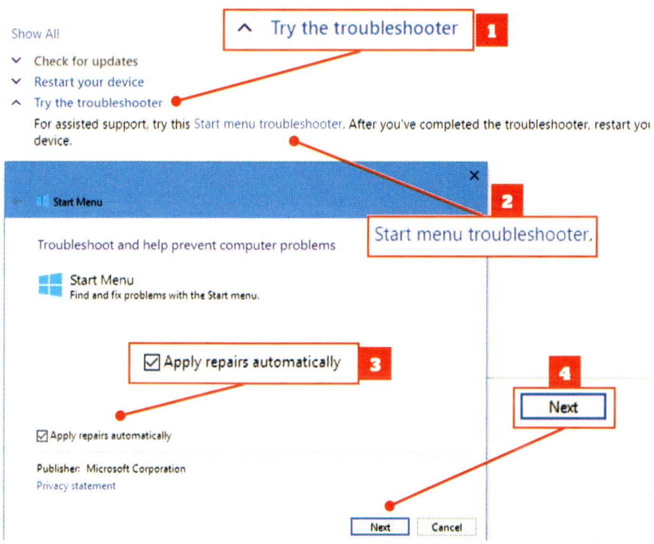

STEP 2 If the problems persist, download Microsoft's free Troubleshooter tool. To do that, go to www.snipca.com/21096, scroll to the five blue links, click the 'Try the troubleshooter' dropdown menu 1, then the 'Start menu troubleshooter' link 2. This downloads the tool to your PC. Open the downloaded setup file, click the Advanced link at the bottom, tick 'Apply repairs automatically' 3, then click Next 4. The tool will now scan your Start menu for any problems and fix them.

STEP 3 After the fix has been carried out, click the 'View detailed information' link at the bottom of the Troubleshooting tool. This gives you a list of problems that were checked 1 and the fixes (if any) that were applied 2. Click the Print icon 3 if you want to print this information for future reference. Now restart your PC and check if the problems have been fixed. If not, Microsoft suggests that you create a new administrator account. To do this, go to www.snipca.com/21096 again, scroll to the 'Create a new local administrator account' dropdown menu 4 and follow the instructions.

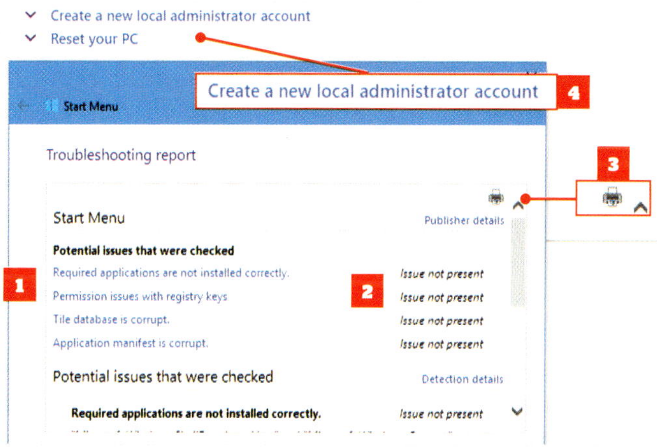

Windows 10 troubleshooting Q&A

Windows 10 is a great operating system, but it doesn't always work perfectly. Here we provide answers to some commonly asked questions

In the first part of our troubleshooting chapter, we've explained how to fix problems with upgrading, compatibility and more. But there are dozens of other problems that don't easily fit into a specific category. So, instead, we've grouped them all together in a kind of offline FAQ.

All the questions in our big Q&A were sent to our sister magazine, *Computeractive*, by its readers, so they're all real problems that we know many people have been experiencing. Since Windows 10 launched last July, *Computeractive* has received thousands of emails from readers requesting fixes to problems they've been having.

So, if you're having a problem with Windows 10 that we haven't solved so far, then check through the following pages to see if there's an answer. You may not suffer from the exact same problem as those featured, but you might be able to apply some of the answers to other troublesome aspects of the operating system. And if you still can't find a fix, then why not try sending it to the experts at *Computeractive* to see if they can offer a solution? *Computeractive* is on sale every fortnight, priced just £1.99 and is packed with computer advice, reviews and workshops. Email them at noproblem@computeractive.co.uk.

What you can do

- Stop Windows 10 slowing down your computer
- Solve problems with graphics cards and displays
- Stop Windows 10 updates repeatedly failing
- Make on-screen text look less blurry
- Fix problems with apps that don't work
- Cure problems with the Windows 10 Start menu
- ...and much more!

1 What's happened to my Windows 10 desktop?

Q I downloaded Windows 10 and I really like it, but for some reason, either my fault or some quirk, the new operating system thought I would prefer giant squares instead of the traditional desktop. These big squares are very easy to add to or remove, but I would like to know what happened, as well as how to go back to the traditional desktop.

A It sounds as if you've inadvertently enabled Windows 10's Tablet mode which, as you can probably guess, is designed to make the operating system easier to use on tablet devices. In Tablet mode, Windows 10 is all about app tiles and live tiles — those big squares you see.

It's surprisingly easy to activate Tablet mode with a wayward click (or tap) in Action Centre, but also just as easy to fix. First, click the Action Centre icon to the left of the clock on the taskbar — it's the little geometric speech bubble. Now just click 'Tablet mode' and your traditional desktop will return.

If, for some reason, the problem persists, click Start, Settings, System then 'Tablet mode' and select 'Use desktop mode' from the 'When I sign in' menu and 'Don't ask me and don't switch' under 'When this device automatically switches tablet mode on and off'.

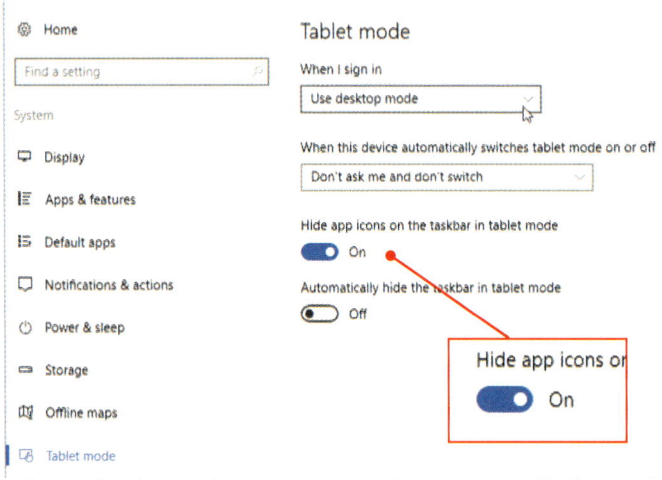

2 Can I take my copy of Windows 10 to a new PC?

Q I feel I know my way around a computer pretty well. However, I'm wondering if I can transfer my copy of Windows 10 from my desktop PC to a laptop that's currently running Vista? The PC is nearly 10 years old, and I fear it may pack up any minute.

A Microsoft's licensing rules are incredibly convoluted. It boils down to how you came by Windows 10 or your original copy of Windows 7/8.1, and if you upgraded from one of those earlier editions.

First, if you bought Windows 10 new – either on a DVD and in a box, or as a paid-for download from Microsoft's website – then you have what the company calls a full-package product (FPP), which you're free to transfer to any PC you please, as long as you remove Windows 10 from the previous PC. The same will apply if you originally bought an FPP version of Windows 7/8/8.1 and upgraded that to Windows 10, as your older licence is subsumed into your new Windows 10 licence. However, if Windows 7/8/8.1 was pre-installed on your PC, then you had an original-equipment manufacturer (OEM) licence, the terms of which were similarly subsumed into your new Windows 10 licence. That means you still have an OEM licence, and Microsoft's terms for these don't allow Windows to be transferred to a different PC.

However, Microsoft will let you transfer an OEM licence to another user, as long as the transfer includes the original device (ie, you can sell your old PC with Windows 10 in place).

Assuming you upgraded a pre-installed copy of Windows 7 to Windows 10, that means you've got an OEM licence that must stay with the machine. To check the terms of your licence, press Windows key+X, then click Control Panel, followed by 'System and Security' and then System. Now click 'Read the Microsoft Software Licence Terms' in the 'Windows activation' section.

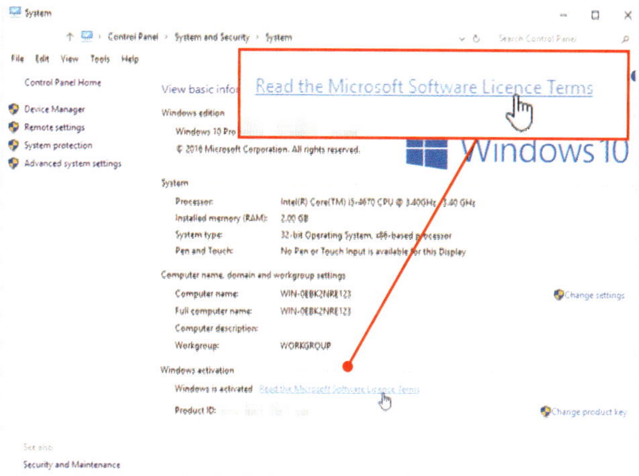

3 How do I update my graphics card driver for Windows 10?

Q When I try to upgrade to Windows 10, Microsoft's tool tells me it wants to make sure my computer was suitable – and it's not. It looks like Windows 10 doesn't support my Nvidia graphics card. I went to Nvidia's website and found the Windows 10 driver for my card, but Windows said it wasn't compatible. How does one get around this stalemate?

A Your solution is to create a Windows 10 installation disc. This bypasses the compatibility check conducted by the standard upgrade procedure. If your PC doesn't have a DVD drive, then you should use a USB stick instead. Then, once Windows 10 is installed and running on basic graphics card drivers, you can download and install the necessary drivers from Nvidia's website.

So, visit Microsoft's Windows 10 website (www.snipca.com/19757) and download the media-creation tool. Double-click to launch the file, then accept the licence. Choose the 'Create installation media for another PC' button, click Next, check the language settings, then click Next. Choose 'USB flash drive' or 'ISO file' (DVD version), click Next then follow the prompts. If you're creating a DVD version, right-click the ISO file and choose 'Burn disc image'. Then follow the prompts. When the process is complete, take your DVD or USB stick and insert it into your Windows 7 PC. Press Windows key+E to open Windows Explorer, navigate to the relevant drive and double-click the setup.exe file to begin the Windows 10 installation.

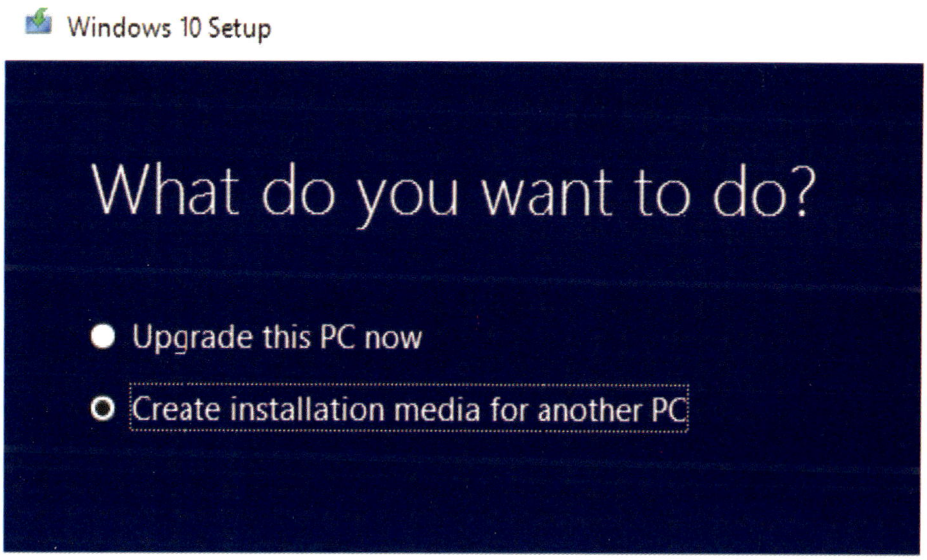

4 How do I stop Windows Update getting stuck?

Q I have a desktop PC and laptop, both have Windows 10 installed and both suffer from the same problem – they get stuck when trying to download updates.

My laptop gets stuck at 36 per cent into the update, and my desktop at 0%. I tried using the Windows Troubleshooter (www.snipca.com/19897), but it was no help. Do you have any suggestions?

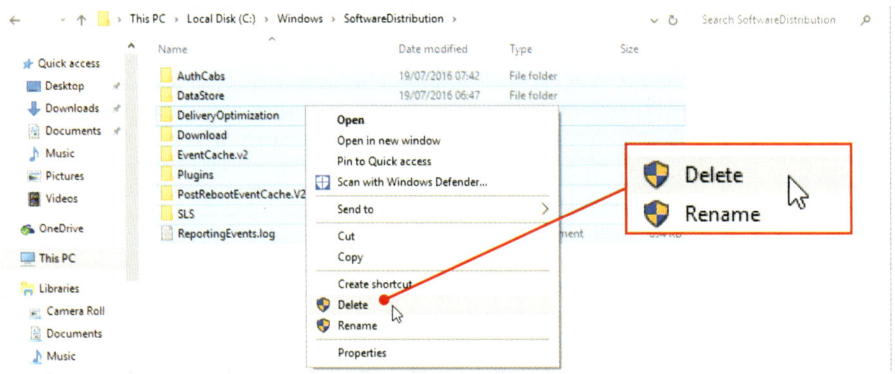

A Reported by many users, this problem is slightly different to the infamous 'reboot loop' that plagued people last year following a dodgy update.

To fix it, you basically need to 'flush out' Windows Update. Restart your PC, right-click Start, then select Command Prompt (Admin). In the window that opens, type the following two commands at the prompt, pressing Enter and waiting for a confirmation message after each one:

```
net stop wuauserv
net stop bits
```

Next, click Start, File Explorer and navigate to the C:\Windows\SoftwareDistribution folder. Press Ctrl+A to select all the items, then right-click your selection and select Delete, then Yes.

If you're unable to delete all the files in this folder, restart your PC, run the above commands, then try again.

Once the folder is empty, go back to the Command Prompt window and type the following two commands, pressing Enter and waiting for a confirmation message after each:

```
net start wuauserv
net start bits
```

When this process has finished, exit the Command Prompt and try Windows Update again.

5 How can I stop my computer hanging on shutdown?

Q I've been having problems with my Windows 10 PC ever since a recent update. The update itself installed okay, but now whenever I shut down my PC, the screen goes blank, but the PC remains switched on, whirring away for about a minute before finally turning itself off. I know it's a small thing, but before the update my computer used to shut off instantly and now it's really bothering me! Is there a fix for this?

A Hanging on shutdown is a problem caused by the Windows 10 November update. The fix for this is simple, but incredibly counter-intuitive. Click Start, type power options, then click Power Options. In the window that opens, click 'Choose what the power buttons do'.

Next, click 'Change settings that are currently unavailable' and scroll down to 'Shutdown settings'. Here, untick the 'Turn on fast start-up' option and click 'Save changes'.

This should solve the problem, but be advised that hanging shutdowns can also be caused by programs and processes not closing down properly, or by driver problems. If you're still having trouble, make sure all your programs, apps and hardware drivers are up to date.

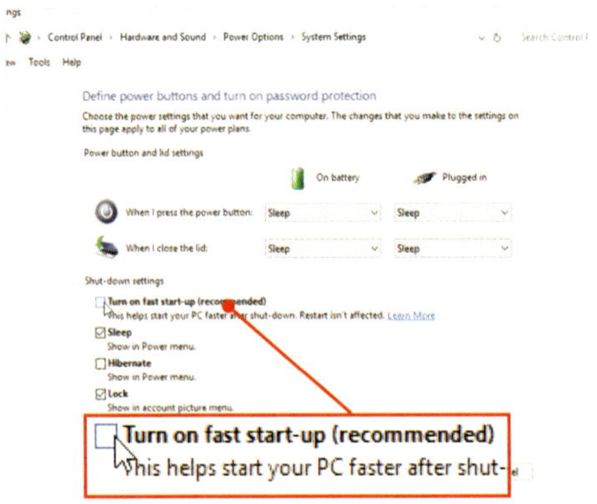

6 How do I reset Windows 10?

Q Whenever I had serious problems in Windows 7, I reset it. It was a drastic fix, but always worked. Can I do the same thing in Windows 10?

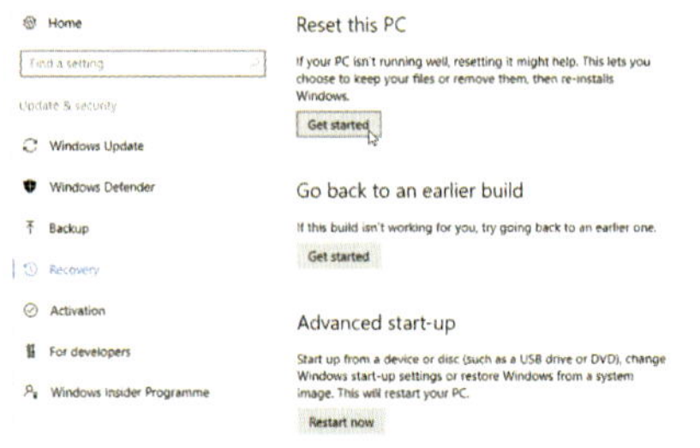

A Yes, and it's simple to do. But remember that it will delete all your programs and third-party apps, so you'll need to reinstall them. You can reset Windows without deleting your personal files, but we thoroughly recommend backing up all your files and data first. When you're ready, click Start, Settings, 'Update & security', then Recovery. Click 'Get started' under 'Reset this PC', select the 'Keep my files' option when prompted, then follow the on-screen instructions. If the problem is so severe that your PC won't start, you should be greeted by a set of recovery options after two failed boot attempts. Click Troubleshoot, 'Reset this PC' then 'Keep my files' and follow the prompts.

7 Why is my display stuck in the wrong resolution?

Q Since upgrading to Windows 10, my screen has been stuck at a resolution of 1024x768, when it should be 1280x768. The monitor is listed as 'Generic PnP' and will not allow me to change the resolution. I have tried every type of alteration, including reinstallation. Is there any way of sorting this problem out?

A This is almost certainly a classic display (graphics) driver problem. Normally, Windows 10 should download and install graphics driver updates automatically but, in some cases, it doesn't and you have to install them manually.

Right-click Start then select Device Manager. Click 'Display adapters', then double-click the adapter listed. In the box that opens, click the Driver tab, then click Update Driver, followed by 'Search automatically for updated driver software'. With any luck, Windows will find a suitable driver and install it. If not, make a note of your display adapter's make and model, then browse the manufacturer's website – usually AMD (www.amd.com), Intel (www.intel.co.uk) or Nvidia (www.nvidia.co.uk) – for the most recent driver. Download and install this yourself.

With the correct driver installed you should be able to select the right resolution by right-clicking the desktop and selecting 'Display settings', then 'Advanced display settings'.

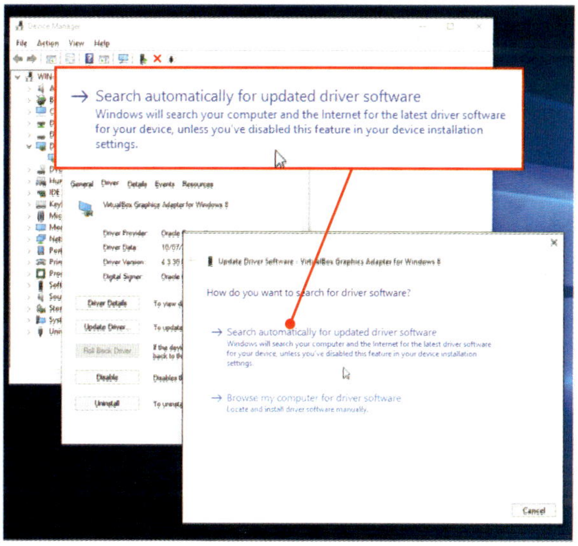

8 How can I get my apps back?

Q I recently lost access to all my Windows 10 app tiles, being unable to open the Start menu pane (or should that be pain?) that contains them. I tried some suggestions I found online and was able to restore Start menu access, but a number of apps – in particular the Windows Store – are now completely unresponsive. I am losing what little hair I have left over this problem! Please help!

A Many users are reporting problems with Windows 10 apps that disappear or won't run. There are different ways to try to fix them. First, head to www.snipca.com/19880 and click 'Run troubleshooter' (see screenshot). This will download a small automated tool for Windows. Double-click the tool to run it, then click Next to see if it can identify and fix any problems.

If you still can't launch your apps or open the Windows Store, try running a second Microsoft troubleshooter at www.snipca.com/19881. You could also try resetting the Windows Store cache. Right-click Start, click Command Prompt (Admin), type WSReset.exe at the prompt and press Enter. Try the Store again.

If none of these solutions work, then you can try reinstalling all your apps from scratch.

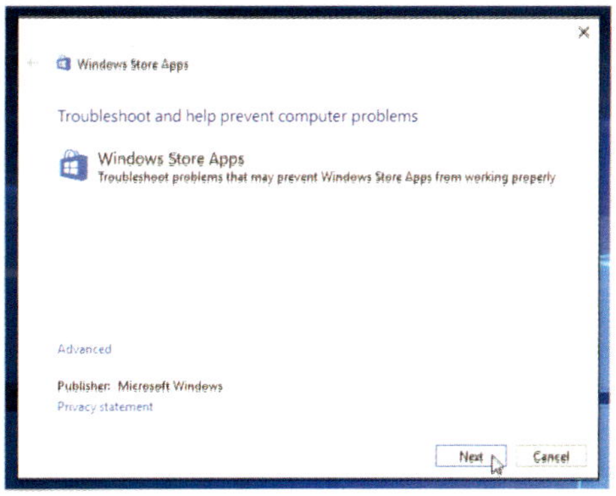

Click Start, type powershell, then right-click the Windows PowerShell listing and select 'Run as administrator'. At the prompt, type the following three commands, pressing Enter and waiting for each command to complete before typing the next.

To prevent any mistakes caused by typing the commands in manually, you can copy and paste the commands directly from our Pastebin page: www.snipca.com/19901.

```
get-appxpackage -packageType bundle |% {add-appxpackage -register -disabledevelopmentmode ($_.installlocation + "\appxmetadata\appxbundlemanifest.xml")}

$bundlefamilies = (get-appxpackage -packagetype Bundle).packagefamilyname

get-appxpackage -packagetype main |? {-not ($bundlefamilies -contains $_.packagefamilyname)} |% {add-appxpackage -register -disabledevelopmentmode ($_.installlocation + "\appxmanifest.xml")}
```

Don't be alarmed if you see any red error messages during the process.

Restart your PC once everything has completed and then try your apps again.

If they're still broken, try running the PowerShell commands once more. Should your apps still refuse to work at this point, then you may need to consider the more drastic solution of resetting Windows – see the 'How do I reset Windows 10?' question earlier for more on this.

9 Why does Edge crash a few seconds after launch?

Q Since upgrading to Windows 10, I have been enjoying the new web browser Edge – or at least I was enjoying it until a recent update seemed to break it completely. Now, whenever I launch Edge, I'm only able to use it for a few seconds before the program window completely disappears. I've tried some of the suggestions found online, but none of them seem to cure the problem.

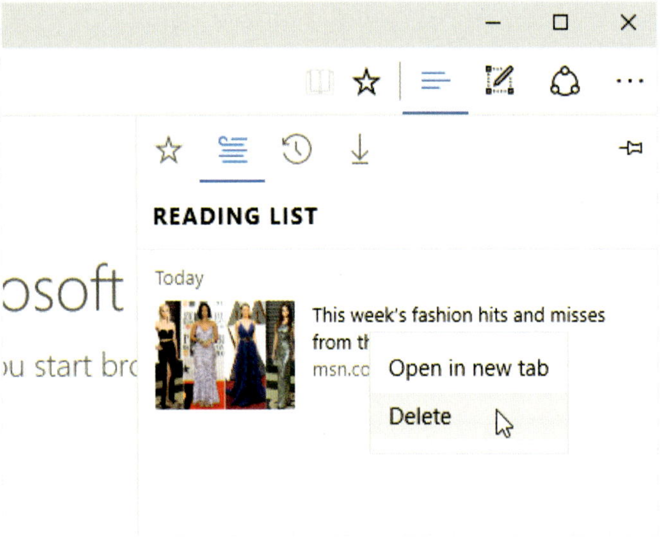

A A number of people have reported similar problems with Edge following the big update that Microsoft issued last November. It's hard to diagnose exactly what's causing the browser to crash, but there are several things you can try to fix it.

First, scan for any corrupt system files. Right-click Start and select Command Prompt (Admin). At the prompt, type sfc /scannow and let the process complete. If that doesn't fix it, try clearing your browsing history – though you'll need to be quick if Edge crashes soon after launching!

Click the menu (three dots) button, then click Settings, 'Choose what to clear', tick all the options and click Clear. You could also try deleting all the items in your Reading List – in some cases this has cured crashing problems. Again, you'll need to be quick.

Launch Edge, then click the Hub (three lines) button, followed by the Reading List icon – right-click anything listed here and choose Delete (see screenshot above). If that still doesn't fix it, then you may have to consider switching to Chrome (www.google.com/chrome) or Firefox (www.mozilla.org/firefox), at least until Microsoft comes up with a solution.

10 How can I stop Windows Update interrupting my work?

Q I'm absolutely fuming because I've just been interrupted in the middle of an important bank transfer by Microsoft choosing to take over my computer and start a lengthy update! Not only that, but when it completed, I went back to browse the web only to be told that Firefox was no longer my default browser. Is there anything I can do to stop this type of thing happening again?

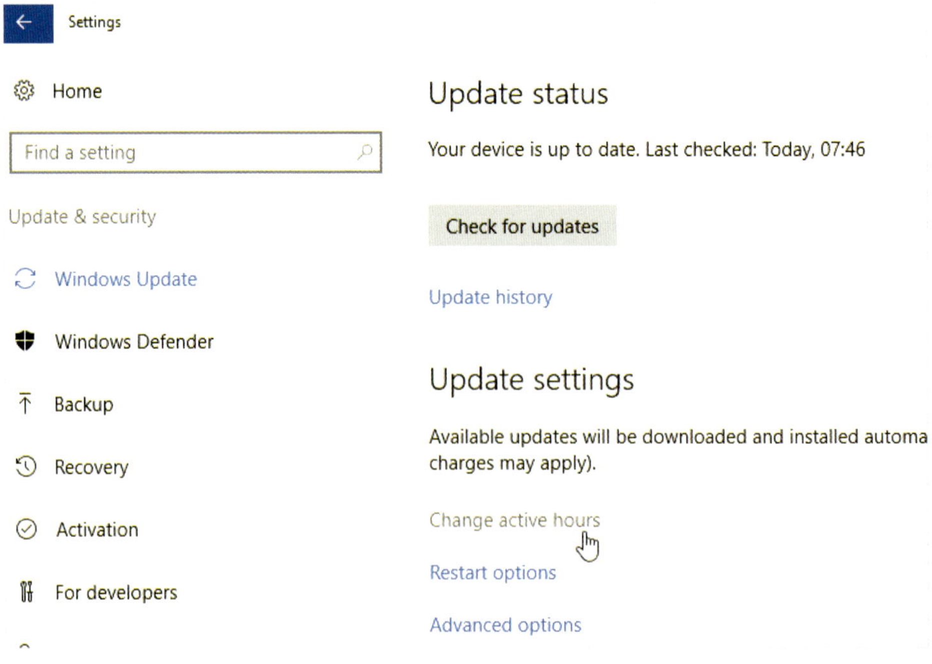

A It's well known that Microsoft has made automatic updates obligatory in Windows 10. However, it is possible to make sure you're never interrupted by updates at inconvenient times. Click Start, Settings, 'Update & security', Windows Update, then click 'Change active hours'. Here you can specify a portion of the day when you know you'll need your PC and you don't want to get interrupted by updates. Select a start and end time, then click Save and you won't be bothered by updates during these hours again.

The second problem described – the default browser being changed after an update – is a widespread problem that can occur after a big update is installed. Other default programs may have been changed, too and, annoyingly, the only way to fix it is to click Start, Settings, System, 'Default apps' and reselect your preferred tools under each category.

11 Can I get Windows Live Mail to work in Windows 10?

Q **I hope to soon migrate to Windows 10 from Windows 7 Home Premium. I currently use Windows Live Mail to manage six different email accounts, but I've read online many cases of people having difficulty migrating Live Mail to Windows 10. Is there a fix for this or can you recommend a suitable alternative that I can use when I upgrade? I would like to stay with an email client rather than a webmail account.**

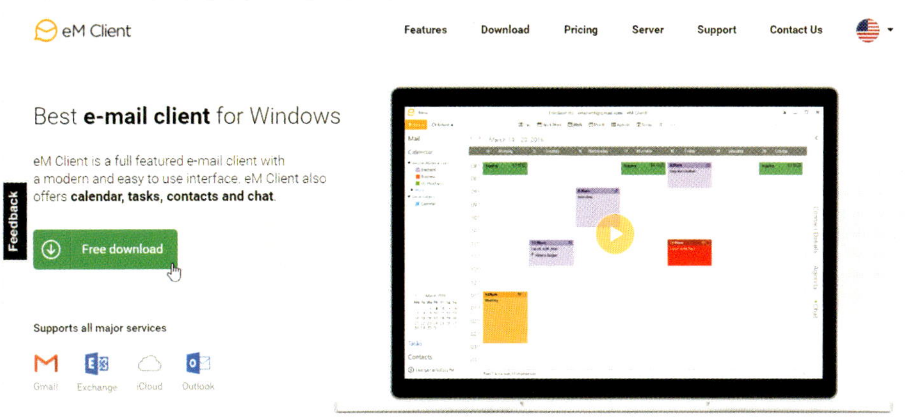

A Windows Live Mail's compatibility under Windows 10 appears to be a bit hit and miss. We were able to download it (free as part of Windows Essentials, from www.snipca.com/19882) and run it without any problems on two separate Windows 10 PCs. But many users are reporting that they're struggling to get it to work after upgrading.

In addition, Microsoft recently announced it has ended support for accessing Outlook.com through Windows Live Mail. Until recently, Outlook.com users have been able to sign into Windows Live Mail with their account and use the program to send and receive messages, or sync calendars and contacts. But from June this year, Windows Live Mail stopped being able to connect to Outlook.com directly, meaning that the program will effectively stop working for anyone currently using it to access their Outlook.com account.

As such, we feel that it might be time to move on from Windows Live Mail, as its functionality is compromised and Microsoft's support for it is clearly waning. We'd suggest backing up all your current messages and contacts in Live Mail (see www.snipca.com/19883 for Microsoft's instructions), then re-importing them into a new email tool once you've upgraded to Windows 10.

As for alternatives, the Mail app that's built into Windows 10 isn't bad at all – we'll demonstrate how it works later on in Chapter 7. Another potential replacement might be Thunderbird (www.snipca.com/19884). Or you could try eM Client (click the Free Download button at www.emclient.com), which works similarly to Windows Live Mail and supports Outlook.com accounts.

12 Can I get an old program to stop crashing?

Q **I upgraded my PC to Windows 10, but the software I use for voice recordings (Creative MediaSource, www.snipca.com/19898) doesn't seem to be compatible with Windows 10 – it always crashes when I run it.**

Is there any way to fix this or can you recommend another similar program? I've tried Audacity but find it too complicated.

A Creative MediaSource is a very old program that was once supplied with Sound Blaster audio cards.

As with any old program, you could try running it in Windows 10's compatibility mode to fix your problems. Locate the program's exe file – it should be somewhere

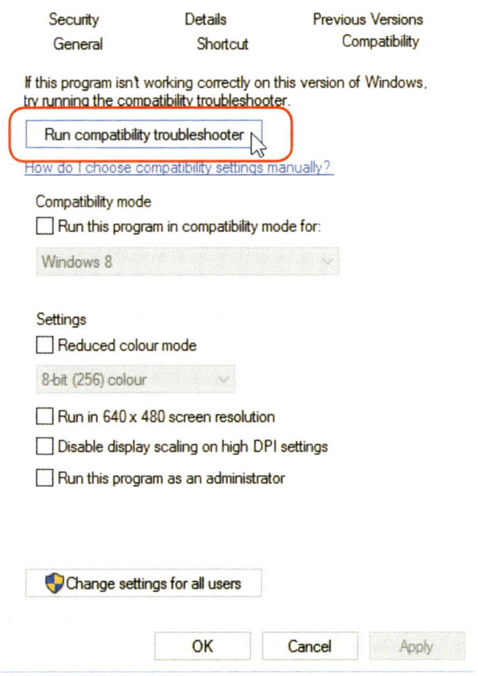

in C:\Program Files or C:\ Program Files (x86) – right-click it and select Properties. On the Compatibility tab, try running the troubleshooter (see screenshot left) and experiment with the other settings available to see if you can get the program to run without crashing. Under 'Compatibility mode', for example, you can run the program as if it were running in a previous version of Windows.

Alternatively, if you only want to be able to make simple recordings, you could instead consider using the Voice Recorder app that comes with Windows 10. Click Start, type voice then click the Voice Recorder link that appears in the Start menu. The Voice Recorder app doesn't have many options, but it's certainly very easy to use.

For more on curing compatibility problems, turn back to page 134 of this guide.

13 Why can't I transfer my data to my new Windows 10 PC?

Q I have tried to use Laplink PCmover (www.snipca.com/19896) to transfer files from my old Vista PC to my new Windows 10 laptop. But when I try to install PCmover on the PC, I receive a message saying 'The Windows Installer Service could not be accessed'. I recently received a similar warning when I tried to install the driver for a new printer. Any idea what has gone wrong?

A But because problems with Windows Installer can affect all versions of Windows, here's what to try if you ever see a similar error message when attempting to install a program or driver. First, right-click Start, then select Command Prompt (Admin).

In the prompt window that opens, type:

net start msiserver

and press Enter (see screenshot below). You should see a message saying 'The Windows Installer service was started successfully'. Exit the Command Prompt and try installing the software again.

If it still won't work, open Command Prompt (Admin) again.

If you're running a 64bit version of Windows, type the following four commands at the prompt, pressing Enter after each one:

%windir%\system32\msiexec.exe /unregister

%windir%\system32\msiexec.exe /regserver

%windir%\syswow64\msiexec.exe /unregister

%windir%\syswow64\msiexec.exe /regserver

If you're running a 32bit version of Windows, type the following two commands at the prompt, pressing Enter after each one:

msiexec /unregister

msiexec /regserver

In both cases, reboot your PC, then try installing the software again.

If you're still having problems, there's another, slightly more involved fix that requires creating and running a Registry key.

See Method 1 on Microsoft's site (www.snipca.com/19870) for precise instructions.

14 Why do my fonts look blurry?

Q I upgraded to Windows 10, but I'm finding it hard to read some of the on-screen text, even though I've enlarged the fonts using the display settings. Is it me, or does the new OS make fonts look blurrier than they did in Windows 7?

A Windows 10 uses a different scaling method than previous versions. The result is that, in some cases, if you increase the scale of your on-screen fonts to anything higher than 100 per cent, they can look blurrier. Reverting to 100 per cent scaling will fix this. Right-click the desktop and select 'Display settings'. Now click 'Advanced display settings', 'Advanced sizing of text and other items', then click 'set a custom scaling level'. Select 100% from the dropdown menu and click Apply, then click 'Sign out now' and log back in.

Text will be sharper, but smaller. If you need larger text, you can tweak Windows 10's Registry so it uses the same scaling technique that previous versions of Windows use. Rather than changing Registry settings yourself, use a free tool called XPExplorer (www.snipca.com/19869). Download and run it, tick the 'Use Windows 8.1 DPI scaling (our fix)' option and select your DPI scale from the dropdown menu (see screenshot). Click Apply then reboot.

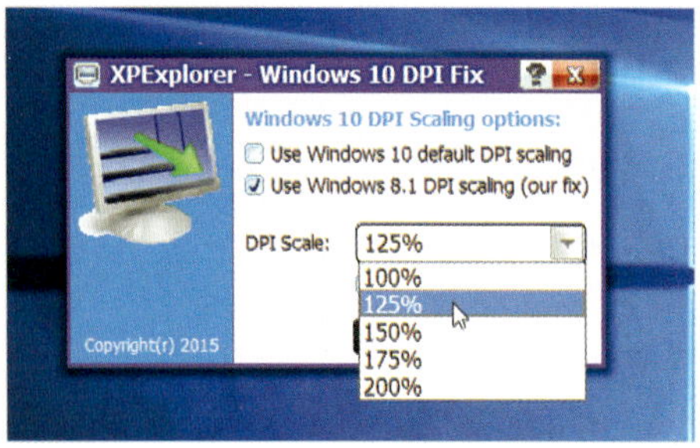

15 Why can't I install MediaPortal?

Q I've installed Windows 10 and much prefer it to its predecessor Windows 8.1, but I wish Microsoft hadn't dropped Windows Media Center (WMC). I tried to install an alternative, MediaPortal (www.teammediaportal.com), and a message came up saying I need to have DirectX 9 installed. In Windows 10 DirectX 12 is installed – so why would MediaPortal need DirectX 9?

A While we think MediaPortal is a great free replacement for WMC, its installer is flawed. The application requires a number of other software libraries to be installed – including DirectX 9. If you check MediaPortal's installation help pages (www.snipca.com/17641), you'll see it says 'DX9 is always necessary, even if a higher DirectX version (eg DX11) already exists on your system'. The same page has links to all the software you need, along with detailed installation instructions.

16 What is this 'Critical error' problem that appears on my PC?

Q I upgraded from Windows 7 to Windows 10 and everything worked fine for a couple of days. Then, when I booted my PC I got the message: 'Critical Error Start menu and Cortana aren't working'. Nothing worked and I couldn't get into the computer. Is there a fix?

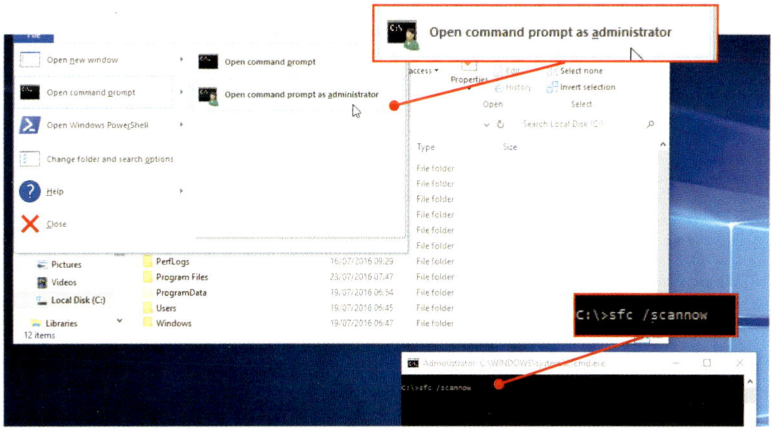

A Many Windows 10 users have reported similar errors. It could be corrupt system files or it may just be an early bug that Microsoft will need to fix via Windows Update. There are a few solutions you can try, though the lack of a Start menu makes navigation awkward. First, double-click the Recycle Bin, click 'This PC' on the left, then click on your C: drive. Click File, 'Open command prompt', then 'Open command prompt as administrator'. At the command prompt, type sfc /scannow and press Enter. This will scan for (and fix) any corrupt system files. Wait for the scan to finish, then restart.

If that hasn't cured the problem, press Ctl+Alt+Del, then click the power icon (bottom right) – hold down the Shift key and click Restart, Troubleshoot, 'Advanced options', Start-up Settings, then Restart. The PC will boot to a screen of start-up options; press F5 for 'Enable Safe Mode with Networking' and log in as normal. The Start menu should work in Safe Mode, allowing you to try a few more fixes. If you use Avast Free Antivirus, for instance, try uninstalling the program and switching to Windows Defender – some users have found that this does the trick. Otherwise try creating a new local (ie, a non-Microsoft) user account, and temporarily switch to using this. Click Start, Settings, Accounts, 'Other users', then 'Add someone else' and follow the steps. Restart and log in as the new user.

If none of these solutions work, you could try a full Reset (click Start, Settings, Update & Security, Recovery, 'Get started', then 'Remove everything'). Be aware, though, this will completely wipe out all your personal files, settings and applications, requiring you to back up everything first.

We recommend holding out for a fix from Microsoft before opting to take this route.

17 Why does Windows think I'm using an old graphics card?

Q I'm currently running Windows 7 Pro (64bit) and am eager to upgrade to Windows 10. But the Windows 10 upgrade tool says my PC won't support the upgrade because it contains an Nvidia 7050 display adapter. But that's not true – I upgraded my PC some time ago with an Nvidia GeForce 8400 GS PCI card. What can I do?

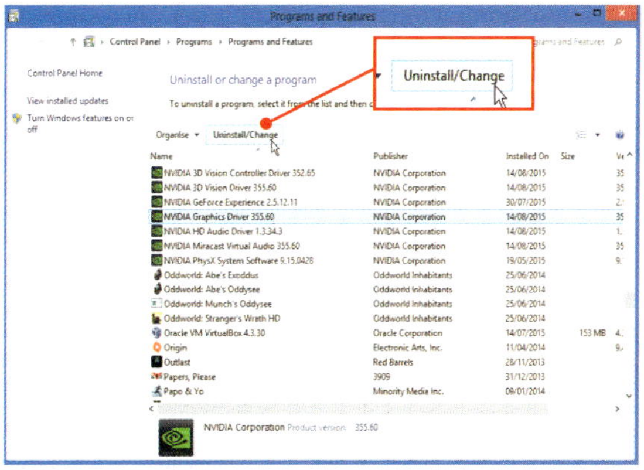

A Lots of people are having problems with compatible graphics and display drivers. In some cases, if your PC's display adapter is very old, the manufacturer may have stopped supporting it, meaning there'll be no official Windows 10 drivers available for it. You can check which display adapters are supported on the websites of Nvidia (www.snipca.com/17634), AMD (www.snipca.com/17635) and Intel (www.snipca.com/17636).

If yours isn't on the list, then you need to buy a new one. Consider the GeForce 210, which you should be able to find for less than £22 on Amazon (www.snipca.com/17640). It is relatively easy to install.

But what's perplexing is that Windows 10 does support your GeForce 8400 GS card. And yet the Windows 10 upgrade tool is mistakenly identifying it as an older, unsupported card. This could be because traces of older drivers are still hanging around somewhere in your system, so one solution would be to first download the latest driver from Nvidia (www.snipca.com/17638). Next, open the Control Panel, click 'Programs and Features', find the driver you want to uninstall, then click 'Uninstall/Change' (see screenshot left). Then install the driver you've just downloaded.

Another option is to go ahead and upgrade to Windows 10 anyway (having backed up first), using the manual method outlined earlier in this section. In theory, Windows should simply install the correct driver itself during the upgrade, though it may install a generic display driver instead – to check, right-click Start and select Device Manager. The GeForce 8400 GS should be listed under 'Display adapters'. If it isn't, then download the Windows 10 driver from www.snipca.com/17638 and install it.

18 Where are all the usual system settings?

Q I have just installed Windows 10 Pro on my laptop which was previously happily running Windows 7 Ultimate. I've struggled to find some tools I like, such as 'Backup and Restore' and Windows Update. Also, I like to know what updates Microsoft is trying to install on my PCs, so I can let it download, but then decide when to install. This option is hard to find. Can you help?

A Let's start with the good news. Most of the system settings are still there, and you don't actually have to look that hard for them. Right-click on the Start button, select Control Panel, and you'll find that the good old Control Panel is still there, ready for duty. Microsoft doesn't really want you to use 'Backup and Restore' anymore because it thinks Windows 10's File History feature and the System Restore options are better.

However, if you disagree then you'll find 'Backup and Restore' in the Control Panel, under 'System and Security', along with a lot of the other system tools that Windows 10 has hidden away.

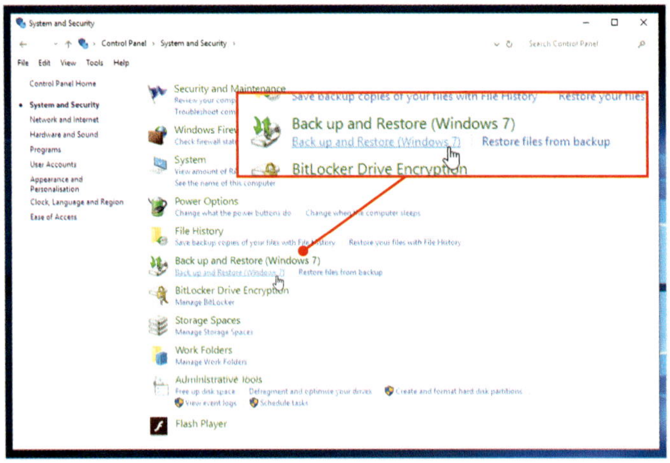

Windows Update is a different story. Controversially, Microsoft will install updates whether you like it or not, but you can – to some degree – decide when they happen by configuring the 'Active hours' option described earlier to set a time of day when at least you won't be interrupted by any updates that are installed.

Some Windows users regard Microsoft's policy on updates in Windows 10 dictatorial, and have accused Microsoft of exerting too much control. However, previously many people failed to install updates, leaving their PC insecure – which is good news only for hackers. At least Microsoft is trying to keep its users safe. It just needs to make sure its updates install more smoothly than they have recently.

19 Why has my trusty printer stopped working?

Q After installing Windows 10 my old and trusty Epson Stylus Photo R300 printer did not appear as a printer. Instead, a USB MFP (Hi Speed) was shown, with 'Driver Unavailable'. I tried a test print and it didn't work. According to the Epson site no drivers are required, because Windows 10 will find everything needed to install it. I can't find the printer's original software installation disc, but I doubt this would solve the problem anyway. Is there a simple solution that escapes me?

A One of Windows 10's more infuriating habits is to tell you that things will just work automatically, then give you no help at all when they don't. One way around this is to manually install the printer. Make sure it's powered on and connected to your PC, then right-click the Start button and select Control Panel. Now look under 'Hardware and Sound' and click 'View devices and printers'. Look in the bar at the top and you should see a link to 'Add a printer'.

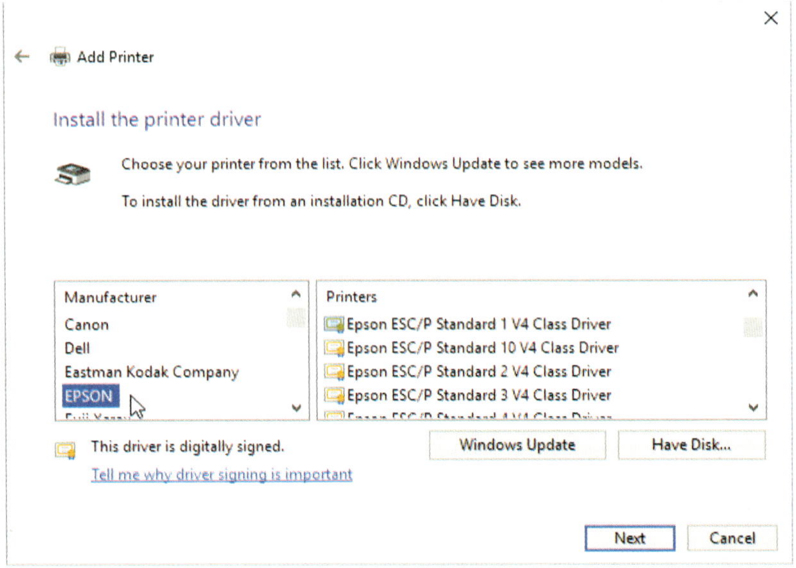

Windows 10 will now search for your printer, but if it fails to come up with the Epson Stylus R300, click the link at the bottom for 'The printer that I want isn't listed'. There are two options here that might help. The first one is 'My printer is a little older. Help me find it'. Select that, click Next and wait while Windows 10 searches deeper.

If that doesn't work, click 'The printer that I want isn't listed' again but this time, click 'Add a local printer or network printer with manual settings' then click Next. Make sure 'Use an existing port' is selected, then click Next. Click the Windows Update button to force Windows to update its list of printers. Now select the printer's maker under Manufacturer and the model number under the 'Printers' heading. Click Next and you should be up and running.

20 Why is my reserve partition too small for Windows 10?

Q I have been trying to install Windows 10 on my Sony Vaio laptop, but all I get is an error message telling me it can't install because of a problem with the System Reserved partition. I tried increasing my System Reserved partition size from 155MB to 500MB, but it made no difference. What should I do?

A First of all, Sony has advised some Vaio owners to wait until compatible drivers are available before installing Windows 10, so double-check with Sony's support website (www.snipca.com/17708) to make sure your model is supported and download any updates that are required.

Before upgrading, make sure you do a full system image backup first. Next, click Start, right-click Computer and select Manage, then click Disk Management to see if there's more than one System Reserved partition. If so, try increasing the size of the other one(s). If you only have one System Reserved partition, you could try making this even bigger than 500MB. You don't mention which tool you used to resize your partitions, but MiniTool Partition Wizard Free (free from www.snipca.com/17642) is a good choice. Right-click the System Reserved partition and select Extend, then use the slider to select how much space to reallocate from your C: drive – try increasing the System Reserved partition to 1GB or even more.

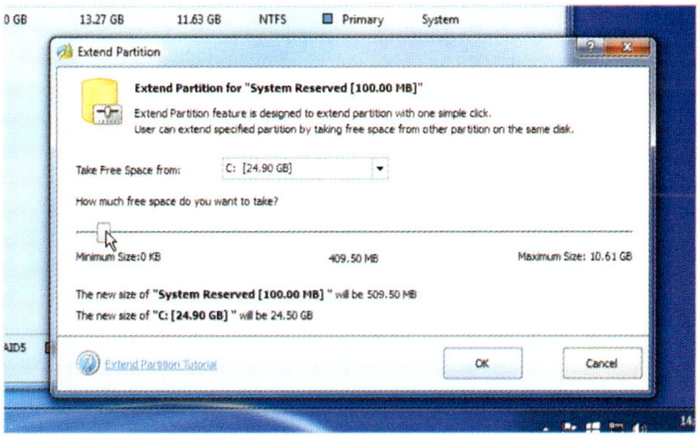

21 Why did Windows 10 wipe my antivirus?

Q I installed Windows 10 with no problems, but then noticed some of my software was missing – including Kaspersky Internet Security 2015. I can only conclude that Windows 10 is so good that it does not need any other antivirus software, or am I missing something?

A Windows 10 can cause problems with older software. If you want to stick with Kaspersky, download the latest version from www.kaspersky.co.uk/product-updates, which supports Windows 10.

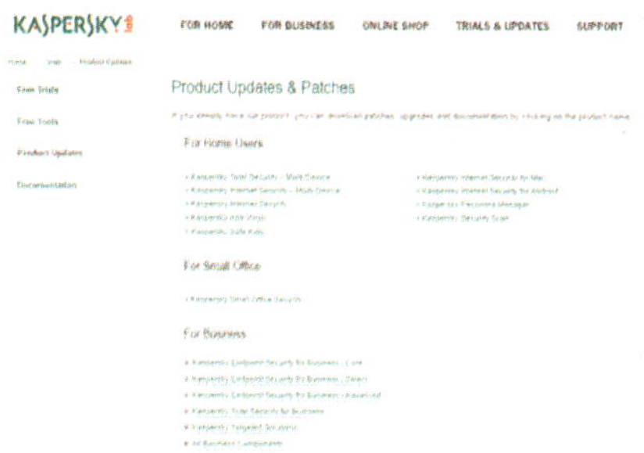

22 Can I get Microsoft Money to work in Windows 10?

Q Microsoft Money won't work in Windows 10, and nor will Money Plus and Money Sunset. Their absence is disastrous for me. I read that I may have to tweak the Registry to fix this, but I'm not confident enough to do that. Is there an easier solution?

A There is now an easier fix for this than when Windows 10 launched. An update to the operating system has fixed a problem that prevented Money Plus Sunset Deluxe (the most recent version) from launching. This is what some people have been fixing using the Registry hack you heard about. So, as long as your version of Windows 10 is up to date, you can download the final version of the retired financial suite from www.snipca.com/17774. We tried it on Windows 10 and it worked perfectly.

However, some people are still experiencing crashes when trying to import bank statement files saved in Quicken Interchange Format (QIF) or Open Financial Exchange (OFX) format. We didn't encounter this problem when we tried but lots of people have complained about it,

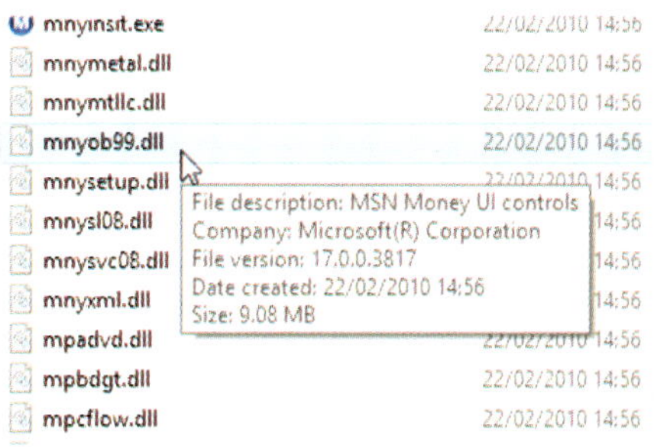

so it's clearly happening. Microsoft may release another Windows 10 update that will fix this glitch.

In the meantime, if you encounter this problem, you'll need to replace a file called mnyob99.dll with a patched version created by blogger Ameridan, who lets you download it for free (www.snipca.com/17775).

Press Win+E to launch File Explorer, and make sure the tool is set to show hidden OS files – click View, Options, View, then scroll down and untick 'Hide protected operating system files (Recommended)'. Click Yes in the warning windows, then click Apply. We'd advise reversing this process once you're done.

Now navigate to C:\Program Files\Microsoft Money Plus\MNYCoreFiles (assuming you installed Money on your C: drive). Select the existing file mnyob99.dll, then press F2 to rename it and type mnyob99.old. Now copy the patched version of the file into this folder and restart your PC.

In the longer term, it makes sense to consider moving on from Money. A good alternative is the free program GnuCash (www.gnucash.org), our favourite free personal finance tool. It offers similar features to Money, and is actively developed and supported by a community of volunteers. It even imports QIF and OFX files; great if you're coming from Money or Quicken.

23 Why can't I install Windows 10?

Q Windows 10 installed fine on my laptop, but not on my two desktop PC. I get the message 'multiprocessor configuration not supported'. This surprised me because the compatibility check had said it would be fine! I've had to reinstall Windows 8.1. What's happened?

A The 'multiprocessor configuration' error could be to do with a setting in your computer's BIOS. Access the PC's BIOS by tapping Delete (Del) or F2 after switching on your PC, then use the arrow keys and Enter to look for a setting labelled 'CPUID Value Limit' or similar. Switch it to Disabled, then restart and try upgrading again.

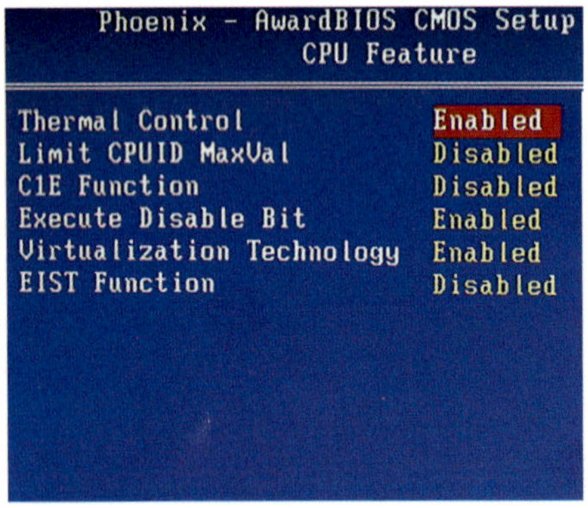

24 Why is my processor running so slowly?

Q Since installing Windows 10, my Acer Aspire 5733's processor is running at around 40 per cent all the time. According to Task Manager it seems to be related to something called 'IAStorDataSvc'. If I stop the process, everything calms down. Can I uninstall this process before my computer melts? I'm sure this has only appeared since Windows 10 has been installed.

A This process belongs to Intel's Rapid Storage Technology (RST), which is basically a set of drivers to make storage devices like hard drives and SSDs work as fast as they can. You should avoid using Task Manager to stop it, because this could lead to data loss.

It's quite common for this and other processes to cause occasional spikes in processor use, but it's not normal for it to be permanently consuming so much of your processor's power. It's possible that your upgrade to Windows 10 failed to update to the latest version of RST. You can get it from www.snipca.com/17782, but remember to back up your data before installing.

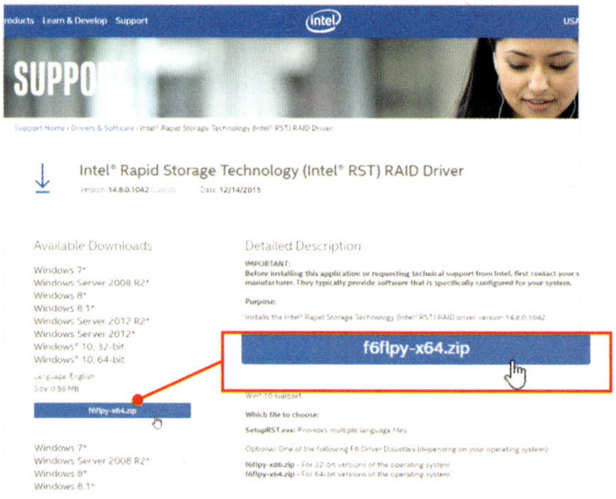

25 Can I stop Windows 10 asking me for a password?

Q I upgraded to Windows 10 from Windows 7 Professional and, aside from having to update the audio driver and reinstall Kaspersky, all went well. I'm the only user of my laptop and never take it out of the house, so it annoys me that Windows 10 insists that I enter a password every time I boot up. Is there a simple fix?

A Yes, and it's an old fix that works just as well with almost all Windows versions – including XP. Press Start or hit the Windows key, type netplwiz and then click netplwiz.exe. Select the Users tab, then click to highlight the user account you'd like to log into automatically (must be an administrator account).

Now untick 'Users must enter a user name and password to use this computer', then click Apply. A new box will pop up asking you to confirm your password. Check the username is correct, then click OK to confirm. Click OK again, and you'll no longer be bothered by requests for your password.

To reverse this in future, just repeat these instructions – but tick 'Users must enter a user name and password to use this computer' instead of unticking.

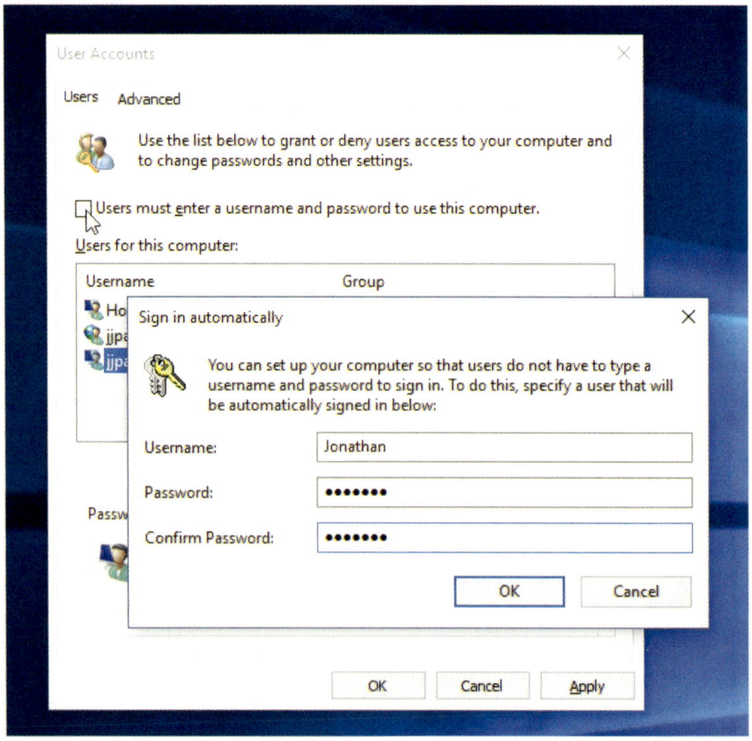

26 Can I remove files from an old PC after upgrading?

Q My previous PC was a nine-year-old Dell. It had served us well but had become tired. I recently bought a new Lenovo PC which came with Windows 8.1. Before upgrading to Windows 10, I used the Windows Easy Transfer (WET) tool (www.snipca.com/17906) to move files from my old PC to my new one. When doing this, would it have transferred unnecessary files that only relate to my old computer? And if so, is there any easy way to identify and remove these? And would the update to Windows 10 have automatically removed unnecessary files relating to Windows 8.1?

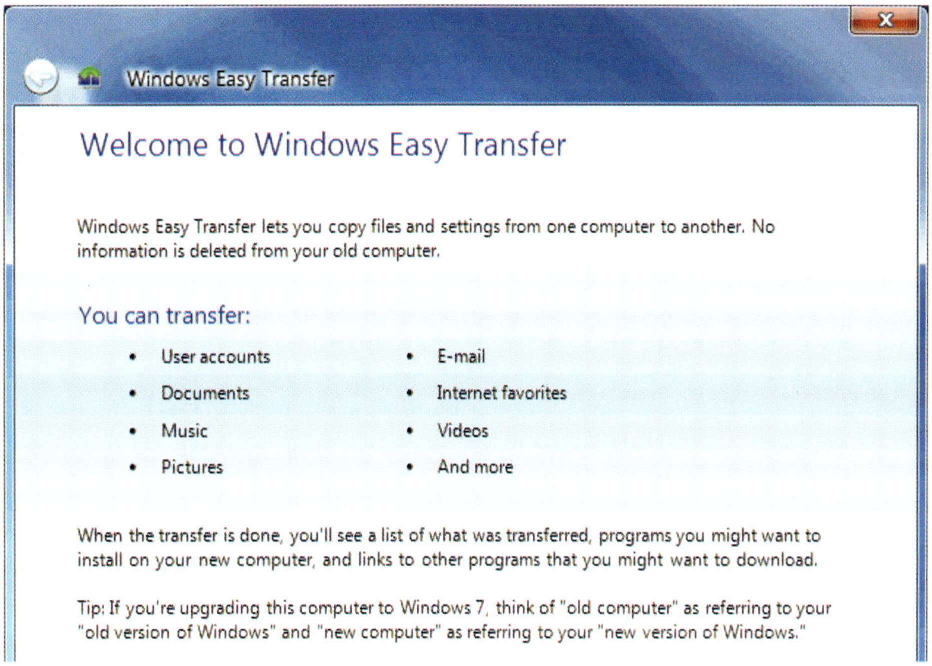

A Windows Easy Transfer focuses on personal files and folders – your documents, photos, music and so on. At your request it will also transfer some personal settings, including user accounts, preferences and configurations for some programs. It will only import these elements to Windows 8.1 from Windows Vista or 7: it offers no export option to Windows 10, which doesn't include WET in any form. However, by upgrading your Windows 8.1 PC to Windows 10 it will automatically inherit whatever you pulled across with WET originally.

There's no single trick to identifying everything that was imported, but you'll know where your personal documents, photos and music are, so delete them if you want.

That just leaves the settings. The storage space these take up depends on the associated programs, but it will be pretty negligible. Again, there's no one way to show all transferred settings, but if they worked well in Windows 8.1, then they should be fine in Windows 10, so there's really nothing to worry about.

And yes, Windows 10 removes lots of redundant Windows 8.1 files, folders, programs and tools.

27 What does error code '080072ee7' mean?

Q When trying to open the Windows Store I get the error code '080072ee7'. I can't find the answer online. Can you help?

A Windows Store errors are usually the result of corrupted settings. We can't say how or why this occurred but, for example, it can be caused by switching off a PC at the mains (rather than using the Power option on Windows 10's Start menu). Microsoft includes a tool for resetting the Windows Store, which fixes most of these problems, but it's hard to find. Press Windows key+R, type wsreset.exe in the Run box (see screenshot) and hit Enter. Windows Store's settings will reset and it should now launch automatically.

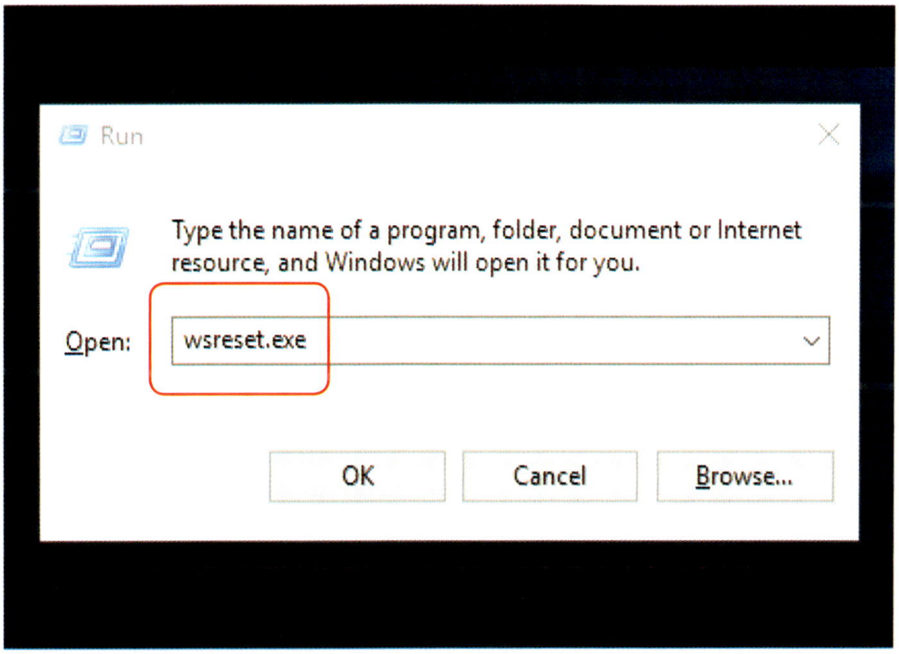

28 Why can't I update apps from the Windows Store?

Q Windows 10 won't update no matter how long I leave my PC on, and I have 21 downloads that are always pending in the Windows Store.

A Windows 10 has recently been updated to put control of Windows Store app updates back into the hands of users, so we think the cause of your first problem is that you have the automatic-update option switched off. Launch the Windows Store app, click your account icon next to the Search box then click Settings. Now slide the 'App updates' switch to On. For the benefit of other readers, if this switch is greyed-out then this may be because Windows 10 is updating itself – wait for this to finish, then it will become available.

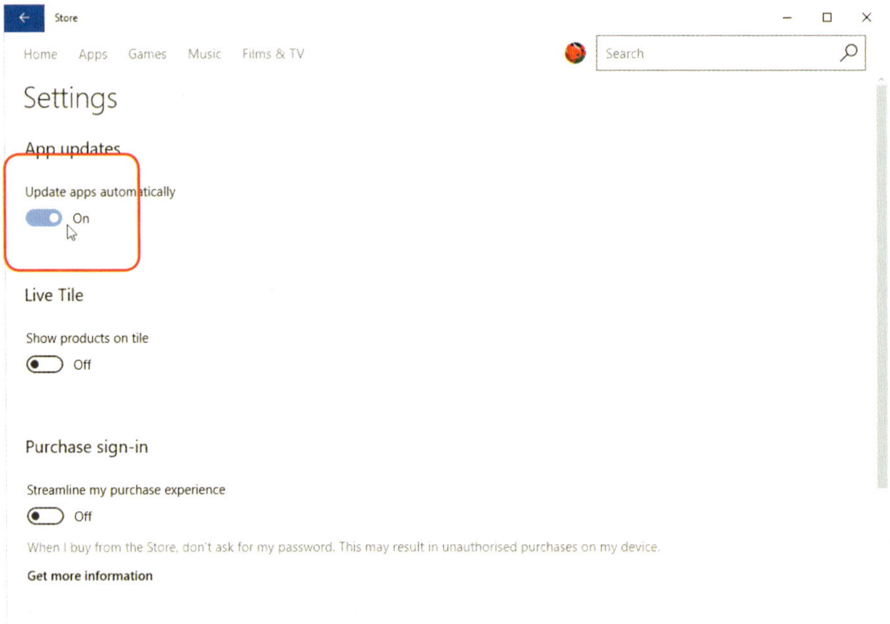

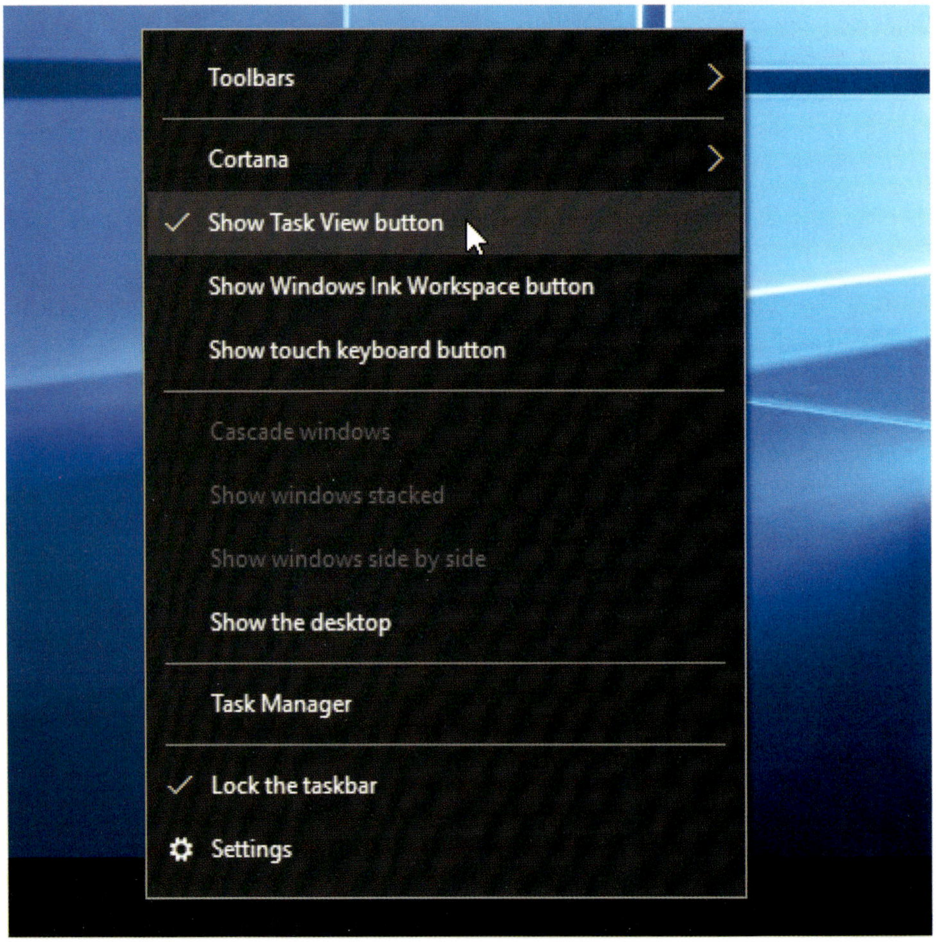

29 Where has Task View gone?

Q When I first upgraded to Windows 10 I had a Task View button on my taskbar, but this has since disappeared. Is there a way of getting it back?

A We're not sure why the Task View button has vanished but an inadvertent right-click may have caused it. It's easy to restore it, though – just right-click a blank part of the taskbar then tick 'Show Task View button'.

30 How have I got Windows Media Player in Windows 10?

Q I read that Windows 10 doesn't come with Windows Media Player, but when I click on 'All apps', there it is in the list of Windows programs. Have I got lucky, or has Microsoft sneaked it in on one of the many updates I've had?

A We think you may have misunderstood what you read, or what you read was incorrect. Windows 10 still comes with Windows Media Player (WMP), but Microsoft has removed Windows Media Center (WMC). WMP as the name suggests is a media player, whereas WMC is (or was) a more general home-entertainment tool that included integration with TV tuner cards for recording live television.

However, if you've installed Windows 10 afresh or upgraded a Windows 7 or 8.1 PC to Windows 10, you'll have lost WMC – and there's no way to get it back. In its place, Microsoft is offering the free, but much more basic Windows DVD Player (www.snipca.com/17907), which downloads automatically if you upgrade a Windows PC (with WMC) to Windows 10 – though if you perform a clean install it costs £11.59.

The DVD player has not been well received by Windows 10 users. Try the free Kodi instead (http://kodi.tv).

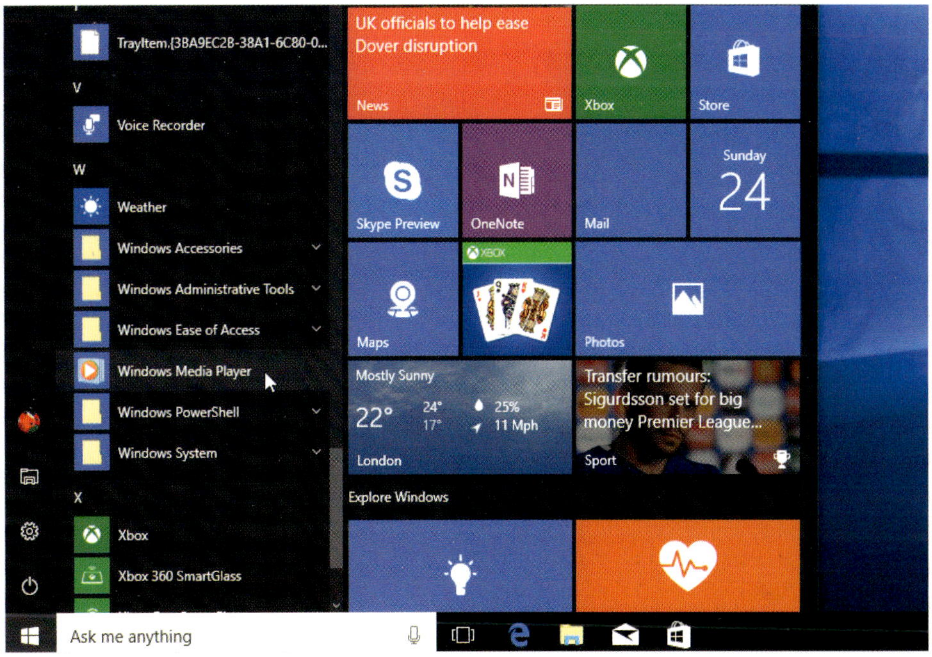

31 Why won't Stellarium work on my Windows 10 laptop?

Q I've recently upgraded to Windows 10 on both my desktop PC and laptop. I had the astronomy program Stellarium (www.stellarium.org) installed on both. It works perfectly on the desktop computer, but not on the laptop, where I always get an error message. Is there a fix for this? I have tried uninstalling and reinstalling.

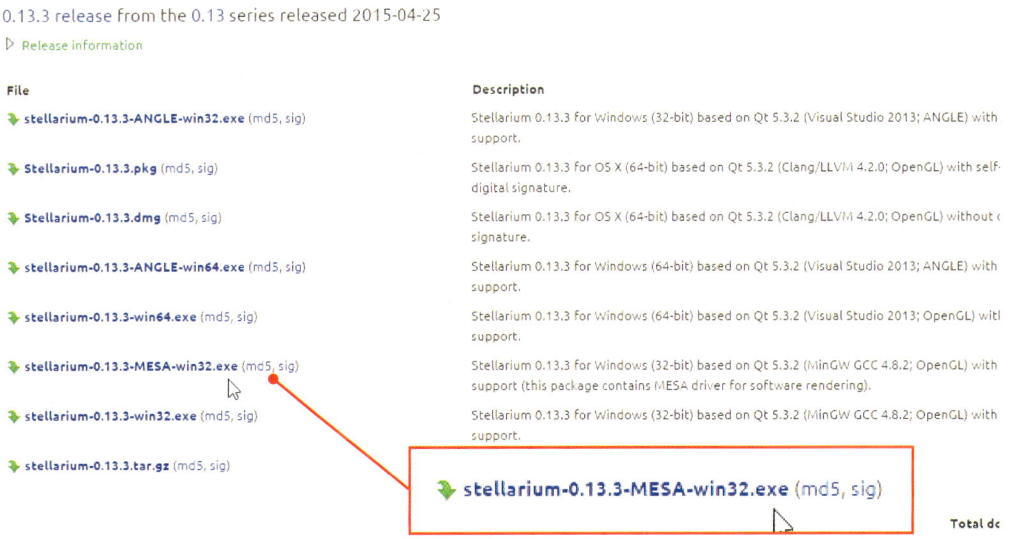

A We're not sure if you upgraded your laptop with Stellarium installed, or re-installed it after upgrading to Windows 10, but the latest version of Stellarium is incompatible with your laptop's Windows 10 graphics drivers. The solution is to use an older version of Stellarium. Visit the program's download page at www.snipca.com/17881 and grab the most recent 'MESA' version (see screenshot).

32 Can I adapt the Windows 8.1 Start Screen to work in Windows 10?

Q I find the Start menu in Windows 10 a mess. Is there any way I can adapt the Windows 8.1 Start screen to work in Windows 10, or can you suggest an alternative?

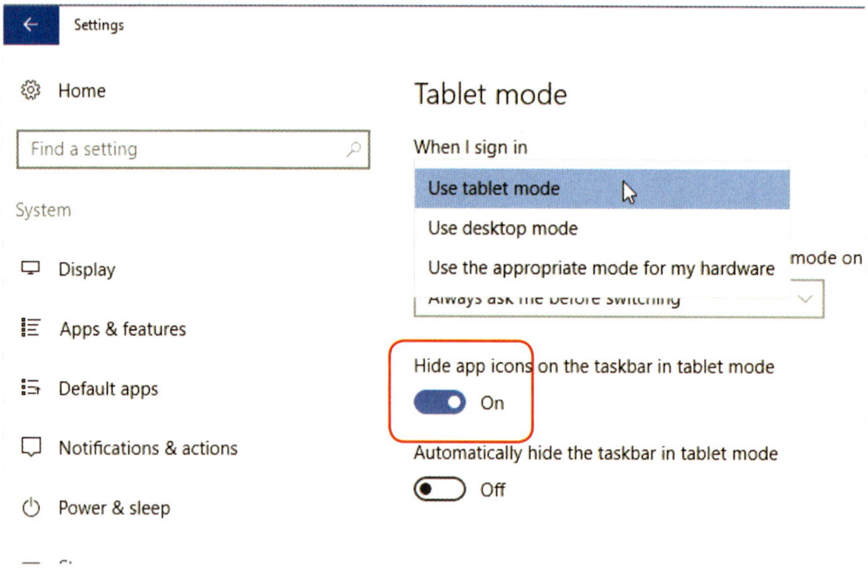

A It's possible to resurrect the full-screen Start by enabling Tablet mode, though this does have at least one significant side effect, which we'll explain as we go along.

First, click Start, Settings, then System, followed by 'Tablet mode' in the left-hand navigation pane. Under 'When I sign in', select 'use tablet mode' switch (see screenshot), and your Start menu will once again be a Start screen.

However, launch an app and you'll see everything now launches in full-screen mode, including traditional Windows programs. If you don't like this, simply reverse the above changes in settings (click Start, then the three top-left horizontal lines). An alternative idea is simply to expand Windows 10's new Start menu so that it virtually fills the screen: this gives you loads of room for extra tiles while retaining the freedom to run apps in full-screen or in windows. To do this, click Start, position your cursor over the top or right-hand side of the menu until it changes to a double-headed arrow, then just click, drag and release at the size you want.

33 How can I sync emails with my calendar?

Q I have tried to use the Mail program in Windows 10 on my PC and set up synchronisation with my Windows Phone. I'd like to be able to synchronise emails with my calendar. But Mail seems to have frozen, showing a 'Not synced yet' message. It's been like that for about a fortnight. Can you suggest a solution?

A Have you checked that Mail is set to sync with your calendar, as well as your emails? Click the cog icon at the bottom of the Mail window, then click Manage Accounts, followed by the relevant account name.

Now click 'Change mailbox sync settings'. Open the dropdown menu under where it says 'Download new content' and choose 'As items arrive'. Now scroll down to the bottom to find the 'Sync options' heading, then check that the Email and Calendar switches are set to On (as well as Contacts, if you also want these synced).

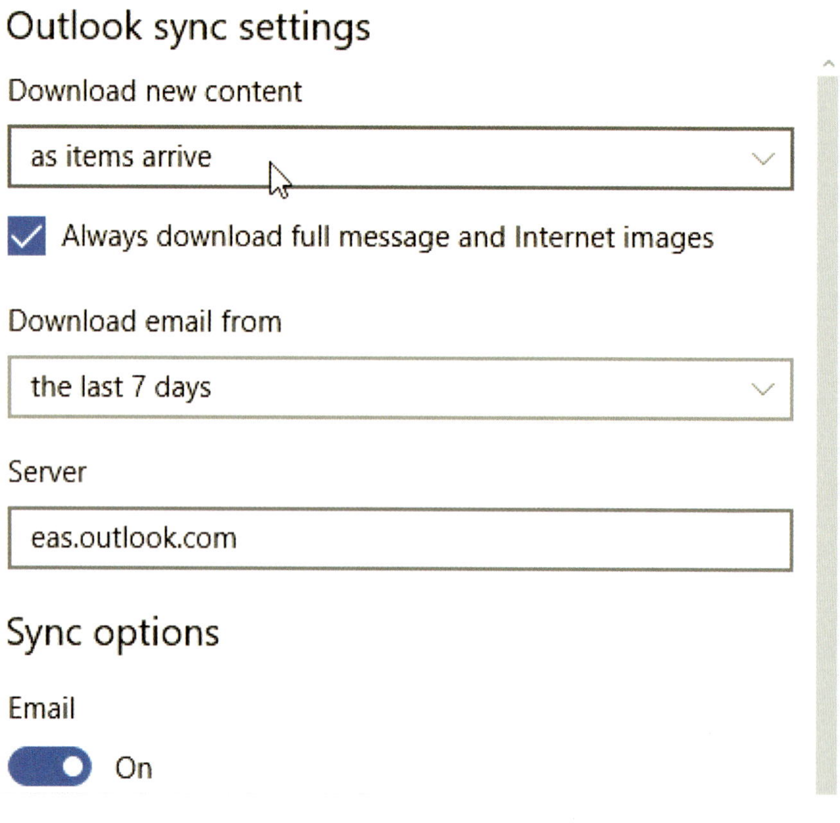

34 Can I store photos under a name in Windows 10?

Q **In Windows 7, I stored my photo albums and collections under group names. It meant I only needed to recall the group name to see the relevant photos.**

But after installing Windows 10, these photos are now shown according to time and date. How do I store them by name, as in Windows 7?

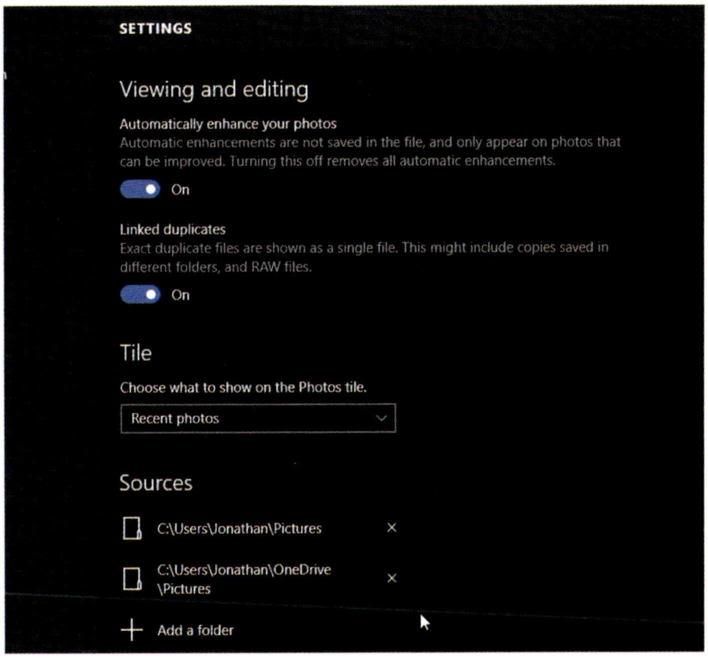

A Your photos remain stored in the same place. What's changed is that you're using Windows 10's new Photos program to view them, which sorts and displays photos by date – as you've discovered. We think you previously used Windows Photo Gallery, which was part of the free Microsoft Windows Essentials suite used by millions of Windows 7 and 8.1 users.

Windows Photo Gallery offered numerous ways to view photos, including by folder (which is what we think you mean by a 'group name'). Windows 10 doesn't remove Windows Photo Gallery, so it should still be installed on your PC: just type photo gallery into the Start menu, then click the program name to launch it.

If it's not there, you can download and install it from www.snipca.com/17888.

Windows Photo Gallery should remember the names of your photo folders, but if not, first launch Windows 10's Photos program then click the cog icon at the bottom left and scroll down to Sources. Make a note of the folders listed here, then close Photos.

Switch back to Windows Photo Gallery, click File, followed by 'Include folder' and then Add. Navigate to one of the folders that you noted down above, click to select it and then click 'Include folder'. Repeat for your other remaining folders.

35 Will upgrading to Windows 10 wipe Movie Maker?

Q **I have Windows 7 and use Movie Maker a lot as I find it very simple and it does everything I need. I've been told that it is not available in Windows 10. As I have Windows Live Essentials installed on my computer, will Movie Maker still work when I upgrade?**

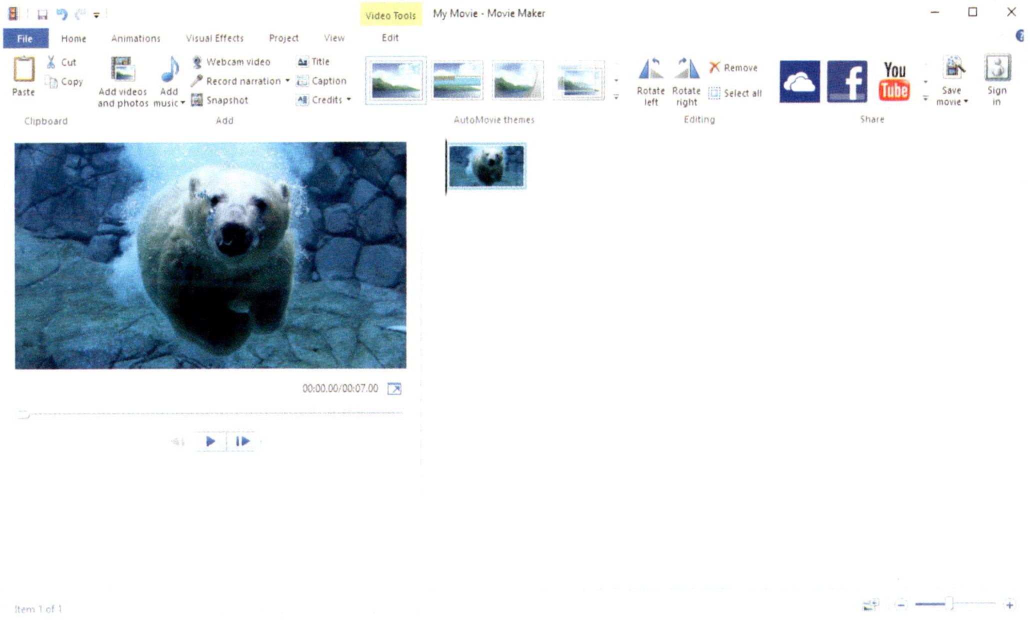

A You're right that Windows 10 doesn't include Movie Maker, but if you already have it installed on your Windows 7 PC and you install Windows 10 as an 'in-place' upgrade, then Movie Maker will remain untouched. However, if you perform a 'clean' install of Windows 10 then everything on your PC will be erased, and Movie Maker will not be reinstalled. Microsoft is not offering official support for Movie Maker in Windows 10, but it's still available to download, and in our tests it seems to work fine. So, if needed, grab Movie Maker from www.snipca.com/17965.

36 How do I set up Microsoft Edge to stop printing adverts?

I received an email with travel tickets to print, but I'm unable to print them in Microsoft's Edge browser without all the adverts also appearing. Why can't I set up Edge to print just the email? I've solved the problem for now by closing Edge and opening the email in Internet Explorer, where I was able to print just the email as usual.

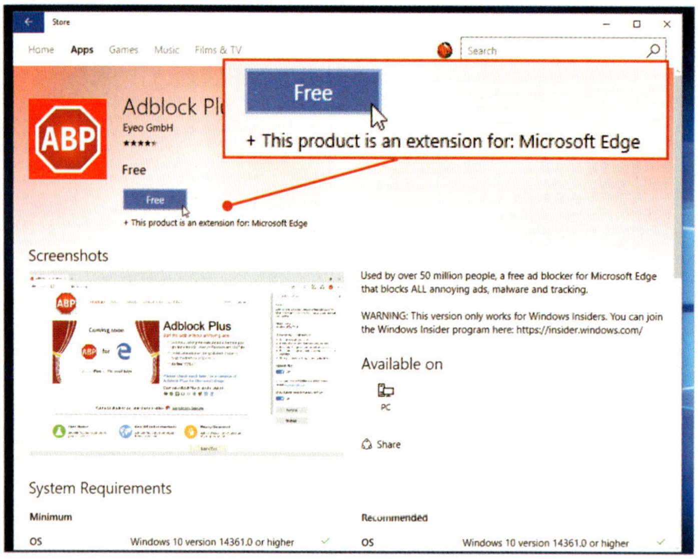

A You're using a web browser to access your emails so you must be using a webmail service, many of which display advertising. Knowing this, our guess is that in Internet Explorer (IE) you've got an ad-blocking add-on installed, such as Adblock Plus (https://adblockplus.org). This works more or less invisibly, so you might've added it ages ago and forgotten about the useful work it does.

Since the big Anniversary Update, Edge now supports add-ons (aka extensions), including Adblock Plus, which you can install by visiting the Windows Store and searching for Adblock Plus. If you can't install extensions in Edge, then it's likely your PC hasn't been updated to the latest version of Windows 10. Microsoft is rolling out the update in waves, so it's possible you haven't received it yet.

Try checking Windows Update (click Start, Settings, 'Update & security', then click 'Check for updates').

If you're still waiting for the update to land, or if you'd prefer not to install it just yet, the easy options are stick to printing in IE (which is still available in the 'All apps' menu under Windows Accessories – you could pin it to the Start menu for easier access), or put up with the ads.

37 Why can't we print from the Mail app?

Q We have two screens on our Windows 10 PC – one for my wife and one for myself. We are unable to print from the Mail app on either screen. The following message appears: 'Nothing was sent to print. Open a document and print again'.

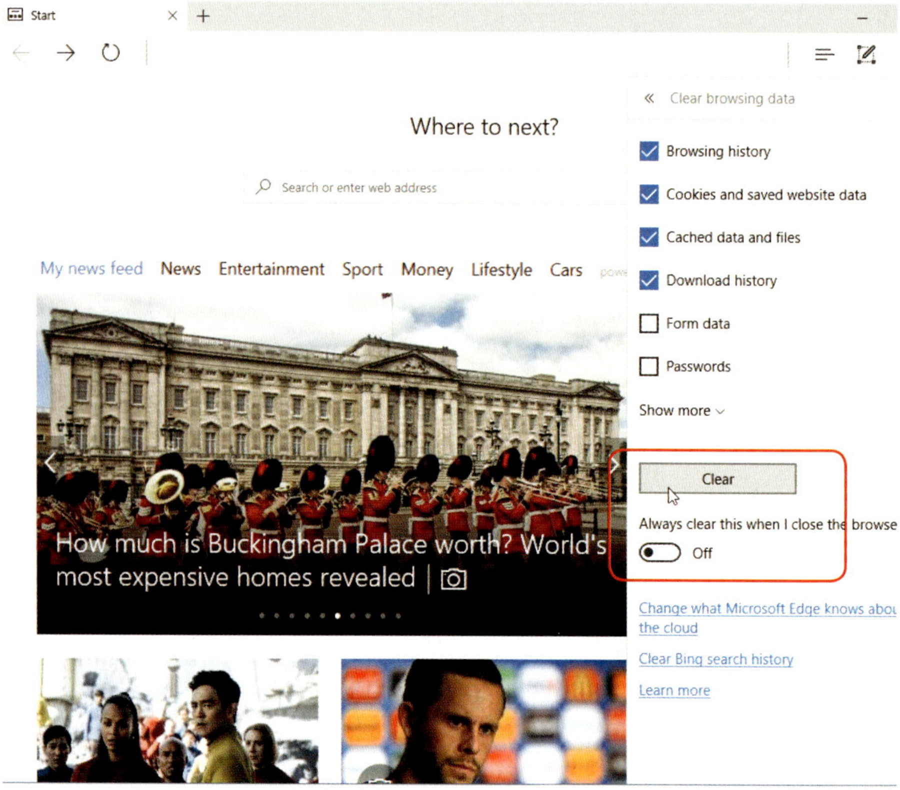

A This problem may be caused by the Edge browser, as elements of Mail connect to this during printing. Clearing Edge's cache and browsing data could fix this. Launch Edge, click the menu button (three dots) at the top right, then click Settings and 'Choose what to clear' under 'Clear browsing data'. Tick the first four boxes, leaving 'Form data' and Passwords unticked. Click Clear, and then try printing in Mail. If it doesn't work, return to Edge and, still under 'Clear browsing data', click 'Show more', then tick the first of the boxes here ('Media licenses'). Click Clear, return to Mail, then try to print. If it still fails, repeat this process until all boxes are ticked.

38 Where have my tiles gone?

Q The Mail and Calendar tiles on my wife's screen have disappeared. Is there any way to get them back? I can't seem to be able to reinstall the apps from the Windows Store.

A To restore lost tiles, click Start, scroll down through the alphabetical 'All apps' list to find the relevant app, then right-click it and choose 'Pin to Start'.

Note that when you do this the app's tile will be pinned to the bottom of the right-hand side of the Start menu, so you may need to scroll down to find it – you can then drag and drop it to wherever you want.

39 How do I make apps full-screen?

Q It may just be me doing something wrong, but when I click on any of the 'boxes' or apps in the Start menu, they come up on my screen, but are not full screen, so I can still see my wallpaper in the background. Is there a way I can make them full screen?

A You're not doing anything wrong – this is the standard way that Windows 10 now works. You can still make an app fill the screen by clicking its Maximize button, which is the little square at the top right (and click it again to reverse).

Preview versions of Windows 10 put an extra menu icon in the title bar of apps that allowed full-screen mode to be set as the default, but that feature didn't make it through to the final version. In the absence of that convenience there's a useful keyboard shortcut you can use instead: Windows key+up arrow. Press this and the current window will instantly maximise, and revert to its previous size when Windows key+down arrow is pressed.

40 Why can't I access Microsoft's personalised ad settings?

Q I'm trying to change my settings for 'Personalised ads', there seems to be a problem with the website http://choice.microsoft.com. I have tried it on different browsers but have not been able to access it. Is there an alternative?

A We also had problems accessing it for a while. Perhaps Microsoft took it offline. It seems to have reappeared now, but if you still can't access it at the address provided, try this alternative address: www.snipca.com/19455. It will redirect you to Microsoft's website, though you may then need to log in using your Microsoft account details before you can access the settings themselves.

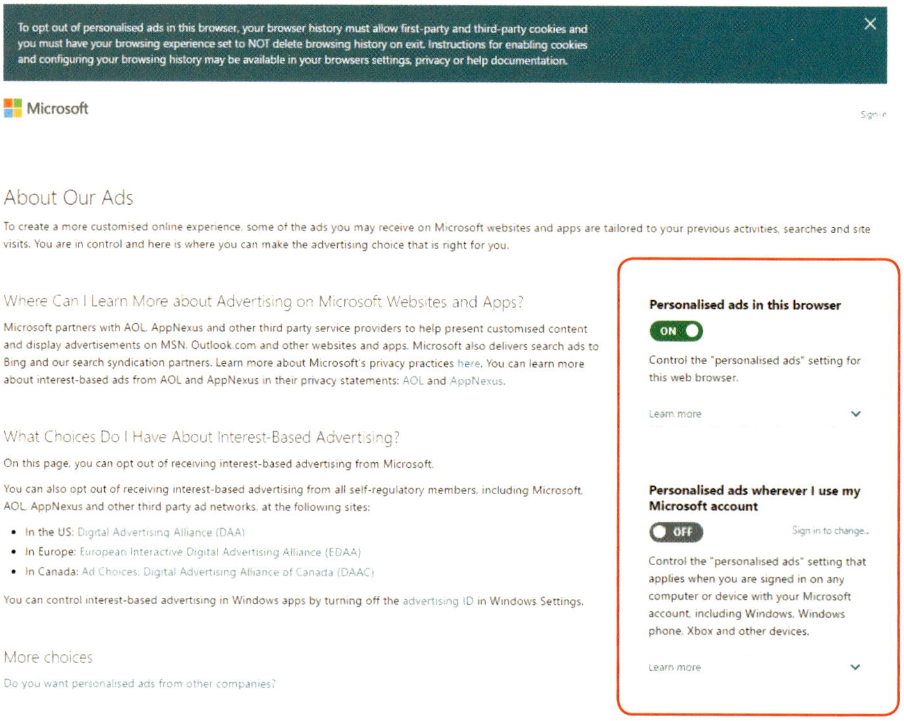

41 Why can't I change my default PDF viewer?

Q I've been trying to click 'Choose default applications by file type' to change default apps in Windows 10. However, this does not seem to work with PDF files. I tried Acrobat Reader and others but, no matter what I do, it changes back to using Microsoft Edge as the default PDF viewer.

A Your PDF problem is a strange Windows 10 quirk that other readers have also experienced. First, try right-clicking a PDF file, then selecting 'Open with', then 'Choose another app'. Select the program you want from the list, then tick the box next to the 'Always use this app to open .pdf files' option at the bottom of the box, before clicking OK. If that still doesn't work, launch Acrobat Reader, then click Edit, Preferences, General. At the bottom of the window, click Select Default PDF Handler. Click Apply, then OK.

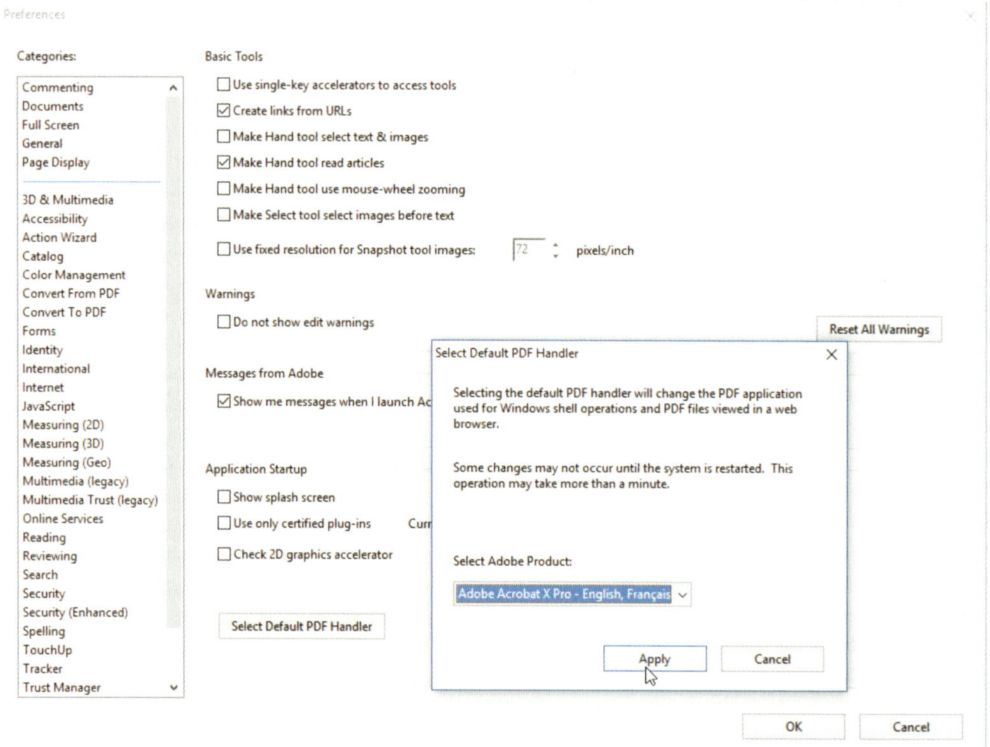

42 Why does my Start button no longer work?

Q **I changed some of the settings in Windows 10. On restarting my computer, however, I discovered that left-clicking the Start button did nothing. I could right-click it, but the Settings button and all the tiles had disappeared. Also, the internet and Mail icons have disappeared from the Taskbar. How do I fix all this?**

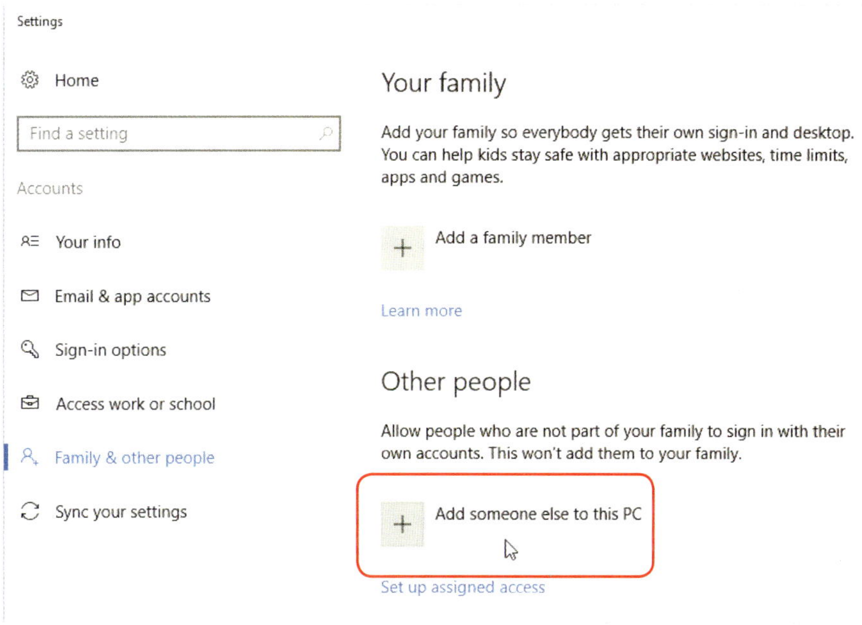

A The problem you describe is widely known to affect Windows 10, seemingly at random. You could try the Start menu tool we demonstrate earlier in this chapter. But if that doesn't work, then the simplest fix is to create a new user account. Right-click Start, select Control Panel, User Accounts, then 'Add or remove user accounts'. Next, click 'Add a new user in PC settings', then 'Add someone else to this PC' and follow the remaining steps (see screenshot left). Once the account has been set up, click 'Change account type', select Administrator then click OK. Log in using this account and your Start menu should be back. You'll need to copy your personal files from your old account and re-apply any other settings, but your apps and programs should be unaffected.

43 Why have my thumbnails turned into icons?

Q **I wanted to speed up Windows 10, so I changed my Visual Effects setting to 'Adjust for Best Performance', but now when I open a folder, it has turned every photo into a red icon. What has happened to my photo files? Have they been deleted by accident?**

A Nothing has happened to them – they are safe. It's quite normal for photos to revert to icons if you choose the 'Best Performance' option. Doing so disables thumbnails, meaning that your photos and other files will be displayed as icons in the default programs they open with, rather than as a miniature preview of the image itself.

Thumbnails are useful for identifying images, but they're cached in your PC's memory and stored on your hard drive, so disabling them is one way to free up system resources and boost performance.

If you prefer to leave thumbnails on, however, right-click Start and select System, then click 'Advanced system settings'. Click Settings under Performance, then choose the Custom option in the Visual Effects screen, and untick all the options below, except 'Show thumbnails instead of icons' (see the screenshot on the right).

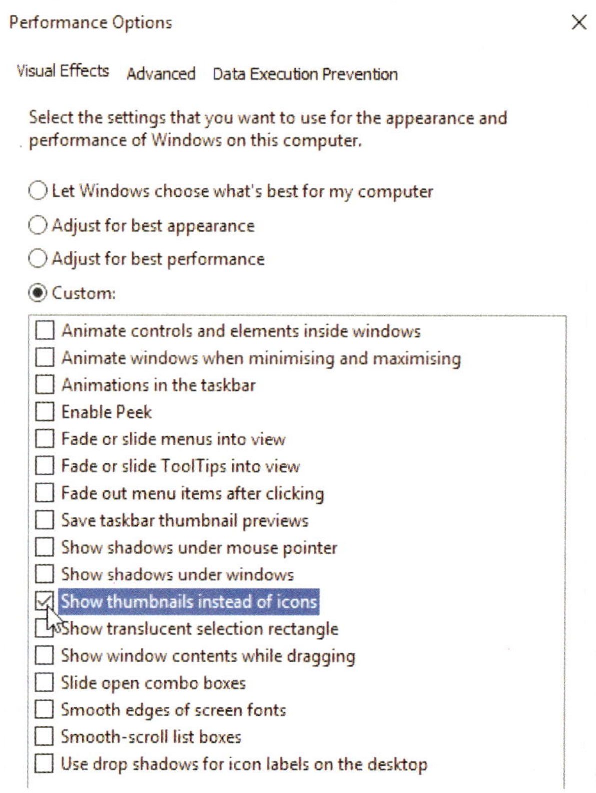

44 Why doesn't Windows 10 include System Restore?

Q I've read that Windows 10 doesn't include the System Restore feature that came with previous versions of the OS. I used to rely on this heavily. Is there any way of installing it?

A Windows 10 does, in fact, include System Restore – but it tends to leave this useful feature disabled by default. Thankfully, it's easy enough to re-enable this useful feature. Right-click Start, select System, then click 'System protection'.

In the window that opens, click your system drive (usually C:), then Configure. Now, click the 'Turn on system protection' option and click OK twice.

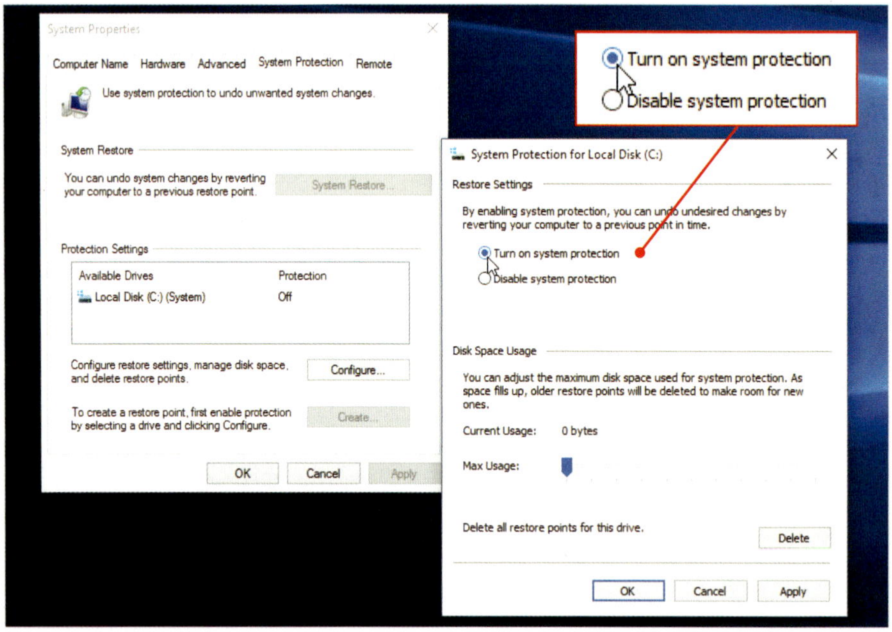

45 Why can't I start Windows 7 after rolling back from 10?

Q I didn't like Windows 10, so I decided to go back to Windows 7. The problem is that now Windows 7 won't start. Instead, it lists a 'StartupRepairOffline' problem with the number '6.1.7600.16385' and 'NoRootCause' listed as problem signature codes. What has happened?

A The most likely explanation is that some of Windows 7's startup files have somehow become corrupted during the rollback process.

There are a few things you can try to fix this. Grab your Windows 7 installation DVD (or borrow one), then start your PC with the disc in the drive. Press a key to boot from the DVD when prompted. On the Install Windows screen, select your language preferences, click Next, then click 'Repair your computer'. You should see your Windows 7 installation listed. Click it, then click Next. From the Recovery Options listed, first try Startup Repair – your error message suggests that Startup Repair was unable to fix the problem, but running the tool multiple times sometimes solves this, so attempt it at least five times before moving on.

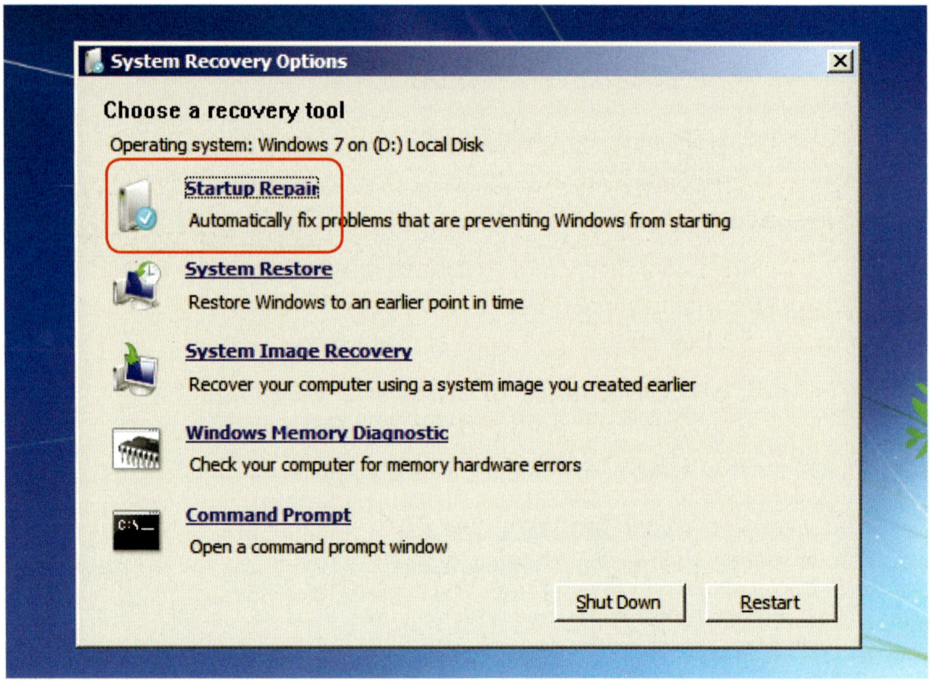

If you still can't start Windows 7, boot to the Recovery Options again and this time click System Restore. Click Next, select a restore point, then click Next, followed by Finish. This may restore the corrupt files. If it doesn't and you have a system-image backup made before you upgraded to Windows 10, you can restore this by attaching your USB stick, booting to the Recovery Options, choosing System Image Recovery and following the instructions.

If you don't have a system-image backup, you may need to reinstall Windows 7 from scratch, though doing this will erase everything on your hard drive, so it's very much a last resort.

Want even *more* advanced Windows 10 tips?

SUBSCRIBE TO WebUser

You'll learn how to...

- Hack it to **unlock more tools**
- Get the best **free software** for it
- Turn off Microsoft's tracking
- Keep it running **smooth and fast**

...AND Prevent Microsoft's updates from **wrecking your PC!**

Web User, the UK's favourite internet magazine, is bursting with practical advice to help you get the best out of the web and your PC.

Pay just £19.99 for 13 issues and get your copies delivered free to your door every fortnight before they're available in the shops.

Order securely online at

dennismags.co.uk/webuser

or call now on **01795 592 926**

Quote offer code: **G1619PW10**

Chapter 7

Windows 10 apps & tools

It's easy to make Windows 10 even better with great apps and programs for everyday tasks

Microsoft's operating systems have always come with their own built-in tools, and Windows 10 is no exception. Not only that, but the OS also features a number of apps – mobile-like mini-programs designed for specific tasks, such as getting a weather forecast or setting an alarm. You don't have to stick with the software that comes pre-installed, though. In this chapter we'll provide you with ways to make more of the apps that Microsoft provides, and show how to dump the ones you don't want. We'll also explain where to find essential free apps and downloads for your PC.

IN THIS SECTION

Fix problems with the Photos app

Time required: 20 minutes

It's easy to write off the Photos app as just another of Microsoft's bundled bloatware tools, but it's actually reasonably good – as long as you fix a few problems first. It doesn't have as many options as some photo managers, and a number of innate quirks can initially make it seem a little annoying. But it's easy to cure these flaws and get Photos working how you want it to. In this guide we're going to show you how to do just that.

STEP 1 SOLVE PROBLEMS IMPORTING FILES

In theory, Windows 10 should pop up a message when you first plug in your camera, smartphone or memory card, asking you what you want to do with the device. But it's easy to miss this, which means new photos don't get imported. To fix this, click Start, Settings, Devices, AutoPlay, then look for your device in the list. Click the dropdown menu underneath your device 1 and select 'Import photos and videos (Photos)' 2 from the available options.

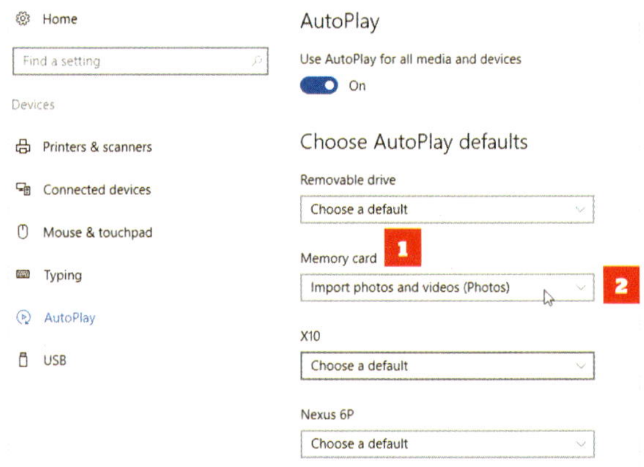

STEP 2 CHANGE WHERE YOUR PHOTOS ARE STORED

By default, Windows 10 saves photos it imports to your Pictures folder, but you can change this if you prefer. Connect your camera, smartphone or memory card and the Photos app will open (assuming you've followed Step 1) and scan the device for new images and movies. When it's done scanning, click Continue, then in the next screen, click 'Change where they're imported' 1. Browse for the folder you want and click 'Add this folder to Pictures'.

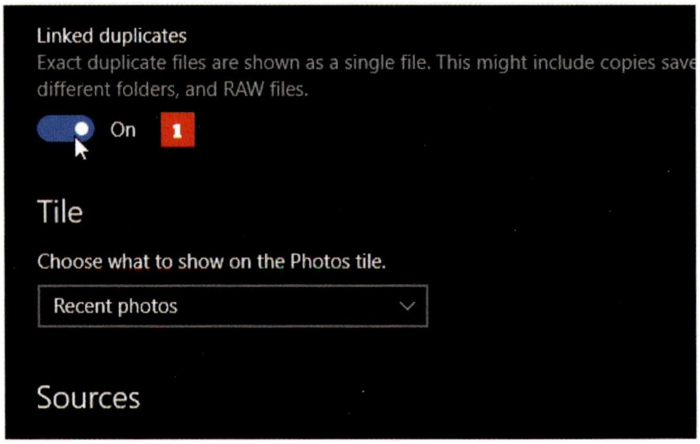

STEP 3 HIDE DUPLICATES

Duplicate photos can occur for a variety of different reasons. You may have edited or enhanced photos and saved them as a new file in order to preserve the original for example, and now both copies show up in Photos. Or you may see both original Raw files and digitally processed copies. Either way, having two (or more) copies of the same image show up in your Photos app can be annoying, so click the Settings (cog) icon and, under 'Viewing and editing' make sure 'Linked duplicates' 1 is switched on. This won't prevent all duplicates but it will help.

STEP 4 TURN OFF AUTO ENHANCEMENTS

Microsoft's Photos app 'helpfully' auto-enhances any photos you import, straightening, brightening and removing red-eye as it sees fit. This doesn't alter the original file in any way, but keen photographers may prefer to view their images as they were taken rather than as Microsoft thinks they should look. Thankfully, it's possible to disable this feature – though doing so will turn off all automatic enhancements, rather than specific photos. Click the Settings (cog) icon and, under 'Viewing and editing', switch 'Automatically enhance your photos' 1 off.

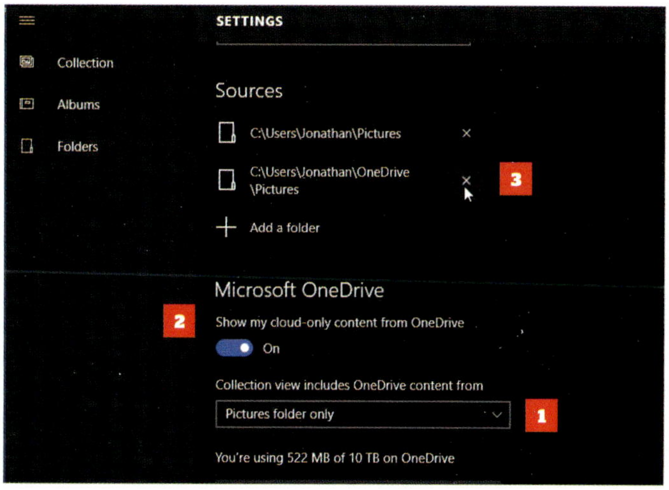

STEP 6 ADD A MISSING FOLDER

If you store photos anywhere other than you Pictures folder or your OneDrive folder, then they won't show up in the Photos app unless you tell it where to look. To fix this, click the Settings (cog) icon and scroll to Sources. Click the plus sign next to Add a folder 1 and then browse to the folder you want to include. When you've found it, click the 'Add this folder to Pictures' button. Any photos included in this folder will now show up in your Collection.

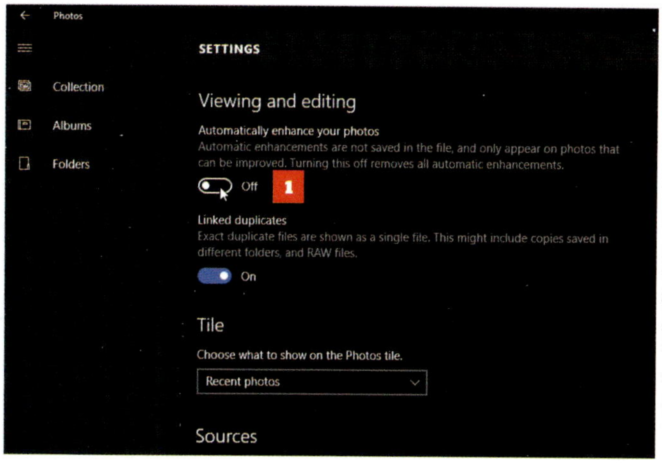

STEP 5 LIMIT OR TURN OFF ONEDRIVE

By default, the Windows 10 Photos app displays any images stored in your OneDrive online storage, as well as those on your PC. But what if you don't want these to show up in your collection? Perhaps the images you keep in OneDrive are for work, for example. Click the Settings (cog) icon and scroll down to where it says Microsoft OneDrive. Here you can either limit the OneDrive files shown to those stored in the Pictures folder (select 'Pictures folder only' from the 'Collection view includes OneDrive content from' dropdown 1), or switch 'Show my cloud-only content from OneDrive' 2 off altogether. You can also click the 'x' next to your OneDrive pictures folder under Sources 3 to remove it.

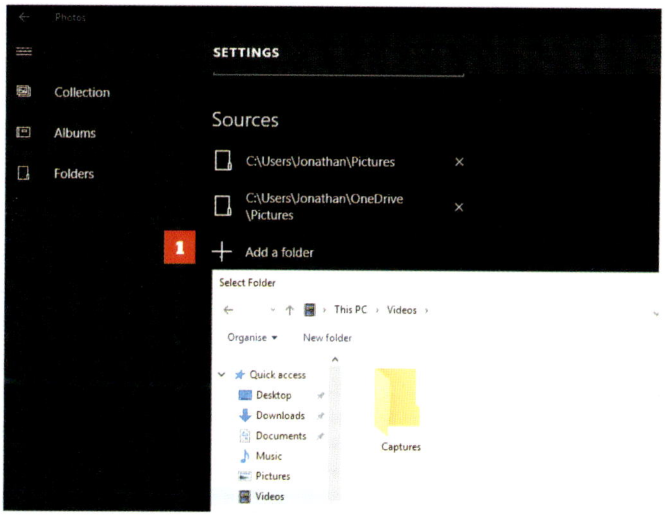

STEP 7 FIX PROBLEMS WITH PHOTOS

The Windows 10 Photos app has a selection of simple, but surprisingly effective tools for editing and enhancing your images. The trouble is, they're not exactly obvious to find or navigate. Open the app and browse to a photo in your collection that you want to improve. Click it and you should see a selection of icons appear along the top. Click the pencil (Edit) icon and two strips of new icons should appear either side of the image. Clicking a category icon in the left-hand strip – Basic fixes, Filters, Light, Colour or Effects 1 – changes the selection of tools available in the right-hand strip 2.

Switch to Windows 10's email app

Time required: 20 minutes

Mail, which comes built into Windows 10 is one of Microsoft's better pre-installed apps. It's easy to use and supports a wide variety of different email account types, including Microsoft's own Outlook.com webmail, which Windows Live Mail (Microsoft's previous own-brand email program) recently stopped supporting.

Whether you're a Live Mail user looking for a replacement, or you just want an easy way to send and receive messages without too much fuss, we'll show you how to switch your account to Mail.

STEP 1 Open the Mail app and click the Settings (cog) icon at the bottom left **1**. Where the Settings panel has slid out on the right, click Manage Accounts. You'll see your existing accounts listed. Click on one if you need to change its settings, or click Add account **2** to add a new one. A 'Choose an account' dialogue box will pop up **3**. Windows 10's Mail is able to set up many types of email and webmail accounts automatically, including Outlook.com, Exchange/Office 365, Google (Gmail), Yahoo! Mail and iCloud. So if you're adding one of those, just click to select it.

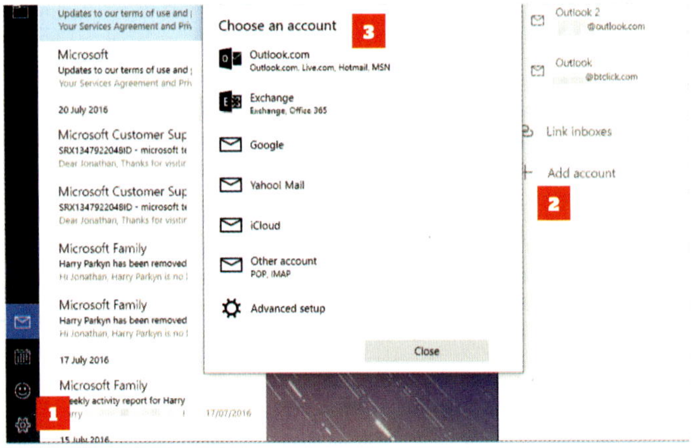

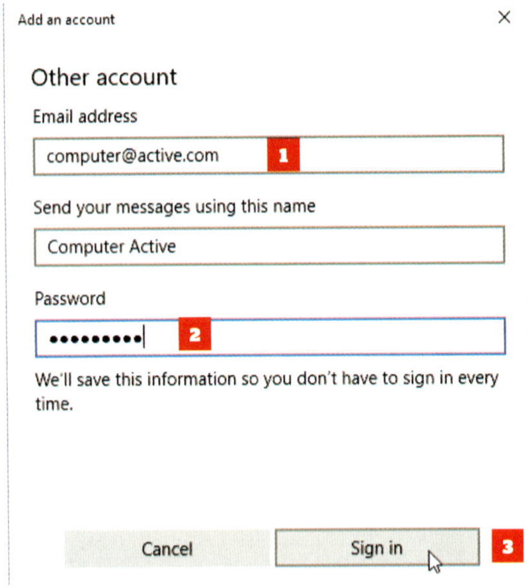

STEP 2 Enter the email address and password for this account, then click 'Sign in'. Mail will configure the account correctly, and messages should start streaming through. If your account doesn't match any of the other categories listed (or you're not sure) click 'Other account (POP or IMAP)'. Mail can still try to configure things automatically. Enter the email address **1** and password **2** for your account, then click 'Sign in' **3**. In many cases, this will be all that's required to set up your account.

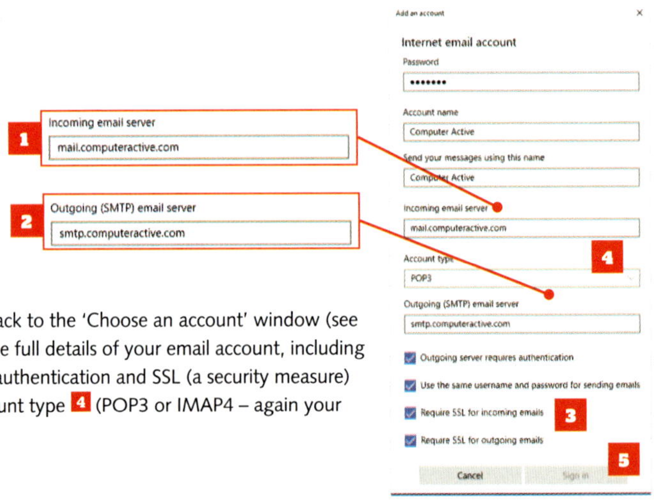

STEP 3 Sometimes, however, you'll need more info to get things working. Go back to the 'Choose an account' window (see Step 1) and Click 'Advanced setup'. Click 'Internet email', then fill out the full details of your email account, including the incoming **1** and outgoing **2** email servers and whether or not the account requires authentication and SSL (a security measure) **3**. You may need to refer to your email provider or ISP for these details. Choose an account type **4** (POP3 or IMAP4 – again your provider will tell you which you need), then click 'Sign in' **5** when you're done.

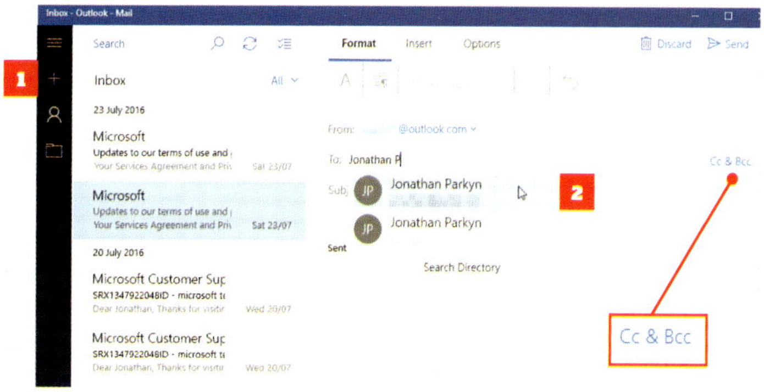

STEP 4 To compose a message, click the plus sign button in the top left 1, then select the account you want to send from (if you have more than one account). Type the name or email address of the recipient into the 'To' field. As you type, Mail will try to match contacts information from the People app 2. Press Enter when the correct one is selected, or after you finish typing the address. You can carry on typing to add further recipients. If you want to Cc or Bcc (blind copy, where recipients don't see each other's addresses) other recipients, click the Cc & Bcc link 3 to reveal these fields in the email.

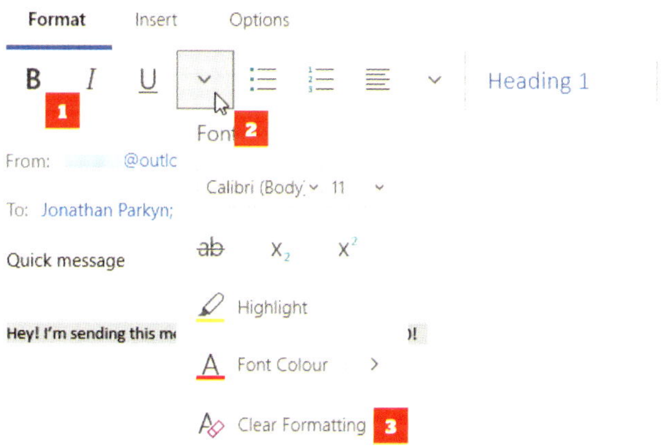

STEP 5 Click in the Subject field and type in a subject line, then click below and start writing your email. Mail has a simplified version of Microsoft Word's ribbon interface. With the Format tab selected, click the B, I and U 1 icons to embolden, italicise or underline text. Click the down arrow next door 2 for further options, including changing the font and size, highlighting text or changing its colour, or you can clear formatting you've already applied 3. The next buttons along on the right add paragraph formatting, such as bullets or numbering, indents or changing the line spacing, just as in Word. You can also select a paragraph style to apply to the text, or create styles of your own.

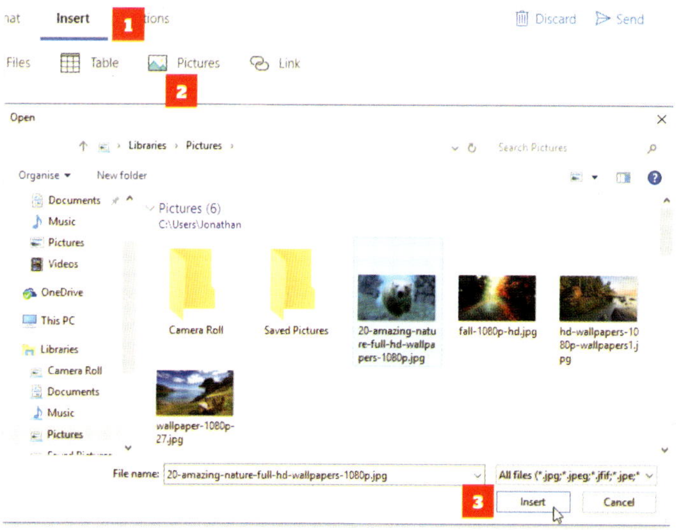

STEP 6 Click Insert 1 to attach a file to the email, or insert a web link or picture. Click the Pictures button 2 and you can use the File Explorer interface to navigate to and select an image file. Now click Insert 3. Once the picture is in place, more tools appear in a new Picture toolbar. Use these to rotate or crop the image or quickly change its size, or click and drag the circular handles on the corners and edges of the frame to resize and rescale it. Click outside the picture when you're finished to continue editing your email. When your email's finished, click the Send button at the top right.

STEP 7 You can manage your inbox by deleting or archiving emails you've read. Deleting gets rid of them permanently. Archiving (not supported by all email or webmail services) takes the mail out of your inbox, but retains it on the server, so you can still search for it later if you need to. Highlight a message, then click the Archive 1 or Delete 2 buttons in the bar above the Preview pane. Alternatively, hover your mouse over an email in your message list and click the dustbin icon that appears to delete it.

Use Windows 10's Contact Support app

Windows 10 comes with a free, built-in tech support app. But how reliable is it, and can it really fix PC problems for you? We put it to the test

Forget, Cortana, Groove Music and 3D Builder. Of all the apps that come pre-installed with Windows 10, Contact Support has the potential to be the most useful.

Unlike Cortana, Contact Support lets you talk to a real person – a Microsoft Answer Desk support operator – who can help you when you have a problem with your PC. You can connect to an operator (or a 'Microsoft Answer Tech,' as the app calls them) in two different ways; either by requesting them to call you back on the phone or by using live chat within the app itself to type your questions directly to an expert. Both are free.

So, just how helpful is Microsoft's Answer Desk? We decided to put it to the test by using Contact Support's live chat option to try and fix four different PC problems.

▲ Chat (almost) instantly with Microsoft

1 Start menu doesn't work

WAITING TIME: 2 minutes
FIXED OR NOT? FIXED

One of the Contact Support app's more obvious failings is that if Windows won't start, or if you've lost key functionality, then you may not be able to launch the app at all. In our case, for example, the Start menu and search box had stopped responding altogether, meaning it wasn't possible to run any apps. We got around this by using the Contact Support app on another Windows 10 PC, and for situations like these, it's worth knowing that you can also live chat with Microsoft's support team from any PC – including those running Windows 7 or 8 – by visiting www.snipca.com/20906 in your web browser and clicking 'Chat with a Microsoft Answer Tech'.

After a brief (two-minute) wait in a queue, a very polite operator came online and we described our problem. The operator asked a few more questions, including which build of the OS we were using and eventually, we were told "your issue may have been caused by some corrupted files, programs and/or system on the background that hasn't been fully upgraded/updated during the upgrade/installation/download process," which was suitably non-specific. At this point, our operator asked if she could take remote control of our system to fix the problem. When we explained we were using Contact Support on another PC, due to the Start menu problem, our operator then talked us through how to set up a remote session on the broken computer, all without needing to use the Start menu. The process was a little fiddly but the instructions given were clear.

Once the operator took over, she was able to launch Powershell and scan for corrupt files. A few commands and a reboot later and the Start menu was back up and running. We were also supplied with a Start menu troubleshooting tool that we could use if the problem ever happened again. Despite the hassle factor of working across two PCs, the Answer Tech solved the problem quickly and impressively.

2 My default programs have changed

WAITING TIME: less than a minute
FIXED OR NOT? FIXED

Windows 10 has a nasty habit of secretly switching its default programs back to Microsoft's own apps. This happened on one of our test PCs following an update, so we fired up the Contact Support app to see whether an Answer Tech would be able to sort it out.

After asking a few questions, our new operator offered to take control of the PC to fix it himself. This time the process was easier, as we were live chatting on the PC that was having the problem – all we needed to do was download a small tool, agree to the terms and conditions and enter a passkey given to us by the operator.

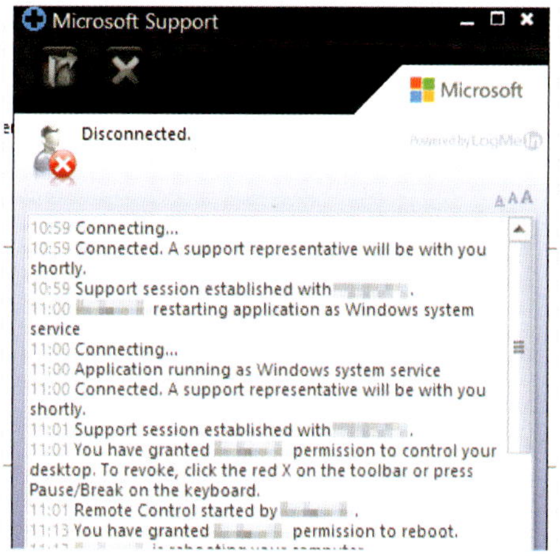

▲ Staff may request remote access to your PC

The first thing he tried was to change the default programs from the Settings app, but this didn't work. So instead, he opened the old Control Panel and clicked Programs, then Default Programs, then 'Set default programs' where he was able to make the necessary changes. At this point, he restarted the PC to check that the changes he'd made had worked. And, indeed, they had.

3 My laptop's screen isn't working

WAITING TIME: 5 minutes

FIXED OR NOT? NOT FIXED

So far, Microsoft's Answer Desk team had been able to fix both of our Windows problems using remote access, so we were curious to find out how they'd cope with a hardware problem. The display on one of our laptops has recently developed a rather peaky looking green-ish cast, along with several unattractive pink streaks running vertically down one side of the LCD screen (possibly as the result of being sat on). Any technical expert worth their salt would be able to diagnose this as a hardware fault or internal connection problem just by looking at it - but would a Microsoft Answer Tech be able to help us fix it via live chat?

This time, we had to wait a little longer in the queue. A message warned that the service was "experiencing higher than normal wait times". Even still, our operator came online in just under five minutes. He asked for more details than our previous operators, including our name, email address, country and phone number. When we asked why the phone number was needed, we were told that it was to contact us if the live chat connection was lost, and were assured that it wouldn't be used for marketing or spam. The operator was able to diagnose the screen problem as a hardware fault within half a dozen questions. Unsurprisingly, he was unable to offer a fix. Instead, he pointed us towards a "Microsoft physical store" for a repair, rather than recommending that we contact the retailer or manufacturer.

4 Can I disable Cortana?

WAITING TIME: 5 minutes

FIXED OR NOT? PARTLY FIXED

Rather cheekily, we wondered what response we'd get from Microsoft if we asked its advice on how to banish Cortana from Windows 10. And, disappointingly, the Answer Desk operator who answered our query simply pointed us in the direction of a Microsoft help page (www.snipca.com/20910). The page shows how to disable Cortana, but it doesn't explain how to clear your search history or delete the information that Cortana stores about you online. When we asked whether following the steps in the web page would prevent Cortana gathering or storing personal information about us and were told that Cortana "doesn't gather information", which is clearly a big fat fib.

Did Microsoft pass the test?

Overall, Windows 10's built-in support app proved pretty useful, though this is somewhat dependent on the type of problem you need solved. Our two Windows-based problems, for example, were both fixed efficiently by the operators concerned. But there are obvious limits to what Answer Desk agents can achieve remotely without physical access to your device – particularly when it comes to hardware problems. And you may find that the information offered isn't always 100 per cent reliable, given the service's strict Microsoft bias and the varying levels of quality you're likely to get from one operator to the next. On one occasion, for example, an operator attempted to take the opportunity to sell us a £100 'service plan'. After each support session you're able to grade and comment on the level of service you've received, so make sure you let Microsoft know exactly how well (or not) it resolved your problem.

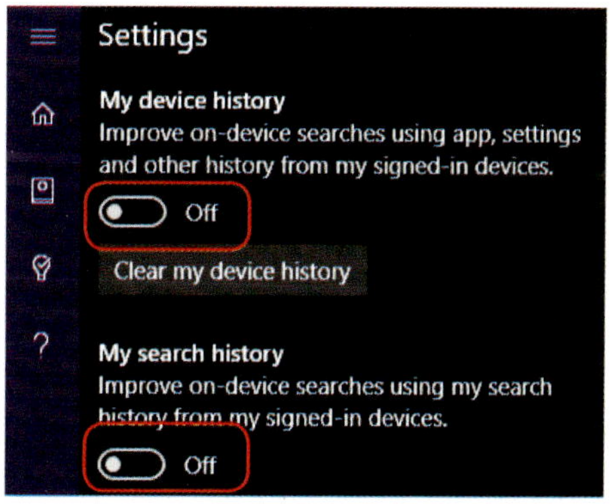

▲ Get advice for almost any Windows problem

How to use the Contact Support app

• To open Contact Support, click Start, type contact and click the link to the Contact Support app. When the app opens, click Getting Started, then type a description of your problem into the box and click Submit.

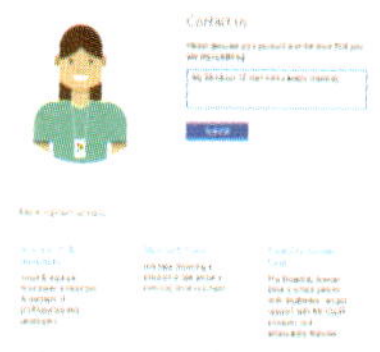

• On the next screen, select the product you're using – Windows, for example – and the category – 'Technical support' – from the two dropdown menus, then select one of the options shown underneath.

• Don't click 'My device' here – this will simply push you towards your PC manufacturer's website. Instead, click Chat for a typed conversation with a Microsoft employee. You can also opt to have a tech support representative contact you by phone – click Call 'me as soon as possible' or click 'Arrange a call' to book a call-back for a specific date and time. Clicking 'Ask the community' will take you to Microsoft's online troubleshooting forums.

• Microsoft Answer Desk's telephone helpline is not a 24-hour service. The 'Call me as soon as possible' option is only available during the services opening hours: 09.00-20.00 Monday to Friday, 10.00-17.00 Saturday and Sunday.

Uninstall Windows 10 apps

Don't let Microsoft control how you use your PC. We explain which Windows apps and features you can get rid of, and show you how to remove them safely

Over the years, Microsoft has gradually added more and more pre-installed programs and tools to its operating systems, and it's safe to say that some of these are more welcome than others.

It can be useful to have built-in media players and so on, but there are often better alternatives available – sometimes for free.

Many of Windows 7 and 8's built-in offerings were limited in their capabilities; others were completely unnecessary – they just get in the way, hogging resources and consuming valuable hard drive space.

Windows 10 goes one step further – not only pre-loading your hard drive with dozens of Windows Store apps, but also making it extremely hard to remove them.

Windows 10 also goes out of its way to try and get you to use these apps, setting them as the defaults for many common tasks, such as listening to music or viewing photos, often because they act as a gateway to one or other of the company's own pay-for services, such as its online music store.

And, while it's possible to change your default programs to ones you want (see the box on page 175), Windows has a nasty habit of switching back to its own apps without any warning. Many users discovered that a recent Windows 10 update sneakily removed certain third-party tools from their PCs and reset Microsoft's apps as their default programs, for example.

But you don't have to put up with software you don't want. As we're about to reveal, there are ways to rid yourself of all the junk Microsoft doesn't want you to uninstall. We'll show you which Windows apps you need to keep, and explain how to banish the ones you don't from your hard drive forever.

In most cases, we'll offer suggestions for other, better alternatives that you can use instead of the apps Microsoft wants you to use, most of which you can install for free.

And we'll be looking at some of these great third-party tools – along with many other brilliant free apps, tools and programs – in greater detail later on in this chapter.

What you can do

- Get rid of useless pre-installed apps and features that you don't need
- Set the programs you want to use as your computer's defaults
- Safely uninstall (and reinstall) Windows 10's built-in apps and tools
- Get rid of unwanted bloat that's slowing down your computer

20 MINUTE TWEAKS

1 3D Builder

WHAT DOES IT DO?

It lets you create and print 3D models.

KEEP OR DITCH?

DITCH. Those who have an interest in 3D modelling may want to give this app a spin, but it's frustratingly low on features and, unless you have a compatible 3D printer (http://microsoft.com/3d), it's pretty useless. We say ditch it.

2 Cortana

WHAT DOES IT DO?

Microsoft's voice-controlled personal digital assistant lets you search your PC or the web, set reminders and more using spoken commands.

KEEP OR DITCH?

DISABLE. Some may find Cortana useful, but it gathers lots of information about you and your activity, and stores this online, which not everyone will be

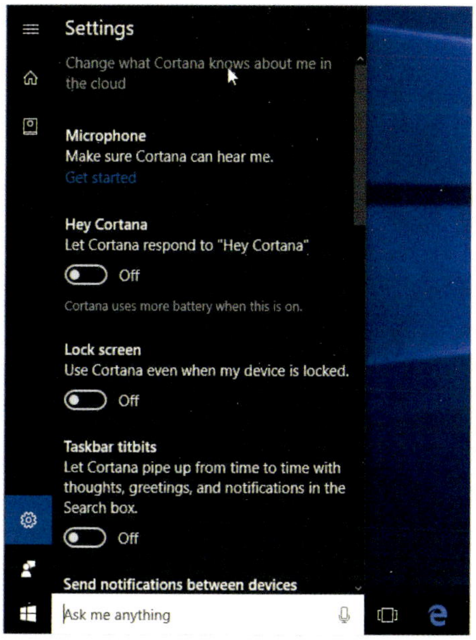

comfortable with. Annoyingly, although Cortana is technically an app, it's hardwired into the OS and you can't uninstall it – not even with the hacks we've outlined on the right. However, you can disable it by clicking the taskbar Search box, then the Settings (cog) icon. Here, switch off all the options available and click 'Change what Cortana knows about me in the cloud' to clear your personal information off Microsoft's servers.

3 Films & TV

WHAT DOES IT DO?

It lets you watch movies and TV shows stored on your PC, as well as those bought or rented from Microsoft's online store.

KEEP OR DITCH?

DITCH. Windows Media Player (which is still included in Windows 10) or VLC (free from www.snipca.com/19249) are much better video players, and there are other ways to get on-demand movies and

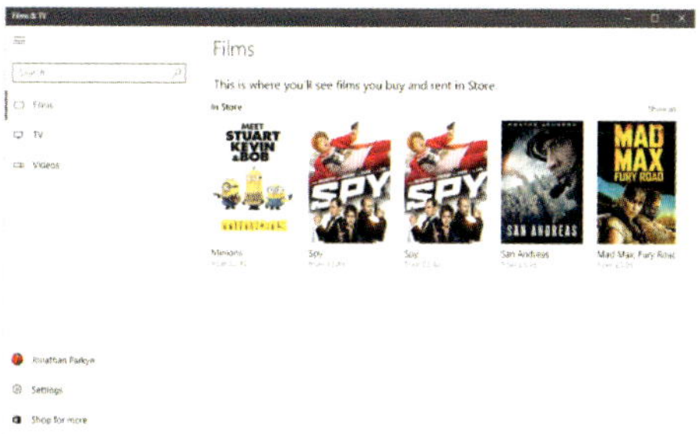

shows, either free from catch-up services like iPlayer, or via the likes of Netflix, Amazon Prime, Google Play, iTunes and others. Unless you're particularly fond of the Windows Store, this is an easy one to ditch.

4 Calendar

WHAT DOES IT DO?

It helps you organise your schedule.

KEEP OR DITCH?

KEEP. The Calendar app is actually pretty useful – it works with Outlook.com, Google Calendar and iCloud, so if you already use one of these services, all you need to do is sign in with the relevant account to view and sync appointments. Removing the app will affect Mail too, so we recommend keeping it.

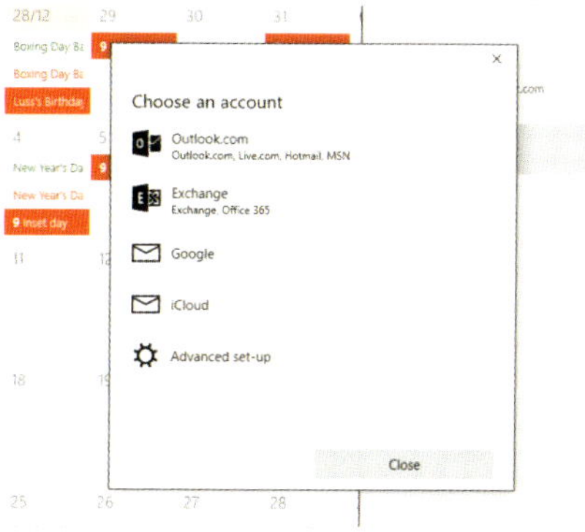

5 Contact Support

WHAT DOES IT DO?

It provides easy ways for you to get help with your PC.

KEEP OR DITCH?

KEEP. It doesn't offer a great deal more than Microsoft's own support website does (www.snipca.com/19248), but it's easy to navigate and lets you chat online with Microsoft support staff. This is one you'll want to keep – which is just as well, as you can't uninstall it anyway!

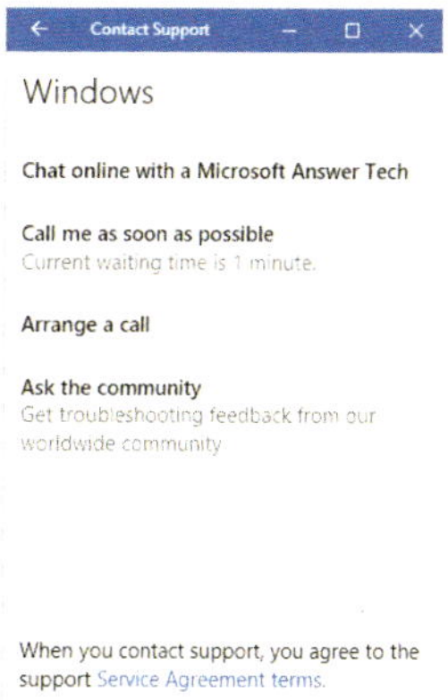

How to completely remove Windows 10's default apps

There are three main ways to uninstall Windows 10's built-in apps. Be warned, though – in some cases it can be hard to get your apps back once they've been removed. See page 172 for more.

1 Right-click
In some cases, it's possible to remove Microsoft's built-in apps from your PC by right-clicking them and selecting Uninstall. This doesn't work for all of them but you can get rid of 3D Builder, Get Office, Get Skype, Get Started, Microsoft Solitaire Collection, Microsoft Wi-Fi, Money, News, Phone Companion, Skype Video, Sport and Sway using this technique.

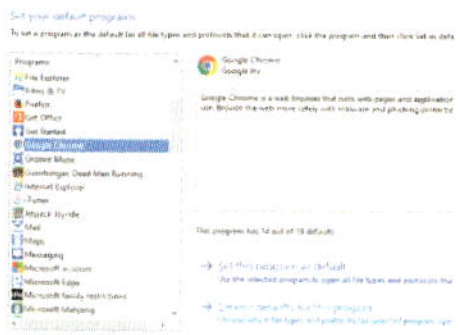

2 Use an uninstaller
Stubborn apps, including Alarms & Clock, Calculator, Films & TV and Groove Music, can be removed using a free tool. 10AppsManager (www.snipca.com/19259) can uninstall 23 of Windows 10's built-in apps. Unzip the tool and run it, then click the icon for the app you want to remove and click Yes. The program maker recommends creating a System Restore point beforehand so you can easily roll back any changes you make. The latest version of Ccleaner (www.snipca.com/19260) can remove even more apps. Click Tools, then Uninstall and you'll see Windows apps listed with all your other programs. Highlight one, then click Uninstall and OK.

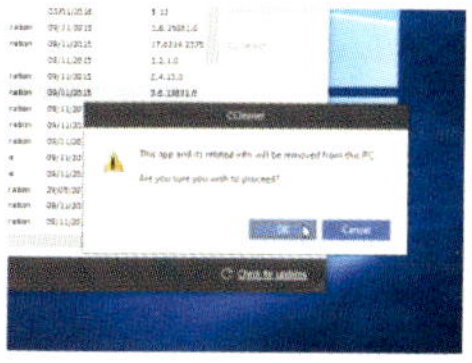

3 Manually remove them
It's possible to use Windows PowerShell commands to manually remove individual apps. We don't recommend using this method, but you may need to use PowerShell to reinstall your apps – see the box on page 172.

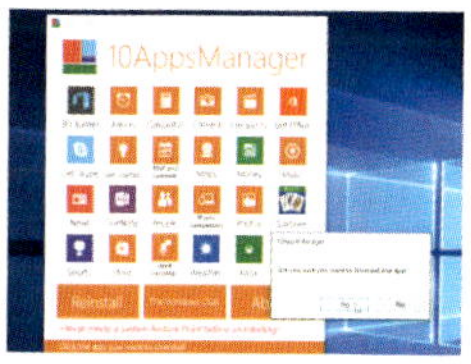

6 Alarms & Clock

WHAT DOES IT DO?

It's an alarm clock, world clock, timer and stopwatch in one.

KEEP OR DITCH?

KEEP. These are all useful functions to have on your PC, so we'd say keep it. That said, Microsoft's app isn't the most reliable – we've heard of cases where alarms fail to sound when they're supposed to. So you may wish to dump it in favour of a free alternative, such as http://freealarmclocksoftware.com.

7 Get Started

WHAT DOES IT DO?

It's a guide to using Windows 10.

KEEP OR DITCH?

DITCH. There are some helpful videos and nuggets of information here about everything from searching and syncing to using Windows 10's new features. But you'll also find the entire contents of this guide online at www.snipca.com/19251, so you can get rid of the app.

8 Get Skype

WHAT DOES IT DO?

This is simply a link to download the desktop version of Skype.

KEEP OR DITCH?

DITCH. This app can be safely uninstalled. If you need to install the desktop version at any point, get it from www.snipca.com/19250.

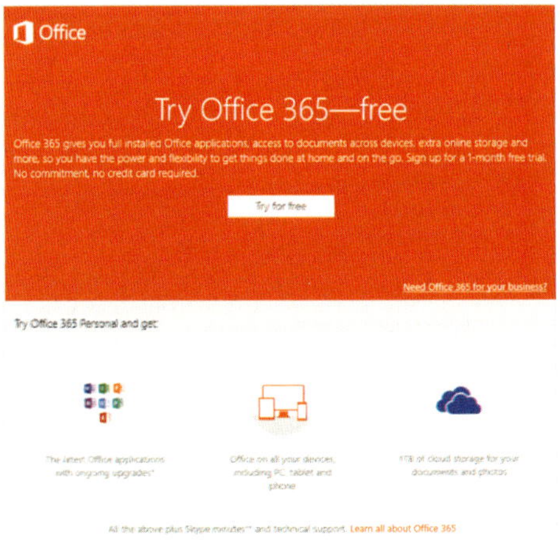

9 Get Office

WHAT DOES IT DO?

It's basically just a link to a free one-month trial of Microsoft Office 365.

KEEP OR DITCH?

DITCH. If you already have Office or have no intention of using it, there's no reason to keep this app. You can get the free one-month trial at any point from www.snipca.com/19264.

10 Camera

WHAT DOES IT DO?

Takes photos and records video clips.

KEEP OR DITCH?

DITCH. If you don't have a camera built into your PC or an external webcam, there's little point in having this app installed. And even if you do, then there are plenty of better camera tools available; your webcam may have come with its own software, or you could try a free tool, such as ManyCam (https://manycam.com).

HOW TO REINSTALL WINDOWS 10 APPS

What if you uninstall an app only to realise you want it back? Luckily, in most cases you can simply re-download the ones you want back individually from the Windows Store. We've found that it's not always possible to do this, however. If you're having problems, then here's something you can try – this will reinstall all the apps you've removed.

Click Start, type powershell, then right-click the Windows PowerShell option and select 'Run as administrator'. At the prompt, type the following command exactly, then press Enter on your keyboard:

Get-AppxPackage -AllUsers| Foreach {Add-AppxPackage -DisableDevelopmentMode -Register "$($_.InstallLocation)\AppXManifest.xml"}

Let the process run until you see the prompt again. Don't be too alarmed if you see lots of red warnings. When it's done, restart your PC and check your Start menu to see if the apps are back. If not, try running the PowerShell command and restarting again – it took us a couple of tries to get our apps back when we tested this.

11 Calculator

WHAT DOES IT DO?

It's a calculator with standard, scientific and programmer modes as well as conversion tools.

KEEP OR DITCH?

KEEP. It might look different to the Windows calculator of yore but there's nothing particularly wrong with it, so we recommend leaving it where it is. If you don't like it, though, there's no shortage of free and pay-for alternatives to try in the Windows Store.

12 Groove Music

WHAT DOES IT DO?

Use it to play your music collection or stream tunes from Microsoft's equivalent to Spotify.

KEEP OR DITCH?

DITCH. Groove Music is far from the best music player. In our opinion, Windows Media Player (also pre-installed) is the better program, while Media Monkey (www.mediamonkey.com) is another simple, free alternative. If you already subscribe to Spotify, Google Play Music or Apple Music or aren't interested in music streaming services, you won't want to pay £8.99 a month for a Groove Music pass, either.

13 Mail

WHAT DOES IT DO?

It's Windows 10's built-in email client.

KEEP OR DITCH?

KEEP. Mail isn't perfect but it's very simple and works with most types of account. If it's not to your tastes, there

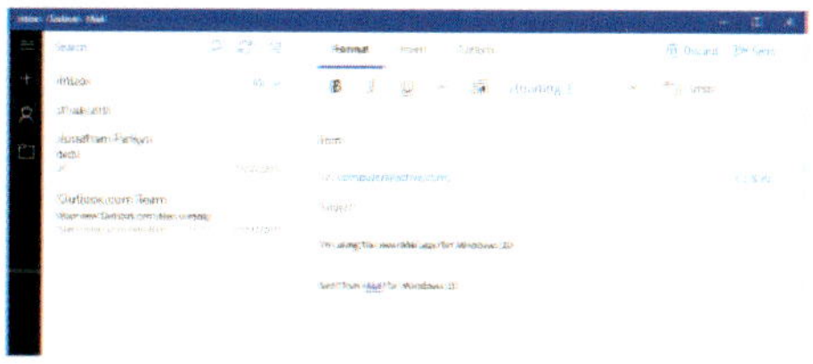

are loads of alternatives. You could install Thunderbird (www.snipca.com/19252), or just login to your webmail via your browser. Even if you're not going to use it, though, we recommend leaving Mail installed, as removing it can affect other apps, such as Calendar.

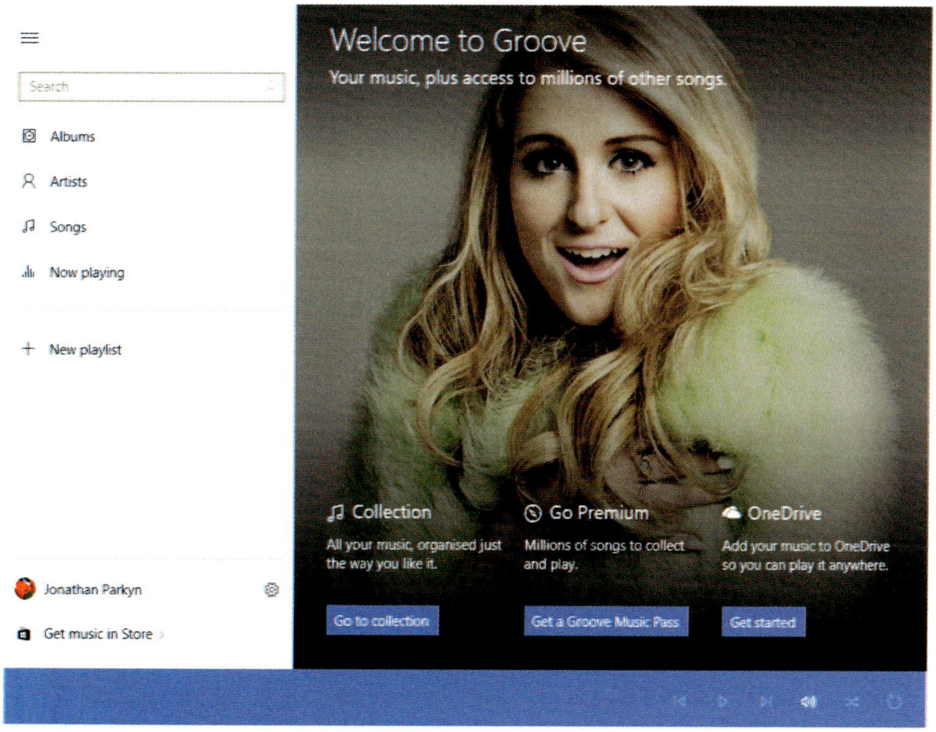

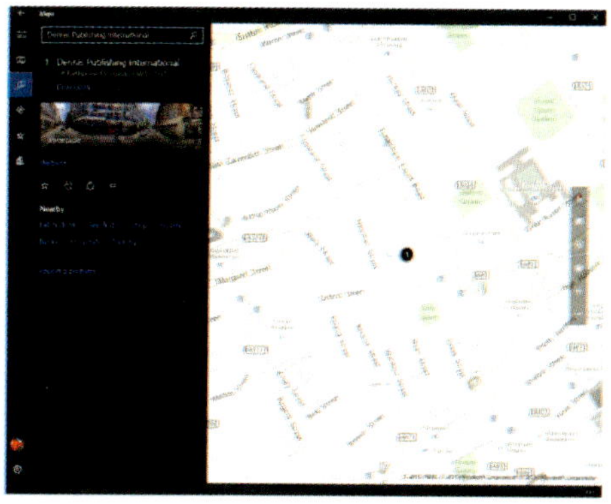

14 Maps

WHAT DOES IT DO?

Maps is Microsoft's equivalent to Google Maps and Apple Maps.

KEEP OR DITCH?

DITCH. Having a map app is useful, even on a non-mobile device, such as a desktop PC, where you can plan routes and journeys, and you can save offline maps, too. However, if you have no need for any of this, you could lose the Maps app and use the map service of your choice – maps.google.co.uk, for example – via your browser, instead.

15 Microsoft Solitaire Collection

WHAT DOES IT DO?

It's a free version of Microsoft's pay-for Solitaire game.

KEEP OR DITCH?

DITCH. Windows has always come with a smattering of built-in games, but Windows 10 only includes only one – Microsoft Solitaire Collection – and asks you to pay (£7.69 per year) to remove adverts and unlock other features. Ditch it and play a truly free Solitaire game (http://solitaireforfree.com) in your browser, instead.

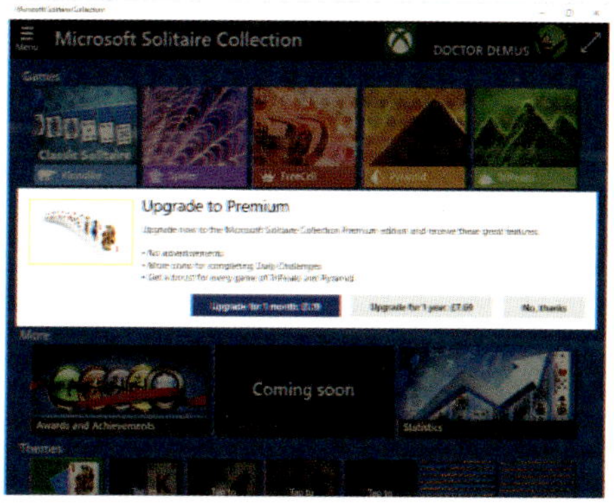

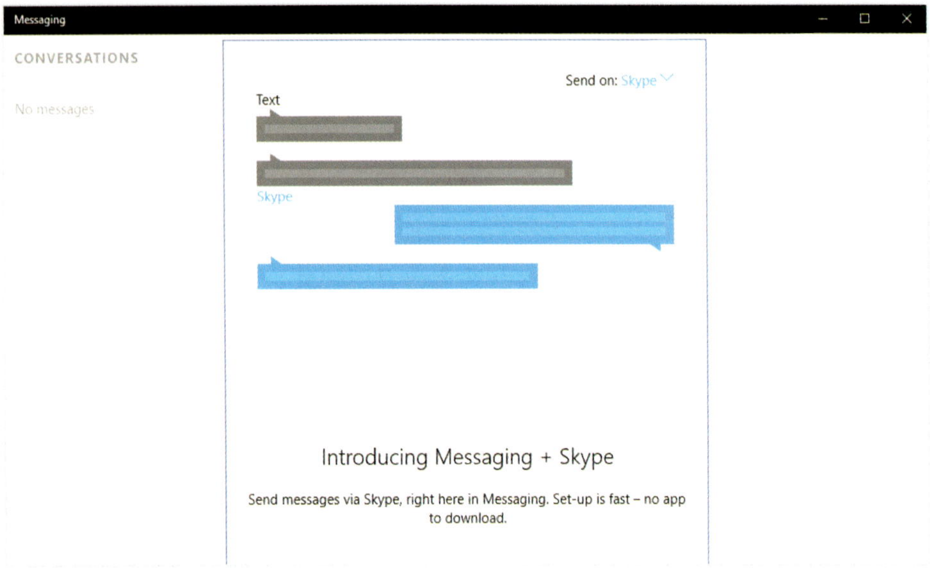

16 Messaging, Phone and Skype Video

WHAT DOES IT DO?

These apps let you send and receive text messages and make voice or video calls.

KEEP OR DITCH?

DITCH. Windows 10's November update took Skype's core functions and split them over three separate new apps: Messaging, Phone and Skype Video. This probably makes sense for some mobile users, but if you're on a PC you'll probably prefer to carry on using the all-in-one desktop version instead (www.snipca.com/19250) and ditch all three apps.

17 Microsoft Edge

WHAT DOES IT DO?

It's the web browser that comes with Windows 10.

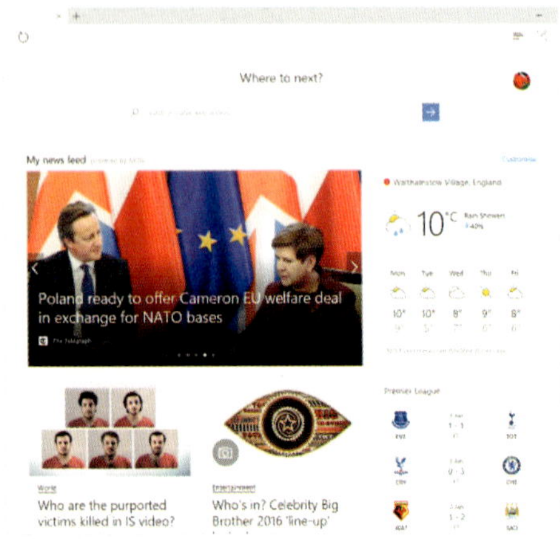

KEEP OR DITCH?

DISABLE. As with Cortana, it's not possible to uninstall Edge. If you don't want to use it, install your preferred browser and make sure it's set as the default, using our instructions on the page opposite.

18 Microsoft Wi-Fi

WHAT DOES IT DO?

This app allows you to buy wireless internet access at hotels, airports and so on, via hotspots that support Microsoft's Wi-Fi partnership scheme.

KEEP OR DITCH?

DITCH. Desktop users can dump this one right away, as they'll almost certainly never need it. Most Wi-Fi hotspots provide alternative methods of getting yourself online too, so this app isn't really needed, even if you're using a laptop and tablet.

19 Money

WHAT DOES IT DO?

It lets you chart markets, get financial news and provides tools to convert currencies, track stocks and more.

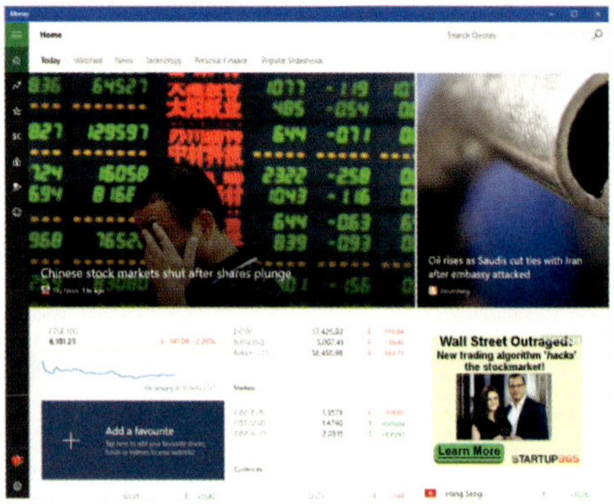

KEEP OR DITCH?

DEPENDS. Not everyone has a portfolio of investments they need to keep an eye on, so this app won't be relevant to every user. For those who follow the markets, however, it's actually a pretty handy tool.

20 News

WHAT DOES IT DO?

Presents you with regularly updated news stories from around the world.

KEEP OR DITCH?

KEEP. While it's not strictly necessary – you can get your fix of current affairs from any number of online sources, or from Twitter – it's actually quite handy to catch a glimpse of the latest headlines whenever you click Start, courtesy of this app's Live Tile.

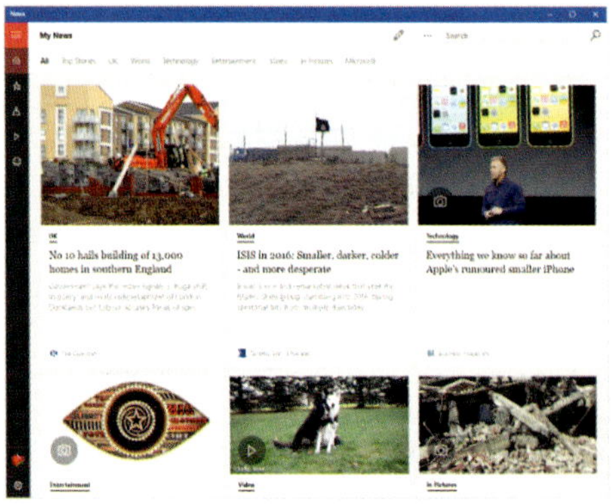

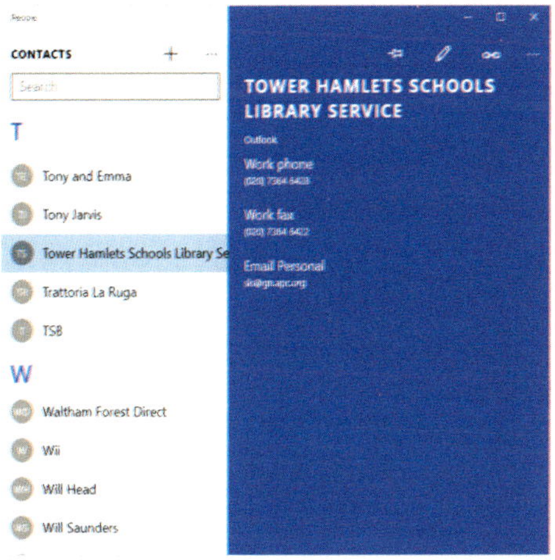

21 People

WHAT DOES IT DO?

It's where Windows stores your contacts.

KEEP OR DITCH?

KEEP. Having your contacts on your PC it very useful and People syncs with not only Microsoft's Outlook.com but also Gmail and iCloud among others. Even if you decide not to make use of it, it's best to leave it installed, as it's linked to the Mail and Calendar apps.

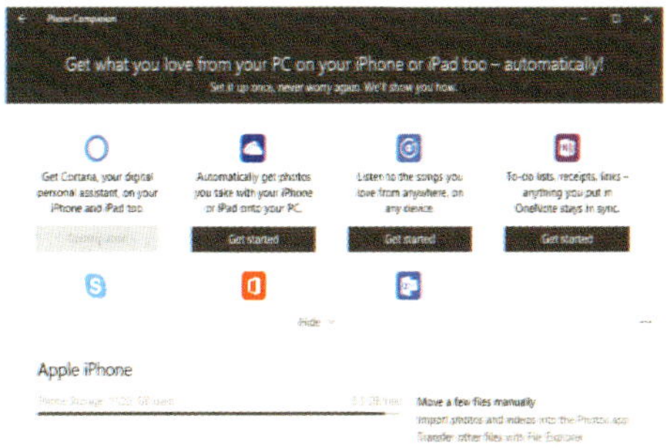

22 Phone Companion

WHAT DOES IT DO?

It's an almost-useful tool that aims to bridge the connection between your PC and your smartphone.

KEEP OR DITCH?

DITCH. In practice, Phone Companion doesn't offer an awful lot to Android or iOS users. It recognises your device and displays storage information but, apart from that, all it does is recommend Microsoft apps (OneNote, Outlook, Skype and so on) to install on your device. Syncing isn't supported and importing photos is handled separately (via AutoPlay).

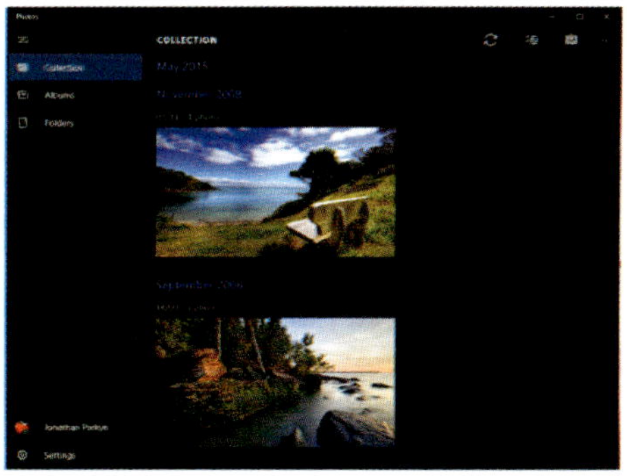

23 Photos

WHAT DOES IT DO?

It lets you import, view and organise your photos.

KEEP OR DITCH?

DEPENDS. Photos is okay – see earlier in this chapter for some tips on how to use it. But it's not the greatest photo organiser by any stretch of the imagination and offers strictly limited editing tools. We recommend giving Google Photos (https://photos.google.com) a go – it's the free online service Google launched last year and it replaces Google's own massively popular Picasa.

24 Sport

WHAT DOES IT DO?

It shows sports-related news and scores.

KEEP OR DITCH?

DITCH. If you're not into sports, this app can be quickly ditched. Those who follow teams, sports or events can personalise the app, but if you're a sporty type, it's likely you already have sites and Twitter feeds that you follow, which renders this app a little useless.

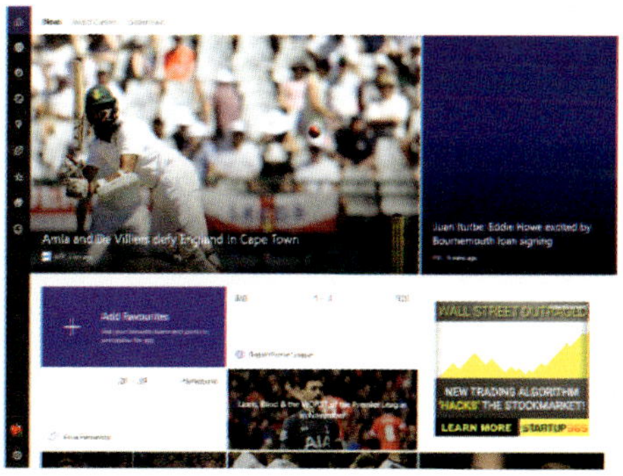

25 Store

WHAT DOES IT DO?

It's Microsoft's marketplace for apps, games, music, films and TV.

KEEP OR DITCH?

KEEP. While it's possible to uninstall the Windows Store using our hacks on page 171, we strongly recommend not doing so. Removing the Store app not only cuts you off from an invaluable source of free tools and games, but it can also cause problems further down the line, should you ever wish to reinstall it.

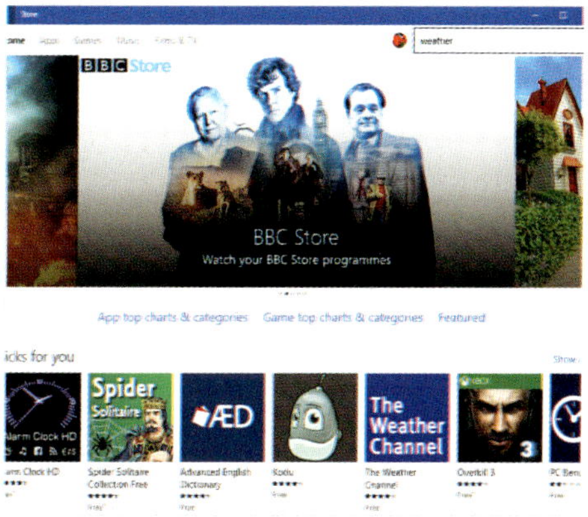

HOW TO CHANGE WINDOWS DEFAULT APPS AND PROGRAMS

If you decide to uninstall Windows' apps or programs, you'll need to tell your PC which applications to use instead. Or, if you'd prefer not to uninstall any of Windows' built-in components, you can simply tell Windows to ignore them in favour of the tools you prefer. The instructions are the same in both cases.

Click Start, type default, then click Default Programs. In the window that opens, click 'Set your default programs' then scroll through the list of available programs and apps and click the one you want – click Google Chrome if you want to set it as your default web browser, for example, then click 'Set this program as default'. Repeat the process for your photo, music, video and any other programs. To refine your selections further, click 'Choose defaults for this program' to specify each individual file type you want to associate with the application.

HOW TO UNINSTALL WINDOWS FEATURES

Most users will already be familiar with Windows' 'Programs and features' tool (right-click Start, choose Control Panel, then 'Uninstall a program'). Its main function is to remove third-party software from your PC. But if you look on the left you'll see an option to 'Turn Windows features on or off'. Click this and a new window will open listing all the features you can enable or disable. If a feature has a plus sign next to it, click this to reveal its individual components. To remove an item, untick it, then click OK. If you see a warning, click Yes. Repeat the process for any other features you want to remove and restart your PC.

However, we'd recommend caution when it comes to removing features. The only ones we'd advise removing (assuming you don't use them) are:

- **Internet Explorer**
Use Chrome, Firefox or Opera instead of Microsoft's built-in web browser? If so, you can safely uninstall Internet Explorer.

- **Internet Printing Client**
There aren't many of us who ever need to print over the internet, so this one can go. Click the plus sign next to 'Print and Document Services, then untick the feature.

- **XPS Services and XPS Viewer**
These two provide support for Microsoft's proprietary PDF-like document format. The thing is, nobody actually uses this format, so it's fairly safe to disable them both.

26 Sway

WHAT DOES IT DO?

It's a presentation tool that lets you share 'stories' made from photos, videos, text and web content.

KEEP OR DITCH?

KEEP. Automatically installed as part of Windows 10's November update, Sway is an intriguing free tool that's also available for iOS (an Android version's on its way). It's possibly something you'll never use, but it's easy to learn and

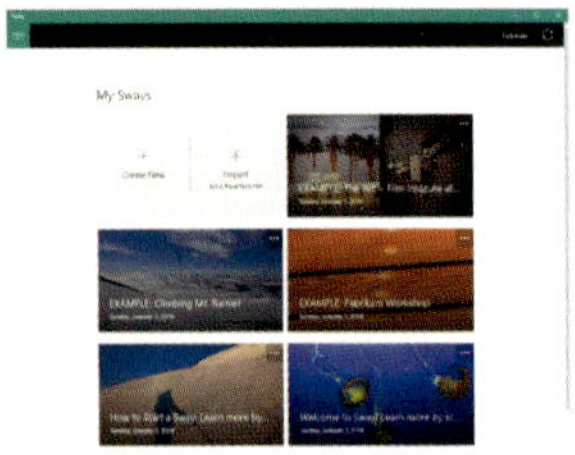

definitely worth having a play with before deciding whether or not to uninstall it.

27 Voice Recorder

WHAT DOES IT DO?

It lets you record voice notes and other sounds.

KEEP OR DITCH?

DITCH. PCs without microphones won't be able to make use of this app at all.

Even if you have a mic, Voice Recorder is low on features – it's better suited to smartphones and tablets. You can record voice notes in note-taking tools, such as Evernote Touch (free from the Windows Store). And for longer-form recordings with better quality and control, use a free sound editing tool, such as Audacity (http://audacityteam.org).

28 Weather

WHAT DOES IT DO?

It provides an up-to-date weather summary and forecasts.

KEEP OR DITCH?

KEEP. This decision is mostly down to personal taste, because there are dozens

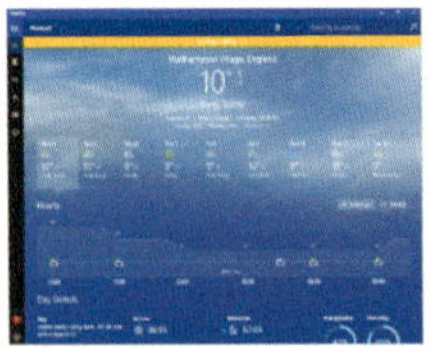

of alternative weather apps available in the Windows Store, some of which offer more detailed information. But we give it the benefit Uninstall Windows 10 apps of the doubt, chiefly because it is well designed, easy to use and, most importantly, provides very accurate forecasts.

29 Windows Feedback

WHAT DOES IT DO?

It allows you to report faults to Microsoft for analysis, suggest features and more.

KEEP OR DITCH?

IGNORE. Using this app means adjusting your PC's privacy settings to allow information about your PC usage to be sent to the company, which you may be

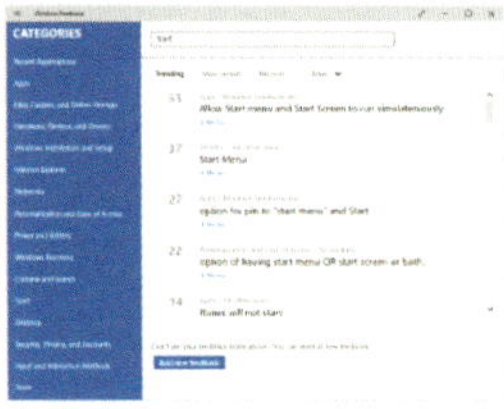

uncomfortable with. Annoyingly, Microsoft won't let you uninstall this app altogether, but you don't have to use it. You may also want to click Start, Settings, Privacy, 'Feedback & diagnostics' and make sure 'Feedback frequency' is set to Never, and 'Diagnostic and usage data' is set to Basic.

30 Xbox

WHAT DOES IT DO?

You can view your gaming achievements, chat with fellow gamers and connect to an Xbox One console.

KEEP OR DITCH?

DEPENDS. The Xbox app will hold little interest for non-gamers, so it's an easy one to dump.

For those interested in games, though, there are plenty features on offer that you won't find anywhere else, such as the ability to stream games and capture footage from an Xbox One console.

31 OneNote

WHAT DOES IT DO?

Microsoft's multipurpose note-taking app is integrated into Windows 10.

KEEP OR DITCH?

DEPENDS. Evernote users can uninstall this; no one needs more than one note-taking tool. If you've never used OneNote, though, it's worth giving it a go. You can jot down ideas, save web

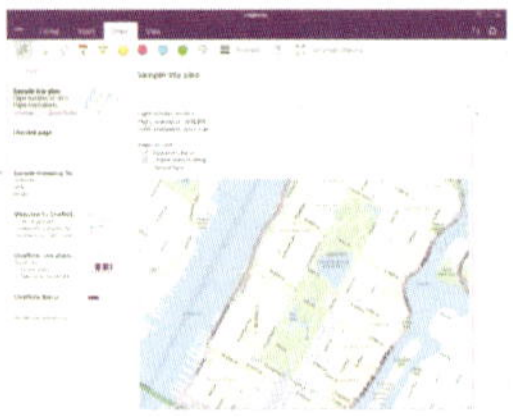

pages, maps and more for later, use it to plan holidays and sync it across all your devices. It's genuinely useful.

Use Windows 10's OneDrive app

Time required: 10 minutes

OneDrive is Microsoft's default cloud-storage service and it comes with 5GB of free storage space. When you first install or upgrade to Windows 10, you'll see an option to sync folders stored in OneDrive to your PC. The most convenient way to use it is through the new OneDrive app, which lets you see all your files without having to download them first. You can also drag and drop files to the app to sync them to your OneDrive account. Here's a quick tour.

STEP 1 Open the Windows Store from your Start menu (or type store into the taskbar's search box and press Enter). Type onedrive into the Store's search box 1 and select OneDrive from the list of suggestions. Click the Free button 2 to download the app. When it's finished you can launch it from the Start menu. If it doesn't appear, type onedrive into the taskbar search box, right-click the app and choose 'Pin to Start' or 'Pin to taskbar'.

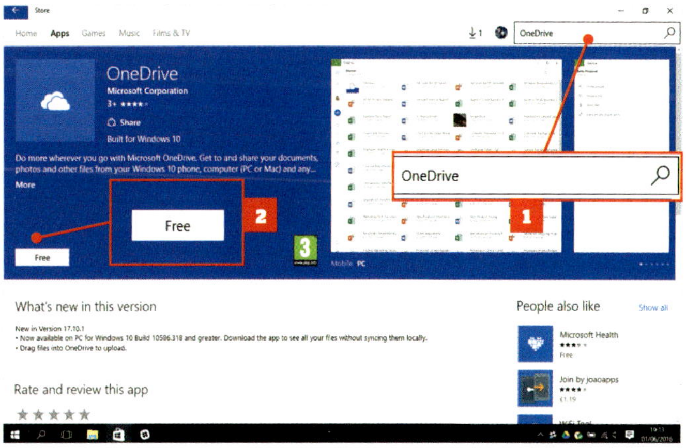

STEP 2 When you first use the app you'll need to click the 'Sign in' button and enter your Microsoft account details. You'll then see all the files in your OneDrive account, not just the ones you've synced with your PC. If you want to edit a file, click it to download it. When you've finished working on it you'll need to save it to your PC, then drag and drop it back into the relevant folder 1 in the app to re-upload it to OneDrive.

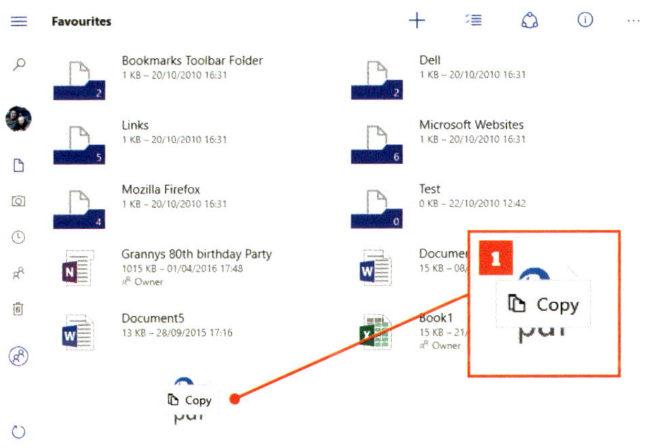

STEP 3 Under your profile picture on the left, you'll find icons to help you view 'All files' and Photos 1. Below that there are options to view files you've recently worked on, files you're sharing with others, and items you've moved to the recycle bin 2. You can also create new documents by clicking the '+' icon; select multiple files to move or delete at the same time; choose how you arrange files (by name, age or size); and create a new folder 3. The menu button 4 lets you switch from List view to Thumbnail view and also lets you refresh the page to show any recent changes.

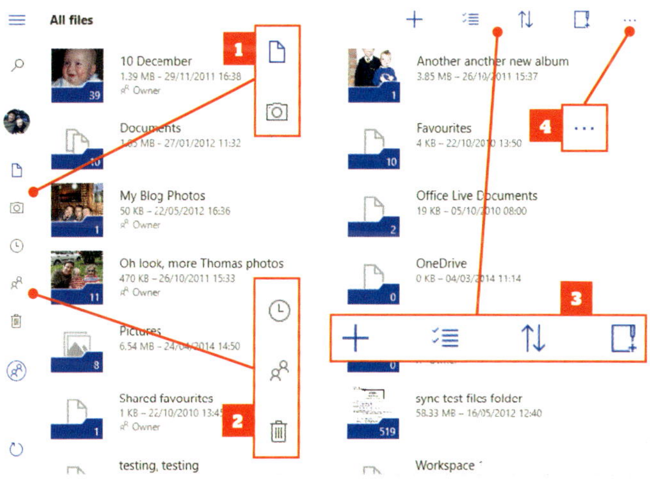

Best free programs for Windows 10

If you've upgraded to Windows 10, you'll want to know the best software to download for the new operating system. We've tested hundreds of tools to find the 15 best ones around

Windows has always been a great platform for software. Every version has allowed you to install tools from a vast pool of brilliant programs, many of which are available completely free of charge. Windows 10 is no different. In fact, it broadens the possibilities by providing access to thousands of Windows Store apps, as well as traditional programs.

The downside to all this choice is that getting the right tools can sometimes be tricky – or even unsafe. Windows 10 has been out for over a year, but there are still tons of programs that haven't been properly updated for the OS. Other tools claim to be free, but aren't – they're either time-limited trials or have had their functionality nobbled in some way that makes them next to useless. And then there's malware... and malware that's disguised as legitimate software.

That's why we've selected 15 of the best Windows 10 tools for you. A few Windows Store apps have made the cut here, but we'll be focussing mainly on traditional Windows programs – you'll find many more apps in our roundup of these from page 186, though.

Apart from that, we set some strict criteria for the tools we've chosen. We're very wary of PUPs – potentially unwanted programs, such as toolbars that get secretly added to your PC when you install some free tools. We've also avoided 'free' rip-offs and programs that start running by themselves. See the box on the right for our full set of selection conditions.

Our conditions

- Completely free. They all work without payment, though some offer paid-for versions with extra features.
- Updated/new for Windows 10. They're all compatible with the new operating system and sometimes contain tools specifically built for it.
- No PUPs. None of our recommendations force you to install unwanted extras (though you may need to untick some boxes during installation).
- No resource hogs. Most of these programs won't automatically run by themselves. Those that do need to run at start-up are relatively lightweight and so won't unduly hamper performance.

1 OutDateFighter

Download from www.spamfighter.com/outdatefighter

There are two very good reasons for keeping your installed programs up to date, especially when running a new operating system. First, the software may need an update to work flawlessly with the new OS. Second, it ensures you're not missing out on any key security fixes, which is especially important for web browsers and software that require regular patching (we're looking at you, Adobe Reader).

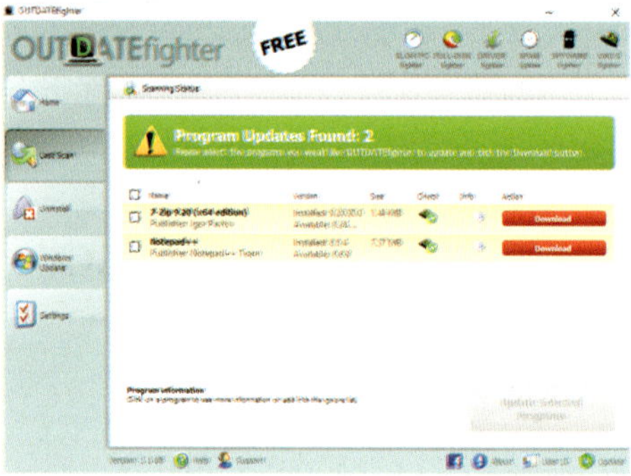

▲ Keep your tools up to date with OutDateFighter

OutDateFighter takes care of this problem for you. It quickly scans your system to see what you've got installed and then searches its database of more than 1.2 million applications to check if there's a newer version of them (we needed to update Notepad++ and 7-Zip in the screenshot above).

If it finds an update, you can download and install it within the program, rather than searching junk-riddled websites

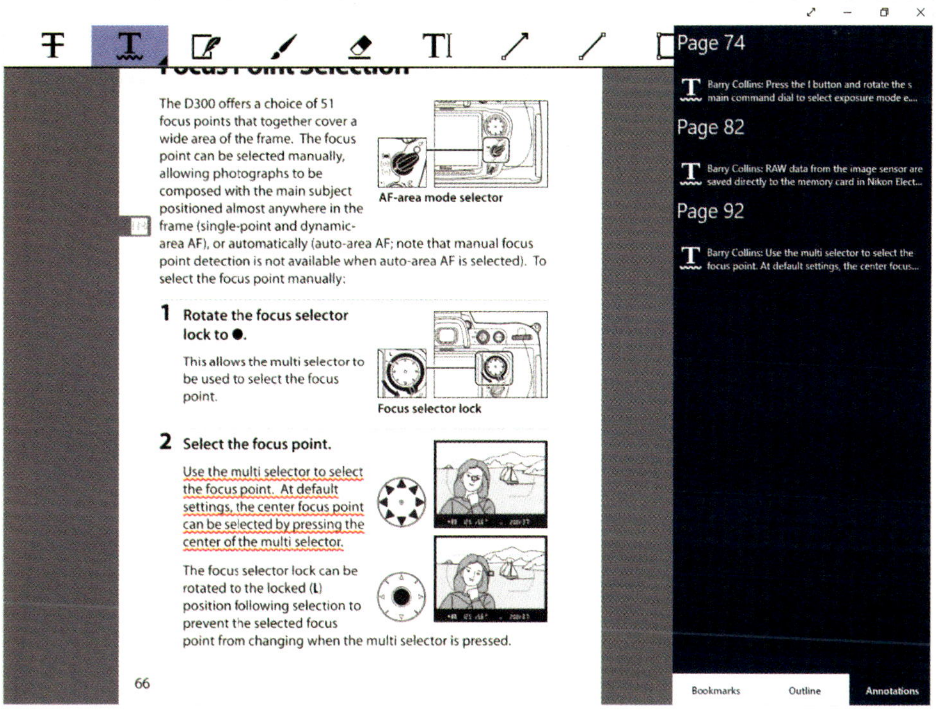

▲ Xodo makes editing PDFs simple – not to mention free!

to find the installer. All downloads are checked for viruses.

What we really like about OutDateFighter is its integrity. The download page isn't trying to sneak other software on to your system, the installer has no pre-ticked boxes for other apps, and it doesn't automatically set itself to run every time you start Windows. It's a lightweight freebie that does no more or less than it promises.

2 Xodo PDF Reader and Editor Desktop app

Download from the Windows Store www.snipca.com/18439

Even as we move into the brave new world of Windows 10, we cannot get by without insurance companies sending policies to sign as PDF documents, or bank statements sent in the format.

But we don't mind too much because we use Xodo's excellent PDF Reader and Editor. All its editing tools appear when you right-click within a PDF. These let you underline parts of the text (see the screenshot on the left above) or add your own comments – handy if you've downloaded a PDF manual for a printer, camera or other piece of hardware and want to make your own notes. Switch to Outline mode, and all those underlined pieces of text are listed separately, meaning you don't need to wade through a 150-page document to find the information you need. If you've got a touchscreen laptop or tablet, you can even sign contracts using your finger or stylus.

3 Ultimate Windows Tweaker 4

Download from www.snipca.com/18462

Originally launched to help Vista users smooth the rough edges of that mostly woeful OS, Ultimate Windows Tweaker (UWT) has regenerated for the Windows 10 era. In this fourth version, you make changes by clicking the Customization option in the left-hand menu, then selecting the Windows 10 tab.

Here, for example, you can disable the whooshy animation that plays when you open the Start menu, making it launch quicker. You can also tweak the colours of Windows 10 apps and menus, and switch off the new 'fly out' menus for battery power and volume controls, going back to how Windows 7 did things. We also like the Context Menu tweaks, which let you add shortcuts to, say, the Calculator or Shut Down option when you right-click your Desktop. Restart your PC to apply these changes.

One final point. Where there are tweaks, there are potential problems, so sensibly UWT creates a System Restore point when you run it. That safety net gives you the confidence to experiment with the changes without having to commit to them.

4 Driver Booster 3

Download from www.iobit.com/en/driver-booster.php

If you've upgraded existing hardware to Windows 10, one of the first things you'll want to do is check that your device drivers have been updated to cope. Recently upgraded to support Windows 10 systems, IObit's Driver Booster 3 lets you fix troublesome drivers in one hit. As with all IObit software, take a little care during the installation. We had to untick a box threatening to install another of the company's tools, IObit SystemCare Free, and decline a newsletter.

It's not the first time we've wanted to put IObit on the naughty step - and it surely won't be the last. But there's a reason why we tolerate this behaviour,

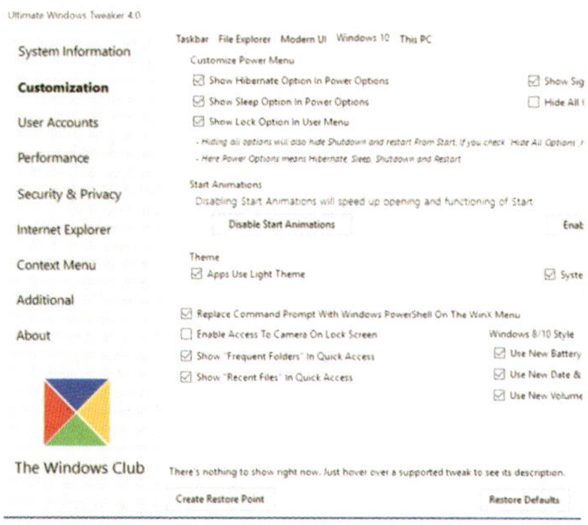

▲ Click the Windows 10 tab to OS settings

and it's this: IObit's tools tend to be very effective. Driver Booster, for example, found seven out-of-date drivers, five of which Glary Utilities, a similar program, missed. It then downloaded the updates in one go, faster than you could say: 'OK, come down off the naughty step now'.

The software automatically creates a System Restore point before installing new drivers so that, should something go horribly skew-whiff, you can revert to a working state. The whole process – from installation to fixing drivers – took a little under 10 minutes in our tests, which is the kind of no-fuss maintenance we like.

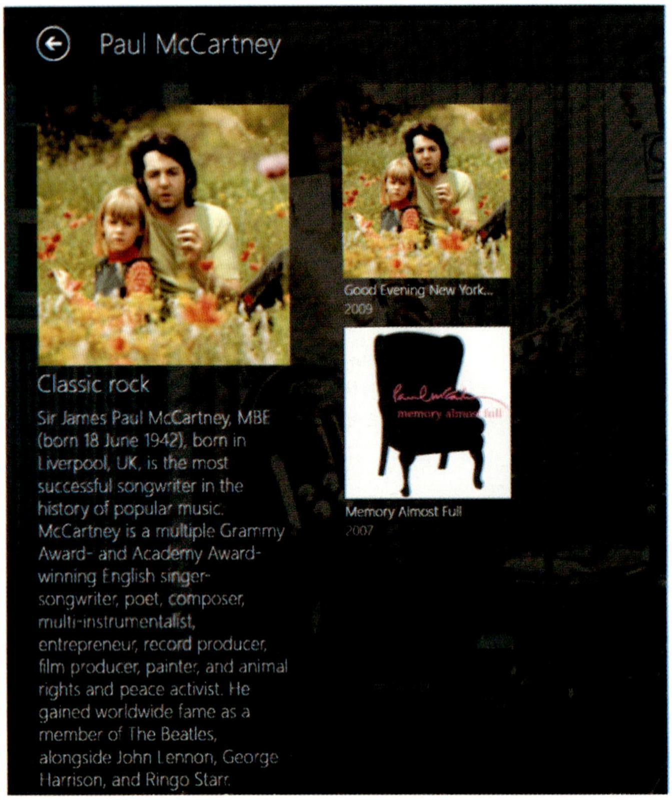

▲ All you need is Plex – it plays your music, videos and photos

5 Plex Desktop app

Download from the Windows Store www.snipca.com/18434

Plex is the home media-server software that keeps getting better and better, and the latest version of its Windows Store app raises the bar even further. It's one of the first 'universal' Windows apps, meaning it can be installed on PC, laptop, tablet and (eventually) Windows phones, providing a familiar look and features across each device.

Plex works like this: download the server software from https://plex.tv/downloads and install it on your main media PC - the one that stores all your music, video and photos. Then install the Plex app on your other devices and stream every track, video clip and photo that's stored on your PC, either across your home network or even from outside the home.

The Windows 10 makeover of the app is beautifully designed and easy to use, whether you're using a regular PC or swiping with your fingers on a Windows tablet. A huge music collection can be sorted by album, genre, play count and many other criteria. Photo collections are easily skimmed through, and as long as there's no heavy traffic on your home network, everything feels fast, as if the files were stored on that device, not a remote PC. Streaming from outside the home requires a decent broadband connection at both ends of the chain.

6 VLC media player Desktop app

Download from the Windows Store www.snipca.com/18429

The days of a catch-all Windows Media Player have long gone. Disappointingly, Windows 10 splits music and video into two separate built-in Desktop apps, neither of which are worth getting excited about. But we like getting excited about software, especially when it's as impressive as VLC.

VLC hasn't always got things right. Its Windows 8 app was a bit messy, but then so were many things associated with that operating system. Happily, the Windows 10 version has been revamped to make it wonderfully easy to play music and video.

Select an artist and a pane emerges from the right with a list of their tracks and albums, along with a short biography (we rather like a bit of Eric Clapton - see screenshot below). Once the track is playing, the song, album and artist names scroll over background graphics, creating a slick-looking screensaver.

VLC still isn't perfect. It crashes from time to time, and gets confused by the compilation albums in our iTunes collection, listing each artist's tracks as a separate album. But coupled with the (also free) VLC software (www.videolan.org/vlc) you get the best of both worlds: an extraordinarily powerful program that plays the DVDs that Windows 10 no longer supports, and an eye-catching Windows Store app for basic music and video.

▲ Select an artist in VLC and you'll see info on the right

7 Mail Desktop app

Pre-installed with Windows 10

If there were football-like awards for software, Microsoft's Mail would win the Most Improved Player gong. Originally introduced with Windows 8, Mail was, frankly, a rubbish way of scanning your inbox. Now, it's right up there with the best mail clients for Windows.

Visually, it really looks the part. The new background images provide a pleasing contrast between menu items on the left and the reading pane on the right, and everything is beautifully spaced. The Live Tile in the Windows 10 Start menu shows little previews of unread messages, meaning you don't even have to open the app to see what's lurking in your inbox.

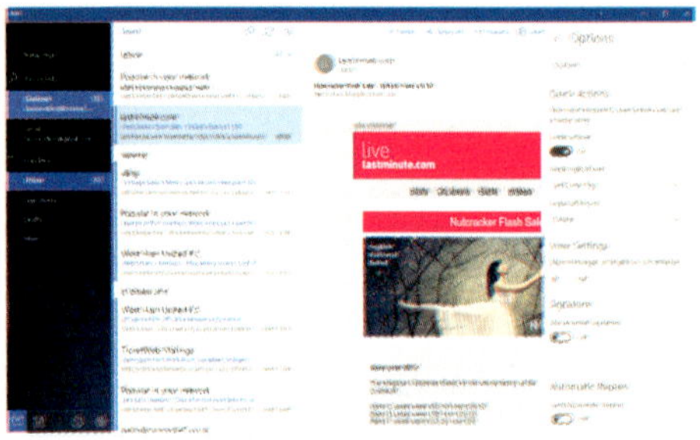

▲ Mail now lets you turn off 'conversation' view

We're not big fans of the Conversation View, where messages on the same topic from the same sender are grouped together in the inbox. But Microsoft must have sensed our disapproval, because it added the option to turn it off in a recent update. Just click the Settings cog,

Options and deselect the option to 'Show messages arranged by conversation' (see screenshot below left). Job done.

8 Audible Desktop app

Download from the Windows Store
www.snipca.com/18435

Audiobooks are wonderful things. They don't just give you the very words that the author wrote, but also the intonation and emotion behind them - especially if it's the author providing the narration. Alas, audiobooks are often fearsomely expensive, but you get one of your choice for free if you download Audible's revamped Windows Store app and sign up for a trial. That freebie book is worth around £25, but if that's all you want don't forget to cancel the free trial before the 30 days are out. If you forget, you'll be charged £7.99 for next month's subscription. This is another 'universal' app, designed for phones, tablets and PCs. You can see that design in action

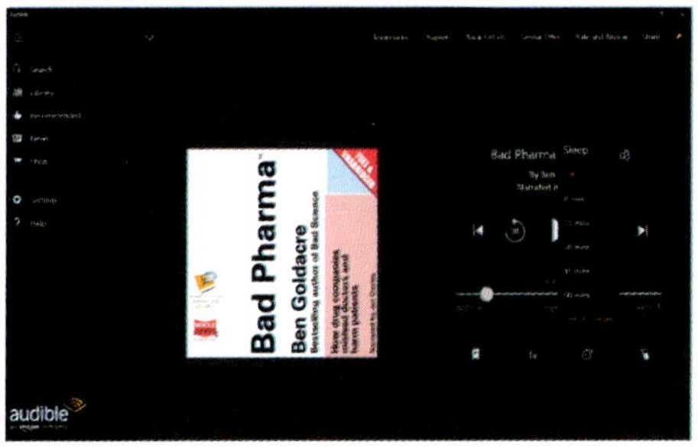

▲ Audible lets you 'snooze' audiobooks

if you shrink the app window to a small square on your screen, with the buttons and menus cleverly rearranged and resized to fit the available space.

The Audible app has some brilliant features. We love the snooze option, which lets you leave the book playing for 10, 15 or 20 minutes - or until the end of the current chapter - before it pauses the playback. The button-free mode on tablets and touchscreen laptops lets you swipe back on the player to rewind 30 seconds and re-listen if you momentarily dozed off (happens to us all the time, after a busy day downloading). On a non-touchscreen PC, use your mouse and keyboard to do this.

9 CCleaner

Download from www.piriform.com/ccleaner

CCleaner has been turfing the clutter from our hard drives for years. Now, at version 5.2, it has been freshly tuned to watch out for junk left behind by Windows 10 apps. Click the Applications tab and you'll see redundant data in apps such as Bing News, Sports and Travel, which are pre-loaded with Windows 10.

It doesn't stop there. CCleaner also ejects unnecessary files from the new Edge browser, Microsoft's replacement for Internet Explorer. It even rummages through Windows 10's built-in antivirus app, Defender, to see if there's stuff it can safely jettison. It still looks in the more obvious places, too. We thought we were pretty good at regularly emptying our Recycle Bin, but CCleaner found more than 10,000MB of unwanted digital photos and other files (see screenshot below). Good riddance!

The only thing we don't like about CCleaner is the website you download it from - it takes more clicks than it should, and contains a booby-trap.

Here's the long-winded process: first, click the green 'Download Free Version' button at the top. That shuffles you to the bottom of the page, where you have to click the green 'Free Download' button. That takes you to another page where you can compare the free and paid-for versions. Click the green 'Download' button and - third click lucky - your download begins. Phew.

But keep your wits about you. When you click that button to start the automatic download, another page appears with a temptingly big, green 'START DOWNLOAD' button. You don't need to click this. On some of our visits to the site, that button has been an advert. It's annoying, but it's worth it – CCleaner is one of the best Windows 10 tools around.

WINDOWS 10 APP STORE: 3 MOST IMPORTANT TIPS

1 If you have more than one Windows 10 device - a PC and a laptop, say - you don't need to pay twice for the same app. Once you've bought it on one device, switch on the other, open the Store, click your profile photo next to the search bar and select My Library. Click the down arrow next to the app to download, without paying again.

2 You can make sure the children (and grandchildren) don't run up horrendous bills in the Store by ensuring any purchase requires a password. Click your profile, then Settings and make sure the slider 'Always check that it's me when I buy things from Store' is set to 'on'.

3 By default apps are set to automatically update. If you want to change this, perhaps to prevent your internet connection from being hogged by a big update, click your profile, Settings, then switch off 'Update apps automatically'.

▼ CCleaner found 10,000MB in our Recycle Bin!

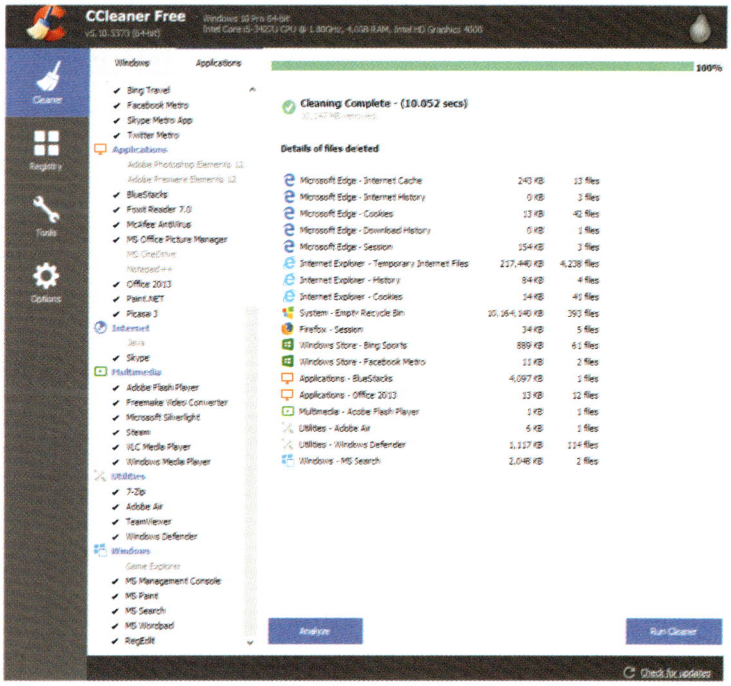

DOES THE W10 STORE HAVE A FUTURE?

The Windows 8 Store soon became a graveyard, with app developers shunning possibly the most unpopular version of Windows ever created. Have things improved with Windows 10? Sort of. Developers are keener now to build apps for the OS, but the vast number of people using iOS and Android means they concentrate first on phones and tablets. Even Microsoft made iOS and Android versions of Word and Excel before releasing them as Windows apps!

But Microsoft is fighting back. One of the reasons it made Windows 10 free is to attract enough users to convince developers that, financially, it will be worth their time and effort building apps for the OS. With more than 110 million devices now running Windows 10, that strategy looks like it could succeed.

Microsoft also introduced 'bridges' - Project Astoria (for Android) and Project Islandwood (for iOS) - to make it easier for developers to port their apps from iOS and Android to Windows. These open-source tools should help to boost the number of apps in the Windows Store, though for now it remains a sparsely stocked corner shop compared with the luxury department stores run by Google and Apple.

10 AdwCleaner

Download from www.snipca.com/18466

Full marks to AdwCleaner, one of our favourite ever programs, for updating within a fortnight of Windows 10 launching. Since then it has been updated a further 13 times (probably more by the time you read this) in its ceaseless mission to remove new types of adware. Recently it has targeted junk within Firefox and Chrome - removing unwanted browser extensions from the former, and eliminating privacy-compromising adware from the latter.

For such a powerful tool, AdwCleaner is pleasingly unobtrusive. Unlike many of its rival programs, which seep into every corner of your system, it's so lightweight that you may even struggle to find it after installation.

If you need assistance, type adw in the Taskbar search menu and it should appear.

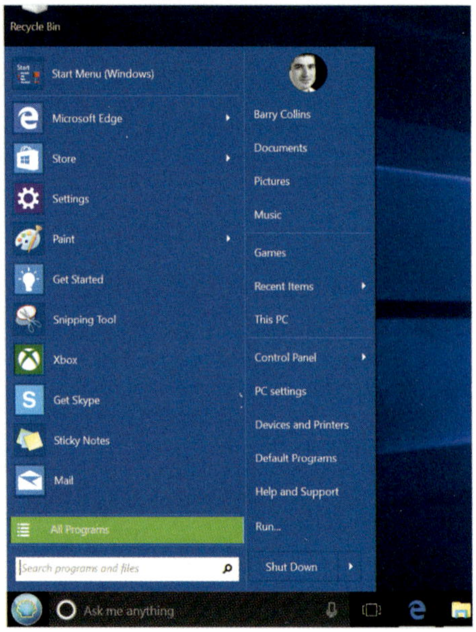

▲ Classic Shell makes W10's Start menu even better

11 Classic Shell

Download from www.classicshell.net

Make no mistake: the default Windows 10 Start menu is a darn sight better than Windows 8's. But we do understand why some of you may yearn for the Windows 7 menu, especially if you have no love for the tiles that come with the new Windows Store apps. If that sounds like you and you've yet to download Classic Shell, please pay attention.

Classic Shell let Windows 8 users place a Windows 7-style (or even XP-style) menu on to their Desktop, in the kind of 'up yours Microsoft' defiance that we can't help but admire. You can now do likewise in Windows 10. Once installed, right-click the remodelled Start button, choose Settings, and tweak the options to get your Start menu just right. Doing this lets you control what appears in the shortcuts menu on the right, change the colour of the skin and choose which power option (ie Shut Down, Restart, etc) should appear by default.

Unlike some other Start menu replacements, Classic Shell blends beautifully into Windows 10's look and feel, and you can still access the live tiles of the default Start menu by clicking a link or holding down Shift when you click the Start button.

Any drawbacks? Well, we're not big fans of what it does to File Explorer. But that's a minor niggle. Everything else can be switched on or off until you find a set-up that works for you.

12 SODAT Privacy Protection Tool for Windows 10

Download from www.snipca.com/18514

Left to run on its default settings, Windows 10 takes several liberties with your privacy. Results from your Start menu searches are automatically beamed back to Microsoft's mothership, location tracking is switched on, and Windows automatically assigns you a personalised ID so that it can show adverts targeted at your interests.

There are also some annoyances that aren't a particular threat to your privacy. You'll be constantly prompted for feedback on what you think about Windows 10 and its apps, for example. And Windows 10's diagnostics tool tracks how you use your PC so Microsoft

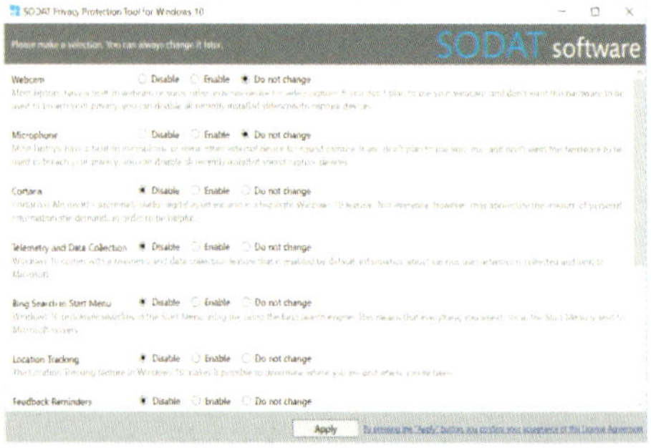

▲ Change Microsoft's privacy settings using SODAT

can "improve the products and features customers use most often and to help solve problems" (read more on the company's website: www.snipca.com/18453).

If all that makes you feel uneasy, use SODAT to plug these holes in one go, doing what the Windows 10 installation screens should have done in the first place. It presents an objective explanation of Microsoft's privacy settings, giving you the relevant details so you can confidently decide which boxes to select. Once you've made your selections, click Apply and SODAT will do the dirty work, saving you from burrowing through various settings menus. Like 10AppsManager, SODAT doesn't need to be installed on your PC – it runs straight from the download.

▲ 10AppsManager lets you remove apps you don't want to use

13 10AppsManager

Download from www.snipca.com/18446

10AppsManager is a useful little one-hit wonder that's probably best used on new Windows 10 PCs or when you first upgrade to the operating system. There's not a lot to it - just a single screen from where you can remove any of the pre-installed apps. Among the pointless apps it offers to remove for you are shortcuts to download Skype and the latest version of Office which remain on your PC even after you've installed them. You can also get shot of the Get Started guide (which is useless once you're up and running), the Camera app (not much use on a conventional laptop or desktop PC) and the Xbox app (worthless if you have no interest in gaming).

10AppsManager doesn't install itself on your system - simply unzip the download package and run the application. Once you've performed the tidy up, bin the 10AppsManager folder and the job's done, without anything being left behind on your PC. See earlier in this chapter for more on removing apps.

14 EarTrumpet

Download from www.snipca.com/18448

This ingenious little tool is so new that the download link is hosted on GitHub, a site where developers share their work. Nevertheless, it worked perfectly in our tests, so we're happy to recommend it before any further updates.

EarTrumpet provides volume controls for every audio-playing app on a Windows 10 PC. Once you've installed it, you'll see a little ear-trumpet icon in the system tray near the clock, giving you a volume slider for every program that's capable of producing audio. This allows you to eliminate one of the biggest annoyances of modern computing – websites that automatically blare out audio adverts in the background. Now you can turn your web browser's volume down to zero and leave your music running, without the risk of The Kinks' Sunny Afternoon suddenly being interrupted by a cheesy voiceover.

It's also handy for managing apps that need to be left running in the background, letting you control the volume of Skype ring tones, for example.

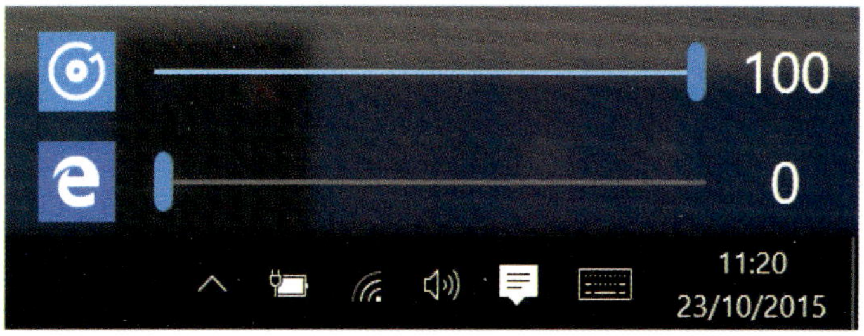

▲ EarTrumpet gives you a volume slider for programs

15 Wi-Fi Analyzer Preview

Download from the Windows Store www.snipca.com/18449

Working out what's going on with an erratic Wi-Fi connection is a dark art. Wi-Fi Analyzer helps you to uncover the mystery by showing you the strength of your router's Wi-Fi, and whether any neighbouring networks are elbowing yours out of the way.

Click the Analyze button at the top and you'll be presented with a graph showing any overlap between your Wi-Fi and others within range.

Most of today's routers, such as the BT Home Hub, automatically assign the Wi-Fi channel. But they can often make bad decisions. Wi-Fi Analyzer is able to recommend which channel you should be on for the minimal possible risk of interference.

If you have a dual-band router with a 5GHz option, you can click the little aerial icon at the bottom of the screen to see how that band looks – it should be clearer.

Expert tips for Windows 10 apps

Get the most from your Windows 10 apps by following these handy tricks

Tablet mode tricks for displaying multiple apps

Most apps from the Windows Store run in a window. Click the maximize button in the top-right corner of the window and the app fills the screen, except for a title bar across the top. If you want the app to display full screen without any title bars or buttons, click the Action Centre button in the notification area on the right of the taskbar and click 'Tablet mode'.

If you have a touchscreen, swipe in from the top and the app shrinks to a window. Drag it to the left or right side to snap it to that half of the screen. Your other apps are displayed in the other half. Tap one to select it and you now have two apps running side by side, filling the screen. This is a great way to work with several apps at once.

Set up the Photos tile

You can personalise the Start menu's Photos tile so it displays an image of your choice. To do this, right-click the Photos tile and select Resize, Large. Right-click it again and select More, 'Turn live tile on'. Open the Photos app, click the gear icon in the bottom-left corner and, in the Tile section, find the menu with 'A single photo' and 'Recent photos'. Use it to choose what to display on the Start menu tile.

Add more folders to Photos

The Photos app only shows images stored in your Photos folder, so if you have a large photo library on an external USB drive, you won't be able to view and edit them unless you tweak the settings. To do this, open Photos and click the gear icon. In the Sources section, click the plus button and select any disks and folders you'd like the Photos app to include. Now you can view and edit all your photos, wherever you keep them.

View traffic and cameras in Maps

Before setting off on a journey, open the Maps app and view your route or the area you're visiting. Click the layers button in the toolbar, turn on Traffic and tick Incidents and Cameras. Roads with stationary traffic jams are drawn in red and should be avoided; orange roads are busy but the traffic is moving steadily; green roads have little or no traffic and no hold-ups. Accidents, breakdowns and other road problems are represented on the map by warning triangles. Click one to read a description of the problem.

The camera symbols on the map, when clicked, show pictures from roadside traffic cameras that are no more than a few minutes old. You can see the traffic, the weather, road problems and so on. London

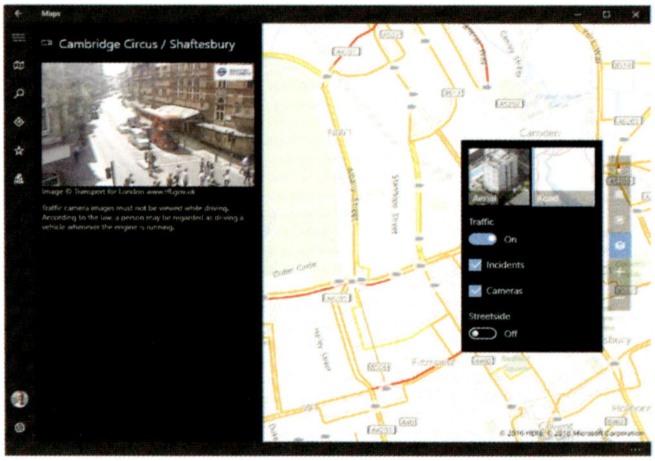

▲ See traffic on the map and through live cameras before your journey

has a lot of cameras, but there are also a few in other large cities.

Take a 3D tour in Maps

Click the 3D Cities button in the top-right corner of Maps and a panel opens listing cities and locations around the world. Click one and a 3D view is displayed in the window. You can change the angle of view by clicking and dragging the grid icon in the toolbar to the left or right. Spin the mouse wheel or push/pull with two fingers on a laptop touchpad to zoom in or out. Hold down the Ctrl key while clicking and dragging the mouse left or right to spin around the 3D view, so you can see it from all sides.

Stream music

You don't have to subscribe to Groove Music Pass or buy music to listen to it in Groove Music – you can play your own music and stream it from OneDrive. Open Explorer and go to the OneDrive folder on your PC's hard drive. If there isn't a Music folder, create one. Copy music files and folders to it.

Open Groove Music and click the gear icon on the left to open Settings. Under 'Music on this PC', click 'Choose where we look for music'. If the OneDrive Music folder isn't listed, click the plus button and add it. You will now be able to play your music via Groove Music on any computer, tablet or phone (iOS or Android). If your music library is on an external USB drive, add the folders in the same way. You can't stream them to other devices but you can manage and play the music on your PC.

Import iTunes playlists

If you previously used iTunes and have switched to Groove Music, you can import your playlists. Click the gear icon in Groove Music, then click 'Import iTunes playlists'. You will only be able to play tracks that are in your library. If you ripped your own CDs, add the iTunes music folder to Groove or copy the music files to the PC's Music folder. If you subscribe to Groove, you have access to millions of tracks and your playlists will work perfectly.

Get all your email in one inbox

If you have more than one email account, you can access them all via the Mail app. Click Accounts in the left panel, move across to the right panel and click 'Add account'. A window opens with several quick setup options, including Google and Yahoo. Enter your email address and password, and setup is carried out automatically.

There is also an 'Other account' option, which lets you add any email account. You just need to know (or find out) the mail server address, username and password. Each new account appears in the left panel and selecting one lists the contents of its inbox, sent mail and other folders.

It is easy enough to select each email account in turn to read your messages but you may prefer to combine all the inboxes from your different accounts into one, to get a unified overview of all your email.

To set this up, click Accounts on the left and then, on the right, click 'Link inboxes'. A list of email accounts is displayed and the tick boxes let you choose the ones you want to combine. These appear in Mail's left panel as 'Linked inbox'. Select it to see all your messages. If you reply to a message, the reply is sent from the account that received it. Click 'New mail' to create an email message, and you'll be asked which account you want to use.

If you decide you would rather go back to displaying your email as separate accounts, return to Accounts and click 'Linked inboxes' to unlink them again.

Define Mail Quick Actions

Select an email account to show the inbox. When you hover the mouse over an email in the list, two icons appear on the right. These are Quick Actions and they let you delete, flag or perform some other actions on emails without opening the message or going through menus. They are a great time saver when you're dealing with lots of messages.

You can choose which actions you want to appear when the mouse hovers over an email in the inbox. Click the gear icon at the bottom of the left panel to open settings, then select Quick Actions. Choose the two actions you want from the two menus. There is an option to apply the actions to all email accounts or to have different actions for each account.

If you have a touchscreen, switch on the 'Swipe actions' option. This lets you swipe left or right over an email in the inbox to perform the first or second 'quick action'. It's a huge timesaver and puts the touchscreen to good use, because you can quickly swipe through lots of emails to clear your inbox.

Invite people in Calendar

If you are organising a party, wedding, business meeting or other event, the Calendar app makes it easy to invite participants. Click the plus button to add a new event and enter the details, including date and location. Click in the box on the right where it says 'Invite someone'. Enter their email address, then continue by adding more people. Calendar sends your invitations and tells you who can make it and who can't.

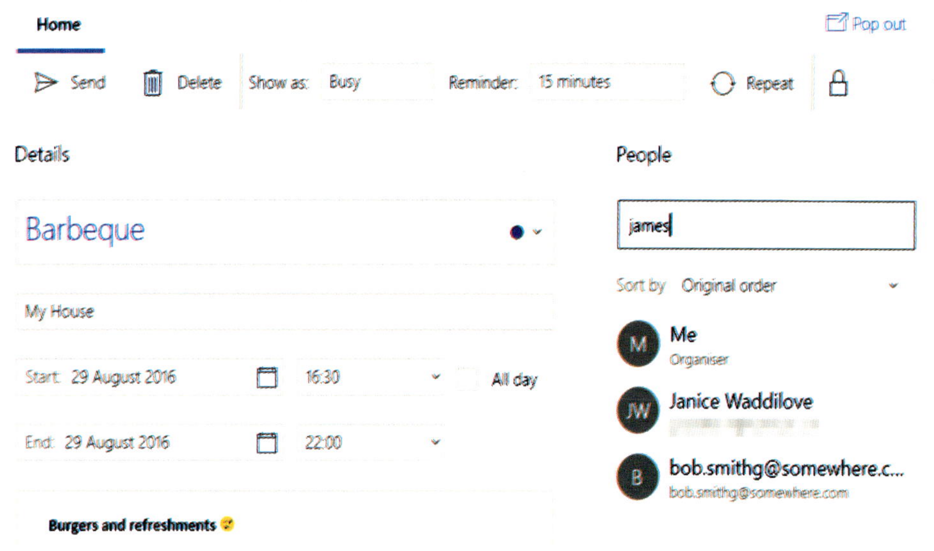

▲ Set up an event and invite people along in Calendar

Get great apps for Windows 10

Some free Windows 10 apps are more than just cut-down versions of full programs. The trouble is, it can be difficult to find the good ones amid all the junk. Here we cherry pick some the best apps currently available from the Windows Store

Anyone who's ever used an Apple or Android device will already know how great app stores are. They make it incredibly simple to install a useful new tool or a fun game.

Apps are small, simple and often very cheap – or even free. Already a massive hit on mobile devices, Microsoft tried to bring apps to the desktop in Windows 8, but largely failed, due to the overall unpopularity of the OS. But all that has changed with Windows 10.

With the Windows Store, Microsoft is making blatant leap for the bandwagon. And why not? After all, apps you download from the Store are much safer than traditional programs, since they don't install in the same way and can't affect your system files. They're convenient too and let you add new functions to your PC quickly and easily. You can still run old-style programs if you want, and Windows 10's great for gaming too.

The Windows Store may not be as well stocked as Google's Play store or Apple's App Store, but it's still home to almost 700,000 apps for PCs and mobile devices. That's a lot of apps to wade through if you're looking for something to install on your computer.

That's why we've tested hundreds of apps for you and rounded up 60 of our favourites for you to try. You'll find apps for helping you get your work done, as well as apps for helping you let your hair down – photo tools, movie players, handy utilities and great games.

1 Flipboard
bit.ly/flipboard396

Part social app, part news app, Flipboard lets you create your own free magazine full of content that interests you. Choose a few topics, such as Gear & Gadgets, Gardening and Bon Appetit, to view articles, photos and videos in an attractive grid layout, which you can swipe through at your leisure. You can also connect your Facebook, Instagram and Twitter accounts to see everything your friends are sharing in one place. Stylish and endlessly fascinating, Flipboard saves you having to buy any magazine again.

2 Autodesk Pixlr
bit.ly/pixlr396

Image editors are often overloaded with tools you'll never use, but Pixlr keeps things simple while still providing lots of useful options. You can apply quick fixes to your photos, such as crop, straighten and resize; balance colours and poor lighting with a single click; and apply 25 effects to your shots. The app also lets you remove red-eye and other imperfections, merge two images and add borders and overlays to your pictures. Additional features are available when you sign up for a free Pixlr account.

3 Wunderlist
bit.ly/wunderlist396

Designed specifically for Windows 10, this app for the popular note taking tool is a brilliant way to organise your life. As well as creating and managing to-do lists, and syncing them with your phone or tablet, Wunderlist lets you share photos and files, set reminders for specific tasks and collaborate on projects at home and work. The app works with Cortana, so you can add items to your to-do lists using spoken instructions, complete with due dates and reminders.

Wunderlist has a Windows program (www.wunderlist.com) as well as an app, but we prefer the latter's lightweight interface, and its compatibility with Cortana is a definite boon.

4 Netflix
bit.ly/netflix396

Netflix is available on virtually every platform you can think of – from mobile devices and games consoles to smart TVs and streaming sticks – so it's no surprise that it also has a Windows 10 app. This is easy to use and adjusts automatically to suit your screen's size and resolution. We also like the fact that when you adjust the volume or use a media button

on your keyboard, a control panel appears, showing you what's playing and providing a volume meter and play/pause, skip and back buttons. You can use Cortana to search for films and TV shows, and if you pin the app to the Start menu, it displays a handy Continue Watching option.

The Netflix app for Windows 10 actually beats watching movies and series in your browser, for the reasons mentioned above and because you can continue to watch while performing other tasks online.

5 Music Maker Jam

bit.ly/music396

Although it's rather large for an app (336MB), Music Maker Jam is a fantastic free download for anyone who wants to create their own tunes. It offers a choice

of four music styles, which you can swap for new ones every month for free, and many more that you can buy as in-app purchases. Choose from a range of professionally produced loops and arrange them however you want, adjusting the pitch, applying effects and mixing everything together across eight channels.

6 ToView

bit.ly/toview396

Who needs a television when you can watch live TV on your Desktop using the new ToView app? You can stream all five national channels in one resizable window, as well as free music, sport

and news channels, while the 24-hour programme guide helps you plan your viewing. ToView even lets you pin your favourite shows to the Windows 10 Start menu, so you never miss them again.

ToView beats having to switch between five separate TV-streaming services and, unlike ITV Hub and All 4, you don't need to register to start viewing.

7 Plex

bit.ly/plex396

Plex makes it easy to browse and enjoy all the music, videos and photos you have

stored on your PC, phone and tablet, as well as media content from the cloud, by bringing it all together. The app is free to use, although to unlock its full potential you need to pay $4.99 (£3.49) for a Plex Pass, which removes all restrictions and syncs your files across all your devices so you can view and play them offline.

8 Earth View Map 3D

bit.ly/earth396

This brilliant app lets you tour the world in 3D from the comfort of your Desktop. There are currently more than 200 locations that you can explore as if you were there on foot or flying above

them in a helicopter, including New York, London, Paris, Rome and the Grand Canyon, while many more are available in flat 2D. You can easily capture screenshots of your favourite 3D views, and use the satellite map to decide where to go.

Although not as comprehensive as Google Earth (earth.google.co.uk), Earth View is a lot simpler and faster, and the quality of its 3D imagery is stunning.

9 The Weather Channel

bit.ly/weather396

There are loads of weather apps for Windows 10, including its own built-in tool, but we're rather partial to the one from The Weather Channel, which is packed with useful features and looks marvellous. It provides hourly and 15-day forecasts in Celsius or Fahrenheit, with

detailed weather conditions that include "feels like" temperature, humidity, pollen alerts and much more. You also get radar maps of rainfall, snowfall, wind speed and other useful information. The app responds to Cortana commands and uses Windows 10's Live Tiles to display at-a-glance updates about current conditions and temperatures for your favourite locations.

The Weather Channel previously had a Desktop program for Windows, but its app is much less bloated, doesn't require the .NET Framework and isn't bundled with junk.

10 Duplicate Cleaner

bit.ly/dupclean400

This Windows 10 app helps you find and remove duplicate files on your device. You can quickly search for a particular type of item (photos, for example), and there are plenty of advanced features available.

11 Web Tiles

bit.ly/webtile400

You can pin any website to the Windows 10 Start menu, but the result is often a bit bland. Web Tiles lets you customise the look of these site tiles, using text, logos and graphics.

12 Realarm Beta

bit.ly/realarm400

This alarm clock is a work-in-progress update of a Windows Phone app. It offers multiple sounds for each alarm, and also lets you use songs from your own music library.

13 LightReader

bit.ly/lightread399

LightReader is an ebook reader for

Windows 10 that lets you manage and read books in ePub format (which is the only format it supports). You can adjust the font size and type to suit your eyes.

14 DI.FM unofficial client

bit.ly/difm399

This unofficial app lets you tune into DIFM, an internet radio station offering

electronic music. There are over 60 free channels to listen to, with styles including trance, house, techno and ambient.

15 Ludo Blitz!
bit.ly/ludo399

This app is a free-to-play reimagining of the classic board game Ludo. You can take on other players over the internet, and special fields add a degree of randomness to the gameplay.

16 Vine for Windows 10
bit.ly/vine398

The official Vine app for Windows 10 lets you watch popular clips, and upload and share 'vines' (six-second looping videos) with friends via social networks. You'll need a free account to unlock most of its tools.

17 Bloom Music Player
bit.ly/bloom398

This is a free music player for Windows 10 devices. You can create your own playlists or set criteria for automatic ones, and browse and buy music from the integrated music store.

18 Newsflow
bit.ly/newsflow398

Newsflow is an attractive RSS feed reader for Windows 10. You can set it to deliver notifications, share news with friends and bookmark favourite stories. Live-tile support shows the latest headlines.

19 Facebook for Windows 10
bit.ly/facebook397

The official Facebook app for Windows 10 shows you what your friends are up

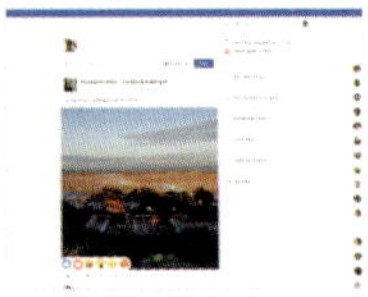

to and lets you share updates and photos. You'll get notifications whenever someone likes or comments on your posts.

20 Messenger
bit.ly/messenger397

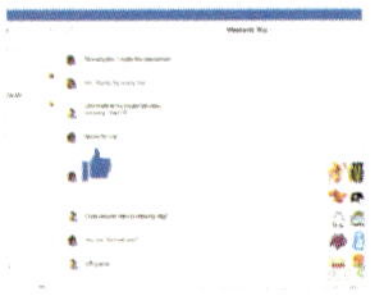

As well as the official Facebook app, there is now also an app for its chat tool. It offers all the essential features, and support for live tiles means you can see instantly when someone has left you a message.

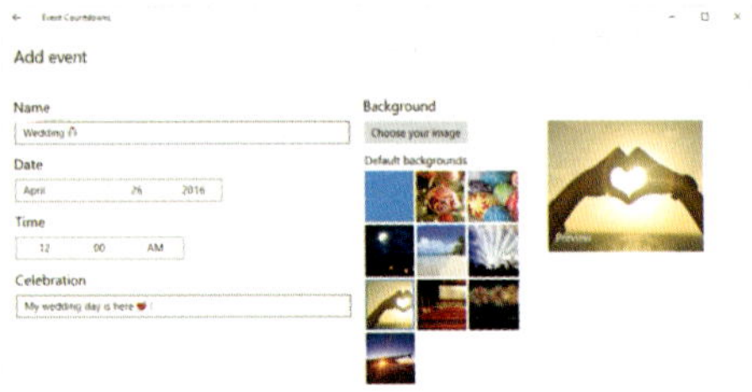

21 Event Countdowns
bit.ly/eventcountdown397

This app can count down to any event, be it a wedding, the birth of a child or the arrival of a new Star Wars movie. You can change the background and view the countdown on a live tile.

22 Lego Juniors: Create & Cruise
bit.ly/legojr396

This app for four- to seven-year -olds lets children create their own Lego

vehicles and mini figures. They can also collect coins to unlock virtual Lego sets, and there are no in-app purchases for parents to worry about.

23 Send Anywhere
bit.ly/sendanywhere396

Send Anywhere is a cloud-based file

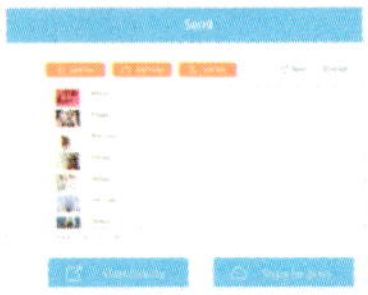

transfer service that lets you send files securely from one device to another. You don't need to sign up for an account to use it, and there's no limit on file sizes.

24 Audiotica
bit.ly/audiotica396

This attractive music player and downloader can import your music collection and play streamed music, with support for Deezer, Last.fm, Spotify and SoundCloud. It even displays lyrics, which is great for those who like to sing along.

25 Disney Magic Kingdoms
bit.ly/disney395

The aim of this game, set in Disney's famous theme parks, is to bring back the magic stolen by evil fairy Maleficent. It features a selection of Disney's most popular characters and has you following leads and undertaking quests.

26 Draw-A-Way
bit.ly/drawaway395

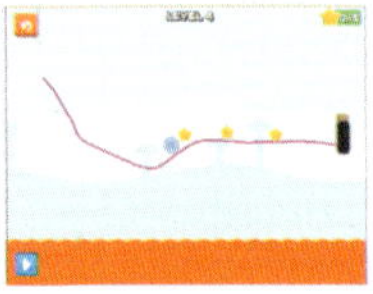

Draw-A-Way is a fun physics-based game in which you draw the path a ball must take to get home. There are 85 levels to play through – and, sadly, the occasional annoying video ad, too.

27 MediaFire
bit.ly/mediafire395

This official Windows app for the popular MediaFire online-storage service lets you upload photos, videos, music and documents to your account and access them from anywhere.

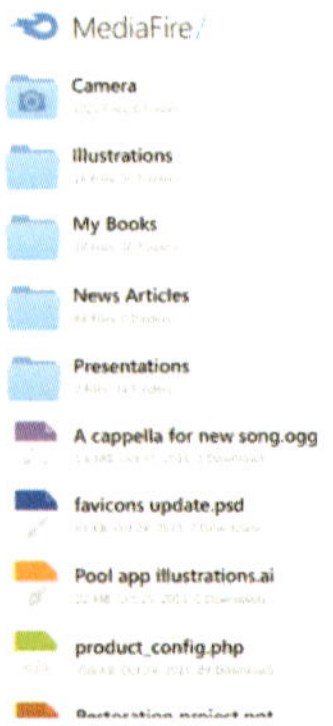

28 Chimpact Run
bit.ly/chimpact394

Chimpact Run is like a simpler version of the Nintendo classic Donkey Kong Country. In this game, you have to time jumps in order to avoid obstacles, and collect bananas and other extras.

29 Plumbago
bit.ly/plumbago393

This oddly named Microsoft Garage project is a digital notebook that offers handwriting smoothing; realistic ink and paper; and the ability to add, trace, highlight and annotate images.

30 Blue Skies
bit.ly/blueskies393

This weather app offers hourly and daily forecasts for multiple locations. There's live tile support and detailed weather information covering humidity, precipitation and wind speed. The app also changes colour based on the weather.

31 Papa Pear Saga
bit.ly/papapear392

In this new game from King, the company behind Candy Crush Saga, you have to shoot pears out of a cannon and try to rack up as many points as possible.

32 Polarr Photo Editor Lite
bit.ly/polarr392

This is a cut-down version of the popular photo editor, which lets you make all sorts of adjustments to your images, crop and tilt them, and apply a range of attractive filters.

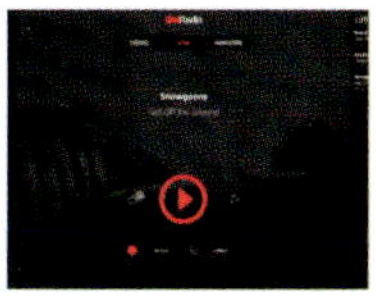

33 Gym Radio
bit.ly/gymradio391

This app plays music designed to motivate your workouts. You can switch between Cardio, Gym and Hardcore modes. You need to link the app to your Facebook or Google+ account to get the most from it.

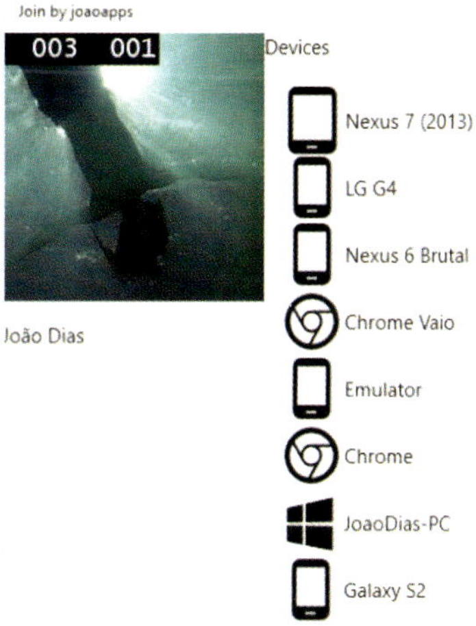

34 Join by joaoapps
bit.ly/join391

The aim of this app (currently in beta) is to "bring your devices together". It can mirror Android notifications on screen and send files to other devices. You can also use it to reply to SMS messages.

35 Boards by Todoist
bit.ly/boards391

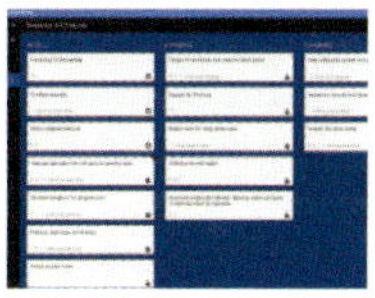

This app for Todoist (en.todoist.com) displays your tasks on Kanban boards. You can track projects and change the status of a task by dragging it to the relevant column: To-Do, In-Progress or Completed.

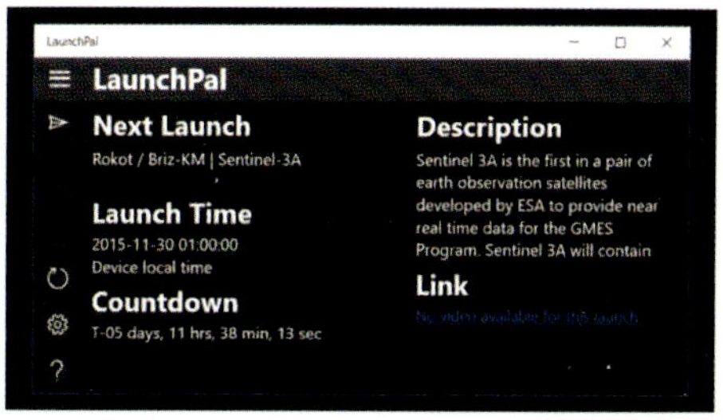

36 LaunchPal
bit.ly/launchpal390

LaunchPal keeps you abreast of all up-and-coming space launches and events. It tells you the purpose of the launch and provides a countdown, and may also point you in the direction of live video.

37 SpotBright
bit.ly/spotbright390

Windows 10 has a lock-screen feature called Spotlight that displays attractive, regularly updated images from the web. SpotBright makes it easy to download these photos so you can use them on your Desktop.

38 Football Hub
bit.ly/footballhub390

This app displays the latest football news, results and information for teams in the top English and Scottish leagues. There are plans to add more leagues in the future.

39 Candy Crush Jelly Saga
bit.ly/ccjelly389

The latest version of King's popular sweet-matching game introduces jelly, which you spread around the grid. There are new candies and boosters, and more than 100 levels to play.

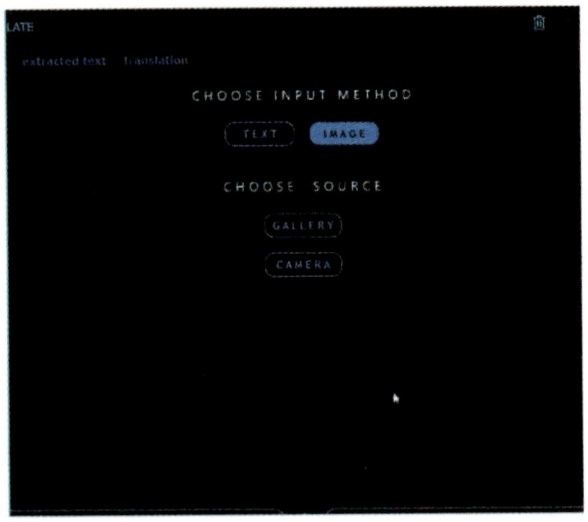

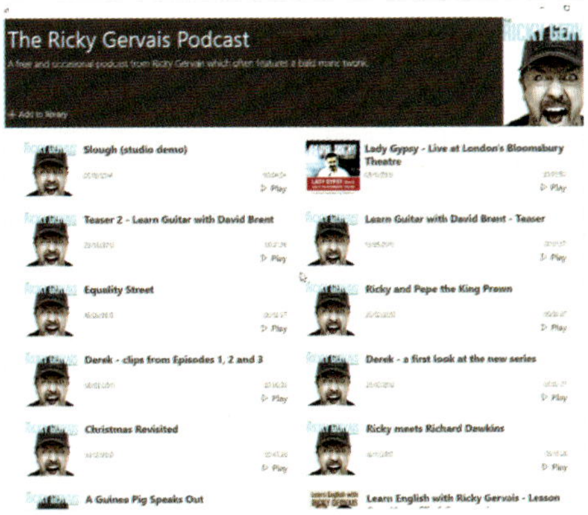

40 Photron Image Translator

bit.ly/photron389

This app can translate text found in images – on billboards, menus or magazines, for example. It supports 21 languages, including Klingon, and can read the text aloud.

41 Daily Mail Online

bit.ly/mail389

The Mail newspaper has a hugely popular website and this app gives you easy access to its content, both online and off. There are sections for News, Celebrity & Showbiz, Science & Tech, Sport and more.

42 Action Note

bit.ly/actionnote388

This app is a note-taking tool with a difference. It integrates with the Windows 10 Action Center to make it easier to access saved notes. You can attach images and sync content.

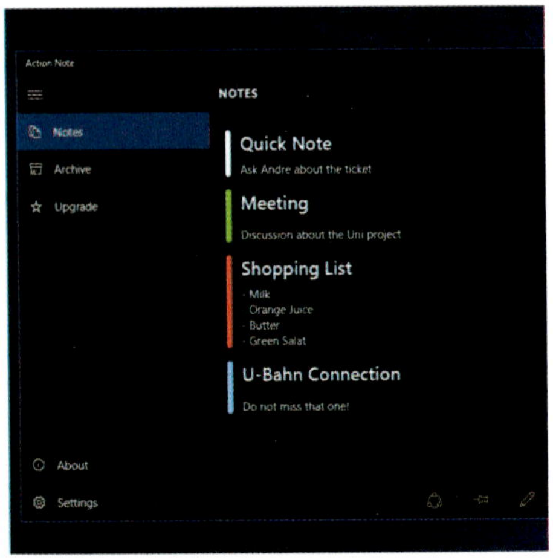

43 Toon Clash Chess

bit.ly/toonclash388

This attractive chess game has a 3D fantasy setting and three different boards to play on. The free version only lets you play against the computer, but you can upgrade to Pro to play against human opponents.

44 Figure

bit.ly/figure388

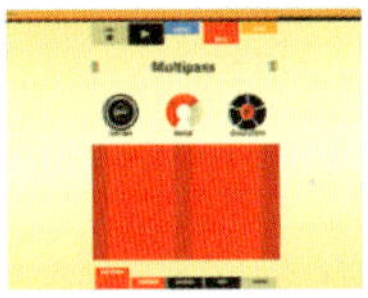

The popular iOS music-making app is now available for Windows 10. It lets you create songs in seconds and share, remix and collaborate with other users around the world.

45 Hear it first!

bit.ly/hearit387

If you're studying a foreign language, you can use this app to hear the pronunciation of any words and save them as MP3s. It offers 11 languages including Chinese, French, German, Italian, Russian and Spanish.

46 Moodflow

bit.ly/moodflow387

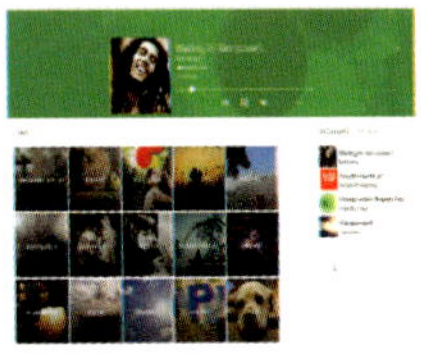

Moodflow plays songs that complement your mood. Select how you're feeling from a list and the app will play matching tunes. You can skip songs, tag them and add them to your favourites.

47 Cast

bit.ly/cast386

This app manages your audio podcasts and synchronises a library across all your Windows devices. You can search for and listen to podcasts directly in the app.

48 BBC Store

bit.ly/bbcstore385

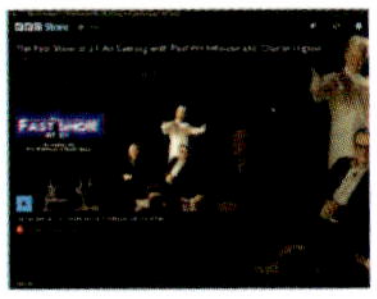

This app lets you stream and download TV programmes you've bought from the new BBC Store, including the latest shows and classic series. You'll need a free account to use it.

49 Loadkit Download Manager

bit.ly/loadkit385

This is a simple download manager that offers http, https and ftp downloading, and lets you filter, sort and search through downloaded files. It works with Firefox and Chrome.

50 Tweakolor

bit.ly/tweakolor385

Open a photo using this app, and it will display it in black and white and let you paint in your own colours. You can adjust the size of the brush to suit your painting requirements.

51 MapFactor GPS Navigation

bit.ly/mapfactor384

This universal app for PCs, tablets

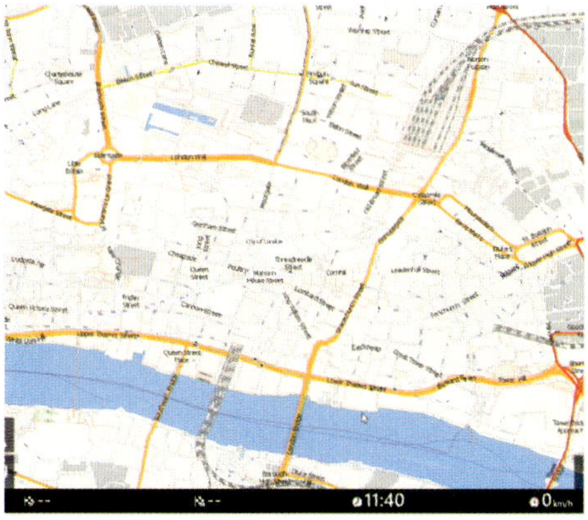

and Windows phones is a turn-by-turn navigation tool that uses OpenStreetMaps data. Maps are downloaded on to your device so you can access them without an internet connection.

52 Trivial Pursuit & Friends
bit.ly/triv384

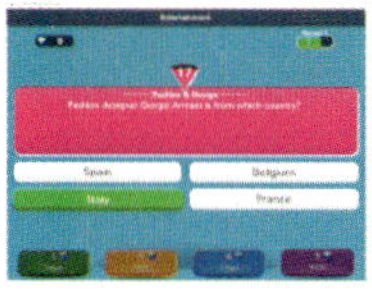

This revamped, social version of the popular trivia game lets you go head-to-head with friends or challenge strangers. Questions are tailored to the country you are playing in.

53 Yahoo Mail
bit.ly/yahoo381

If you use Yahoo Mail, it's definitely worth installing this new, official app. It displays recent emails in a live tile and also alerts you to new messages via desktop and lockscreen notifications.

54 Route Z
bit.ly/routez381

The zombie apocalypse is here, and you'll need to drive to survive in this fun action game. As well as escaping the zombie hordes, you need to collect fuel and armour.

55 Cosmo Run
bit.ly/cosmo380

This fun arcade game involves you guiding a beam of energy through an ever-changing game world. Just tap Space to change direction.

56 Duolingo
bit.ly/duolingo380

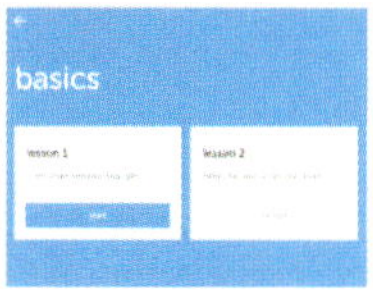

This free language-learning app helps you master French, Spanish, German, Italian, Dutch and Danish. It's now Windows 10-compatible, and has added Esperanto and Norwegian to its list of languages.

57 Newsmator
bit.ly/newsmator380

A simple feed reader that pulls in news from more than 150 supported sources. You can also add custom newsfeeds yourself from the web, view an article history and bookmark content.

58 Fitbit
bit.ly/fitbit379

Updated for Windows 10, this app lets you track your fitness and is compatible with all Fitbit hardware. Features include updated live tiles, and Cortana and Notification Centre support.

59 Aerize Optimizer
bit.ly/aerize379

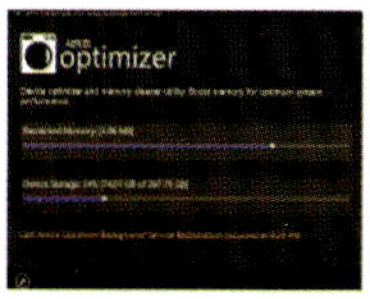

A memory-boosting app that claims to be able to clean device memory with a single click. You can set it to automatically overcome performance bottlenecks.

60 Pic Collage
bit.ly/piccollage378

Pic Collage lets you combine photos, text, stickers, drawings and cut-outs to create your own collages. It's very easy to use and works with both touch and keyboard and mouse.

Computer active

SUBSCRIPTION OFFER

Subscribe to Computeractive

for jargon-free help on using **Windows 10**

Every issue contains tips on how to get the best out of Windows 10, including:

- Every new tool in updates
- Foolproof fixes for problems
- Security flaws Microsoft keeps secret
- New web extensions for Edge
- How to stop Microsoft spying on you

PLUS: Reverse the settings that Microsoft changes

Pay just £19.99 for 13 issues (that's **just £1.54** an issue), you'll also get your copies delivered **FREE** to your door every fortnight before they're available in the shops.

Order securely online
dennismags.co.uk/computeractive
or call **0844 815 0054** quote code **G1619PW10**

Calls will cost 7p per minute plus your telephone company's access charge

Jargon buster

32bit
A measure of how much information a computer can process at once.

64bit
PC technology that processes information in larger chunks.

1080p
High-definition video.

Add-on
A small program that adds extra features to your web browser or to other applications.

Adware
Software that displays adverts.

Back up
The process of copying your important files to protect against loss of the originals.

Bandwidth
A measure of the amount of data that can be transferred over a connection at any one time.

BIOS
Basic Input-Output System. Software built into PCs that connects the vital components.

Bluetooth
A technology that allows devices to communicate wirelessly over short distances.

Browser
Short for web browser – a program or app that lets you view pages on the internet.

Cache
A temporary space for storing information.

Cloud
A nickname given to web-based services, such as online storage and syncing tools.

Driver
A software file that tells Windows how to work with hardware and peripheral devices and provides functions for the device.

Firmware
Software permanently stored on a device, such as a mobile phone, that controls its basic operation.

GHz
Gigahertz. A measure of how many instructions a chip can process per second.

THE A-Z JARGON BUSTER BOOK

ON SALE NOW

This A-Z guide contains over 900 definitions of computing jargon, helping you take back control of your PC

ON SALE NOW FROM AMAZON:
www.snipca.com/21272

DRM
Digital Rights Management. Software that limits the usage and copying of a file.

Encrypt
To scramble data so that it can only be read by those with a key or a code.

EXIF data
Refers to the metadata (date, time and other details) recorded within photo files by most digital cameras.

GPS
Global Positioning System. Technology used to pinpoint an exact position on the planet.

Graphics card
A component in a PC that produces the monitor image.

HDMI
High Definition Multimedia Interface. A type of connection that transmits HD video and audio.

Hotfixes
Software files that fix problems with an existing program.

Hotspot
A public area covered by a wireless network that allows you to access the internet.

IMAP
Internet Message Access Protocol. A standard for retrieving email from a server

iOS
The operating system used by portable devices from Apple, such as the iPhone and iPad.

ISO
An image file that contains all the data from a CD or DVD disc.

IP address
Internet Protocol Address. A unique set of numbers, used to identify computers and websites on the internet.

Linux
Open source software that's used as the basis for many operating systems, including Android.

Megapixel
A measure of the amount of detail that can be recorded by a digital camera or cameraphone.

Memory
(Also RAM) A device's temporary storage area, usually measured in gigabytes (GB).

Jargon buster continued

Memory card
Small, plastic cards that can be used by some phones and tablets to expand storage capacity.

Metadata
A set of data embedded within a file that provides additional information about the file.

Motherboard
The main circuit board inside every PC into which all other parts connect.

MP4
A type of digital movie format often used by portable devices, such as tablets and phones.

Multi-touch
The ability of a touchscreen to accept input from multiple points on a screen simultaneously.

NAS
Network-attached storage. A hard drive attached to a network that can be shared by other PCs.

NFC
Near-field communication. A technology that allows two devices to communicate wirelessly by being touched together.

Notification area
An area bottom-right of the screen in Windows, which shows alerts, shortcuts to running programs and more.

Operating system
Software that governs the way that the hardware and software in a computer or mobile device work together.

Plug-in
A small tool that adds extra features to web browsers or other applications.

POP3
Post Office Protocol 3. A protocol for remotely accessing and retrieving messages from an ISP or email provider.

Processor
The processor is the 'brain' of a computer or a device, governing performance. Also known as a CPU.

Quad-core
A computer that has four processor cores on a single CPU chip.

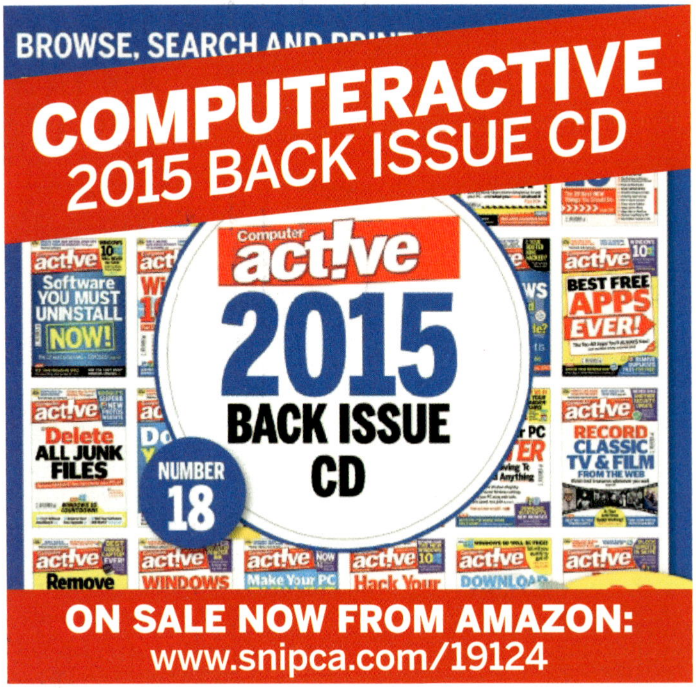

RAM
(Also Memory) Random-access memory. The computer's working area, used for data storage while the computer is switched on.

Registry
A file integrated into Windows that stores important information about all your PC's hardware and software.

Resolution
The amount of detail shown in an image, whether on-screen or printed.

Rip
To digitally copy the data from one format, such as an audio CD, to another format, such as MP3.

Router
A device used to connect PCs and wireless devices, such as smartphones to the internet.

SATA
Serial ATA. An interface for connecting hard drives.

SD card
And microSD. Popular types of memory card used for storage in some PCs, phones and tablets.

Server
A computer device on a network that distributes information to other PCs and devices.

Speech recognition
A technology that recognises the spoken word and translates it into commands or text.

Spyware
Software installed (usually surreptitiously) to monitor and report back on a PC's use.

SSD
Solid-state drive. Storage that uses no moving parts.

Streaming
A way of transmitting audio or video data without having to download an entire file first.

Stylus
A pen-like input device sometimes used for writing directly onto touch-screen devices.

Thumbnails
Smaller preview versions of pictures or videos.

Tethering
A technique that allows you to set up a portable hotspot using your smartphone's data connection.

Two-step authentication
A system that uses two different means to identify the user.

USB
Universal Serial Bus. A common standard for connecting devices and computers.

Virus
Malicious software designed to multiply itself and spread from device to device.

Wi-Fi
An umbrella term for various types of wireless networking technology.